Violence and Occupation

This groundbreaking history traces the Red Army's advances across central Europe and the Balkans in 1944–1945. It focuses on the 2nd and 3rd Ukrainian Fronts that occupied Romania, Bulgaria, Yugoslavia, Hungary, and Austria. Utilizing material from archives across Russia, Ukraine, and Serbia, alongside diaries, memoirs, and interviews, Vojin Majstorivić examines the official policies and troops' behavior in each country and analyzes military violations, from deserting and looting to widespread sexual violence. His findings show that the Red Army was an ill-disciplined force, but that military personnel committed fewer crimes against civilians in "neutral Bulgaria" and "friendly" Yugoslavia than in "enemy" Romania, Hungary, and Austria. To explain the variation in troops' conduct, he stresses the interaction of several continuously evolving factors: Kremlin's policies, the severity of the fighting, the command's policies toward criminals, the official propaganda, and troops' martial masculinity, identity, and views of the local populations.

Vojin Majstorović is a military historian at the University of North Texas. He examines the Red Army from the standpoint of frontline soldiers, military commanders in the field, the high command, and armies and civilians who encountered the Red Army.

Cambridge Military Histories

The aim of this series is to publish outstanding works of research on warfare throughout the ages and throughout the world. Books in the series take a broad approach to military history, examining war in all its military, strategic, political and economic aspects. The series complements *Studies in the Social and Cultural History of Modern Warfare* by focusing on the 'hard' military history of armies, tactics, strategy and warfare. Books in the series consist mainly of single author works – academically rigorous and groundbreaking – which are accessible to both academics and the interested general reader.

A full list of titles in the series can be found at:

www.cambridge.org/militaryhistories

Violence and Occupation

The Red Army in the Balkans and Central Europe, 1944–1945

Vojin Majstorović
University of North Texas

CAMBRIDGE
UNIVERSITY PRESS

CAMBRIDGE
UNIVERSITY PRESS

Shaftesbury Road, Cambridge CB2 8EA, United Kingdom

One Liberty Plaza, 20th Floor, New York, NY 10006, USA

477 Williamstown Road, Port Melbourne, VIC 3207, Australia

314–321, 3rd Floor, Plot 3, Splendor Forum, Jasola District Centre,
New Delhi – 110025, India

103 Penang Road, #05–06/07, Visioncrest Commercial, Singapore 238467

Cambridge University Press is part of Cambridge University Press & Assessment,
a department of the University of Cambridge.

We share the University's mission to contribute to society through the pursuit of
education, learning and research at the highest international levels of excellence.

www.cambridge.org
Information on this title: www.cambridge.org/9781009652445

DOI: 10.1017/9781009652438

When citing this work, please include a reference to the
DOI 10.1017/9781009652438

First published 2026

Cover image: Galerie Bilderwelt / Hulton Archive / Getty Images

A catalogue record for this publication is available from the British Library

*A Cataloging-in-Publication data record for this book is available from the
Library of Congress*

ISBN 978-1-009-65244-5 Hardback

Contents

Figures

Maps and Tables

Maps

Tables

Acknowledgments

This book originated as a dissertation, which I began actively working on in 2012. Over the years, multiple institutions have supported my research, including the Social Sciences and Humanities Research Council of Canada, the Ontario Graduate Scholarship, and the United States Holocaust Memorial Museum. At the University of Toronto, where I got my PhD, the Department of History, the School of Graduate Studies, and the Anne Tanenbaum Centre for Jewish Studies have supported my research. The Center for Holocaust Studies at the Leibniz Institute for Contemporary History and the Vienna Wiesenthal Institute for Holocaust Studies have awarded me research fellowships, where I was able to work on the book while also researching my next project. I am also thankful to the Holocaust Education Foundation at Northwestern University and the European Holocaust Research Infrastructure. At the University of North Texas, I received support from the Department of History, Military History Center, and College of Liberal Arts and Social Sciences.

My research in archives in Russia, Ukraine, Serbia, Germany, and the United States was assisted by numerous historians and archivists who shared their expertise of local sources with me. I am grateful to all of them, but I want to mention, in no particular order, Ljubinka Škodrić, Anna Sheremeteva, Alexey Timofeev, Leonid Terushkin, Giles Bennett, Vincent Slatt, Nevenko Vlaisavljević, and Vadim Al'tskan. Oleksandr Marinchenko, a specialist on the Red Army and archives in Ukraine, always gave me expert advice on archives in Ukraine. Sadly, he died prematurely during the Russian aggression against Ukraine in his beloved native Dnipro in 2022.

Over the years, I had many informal and formal conversations about my research. They all contributed to my work, including Francesca Silano, Seth Bernstein, Oleksandr Melnyk, Kristina Pauksens, Lilia Topouzova, Maris Rowe-McCulloch, Marilyn Campeau, Anka Hajkova, Aleks Pomiećko, Ben McVicker, Konstantin Fuks, Stephanie Corazza, Ryan Masters, Alison Smith, Piotr Wrobel, Jeffrey Kopstein,

Andrew Rossos, Tracy McDonald, Eva Kovacs, Nicole Eaton, Oleg Budnitskii, Barbara Stelzl-Marx, David Stone, Kenneth Slepyan, Roger Reese, Edward Westermann, Grant Harward, Kerstin Bischl, Jadwiga Biskupska, Brandon Schechter, Ruth Lawlor, and Alexander Hill.

In Toronto, Anna Shternshis encouraged my interest in the Holocaust. Doris Bergen, always generous with her time, taught me to view atrocities as inseparable from the wider war. Lynne Viola was an outstanding supervisor; a great historian of Stalinism with unrivaled knowledge of Soviet archives, caring, quick to help, and always finding the right balance between guiding her graduate students while treating them as adults.

The Department of History at the University of North Texas has always been supportive of my career and research. I am grateful to Michael Leggiere (who has gone to the University of Florida), Geoff Wawro, Harold Tanner, Jennifer Jensen Wallach, Rachel Louise Moran (who has gone to Texas A&M), and Michael Wise for their support.

My maternal grandparents, Dušan and Vera Protić, as well as my parents, Jelisaveta Protić and Ivan Majstorović, have always encouraged me and my interests. I am so grateful to them.

I married Irina just before starting my PhD program. Since then, we have lived in at least four cities in three countries and had extended research stays in five additional cities. She was a supportive, loving, and joyful companion while changing professions and practically building our house in the Dallas area. In the process, we had two children, Lydia and Vera, the former coming into the world in the closing stages of the dissertation and the latter in the closing stages of the book. Irina, Lydia, and Vera have made the fun process brilliant. I dedicate this book to them.

Abbreviations

ACC	Allied Control Commission
AJ	Arhiv Jugoslavije (Archive of Yugoslavia)
BA	Blavatnik Archive
BKP	B'lgarska komunisticheskaia partiia (The Bulgarian Communist Party)
GlavPURKKA	Glavnoe politicheskoe upravlenie Raboche-Krest'ianskaoi Krasnoi Armii (Main Political Administration of the Red Army)
IAN	Istorijiski arhiv Negotin (Historical Archive of Negotin)
IAN RAN	Istoricheskii arkhiv rossiiskoi akademii nauk (Historical Archive of the Russian Academy of Sciences)
IAS	Istorijski arhiv Subotica (Historical Archive of Subotica)
IAZ	Istorijski arhiv Zaječar (Historical Archive of Zaječar)
KPJ	Komunistička partija Jugoslavije (The Communist Party of Yugoslavia)
NKO	Narodnyi komissariat oborony SSSR (People's Commissariat of Defense of USSR)
NKVD	Narodnyi komissariat vnutrennikh del SSSR (People's Commissariat of Internal Affairs of the USSR)
Partisans	Narodnooslobodilačka vojska Jugoslavije (The National Liberation Army of Yugoslavia)
RGASPI	Rossiiskii gosudarstvennyi arkhiv sotsial'no-politicheskoi istorii (Russian State Archive of Social and Political History)
RGVA	Rossiiskii gosudarstvennyi voennyi arkhiv (The Russian State Military Archive)

RKKA	Raboche-Krest'ianskaia Krasnaia Armiia (Worker-Peasant Red Army)
SMERSH	Smert' shpiunam (Death to Spies, the military intelligence agency)
Stavka	Stavka Glavnogo Komandovaniia Vooruzhennykh Sil Soiuza SSR (Headquarters of the Supreme Command of the Armed Forces of the Union of Soviet Socialist Republics)
TsAMO, RF	Tsentral'nyi arkhiv Ministerstva oborony, Rossiskoi Federatsii (The Central Archive of the Ministry of Defense of the Russian Federation)
TsDAGO	Tsentral'nyi gosudarstvennyi arkhiv grazhdanskikh ob'edinenii Ukrainy (Central State Archives of Public Organizations of Ukraine)
USHMM	The United States Holocaust Memorial Museum
VA	Vojni Arhiv Srbije – The Military Archive of Serbia
VKP(b)	Vsesoiuznaia Kommunisticheskaia partiia bol'shevikov (All-Union Communist Party of the Bolsheviks)

Introduction

On 12 July 1944, Colonel Zolotukhin, a high-ranking official in the powerful Main Political Administration of the Red Army (GlavPURKKA), sent his superiors in Moscow an alarming report about the breakdown of discipline in the Red Army's ranks in Romania. After he inspected the 2nd Ukrainian Front (army group), which had recently occupied parts of Romania and Moldavia, he reported that there was an explosion in instances of desertion, self-inflicted wounds, drunkenness, and venereal disease.[1] Zolotukhin specified dozens of examples that illustrated the deteriorating situation, including instances of rapes of civilians, widespread use of prostitutes by officers in Romania, the leadership's brutal treatment and neglect of the new recruits, large-scale looting, and drunken violence between Soviet officers. This book explores the disintegrating discipline that Zolotukhin's report vividly illustrated in the context of the 2nd and 3rd Ukrainian Fronts' encounter with the countries of the Balkans and Central Europe.

The Red Army's *Disciplinary Regulations of the Red Army*, issued in 1941 by the Commissar for Defence Marshal Semen Timoshenko, defined Soviet military discipline as: "knowledge of and strict compliance with the established Red Army procedures (*poriadka*), based on the laws of the Soviet government and on military regulations, which regulate the life (*zhizn'*), everyday life (*byt'*), and military activities of the armies."[2] In official documents, violations of the disciplinary regime were known as either violations (*prostupki*) or crimes (*prestupleniia*). The latter term was usually used to describe the troops' actions that were covered by the criminal code, such as committing robberies or rapes, whereas the former was used to describe violations of military regulations, such as sleeping on duty or loss of personal documents.

The wartime Red Army was the largest military in Europe. An estimated 34 million Soviet citizens served in their country's military between 1941 and 1945.[3] In the summer and early fall of 1944, some 6,714,300 Red Army soldiers and officers faced the forces of the Axis in Europe.[4] They were organized into nine army groups, which received their names from their geographic locations: three Baltic fronts, two Belarusian fronts, and four Ukrainian fronts.

The 2nd and 3rd Ukrainian Fronts, the focus of this study, fought at the southern end of the Soviet-Axis frontlines. Although these two army groups' numbers constantly fluctuated in the period under discussion, the 2nd and 3rd Ukrainian Fronts numbered 1,314,200 during the Iasi – Kishinev Operation in late August 1944, when the Soviet forces broke through German and Romanian defenses in the Balkans.[5] After Romania, the two army groups fought in Bulgaria, Yugoslavia, and Hungary, finishing the war in Austria.

Violence and Occupation: The Red Army in the Balkans and Central Europe, 1944–1945 focuses on two related issues: the decline in discipline and the soldiers' encounter with Europe. The book illuminates the Soviet troops' ill-disciplined conduct and criminality from above and below, both from the perspectives of the political and military leaderships and the frontline soldiers and officers. The study also tries to give a voice to European civilians who experienced the Soviet occupation, especially the victims of Soviet-perpetrated sexual violence. The book asks questions such as: How did the army's leadership want its troops to behave? What were the army's disciplinary policies toward the criminals in the ranks? What were the typical punishments for violators of discipline? What message did the leadership try to convey to the rank and file through propaganda? When it comes to the frontline troops, the study seeks to illuminate issues such as: How did the soldiers view each country that they occupied? What was their identity? Why did soldiers fight? How did they view women and sex? Why did they commit so many acts of sexual violence? Did Soviet soldiers engage in nonviolent sex with European women?

Military violations and criminal code violations committed by the Soviet troops, as defined by the Red Army's regulations, included getting drunk and shirking from duties, which usually took the form of straggling and deserting. The troops also committed many acts of robberies, rape and, more rarely, murders. Usually, these crimes were linked to each other. An upsurge in one set of crimes meant that there was an increase in other crimes.

The study pays attention in particular to the issue of sexual violence and what these crimes tell us about the Red Army – both the troops' attitudes and how discipline was enforced in the military. Rape was one of the more common crimes the Soviet troops committed. For many Europeans, assaults on women came to symbolize the Soviet occupation, and rapes had a profound impact on European societies. The Red Army personnel committed more rapes in "enemy" Romania, Hungary, and Austria than in "neutral" Bulgaria or "allied" Yugoslavia. Moreover, as historian Miriam Gebhardt noted, in 1945, authorities and societies understood rape to be forceful vaginal penetration with the use of force and credible resistance by the victim. More respectable women, such as married and older women, were more readily believed than young and single women.[6] Thus, the number of victims of sexual violence was much higher than the victims of rape, but neither Soviet nor European officials bothered to record them. The study also discusses other sexual encounters between European civilians and Soviet soldiers, which often fell in the gray area between outright rapes and consensual relations as we would understand them today.

The book tries to make sense of the world in which the soldiers and officers of the two army groups lived and acted. Whenever possible, the study provides figures and estimates. A comparative perspective is also important. It often references the research on the Red Army's peer armies, which helps contextualize the Red Army's experience. The comparative perspective is, in particular, developed in the conclusion. This is a study about a relatively large collective, but it also employs techniques of microhistorians, who analyze everyday stories to make larger points.[7] In every chapter, the book dwells on individual stories of soldiers, officers, or civilians that illuminate larger events. The Red Army's treatment of civilians and the leadership policies differed across the phases of military campaigns and the countries occupied by the two army groups. Most thematical chapters follow this chronological order.

The book also uses the troops' behavior as a prism to make sense of other important issues pertaining to the Red Army at war. The army leadership's often unsuccessful struggle to limit straggling and prevent the outbreaks of unsanctioned violence against civilians helps us understand the limits of the high command's ability to shape the frontline troops' worldviews and conduct while illuminating how discipline was enforced in the Soviet army. Focusing on the high command's attempts to control the rank and file, ultimately, illuminates how the Kremlin governed the Red Army during the war. The frontline soldiers' and officers' subculture, which enabled the violence against civilians to flourish, illuminates their attitudes and identity. It is impossible to grasp troops' fury and behavior without thinking about their growing nationalism, assertiveness, their conception of masculinity, vengefulness, and sense of entitlement vis-à-vis their commanders and the Europeans that they conquered. A discussion about the proliferation of stragglers and deserters leads us to evaluate the Red Army's cohesiveness and military effectiveness. Focusing on the issue of discipline, especially violence against the civilian population, can also help us understand how Europeans experienced the closing stages of World War II and how they viewed and interacted with Soviet troops.

I.1 Sources

Violence and Occupation relies mostly on Soviet documents. The Central Archive of the Ministry of Defense of the Russian Federation TsAMO RF the Red Army's principal wartime depository under the jurisdiction of the conservative Ministry of Defense, is mostly closed off to foreign researchers. However, thousands of documents have been published in various documentary collections. More significantly, archives in union republics or friendly countries, as well as many Soviet agencies, institutions, and commissariats (ministries) received documents from TsAMO RF after the war or were copied into the army's correspondence while generating their important information about the war. These collections are now largely available to researchers, or at least they were until 2022. Finally, I obtained hundreds of pages of documents from TsAMO RF from a colleague.

The study relies most heavily on documents from the Russian State Military Archive (RGVA), under the civilian Federal Archival Agency. RGVA holds documents from the NKVD Army for the Protection of the Rear of the Red Army (the NKVD Army). The NKVD Army was part of the People's Commissariat for Internal Affairs, but it was under the Red Army's operational control. The NKVD Army in the field was also divided into fronts, and the NKVD Armies of the 2nd and 3rd Ukrainian Fronts reported to and received orders from their respective army group commanders. Four types of NKVD Army documents are particularly important: the orders that the NKVD Armies of the 2nd and 3rd Ukrainian Fronts received from their front commanders, the NKVD Army's reports on the behavior of Soviet soldiers as it related to the issue of violence against civilians and desertion, and the reports on the mood of civilians in the occupied countries. The fourth type of documents used are documents about discipline in the two NKVD Armies, which tell us something about the occupying Soviet forces in general.

Other Red Army documents utilized are from the United States Holocaust Memorial Museum (USHMM), the Military Archive of Serbia (VA), the Central State Archives of Public Organizations of Ukraine (TsDAGO), and the Historical Archive of the Russian Academy of Sciences (IAN RAN). Other sources have been published in documentary collections. The study also relies on the Communist Party of the Soviet Union (CPSU) records in TsDAGO and the Russian State Archive of Social and Political History (RGASPI).

The book uses personal sources. It relies extensively on the website, "Reminiscences of the Veterans of the Great Patriotic War" (*Ia pomniu*), which holds hundreds of interviews with Red Army soldiers and officers.[8] Furthermore, it utilizes Jewish soldiers' sources from the Russian Research and Educational Holocaust Center (Tsentr Kholokost) and the Blavatnik Archive (BA). The study also utilizes diaries and memoirs (when it is possible to find them) written by veterans from the 2nd and 3rd Ukrainian Fronts and letters from archives and published collections.

Although the Red Army sources extensively discuss the issue of murders, sexual violence, and robberies, they rarely offer a close look into acts of violence and seldom depict the victim's perspective. Available Soviet sources typically state tersely the nature of the crime, sometimes noting the punishment meted out to the perpetrators and actions taken to avert such behavior in the future. The military officials writing these reports were practically never interested in victims or what happened to them afterward, viewing the crimes primarily as a disciplinary issue or a political problem. More details could likely be found in the documents generated by the army's Military Tribunals that prosecuted and sentenced the perpetrators, since the prosecutors and judges would typically use victim and witness statements. Military Tribunal records, however, are in TsAMO RF and are inaccessible even to Russian historians who are allowed to work in the archive.[9] At best, partial information about the activities of Military Tribunals can be occasionally gleaned from internal military reports about the morale of the troops.

The book seeks to give a voice to the occupied populations. It uses extensively Serbian-language sources, including Yugoslav army and police documents from VA, the records from the Communist Party of Yugoslavia collection in The Archive of Yugoslavia (AJ), as well as three provincial Historical Archives of Zaječar (IAZ), Negotin (IAN), and Subotica (IAS) that hold municipal government and court records. The author conducted twenty-two interviews in Serbia with former soldiers and civilians of various political persuasions. The book also utilizes numerous published Austrian, Hungarian, Romanian, Yugoslav, and Bulgarian primary and secondary sources, including diaries and memoirs in various languages, to give voice to the occupied populations and victims of Soviet sexual violence.

Yugoslavia gets more attention than other countries that the 2nd and 3rd Ukrainian Fronts occupied for two reasons. First, we know almost nothing about how Yugoslavs reacted to the Red Army and how the Soviet troops behaved in the country. In contrast, there is some literature on the Soviet occupation of Austria, Hungary, and Romania, although not as nearly as there is on the Red Army in Germany.[10] Second, the author is fully fluent in Serbian, making research possible in the country.

It should be mentioned that the vast majority of Soviet soldiers in Yugoslavia fought only in Serbia and headed north into Hungary, instead of moving further west into Bosnia and Hercegovina and Croatia. Thus, they did not encounter Muslim and Catholic populations who were historically less sympathetic to the Russians than the Serbs. Throughout the text, the term "Yugoslavs" rather than "Serbs" is used because not all the civilians and especially not all the Partisans in Serbia were ethnic Serbs, while many who were would have identified as Yugoslavs. Furthermore, Serbs were citizens of Yugoslavia, so the term Yugoslavs is formally accurate.

***

The book is divided into three parts. The first part of the book provides the context for the rest of the study. Chapter 1 examines the 2nd and 3rd Ukrainian Fronts before they stormed into Europe in August 1944. The two army groups began their westward advance at Stalingrad and Kursk in 1943, pushing the Axis across southern and eastern Ukraine throughout 1943 and 1944. On the eve of their entry into Europe, the majority of the troops of the two army groups were recent recruits, mostly from Ukraine. The chapter outlines the major operations fought by the two fronts and their extremely high casualties. It also explores the soldiers' worldview, their brutal treatment by the high command that often viewed them as little more than cannon fodder, and how many of them were eventually integrated successfully into the army.

Chapter 2 discusses the military operations of the two fronts in Europe, and it traces the Soviet casualties. Crucially, it also discusses the rapid growth of military violations in the ranks. There was an increase in all types of military violations, including alcohol consumption and straggling. However, the attacks on civilians increased drastically, especially sexual assaults. The chapter also seeks to illuminate the approximate number of rape victims in each European country.

The second part of the book explores the role of political and military leadership in the rapid growth of military violations. Chapter 3 focuses on the Kremlin and its policies in Romania, Bulgaria, Yugoslavia, Hungary, and Austria. It argues that the Kremlin set the tone for the army on how to deal with the local population by ruthlessly exploiting the region's economy for the war and by exacting war reparations.

Although much has been written about the Soviet anti-German indoctrination campaign that was used to mobilize Soviet society for war, we know very little about the information given to the rank and file about Romania, Bulgaria, Yugoslavia, Hungary, and Austria. Yet, the official discourse is vital to understanding the troops' conduct as it communicated to them how to view these countries and what kind of behavior was acceptable. Chapter 4 discusses the content of the propaganda about each country that the two army groups occupied.

Chapter 5 examines the Red Army's repressive institutions, which historian David Glantz called "control organs."[11] These institutions' activities played a vital role in implementing orders from above and in signaling to the rank and file what they could get away with (or not). It discusses the laws and regulations in the Red Army, how they were enforced, and the orders issued to the armies in the field by the command. It also considers the types of punishments meted out to perpetrators of various kinds of crimes.

The third part of the book switches the focus to soldiers and officers in the field. Chapter 6 examines the troops' actual attitudes toward Romania, Bulgaria, Yugoslavia, Hungary, and Austria. These views reflected how the troops behaved in each country. This chapter underlines that there was no "single" view of Europe.

Chapter 7 seeks specifically to explain the sexual violence committed by the troops. It builds on Chapter 6 by examining the troops' views of women. The final chapter, Chapter 8, discusses the period after the war. It illuminates the difficult process of the high command's struggle to rein in the troops in the new postwar context.

Part I

The Front

Map I.1 Map of Eastern Europe with key cities in 1945 borders.

1 On the Eve of the Balkan Offensive

Petr Mikhin was a twenty-year-old mathematics student in Leningrad when the Axis invaded the Soviet Union in June 1941. By the time the 2nd and 3rd Ukrainian Fronts marched into Romania in the summer of 1944, he had risen to the rank of captain and commanded an artillery battalion. In the three years that it took the Red Army to expel the Germans and their allies from the Soviet Union, Mikhin learned to hate Germans, completed a military school, joined the Communist Party, became an experienced officer, took in hundreds of recruits teaching them how to handle artillery guns, was wounded three times, and according to his count had twenty-nine close brushes with death. He fought at Rzhev around Moscow and at Kursk, as well as in many other lesser battles. He destroyed countless German tanks, guns, and soldiers.[1] Mikhin and hundreds of thousands of other soldiers and officers who were steadfast in their commitment to the victory may not have been representative of the entire 2nd and 3rd Ukrainian Fronts, but they were one of the main reasons why the Red Army managed to expel the Germans from Soviet territory.

By the time the 2nd and 3rd Ukrainian Fronts crossed the Soviet Union's international border in the spring of 1944, few doubted the Red Army would eventually prevail over Germany and its allies. Many of the troops' experiences and attitudes toward their service, the enemy, and women, which shaped their conduct and treatment of civilians in the Balkans and Central Europe, were already formed by the summer of 1944. This chapter offers a historical background of the 2nd and 3rd Ukrainian Fronts, providing necessary information to contextualize the soldiers' conduct in Europe.

1.1 The Profile of 2nd and 3rd Ukrainian Front Soldiers

The two army groups participated in the war's major battles before they stormed into Romania. The Southwestern Front, the 3rd Ukrainian Front's precursor, fought at Stalingrad, the first major Soviet victory and the first decisive Axis defeat of the war. Subsequently, it participated in the liberation of Donbas in August and September of 1943. The Steppe Front, the 2nd Ukrainian Front's predecessor, participated in the defense of Kursk in July 1943. The Battle of Kursk marked a watershed moment in the war, as it was the last large-scale German offensive attempt to decisively reverse its dwindling fortunes on the Eastern front.[2] Moreover, the Red Army never lost the strategic initiative after Kursk, relentlessly advancing westward. After Kursk, the Steppe Front liberated the large Ukrainian cities of Kharkiv in August and Chernihiv and Poltava in September.

In the Red Army, army groups received their names from their geographic locations and operational axis.[3] Therefore, the Steppe and Southwestern Fronts were renamed respectively the 2nd and 3rd Ukrainian Fronts in October 1943.[4] The two army groups, along with the 4th Ukrainian Front, liberated Melitopol, Zaporizhzhia, and Dnipropetrovsk between 26 September and 20 December 1943.[5] From December 1943 to 17 April 1944, the 2nd and 3rd Ukrainian Fronts took numerous important cities in right-bank Ukraine: Kryvyi Rih, Kherson, Mykolaiv, Uman, and Odesa (Figure 1.1).

The Soviet military carried out wholesale mobilization of all men in the territories that it liberated. Comprehensive and systematic data on the background of soldiers is hard to come by. However, the available

Figure 1.1 Celebrating soldier. Source: Ullstein Bild via Getty Images.

information makes it clear that on the eve of their entry into Europe, the majority of troops in the 2nd and 3rd Ukrainian Fronts were Ukrainians. According to the Main Political Administration of the Red Army (GlavPURKKA) estimates, soldiers from the newly liberated territories, which presumably consisted mostly of Ukraine but also occupied parts of Russia (North Caucasus and southern Russia), comprised two-thirds of the 2nd Ukrainian Front in July 1944.[6] The 38th Rifle Division of the 2nd Ukrainian Front on 1 July 1943 had 52 percent Russians and 8 percent Ukrainians, on 1 January 1944, the Russians comprised 40 percent and Ukrainians 46 percent, and on 1 July, there were only 30 percent Russians and 63 percent Ukrainians.[7] Some units had even more Ukrainians. German intelligence estimated, also in July 1944, that the 41st Guards Rifle Division of the 4th Guards Army of the 2nd Ukrainian Front was composed of 80 percent Ukrainians and 20 percent Russians.[8]

Although there is no systematic information for the 3rd Ukrainian Front, between December 1943 and April 1944, the 3rd Ukrainian Front numbered 336,900 troops, many of whom were from Donbas.[9] Yet, it replenished its ranks with 110,000 recruits just from the Odesa and Mykolaiv regions from 1 March to 14 April 1944.[10] Most infantry units of the 37th Army of the 3rd Ukrainian Front comprised more than 70 percent of the new intake.[11] The 3rd Ukrainian Front would have also recruited hundreds of thousands of soldiers in Dnipropetrovsk, Zaporizhzhia, and Kryvyi Rih, although I did not find the relevant information. Therefore, it is safe to presume that in the 3rd Ukrainian Front, just like in the 2nd Ukrainian Front, recruits from occupied territories comprised around two-thirds of all troops as they entered Europe.

The Red Army faced critical manpower shortages during this period. Many rifle divisions had an effective strength of 2,000, while the required strength was 12,785.[12] The speediest, cheapest, and easiest way to fill the manpower shortages was to conscript locally in the newly liberated territories. There is no evidence that the command attempted to use Ukrainian soldiers as cannon fodder simply because they were Ukrainian; the Red Army leadership also threw Russian recruits into battle en masse. For example, in April 1943, the 79th Guards Rifle Division of the Southwestern Front was replenished with new conscripts while it was still stationed on the territory of Russia, near the border with Donbas. The conscripts were 87.5 percent Russian, 5 percent Ukrainian, and 11.5 percent from other nationalities.[13]

The shift away from Russians to Ukrainians in the Red Army was particularly evident in the composition of the four Ukrainian fronts that fought in Ukraine, but it was also captured in general statistics on the ethnic composition of the Red Army. In January 1943, when all of

Ukraine was still under Axis control, Russians comprised 64.6 percent and Ukrainians 11.8 percent of all Red Army troops. In April 1944, when most of Ukraine was back under Soviet rule, the Russian element dropped to 58.32 percent, whereas the portion of Ukrainians almost doubled to 22.27 percent.[14] Thus, there were so many Ukrainians in the two fronts because there were many men of military age in the newly liberated territories available for service.

The newly conscripted soldiers, having often received impromptu training, were injured or killed in large numbers. For instance, Lieutenant Mansur Abdulin, a Komsomol organizer in the 2nd Ukrainian Front, recalled that "the war brutally and mercilessly devoured people."[15] He went on to explain that from the middle of October to early November 1943, recruits from the Ukrainian city of Poltava, which his division liberated, predominated in the unit. However, by the end of November, only a handful of soldiers from the Poltava region were left in the division.[16] Mikhin came close to being killed many times, although as an artillery officer, he was less exposed than an infantryman. He explained:

> On the offensive, a private on average lasted for a couple of assaults; a platoon leader lived for a day, a company commander for a week, and a battalion commander for a month.... one couldn't survive the whole war on mere luck. A bullet or a piece of shrapnel always found a man sooner or later. This happened every day, every hour, every minute. The problem was one never knew when this would happen – in an assault, under a barrage, while getting your grub, in one's sleep, or even at some more inconvenient moment. Of course, each man prayed and secretly hoped to survive, but with men constantly dying all around you, you knew your turn would come eventually.[17]

Given the realities of combat on the Eastern front, after the liberation of Ukraine, the relative number of Ukrainians in the 2nd and 3rd Ukrainian Fronts started to diminish.

After the liberation of Moldavia was completed in August 1944, the Red Army conscripted 256,800 Moldavians.[18] Most of these soldiers ended up in the two army groups because they were the only Red Army fronts that operated in Moldavia. Some units became predominantly Moldavian. For instance, the 25th Guards Rifle Division of the 2nd Ukrainian Front had 60 percent Moldavians in its ranks.[19] Thereafter, the 2nd and 3rd Ukrainian Fronts took heavy casualties in Romania, Yugoslavia, Hungary, and Austria. Replenishments for the lost troops came from the Soviet Union and locally from the liberated forced laborers and prisoners of war. These soldiers were more representative of the Soviet Union as a whole than the soldiers recruited in Ukraine.

There is little information on the Ukrainian Fronts' ethnic makeup after they stormed into Europe in August 1944, but it seems that the

Ukrainian element dropped precipitously. For instance, the 59th and 60th Armies of the 1st Ukrainian Front in January 1945 had 33 and 44 percent Ukrainians in their ranks, respectively.[20] Similarly, the 15th Guards Rifle Division of the same front was 50 percent Russian and 50 percent Central Asian in April 1943, but by November 1944, the same unit was 90 percent Ukrainian, and in January 1945, it was two-thirds Russian and one-third Ukrainian.[21] Almost certainly, the situation was similar in the 2nd and 3rd Ukrainian Fronts as in the 1st Ukrainian Front – the Ukrainian element dropped to well under 50 percent after the heavy fighting in Europe. European civilians who could communicate with Soviet troops and came into prolonged contact with them also noted that there were many Ukrainians in the 2nd and 3rd Ukrainian Fronts.[22]

Another characteristic of the Red Army was its youthfulness, especially of the officer cadres. A significant part of the officer corps was wiped out in 1941 and 1942, particularly the lower-ranking commanders in the field.[23] The Red Army lost more than 2 million officers during the war, the vast majority of them serving as command cadres. Throughout the war, the high command trained, promoted, and called up from the reserves 4,140,000 officers, among them Petr Mikhin, mentioned at the beginning of the chapter.[24] These were mostly young officers who compensated for the lack of proper training with enthusiasm and battlefield experience. They became the core of a military that absorbed successive waves of recruits, providing experience and commitment to the military, which due to high casualties was in a permanent state of flux. At the same time, their young age gave them self-confidence, sometimes to the point of arrogance.[25]

The composition of the NVKD Armies of the 2nd and 3rd Ukrainian Fronts did not fluctuate since the NKVD suffered fewer casualties. Thus, they were more representative of the Soviet Union as a whole than the Red Army. The NKVD Army of the 2nd Ukrainian Front on 1 April 1944, had 4,059 officers, sergeants, and soldiers. Among the latter, Russians comprised 79 percent and Ukrainians 14 percent. Out of 645 officers, Russians made up 55.1 percent and Ukrainians 17.4 percent.[26] In the NKVD Army of the 3rd Ukrainian Front, out of 729 officers, 69.1 percent and 23 percent were Russian and Ukrainian, respectively.[27]

There was no shortage of Ukrainians in the highest leadership as well. Marshal Rodion Malinovskii, commander of the 2nd Ukrainian Front, and Marshal Timoshenko, who coordinated the two fronts' activities on behalf of the Main Command of the Armed Forces of the USSR (Stavka), were both from the Odesa region.[28] Lieutenant General Ivan Gorbatiuk, the Chief of the Main Directorate of the NKVD Army for the Protection of the Rear of the Red Army and the direct boss of the chiefs of the NKVD Armies of the 2nd and 3rd Ukrainian Fronts, was also a Ukrainian from Odesa.[29] General Zhmachenko, who commanded the 40th Army of the 2nd Ukrainian Front, was born in the Zhytomyr region and died in his Kyiv home after the war.[30] Lieutenant General Andrei Grigor'evich Kravchenko, commander of the 6th Guards Tank Army, the two army groups' most formidable mobile armored formation, was born in a village in today's central Ukraine.[31] Kuz'ma Nikolaevich Derevianko, best known for eventually accepting Japanese unconditional surrender on behalf of the Soviet Union, was Chief of Staff of the 4th Guards Army of the 3rd Ukrainian Front. He was from a village in today's Cherkasy region.[32] Aleksei Sergeevich Zheltov, born in Kharkiv, was a member of the Military Council of the 3rd Ukrainian Front.[33] General Kiril Semenovich Moskalenko, commander of the 38th Army that was transferred between the 1st, 2nd, and 4th Ukrainian Fronts during the Soviet offensives in Ukraine, was a Ukrainian from the Donetsk region.[34]

In sum, when the 2nd and 3rd Ukrainian Fronts entered Romania in August 1944, up to two-thirds of the troops were from the German- and Romanian-occupied parts of the Soviet Union. These two-thirds were mostly Ukrainian, but some were from Moldavia and occupied parts of Russia. Thus, the vast majority of Soviet soldiers who conquered and occupied Romania had experienced Axis rule directly, and a minority of troops had been fighting Germans and their allies since 1941 or 1942. The soldiers were unusually led by young officers, much more so than was the case in other armies. The NKVD Army soldiers and officers and regular army officers suffered far fewer casualties than the frontline troops after the Battle of Stalingrad. Their profile was much more stable and consistently representative of the Soviet Union as a whole.

1.2 Soviet Soldiers and Death

Soldiers from the 2nd and 3rd Ukrainian Fronts who made it to Europe in late August of 1944 were in many ways the fortunate survivors of successive waves of Stalinist and Nazi violence. The vast majority of troops were youths or adults who experienced Stalin's revolutions from above in the 1930s and associated repressions. Since many soldiers were from southern and eastern Ukraine, they often discussed in personal sources how they lived through the Holodomor, the man-made famine organized by the Stalinist leadership. The famine took 3–4 million lives in Ukraine in 1932–1933.[35] The future soldiers survived the famine by variously living off rook's eggs, beets, cherry leaves, or through the assistance of relatives living in the West.[36] Numerous soldiers reported that their close relatives starved to death, that they were aware of instances of cannibalism, and their accounts of the 1930s-era countryside were replete with images of bloated stomachs and other images associated with severe famine.[37] Mariia Rist (Fedorko), a signaller, was born in Kharkiv, Ukraine. She said that she had not experienced anything more terrifying in her life than the famine of 1933. This was a powerful claim, considering it came from a woman who was wounded twice during the war. She explained her position by saying that "people ate people, cats, dogs, everything they could get their hands on."[38] Other soldiers talked about the deportation of their neighbors from their villages to the Soviet Union's more remote parts such as the far north or the far east.[39]

The Red Army leadership was one of the most prominent victims of the Great Terror during 1937–1938. The military elite was ravaged.[40] Yet service personnel of the 2nd and 3rd Ukrainian Fronts rarely mentioned the Great Terror of 1937–1938 in their sources. This was because the terror was largely aimed at the higher-ranking officers in the army. Therefore, it did not personally affect the overwhelming majority of the troops from 1944 and 1945, who at the time were civilians.

A substantial portion of the soldiers who were recruited into the Red Army as it marched westward across southern Russia and Ukraine were veterans of the disastrous 1941 and 1942 campaigns. Comprehensive data is unavailable for all of the 2nd and 3rd Ukrainian Fronts. Instead, the available information is fragmentary. For instance, the 28th Army conscripted 4,739 soldiers in the city of Mykolaiv and surrounding villages between 28 March and 7 April 1944. Out of these conscripts, 1,090 or 23 percent were former service personnel.[41] Major-General Mikhail Mikhailovich Pronin, head of the Political Department of the 4th Ukrainian Front, recalled that during the liberation of Donbas, which was carried out jointly by the 4th and 3rd Ukrainian Fronts, his army group conscripted 125,000 soldiers. According to him, almost 80 percent of these soldiers had previously served in the army.[42] The number of conscripts and those who had previously served in the Red Army would have been similar in the 3rd Ukrainian Front.

Some soldiers who served in 1941 and again from 1943 or 1944 went straight to their homes in occupied territories after the Red Army was defeated, instead of falling into German captivity or trying to break through to Soviet lines. Other soldiers who served in 1941 and again in 1943–1944 experienced German captivity. The fate of Soviet soldiers captured in 1941, when most were taken prisoners, sometimes depended on their nationality and political affiliation. The Germans set up commissions that screened the prisoners for their ethnicity and politics.[43]

During this period, the Nazis released some Ukrainians whom they needed to work on the land, especially after the early phases of Operation Barbarossa ended. However, they tended to starve the Russians and Ukrainians that they did not release, while systematically murdering Jews and members of the Communist Party.[44] Soldiers who escaped or were released from German captivity were very fortunate, as 3.3 million prisoners of war perished in German captivity out of 5.7 million that fell into German hands (57.5 percent), although the death rate in the winter of 1941–1942 was much higher.[45] According to historian Christian Streit, "Except for the Jews, Soviet prisoners of war suffered the worst fate of all the victims of National Socialist Germany."[46] Thus, a substantial percentage of soldiers that this study examines were among the fortunate few who survived German captivity.

It's noteworthy to compare the fate of the Western prisoners of war in German hands. Out of 232,000 British and American troops in German captivity, 8,348 (3.5 percent) died, whereas the same number of Soviet prisoners died on a single day in the fall of 1941.[47] The vast differences in the fate of Soviet and Western prisoners in German captivity are illustrative of the particular German animosity and brutality toward the Red Army that was characteristic of the Eastern front. In contrast, Mark Edele argued that although the Soviets committed many war crimes against German prisoners of war, their war crimes were more similar to prisoner executions in other wars than to the Germans' premeditated war of extermination.[48]

Hitler called his war against the Soviet Union "the war of annihilation."[49] The invasion had the short-term goals of eliminating the potential Soviet enemy and obtaining vital resources that Germany needed to sustain a longer war against the West. Hitler's long-term objective was to seize *Lebensraum*, the living space for Germans.[50] To fulfill this ghastly vision, the German planners intended to murder all Jews, starve 30 million urban dwellers of the European Soviet Union, subjugate the remaining Slavs to brutal exploitation, and eventually populate the region with ethnic German colonists.[51] The German thirst for resources was accompanied by vicious racism toward East Slavs. One collaborator, who was in frequent contact with high-ranking German officials, recalled after the war: "Indeed most Germans, and certainly almost all [Nazi] party members, did look upon the Russians as livestock, undeserving of pity if a million of them died."[52] According to historian Karel Berkhoff, peasants, who comprised the majority of the population, were treated worse than slaves because slaves were traditionally shown some consideration or concern, which was not the case with the peasantry under the Nazis.[53] The Romanian occupation of Transnistria was, overall, less brutal than the German occupation, but it was also aimed at the ruthless exploitation of Ukrainian territories.[54] Thus, all soldiers who were conscripted in 1943 and 1944 in the liberated territories lived through the genocidal German and Romanian occupations.

When it became clear that the Axis would not achieve a quick victory in 1941, the occupiers' policies shifted somewhat. Now, the Germans concluded that they would need the help of the local population to win, leading to some relaxation of the harshest policies. However, when the Red Army began pushing the Axis westward, the German military launched one of the most brutal phases of occupation: anti-partisan operations and scorch earth policies that systematically strove to destroy assets that the Red Army could potentially use, while also marching millions of men westward so that they would not be conscripted by the advancing Red Army. These policies were implemented under the doctrine of military necessity, which held that the German Army could do whatever it thought was necessary to preserve its combat efficiency.[55] Thus, what liberating Soviet soldiers saw was usually the worst of the German occupation: burnt villages, destroyed factories, and men and women marched west under the barrel of the gun.

As a result of these Axis policies and the war, Ukraine (in its post-1954 borders) lost 7 million people.[56] This number included anywhere from 1,475,000 to 1,550,000 of Ukraine's Jews who remained in Ukraine during the occupation (of whom only 23,000 to 32,000 survived).[57] The Germans deported an estimated 2,402,234 Ukrainians for forced labor to the Third Reich.[58] They were transported in freight cars and treated with particular ruthlessness as the so-called *Ostarbeiter*.[59] The treatment of civilians in the northern Caucasus and southern Russia, where the 2nd and 3rd Ukrainian Fronts fought before entering Ukraine, was similarly brutal, although the German occupation there lasted a shorter period.

The Soviet Union lost 26.6 million people during the war, but the estimates for the proportion of irrecoverable military losses (killed, missing in action, taken prisoner, died of wounds, or sentenced by tribunals) vary anywhere between 11.3 and 14.6 million, indicating that the Soviet Union lost 12–15.3 million civilians.[60] The war's other major belligerents suffered a lot less. Germany lost almost 4.5 million soldiers and 1.5 million civilians. Almost 500,000 French civilians and soldiers were killed during the war, 300,000 British citizens, and 310,000 Italians. Poland suffered proportionally the most: 6,028,000 were killed, including 3,000,000 Jews.[61] The Germans were also much more brutal toward Soviet women than in other occupied European countries. Wehrmacht and SS commanders believed that their soldiers needed to have sex to perform effectively as combatants, but they seldom ordered their troops to commit acts of sexual violence.[62] Instead, German military leaders arranged for the rank and file to use brothels for sex. In Western and Central Europe, Wehrmacht took over existing brothels. However, since the Stalinist Soviet Union did not allow brothels to exist, the Germans had to set up the brothels in 1942.[63]

According to historian Maris Rowe-McCulloch, who studied German brothels in the Russian city of Rostov on Don, Soviet girls and women were forced to seek work in brothels by starvation, threats of deportation and torture, or they were simply snatched off the streets.[64] The girls and women, whom Rowe-McCulloch described as sex slaves, could not leave brothels, their communications with each other and the outside world were severely curtailed, and they were subjected to extremely invasive medical examinations and psychological and physical abuse. They were threatened with executions if they became infected with venereal diseases. Each sex slave was expected to have intercourse with eighteen men per day. The brothels were run by German officers.[65] The situation was not specific to the brothel in Rostov. A German civilian administrator recalled after the war that the women deployed in the Wehrmacht brothel in Poltava were very young, with 85 percent of them being virgins.[66] Historian Wendy Jo Gertjejanssen argued that German policies in the East amounted to a system of sexual slavery.[67] It is not clear how many brothels Wehrmacht operated in the Soviet Union. The Italian army also created as many as thirty-six to fifty brothels in the Soviet Union, although their brothels seem to have been somewhat less coercive and violent.[68]

Beyond the systematic rape of Soviet women in brothels, soldiers could commit sexual violence with impunity, as punishments were very relatively rare. Regina Mühlhäuser, the foremost historian of German-perpetrated sexual violence in the Soviet Union, argued that sexual violence was an integral part of German warfare in the East.[69] At least some Italian, Hungarian, Romanian, and SS officers had their underlings procure women so they could rape them.[70] Sexual exploitation of women was an essential part of the broader Axis' drive to control and exploit Soviet territories.

When the 2nd and 3rd Ukrainian Front soldiers were conscripted into the Red Army in 1943 and 1944, the most catastrophic phase of the Soviet–German war was over for the Red Army. The bleakest period lasted from 22 June 1941, to January 1943, when the Red Army checked the advance of Germans, Romanians, Hungarians, and Italians at Stalingrad. In the initial eighteen months of the war, the Red Army suffered anywhere between 6,395,889 and 8,733,400 irrevocable losses.[71] Yet the war on the Eastern front remained vicious even after Stalingrad, if to a lesser degree. The Red Army respectively suffered anywhere between 2,312,429 and 2,927,900 irrecoverable losses in 1943, 1,763,891 to 2,068,700 in 1944, and 800,817 to 924,000 in

1945.[72] Clearly, the Red Army did not suffer as severely from January 1943 to May 1945, as in the period from June 1941 to December 1942. Nonetheless, the war remained extraordinarily lethal by any measure. For comparative purposes, the three major Western allies (the United States, the United Kingdom, and France) combined suffered 879,842 military deaths on all fronts from 1939 to 1945 (Figure 1.2).[73]

Figure 1.2 Border restored. Source: Victor Temin/Slava Katamidze Collection via Getty Images.

According to the available data that most likely underestimates Soviet casualties, the Steppe/2nd Ukrainian Front, from the Battle of Kursk in July 1943 until 17 April 1944, when the forces entered the northern Romanian city of Botosani, suffered 544,351 losses, of which 66,059 were irrecoverable casualties.[74] The Southwestern/3rd Ukrainian Front, from the Donbas Strategic Operation in August 1943, until 17 April 1944, when its forces liberated Odesa and its environs, suffered 593,653 casualties, of which 130,093 were irrecoverable.[75] The two army groups' advance ended temporarily in the middle of April after they seized Botosani in Romania, parts of Moldavia, and the Odesa region. The frontlines did not change significantly from 17 April until August 21, when the Soviets broke through the Axis lines and occupied Romania. Nonetheless, the fighting did not cease in this period. The Kremlin ordered the 2nd and 3rd Ukrainian Fronts to invade Romania in April and May, which ended as a failure for the Soviets.[76] According to historian David Glantz's estimates, the 2nd and 3rd Ukrainian Fronts suffered 150,000 casualties, irrecoverable and wounded, during these early botched attempts to enter the Balkans.[77]

In all, during the twelve months preceding their entry into Europe, the 2nd and 3rd Ukrainian Fronts suffered 1,288,004 losses, of which 221,652 were irrevocable casualties. These losses were dipterous as the two fronts' size during this period ranged between 901,400 in August and September of 1943 and 1,294,200 in August 1944.[78] It should be mentioned that although the Red Army soldiers suffered heavily, they also inflicted devastating losses on the Axis. During the war, the Red Army inflicted on Germany and its European allies anywhere between 5,980,300 and 8,649,200 irrecoverable casualties.[79] The ratio of Soviet to German losses (including the two major belligerents' allies) for the entire war has been variously estimated to be 1,3 to 1 and 2,5 to 1 in favor of the Germans.[80]

1.3 The Treatment of Conscripts by the Red Army

The People's Commissariat of Defense ran a network of recruitment centers throughout the Soviet Union, which were responsible for inducting conscripts and providing them with preliminary military training.[81] However, after the Red Army started liberating new territories, it became easier for the Red Army to recruit soldiers locally. Thus, after the first Soviet offensive of the war in the winter of 1941–1942, Stalin, on behalf of Stavka, ordered armies in the field to establish the reserve regiments, which were tasked with recruiting, training, and equipping soldiers close to the frontline.[82] Conditions in reserve regiments were terrible. The training was supposed to last only thirty-five to forty-five days, after which the reserve regiments were expected to transfer the soldiers to frontline units.[83] In reality, these troops were often not properly trained, which contributed to the Red Army's colossal casualties, as one officer who led new soldiers into battle put it.[84]

There were two main reasons why the authorities did not follow proper procedures with conscripts. First, there were extreme manpower shortages in the frontline units, and the new soldiers were needed to plug the holes on the frontlines before they completed their training. Moreover, continued economic difficulties made it difficult to properly equip the new troops. Second, senior commanders had little respect for the value and dignity of the lives of ordinary soldiers, referring sometimes to their casualties as "burnt matches" or "broken pencils."[85] The indifference toward the rank and file was displayed vividly by the prevalence of corporal punishment in the Red Army, which was formally illegal. Political departments collected information on instances when officers employed violence against their soldiers or lower-ranking officers. Although the command sometimes punished the offenders, violence against underlings happened often enough that it cannot be characterized as exceptional.[86]

Command in Moscow and at the levels of front and armies were particularly indifferent to the indignities and suffering of the troops from the occupied territories. The captivity of Soviet soldiers by a foreign army was criminalized even before the war started, but these laws were radicalized after Operation Barbarossa was launched.[87] Accordingly, the authorities automatically viewed all those from occupied territories suspiciously and felt free to subject them to cruel treatment. The army's representatives who carried out recruitment were popularly known as "buyers," illustrating how the Red Army's system regarded new conscripts.[88] "Buyers" typically procured goods, slaves, or cattle, not soldiers. In some instances, "buyers" from different armies competed with each other to induct as many men as possible into their units.

For instance, the 3rd Ukrainian Front ordered all recruits from the city of Kryvyi Rih to join the 46th Army. However, officers from the 37th Army continued mobilizing men in the city despite the orders. Evidently, to conceal their transgression, "buyers" from the 37th Army did not leave any documentation on the number of recruits.[89] In this situation, "buyers" from the 37th Army were unlikely to have followed regulations aimed at soldiers receiving proper training and uniforms. I. G. Popov, a regimental commander in the 4th Guards Army, recalled that an officer sent 800 recruits into various units without verifying their training or skills. As a result, he sent trained artillerists to infantry, and he directed infantrymen, who had never seen artillery guns, to operate batteries.[90] Popov described this incident as "characteristic," indicating that such recklessness with soldiers' lives and professional expertise regularly accompanied the mobilization process in the newly liberated territories.[91]

The musings of Ukrainian General Zhmachenko, who commanded the 40th Army of the 2nd Ukrainian Front, vividly illustrate Soviet officers' disdain for recruits. He wrote after the war in his unpublished diary that in the summer of 1944 his army's reserves included 120,000 recently mobilized troops from the right-bank Ukraine.[92] He went on to say that the reserves lacked basic provisions and equipment such as shirts, shoes, and weapons.[93] Archival documents confirm Zhmachenko's description of the poor state of recently recruited soldiers in reserve regiments. In this period, for example, out of a group of 240 such soldiers, 80 to 90 percent did not have shoes, while 15 soldiers walked around only in their undergarments.[94] However, Zhmachenko did not express even the slightest compassion for the soldiers. Instead, this is how he described them: "Among them were many deserters, who in 1941 stayed at 'home, [thinking that] all is over, why to fight on, when my house is under the German [control].'"[95] Zhmachenko evidently believed that many of his soldiers were cowards and traitors for having lived under German occupation, and implicitly, he justified their brutal treatment in the Red Army.

The military and civilian leadership expected new soldiers to engage in mass self-denunciation for having lived in occupied territories. For instance, the new troops from Donbas at a mass meeting were compelled to collectively pledge: "We are guilty before the Soviet power, we are ashamed [for having lived under occupation], and we give our word, that we will justify ourselves [on the battlefield]."[96] In this way, the troops accepted their supposed guilt and responsibility before the Stalinist state for something that was beyond their control, while promising not to let down again their forgiving authorities a second time.

Some Red Army personnel even took pleasure in the suffering of civilians under German rule. Daniil Vladimirovich Fibikh, a military correspondent, wrote in his diary: "You read about German atrocities against the peasant population, and you experience a sense of satisfaction. You did not leave with us, you waited for the Germans, maybe you were even happy that they arrived – so accept [the German abuse], eat their food, Sir peasants."[97] Firbikh blamed the peasants for not abandoning their homes and families and for failing to follow the Red Army when it retreated in 1941. However, the Kremlin never ordered or expected all Soviet citizens to evacuate, nor could the Soviet authorities house and feed tens of millions of refugees in the rear who ended up living under the German occupation.[98] Fibikh's cruel gibe embodied the Stalinist hostility to all perceived or potential disloyal subjects.

Some lower-ranking officers, in immediate contact with new soldiers, as well as other frontline soldiers, did not view the new troops as trustworthy. Mark Papish, a junior commander, did not respect them, describing their martial skills as a joke and accusing them of being guilty. He also suspected them of not wanting to serve and of being most likely to inflict self-injuries.[99] Another soldier, Grigorii Rabinovich, gave a more nuanced response. He said that there were those who fought well and those who had learned how to be adaptable under the Germans, by which he meant that they cooperated with the Nazi occupation authorities. Subsequently, the supposedly adaptable soldiers assumed the safe positions of orderlies and clerical duties in the Red Army.[100] Clearly, Rabinovich believed that some of the recently recruited soldiers survived only because they had served the Germans.

The majority of the new soldiers were Ukrainian. Hostility toward these troops by the longer-serving soldiers and officers occasionally took on a national character. Abdulin said that the veterans in his unit called the new recruits from the Kryvyi Rih region, still dressed in civilian clothes, corn men, presumably because corn grows in the Ukrainian steppe.[101] A sergeant, who had served since the beginning of the war, claimed that in the summer of 1944, the veterans referred to the infantry as "khokhliatskoi" (a Russian-language ethnic slur for Ukrainians) since most of the frontline soldiers were Ukrainian.[102] Milovan Đilas, a high-ranking Yugoslav communist, recalled that during an official visit to Moscow, his Russian driver cursed Ukrainians because they did not fight effectively, forcing the Russians to liberate them.[103] The Ukrainian losses were so high that some members of the Soviet Ukrainian intelligentsia expressed concern about the inhumane nature of mobilization, the fact that Soviet authorities viewed all people from occupied territories as guilty, and they expressed fear that there would be no people left in Ukraine after the war.[104]

Of all nationalities that were represented in larger numbers in the 2nd and 3rd Ukrainian Fronts, Moldavians faced the most difficulties. They were Romanian-speaking and having become part of the Soviet Union only in 1940, many did not speak Russian or another Slavic language. Speaking or at least understanding Russian increased one's chances of survival within the army – it was a prerequisite to promotion or assignment to safer tasks in the infantry in the rear, and it was necessary to be integrated into the army and to be accepted by the majority of Slavic-speaking soldiers. More problematic than the linguistic barrier was the fact that Moldavians' Russian and Ukrainian comrades often viewed them as foreign. One popular stereotype, shared by Russians and Ukrainians, was that Moldavians were dirty, indicating how Moldavians were othered by their comrades.[105] It is unsurprising, therefore, that Moldavians were more likely than other soldiers to desert from the army.[106]

Soviet troops from the 2nd and 3rd Ukrainian Fronts appear to have treated Moldavian civilians worse than Ukrainians or Russians. The murders, rapes, and looting began to intensify just as the two fronts occupied parts of Moldavia. The commander of the 3rd Ukrainian Front issued an order on 19 May 1944, which was read to all the officers of the front. The commander proclaimed that soldiers had started drinking more, which was accompanied by murders, assaults, rapes, and attacks on property. He explained this phenomenon by the fact that alcohol was more readily available in Moldavia and the neighboring Odesa region.[107] However, the upsurge in violence was also connected to the foreignness of Moldavians to the predominantly Slavic soldiers. One Moldavian officer claimed that he was instructed to introduce order in several villages around the town of Orhei, Moldavia. According to him, the Soviet troops' numerous crimes led to antagonism toward Russians on national grounds in Moldavia.[108] A report by the prosecutor's office in Moldavia also concluded that Soviet soldiers had "an intolerant attitude towards the local population," committing many robberies and rapes.[109]

The conscripts were shocked by their treatment in the Red Army. Leonid Gurvits escaped from German encirclement and prisoner-of-war camps to the Red Army in 1942. With a group of soldiers from occupied territories, the NKVD interrogated him repeatedly. Subsequently, he was sent to a reserve regiment. In the reserve regiment, according to him, there were no uniforms, no discipline, and the food was terrible. As he put it, the reserve regiment, where the soldiers were trained, equipped, and screened for loyalty, reminded him more of a prisoner-of-war camp than an army.[110] This comparison, coming from a Jew who survived German captivity, revealed how poorly the Red Army treated soldiers in training. Furthermore, Mikhail Ivanov, a soldier from the Stalino (now Donetsk) region said: "Excesses [against the recruits] were horrible … we could not immediately understand why they had such an attitude to us, and only gradually did we get that they viewed practically all of us as enemies because we had lived under occupation."[111]

At the same time, many of these soldiers were eventually integrated into the army and became part of it if they survived their first battles. Gurvits became a signaller in the army, a relatively trusted and coveted position. Ivanov, soon after his mobilization, was promoted to an artillery spotter, and eventually, he became chief of staff of an artillery regiment.[112] Moreover, some of the recruits reported that the established soldiers welcomed them. One soldier from the Odesa region recalled that once he arrived in the unit, the new soldiers were received well and supported by their more experienced comrades.[113] Certainly, the longer-serving soldiers and officers related that they treated the new soldiers well, sharing their experiences about the war. Abdulin recalled, "I felt great despair and anguish when I witnessed the death of our soldiers, who had just arrived from the rear. I wept. I could not contain my emotions."[114]

Soldiers often had comradely and friendly relations with their fellow fighters, and in the context of a brutal war, they seem to have forged close friendships in short periods. As evidence of this camaraderie, soldiers became "honorable" sons to parents of fallen comrades, or they married their fallen friends' sisters.[115] Here is how Mikhin, the artillery officer, described the time that he spent in the trenches and dugouts in Ukraine in the winter of 1943 and 1944:

> We talked about all sorts of things in those three winter months, but mainly about the things we missed the most – home, women, pre-war parties and holiday gatherings. Every inhabitant of a dugout knew all about each other – his family, friends, and even neighbors. We also liked to listen to all sorts of tales and unusual stories. I spoke a lot about Leningrad [his home city], its palaces, museums and theatres, and the books that I had read.[116]

For many soldiers, having circles of friends helped them overcome fear, loneliness, and separation from family.[117]

Difficulties with integrating recruits into a fighting army were not unique to the Soviet armed forces during the war. The US Army also faced severe problems in properly training and quickly sending the recruits to replenish the degraded frontline units in France. Viewing them as clumsy and doomed, the veterans tended to keep their distance from them until they gained combat experience after the first battle.[118] However, the situation was greatly exacerbated in the Red Army by the Soviet leadership's greater indifference to the suffering of ordinary soldiers and the suspiciousness with which the system viewed everybody who lived under occupation. The economic situation was also objectively much worse in the Soviet Union, which greatly contributed to the problems that newly recruited soldiers faced. In the 2nd and 3rd Ukrainian Front, the issue of new conscripts also intersected with the nationality question, as most newcomers tended to be Ukrainians and then Moldavians, whereas the more experienced soldiers were mostly from Russia and other unoccupied parts of the country.

1.4 Motivations to Serve

Given how they were treated, it is unsurprising that a comparatively large number of Soviets refused to serve. The Red Army was the only military among the major belligerents in Europe to produce 117,000–251,000 defectors who crossed the lines to join the enemy. In addition, the Red Army had 1.5 million draft dodgers, stragglers, and deserters.[119] Active opposition, however, was a minority position among the 34 million men and women who served in the Red Army. The vast majority of Soviet citizens were neither active opponents nor supporters of the regime during the war. Instead, as historian Timothy Johnston put it, most people "just got by."[120] Most of the 2nd and 3rd Ukrainian Front soldiers, when they were initially conscripted into the Red Army in 1943 and 1944, fit this mold. As the two army groups moved across southern and eastern Ukraine and Moldavia, there were neither scenes of mass volunteering nor mass desertions. For new recruits to get by meant to accept their induction since either volunteering or deserting carried greater risks than going along with the state requirements.

There is an important difference, however, between the attitudes toward service before conscription and sustaining morale in the army. Historian Roger Reese wrote on the subject of Soviet soldiers' motivations to serve, and his findings apply to the 2nd and 3rd Ukrainian Fronts. He argued that Soviet soldiers served because of self-interest (wishing to be promoted socially based on service), hatred of the Germans generated by personal experiences, an appreciation of the benefits of Stalinism such as social advancement, a broad sense of patriotism, the fear of consequences of evading conscription if caught, hate promoted by official propaganda, and social pressure to conform.[121] Reese also argued that soldiers at the level of a platoon, or even just a few soldiers in a platoon, developed deep bonds that helped them sustain through combat. According to Reese, the high rate of attrition meant that the troops had to make new connections frequently but did not prevent the emergence of groups of buddies.[122]

It is important to note that patriotism was one of the Red Army's primary driving forces, but how the troops understood patriotism varied greatly. Many troops identified with the Soviet state and, to a lesser extent, with Stalin as their commander-in-chief. Governments tend to increase their legitimacy in victorious and just wars (as understood by the majority of the population), and the Stalinist regime was no exception. This fact is best illustrated by the speedy growth of the Communist Party in the trenches.[123] Soviet propagandists managed to construct a link between soldiers' emotional connections to their homes and families with the patriotic notion of *rodina* (motherland).[124] For many soldiers, patriotism was about their families and homes. Soldiers' sense of patriotism could also entail belief in the socialist experiment without endorsing Stalinism.[125]

Patriotism could also mean loyalty to a soldier's particular ethnic group or national language. The example of Jews in the Red Army illustrates most clearly how Soviet troops could have complex motivations to fight. As scholar Anna Shternshis argued, in the 1920s and 1930s, Jews developed a secular and ethnic identity in association with the Soviet regime.[126] Once the war started, Soviet Jews came under existential threat from the Germans, Romanians, and Hungarians, as well as Cossacks, Ukrainian nationalists, and Bessarabian peasants. Therefore, they started to identify even more with Soviet power, while the attacks against them reinforced their Jewishness. Vol'f Zelenyi, a nineteen-year-old Jewish soldier, sent a letter to his parents on 20 February 1943, which vividly illustrated this point:

> Dear daddy and mommy! For all of our multi-national people, but especially for the Jewish people, a tough moment has arrived. Hitler's bloody hands want to enslave them, even worse, to "remove" them from the face of the planet, but he will fail. The Jewish people will show the truth, they will avenge their tormented daughters and sons. Being a son of Jewish people...and being aware of all of this, I have fought with the enemy fearlessly and heroically, not regretting my strength and life...Dear daddy and mommy! I give you my word that in the future I will continue, with honor and gratitude, to serve my Motherland, the party, and the government, which have so highly appraised my humble deeds [he was awarded a medal for participating in the liberation of Stalingrad].[127]

Zelenyi clearly understood Hitler's policies toward Jews, and he did not see a contradiction between his fidelity to Soviet Union and the Jewish people.

Boris Slutskii's war experience also illustrated how Soviet and Jewish motives coexisted among Jews in Red Army uniforms. Slutskii was a quintessential Soviet *intelligent*, having studied law and literature in Moscow prior to the war.[128] He started the war as a simple infantry soldier in 1941 and ended it as a major in the political department of the 3rd Ukrainian Front. His memoir, which he wrote in the summer of 1945, makes it clear that he fully identified with the Red Army.[129] He used "we" when writing about the Soviet Union and the Red Army's greatest achievements, as well as its atrocities against German prisoners and the rape of women in enemy European countries. At the same time, he paid a great deal of attention to issues that affected Jews: the growth of nationalism among Russian soldiers and officers, the proliferation of antisemitism in the army and among civilians, and collaboration in the Holocaust. He was also very attentive toward the Jews of European countries.[130] Reading his memoirs, there is little doubt that Slutskii was both Soviet and Jewish.

Considering that so many soldiers were Ukrainian, it is necessary to consider their national identity. One study of the Kherson Region suggested that the significant majority of residents had a Soviet identity. However, the Red Army's defeats in 1941 and German propaganda drew some of these people away from the Soviet vision. Yet, when the Red Army returned, residents of Kherson quickly reembraced Soviet identity.[131] Another study found that in Romanian-run Transnistria, a small piece of territory centered on Odesa, the identities were very fluid. Even the resisters had overlapping and fluid identities that fluctuated between pro-Soviet and pro-Ukrainian.[132] According to Berkhoff's meticulous study of the Reichskommissariat Ukraine, the issue of national identity was vague. Most Ukrainians used *svoi* or *nashi* (our) when describing Russians, even those who had a strong Ukrainian national consciousness. Berkhoff concluded that the majority of people in Dnepr Ukraine (southern, central, and eastern Ukraine), thought of Ukrainians as a subgroup of Russians.[133] For many contemporaries, Ukrainian was not exclusive with the Soviet and even Russian. Wendy Jo Gertjejanssen claimed that women she interviewed in the central Ukrainian city of Cherkasy fully identified with the Russians, and that "when they spoke of the approaching Red Army they spoke with genuine happiness, 'ours, ours came!'"[134] Thus, Ukrainian national identity largely aligned with the Kremlin's line that Russians were the older brothers in the family of Soviet nations, which left room for Ukrainian cultural expression.[135]

None of this is to deny that there was widespread hostility to Soviet power. Opposition to collective farming was very common, while preference for more democracy was somewhat common.[136] In pre-1939 Soviet Ukraine, there was a network of hundreds of local anti-Soviet activists. They consisted of members of the defunct Ukrainian People's Republic from the Civil War period, the clergy of the Ukrainian Autocephalous Church, the Ukrainian-speaking intelligentsia, and local peasants, all of whom were anti-Soviet and connected to the center of armed insurgency in western Ukraine.[137] However, it should be kept in mind that the 2nd and 3rd Ukrainian Fronts never operated in western Ukraine, which was the epicenter of Ukrainian nationalism. Moreover, popular anti-communism in Ukraine did not necessarily amount to the desire for political independence or anti-Russian attitudes. Even in Vinnitsya, the westernmost part of pre-1939 Ukraine and therefore the least Russified and most exposed to Ukrainian nationalist influence, Ukrainians believed that there was a clear difference between Soviet power and Russians. They viewed Russians as their own and Bolsheviks as foreign. At the same time, residents of Vinnitsya were puzzled over Galicia-based Ukrainian nationalist fighters' venomous hatred of the Russians.[138] In any case, given the Axis treatment of the local population, and the lack of viable alternatives, many residents of Reichskommissariat Ukraine and Transnistria welcomed the Red Army's return and the departure of the Germans and Romanians.[139]

It should also not be overlooked that Ukrainians were overall relatively privileged in the hierarchy of Soviet nationalities, second only to the Russians.[140] The Kremlin promoted Ukrainian patriotism within the Soviet context from the earliest days of the war. On 24 June 1941, only three days after the war started, the central party mouthpiece *Pravda* published a patriotic poem in Ukrainian.[141] The Red Army leadership, especially when it advanced into Ukraine, sought to use Ukrainian identity and patriotism to mobilize the troops. For instance, these were some of the lectures and topics that the Communist Party cells were required to discuss and study in 1944: "Love towards fatherland … Glorious Traditions of the Russian and Ukrainian People," "Crimes by the German-fascist Conquerors in Ukraine," and "The Fight for the Unification of the Great Ukrainian Nation."[142] Other lessons include: "The Friendship between People of USSR is Growing and Strengthening."[143] Meanwhile, military agitators sometimes wrote propaganda materials in the Ukrainian language, and more often, they addressed the new conscripts in Ukrainian.[144] Ukrainians were the only Soviet nationality that had a Soviet military order (Bohdan Khmelnytsky) named after a non-Russian.[145] Clearly, the Kremlin's narrative of Soviet history and the war allowed for Ukrainian patriotism and culture to coexist with the wider Soviet system, allowing Moscow to effectively mobilize Ukrainians in the war.

There were also very pragmatic reasons for Ukrainians to fight. In 1941, the Axis troops were victorious, and it seemed that Soviet power would not return to Ukraine. However, by 1943, it was clear that the Germans and their allies were neither invincible nor benign, while with every passing day, it seemed more likely that Soviet power would return for good to Ukraine. The Axis atrocities and exploitation of the local population made it clear that continuing to live under their occupation was not feasible. Therefore, serving the Soviet regime became more necessary than was the case in 1941. All of these factors help explain why Ukrainians served in the 2nd and 3rd Ukrainian Fronts, overall, loyally in 1944 and 1945. Most Ukrainians' conception of their identity as part of broader Soviet or Russian identities, even if they were unhappy with Stalin's policies, does help explain why the 2nd and 3rd Ukrainian Fronts in 1944 and 1945 managed to crush the Wehrmacht and its allies in their sectors of the front.

Significantly, it is wrong to extrapolate a soldier's identity solely based on how civilians viewed the world. Intensive military training and combat transformed old identities, while also generating new identities and loyalties that set soldiers apart from civilians. Whatever Soviet soldiers may have thought about Stalin and Hitler before the war, once in combat, they were either going to kill or be killed. The Red Army's undeniable successes in the field in this stage of the war also created a sense of pride, while many soldiers began identifying, at least in part, with the Soviet government. At the same time, the army's coercive powers – fear of punishment for desertion, dereliction of duty, or committing crimes – were also vital in sustaining the troops in combat. Historian Roberto J. Carmack argued that Kazakh soldiers, who as ethnic outsiders were repeatedly excluded and discriminated against by the Soviet system, were eventually integrated by their military service into the Soviet Union's social and political structures.[146] Carmack's arguments are even more valid when it comes to Ukrainian soldiers who were not ethnically foreign.

1.4.1 The Duty to Hate

The barbaric conduct of the German and Romanian occupiers and the soldiers' suffering on the frontlines ensured that the thirst for vengeance was felt viscerally by many soldiers. However, Soviet propaganda, which for years encouraged soldiers to hate the "enemy" while urging them to exact revenge against the Germans and their allies, shaped the soldiers' perceptions and conduct in "enemy" countries. An important feature of Soviet propaganda was that the troops had to express the desire for revenge to be fully accepted into the Red Army by their officers and other soldiers.

The soldiers' hatred of the enemy and their desire for vengeance were often genuine and caused by the behavior of Axis soldiers. The few veterans in the 2nd and 3rd Ukrainian Fronts in 1944, who had been in service since 1941, claimed to have learned to hate early in the war. A tank officer from the 2nd Ukrainian Front recalled that during the Red Army's retreat in 1941 in the Zhytomyr region, he saw by the road the corpse of a young woman, who had been killed by a German dive-bomber. Next to her was a screaming one-year-old baby. After knocking on the doors of several houses, he found an old woman who agreed to take the baby. He claimed that after this episode: "I had only one thought in my head then: the German is an enemy that must be destroyed! And until the end of the war, we did not take any prisoners without particular necessity."[147] As historian Matt Lenoe argued, Soviet soldiers tended to associate child victims of atrocities with their children, leading to a deep-seated craving for revenge.[148]

The Red Army maintained close links with the civilian population as it pushed the enemy westward. Many of the contacts were informal, but they were also facilitated by official policies. The Red Army organized cinema sessions for the liberated population and rallies in which rank-and-file soldiers and civilians participated.[149] It also assisted peasants with spring fieldwork, and it helped restore the destroyed property.[150] Moreover, the Soviet leadership created the so-called Military Commissions, which investigated "enemy" war crimes. These commissions consisted of officers and local civilians, and their findings were used in hate propaganda.[151] These contacts between civilians and the army facilitated the flow of information to the troops about the occupiers' genocidal policies. For example, one soldier wrote home from liberated territories that peasants were telling the troops about hunger, beatings, executions, and being taken for forced labor to Germany, illustrating the flow of information between frontline soldiers, liberated civilians, and civilians in the rear.[152]

Encountering and learning about the Axis' atrocities further cemented the troops' desire for revenge against the enemy. Iosif Drakhlin, a Jewish soldier from Ukraine, wrote to his wife that all Jews in Kharkiv and Voroshilovgrad (Lugansk now) had been killed. He went on to say: "There is not one person whose heart is not burning with hate for these hangmen (*palachy*). And they deserve one thing only – death. And not just death, but a torturous death."[153] Mansur Abdulin, a Komsomol organizer, discovered in a village near Kharkiv a horrid scene: A mutilated Red Army officer was dumped in a well, along with corpses of (presumably raped) naked girls and women, and at the end of the hamlet he saw that all the villagers had been shot and stretched out along the road. "The infantrymen, taking off their caps, slowly walked past the several hundred shot women, old people, and children. We felt ashamed. I sobbed violently, beside myself with anger and rage. I promised myself to avenge these people, to get as many Nazis and our traitors as I could!"[154]

He wrote in another part of his memoir: "I was consumed by the idea that while alive, I would have my revenge on the Germans in advance: for I never expected to survive that slaughter. Once, on my initiative, we shot no less than 200 wounded Nazis in a vegetable store."[155] For other soldiers, the suffering of their family members was enough to incite hate and a desire for vengeance against the Germans. A Ukrainian officer wrote in his unpublished memoirs that during the occupation, Germans burnt his house down, shot his parents, took his sister to Germany for forced labor, arrested his brother for cooperation with the Partisans, and beat his wife to death. According to him, this was the main reason why Soviet troops hated Germans and were encouraged to fight against them.[156]

Undeniably, an important reason for the widespread hatred for the Germans and Romanians was their deliberate humiliation and genocidal treatment of Soviet civilians and prisoners of war. At the same time, as historian Serhy Yekelchyk argued, the regime expected civilians to feel hate, but that hate played a secondary role to positive civic emotions that they were supposed to express, a love of the Motherland and gratitude to Stalin.[157] However, when it comes to soldiers, the country's leadership held that the troops' primary emotion should be hate. A 1943 report about Soviet propaganda, which was submitted to Georgii Aleksandrov, who was in charge of the Central Committee's Propaganda and Agitation Department, stated that propaganda aimed to mobilize Ukrainians in the war by cultivating hate, anger, and the desire for revenge toward the Germans, as well as to encourage bravery, patriotism, and belief in the ultimate Red Army victory.[158] Thus, the troops' desire for revenge was legitimized and incited by Soviet authorities. Soldiers were expected to feel and express hate, and no doubt, some of these expressions were performative. However, the Soviets did have valid reasons to hate and want revenge, and they responded positively to the hate propaganda.

The Kremlin was well aware that it was able to win over some troops, even those who were not supportive of the Stalinist regime and its policies, through nationalism and anti-German hate. Cultivating hate was a way to socialize soldiers into the Red Army's culture, and expressing hate helped new soldiers integrate into the existing military collective by demonstrating loyalty to it. For this reason, the Red Army hate propaganda was not only distributed to soldiers, but agitators sought to involve soldiers in a political theater in which they had to express hate. The military hierarchy went to great lengths to enflame "irreconcilable hate," as one document described the goal of propaganda.[159]

One method that agitators widely used to involve soldiers in hate propaganda was mass demonstrations, sometimes referred to as "meetings of revenge." At these events, soldiers read letters from home that informed them about the Axis atrocities, while liberated civilians related the horrors of Nazi occupation to the troops, or soldiers spoke of the victimization of their family members. At these events, the tone of the language was usually righteous anger while the speakers appealed to Soviet troops' most bloodthirsty urges. For instance, the troops were riled into a frenzy by being told stories of Axis atrocities in the city of Dnipropetrovsk. Afterward, soldiers swore to take revenge against the occupiers in the most bloodthirsty terms possible. The meeting of revenge ended in a mass oath by soldiers:

> *Frau*, can you hear our screams? You who sent your beasts to murder children and old people of our country?...We, the soldiers and commanders of Mykolaiv

Red Banner Border Guard Regiment who have gathered at this meeting, we are swearing an oath that we will exact revenge against German conquerors for all the villainy and criminal acts that they committed against the citizens of our Soviet country. We are propelled westwards by our burning hatred for you Hitlerland (*gitleriia*), who has drenched in blood dozens of countries around the world. We will force you, fascist Germany, to wash out with your tears the world which has been drenched in blood of millions murdered and buried alive citizens of our Soviet socialist fatherland.[160]

At another meeting of revenge, a soldier read a letter to the comrades from his unit. He received a letter from the inhabitants of his recently liberated village in the Leningrad region, informing him that his entire family had been killed by Germans. The soldier announced to the troops of his unit: "I have nothing left except revenge and more revenge. I will destroy the fascist scum (*gadov*) without pity, wherever I may encounter them."[161] After his speech, other soldiers and officers spoke, expressing support for him and promising revenge against the Germans.[162] There is no doubt that the meetings of revenge were performative. However, there is also no doubt that for some troops these meetings legitimized violence against civilians in the name of revenge.

Agitators in some instances came up with creative ways to involve soldiers in participating in hate propaganda. In the autumn of 1944, a Red Army newspaper, *Sovetskii Boets*, ran a competition on the question, "Why I want to kill every German." Hundreds of soldiers submitted essays on how German crimes afflicted them, forcing them to dwell on and magnify their suffering.[163] Another resourceful tactic that agitators used to involve soldiers in expressing hate while intensifying the desire for revenge was the so-called revenge scores. Political Department officers interviewed their soldiers and collected information on how they were affected by the war. Before the battle, agitators made posters in which they recorded how many of their soldiers' relatives were killed and taken as slave laborers. In one battalion, soldiers of the unit before the battle were instructed to take revenge for 775 killed relatives, 909 forced laborers, 478 burnt-down houses, and 303 destroyed farms.[164]

Hate propaganda resonated profoundly with the troops. Arguably, almost all soldiers could identify with the Kremlin's anti-German message, since most had one or more relatives killed in the war, and they likely lost many comrades. Propaganda that glorified Lenin, Stalin, and the communist system must have seemed hollower to many soldiers. However, what made propaganda in the Red Army so effective was not only that many soldiers could relate to it but also that it was interactive. The hate campaign was not limited to agitators reading lectures, although this was certainly part of it. Instead, the hate campaign involved soldiers because they had to participate in it by drawing on their own experiences with the Germans, making it more personal and thereby more effective.

The Soviet regime had good reasons to deploy hate propaganda. The Red Army was an ill-disciplined force. Many Soviet citizens did not want to fight in the war, whether because they were reluctant to serve the regime or because they were afraid of being killed or maimed. Moreover, as military specialists have noted, soldiers' fighting morale on the battlefield is mainly sustained by their friendship and sense of camaraderie with other soldiers.[165] The influx of hundreds of thousands of new soldiers into the 2nd and 3rd Ukrainian Fronts in 1943 and 1944 must have sapped some of the cohesiveness of units on a micro-level. What virtually all Soviet soldiers had in common – the new recruits, experienced soldiers, and their officers – was that they had strong reasons to hate Germans. The hate, thus, was useful in uniting disparate groups of soldiers around the regime's ultimate goal of defeating the Axis.

Soviet hate propaganda was officially aimed at enemy armies and their leaders, and not against Romanian, Hungarian, and German civilians. Even Stalin emphasized that German soldiers were the targets of Soviet fury, in his famous speech on 6 November 1941. On that occasion, the Soviet dictator said:

> The German conquerors want a war of extermination with the peoples of the U.S.S.R. Well, if the Germans want to have a war of extermination, they will get it. From now on our task, the task of the peoples of the U.S.S.R., the task of the fighters, commanders, and the political workers of our army and our navy will be to exterminate every single German who has set his invading foot on the territory of our Fatherland. No mercy to the German occupiers! Death to German occupiers.[166]

Yet, as Karel Berkhoff noted, propaganda blurred and sometimes erased the distinction between "fascists" and "Germans."[167] Moreover, even if aimed formally at enemy forces, the language accompanying the hate propaganda was so aggressive and vivid that, in the eyes of Soviet soldiers, it contributed to the collapse of the important distinction between enemy soldiers and civilians. Propaganda regularly referred to enemy soldiers as Hitlerites, fascist scum, monsters, villains, bandits, rapists, and murderers, to cite just some of the epitaphs. On the eve of the Red Army's entry into Europe, Soviet soldiers and officers hated and were eager to wreak havoc against the enemy.

1.4.2 Food

The Soviet Union faced severe food shortages throughout the war. Devastated by war, the Soviet Union produced in 1945 less than half of the food that it produced in 1940.[168] According to one estimate, the famine took the lives of 1.5 million Soviet civilians, excluding up to 800,000 people who starved to death in besieged Leningrad.[169] Although the Red Army also went hungry, especially in 1941 and early 1942, the Stalinist regime prioritized feeding its military machine over civilians.[170] Soviet troops began to eat much better in 1943 after they went on the offensive, but the civilians continued to starve, with cases of cannibalism proliferating in central Russia in the winter of 1943–1944.[171] As late as 1944, malnutrition was the leading cause of death of adult civilians.[172] Although soldiers were supposed to be the best-fed group of people in the Soviet Union, there simply was not enough food to feed them properly, nor was it always possible to deliver food to the frontlines. One officer recalled that his troops were so hungry that they ate grass in the early winter of 1942.[173] Almost all troops in the rear undergoing training complained of hunger.[174]

The situation began to change for the better once the Red Army went on the offensive and began capturing German food supplies, which were taken from the occupied territories. Moreover, Ukraine had more readily available corn and vegetables for soldiers to seize than was the case in Russia.[175] The food situation started to improve in 1943, but Soviet soldiers were rarely fed according to the Red Army's own standards. A special investigation in the 3rd Ukrainian Front, which the front command ordered to find out whether the soldiers were fed and supplied properly, revealed that the quartermaster service responsible for feeding the soldiers of the front had made significant improvements in the second half of 1943. Nonetheless, it also found that there were shortages of sugar, butter, and animal fats.[176]

Similarly, the 2nd Ukrainian Front Command investigated in January 1944, which revealed serious shortcomings in how soldiers were treated. The investigation revealed that some soldiers had not bathed and changed their undergarments in three months. Furthermore, the investigative report maintained that soldiers lived in dugouts, sleeping directly on the ground; the food was below official standards, as it was served irregularly and cold. The commander of the 2nd Ukrainian Front characterized the officers responsible for this situation as "criminal" and "heartless."[177] Similarly, a sanitary inspection of the 4th Mechanized Corps of the 3rd Ukrainian Front reported in September 1944 that the quality of food served was low, tasteless, without necessary vitamins, and of insufficient caloric value. One soldier described the food as "swill."[178] Although there were clear improvements in how soldiers were fed, the soldiers' most basic needs were never properly met during the war on Soviet soil.

1.5 Conclusion

When the 2nd and 3rd Ukrainian Fronts entered Europe in the summer of 1944, the soldiers were mostly Ukrainians, since the Red Army recruited locally. They were survivors of numerous violent Stalinist campaigns, including dekulakization, the man-made famine of the 1930s, and the Stalinist repressions. They also lived through the genocidal German occupation and had experience with extraordinarily lethal warfare. Their high command viewed them as little more than cannon fodder, often throwing them into battle with little training. As the Soviet forces suffered heavy casualties in Europe, the ethnic profile of the two army groups became more representative of the Soviet Union.

The vast majority of soldiers accepted their enlistment. They were motivated by a mixture of patriotism broadly understood, a desire for revenge, and perhaps most importantly in this stage, an absence of viable alternatives. In 1944, it was clear that the Soviet power would be permanently restored throughout the western Soviet Union. Once in the army, the ordeals of frontline service – combat and camaraderie – tended to reinforce many soldiers' ties to the cause and the system as they forged new identities as Soviet warriors. This situation was not unique to the Red Army. With regards to the Wehrmacht, Omer Bartov argued that ideology, high casualties, and a breakdown in supplies contributed to the physical and psychological hardship of German soldiers, which in turn led to their brutalization.[179] There is little doubt that Soviet soldiers, according to these standards, were even more brutalized as they entered Europe.

2 2nd and 3rd Ukrainian Fronts' Operations and Rampage in Europe

Pavel El'kinson, a scout in the Red Army, recorded his attitudes to the war in his diary on 27 August 1944, as his unit was preparing to cross the River Prut, the border between Romania and the Soviet Union:

> Finally, on our sector of the front, the long-awaited day of the complete expulsion of Germans from our country has arrived ... at six o'clock, we crossed the Prut. Did I ever think that I would have a chance to go abroad? Now, the time has come for this. I really want to remember and record everything that I have seen ... I am so happy to observe all our weaponry on the move. What might! There is so much dust that vehicles are hitting each other in broad daylight. And we will swallow the dust. We are passing by the first [Romanian] village. It is burnt to the ground. There are almost no inhabitants.[1]

Remarkably, El'kinson recorded his war experiences since it was illegal to keep a diary on the frontlines, and only a few such documents have survived and been recovered by scholars.[2] El'kinson's musings offer important insights into the Soviet frontline troops' attitudes as they marched into the Balkans and Central Europe in the last year of World War II. Like many of his comrades, El'kinson was very proud of the Red Army's strength and its victories over the Axis. He was curious to see new countries and completely indifferent to the fate of the enemy population, whose houses the Red Army burned while murdering the inhabitants or forcing them to flee.

The magnitude of military violations committed by Soviet troops in Europe grew considerably. These excesses happened in and were shaped by the context of military operations and specific historical locations. This chapter outlines the major operations of the 2nd and 3rd Ukrainian Fronts in 1944–1945, and it seeks to measure the growth of violations. Its purpose is to provide context for the subsequent chapters.

2.1 Romania

When the troops of the 2nd and 3rd Ukrainian Fronts unleashed a wave of robberies, rapes, and murders in 1944 in Romania, it was only the most recent episode in a longer Soviet–Romanian conflict characterized by violence. The relations between Moscow and Bucharest were riddled with territorial and ideological disputes from the establishment of the Soviet state. Moscow never recognized the incorporation of Bessarabia and northern Bukovina by Romania after the First World War. The Kremlin annexed these regions in 1940 as part of the Molotov–Ribbentrop Pact, arresting and deporting 31,419 residents.[3] An additional 53,356 persons were mobilized for compulsory labor in different parts of the Soviet Union.[4]

Soviet aggression contributed to Bucharest's decision to join the Axis. Romania played an important role in the German-led war against the Soviet Union. In total, Romania had 686,258 men under arms in 1941 and 1,174,147 in June 1944, deploying more troops on the Eastern front than all the other German allies combined.[5] In addition, Bucharest reannexed territories that it had lost to the Soviet Union in 1940, and it occupied Transnistria, a large section of southwestern Ukraine between the Dniester and Southern Bug Rivers with Odesa at its center. However, Bucharest's decision to join the German-led bloc was not simply a reaction to Moscow's initial seizure of Bessarabia and northern Bukovina. The Romanian leadership expected Germany to emerge as the dominant power in Europe after the war, and by fighting loyally alongside the Wehrmacht, it hoped to win Hitler's favor so that he would reconsider his decision to give part of Transylvania to Hungary.[6] Moreover, Bucharest's realignment with Germany reflected the Romanian leaders' commitment to Germany's crusade to defend Christian civilization from the threat of the so-called Jewish Communism.[7] Historian Vladimir Solonari persuasively argued that Ion Antonescu, the wartime Romanian leader, doggedly pursued a policy of recreating Greater Romania and forcefully cleansing it of more than three-and-a-half million so-called foreign elements.[8] Antonescu could only fulfill this vision in alliance with the Nazis.

Bucharest pursued its genocidal policies in Transnistria, using the territory as a dumping ground and killing site for Jews from Bessarabia and Bukovina. In total, the Romanians murdered 250,000 Soviet and Romanian Jews.[9] The nationalism of the Romanian leadership was also, at times, anti-Slavic. Mihai Antonescu, the second most powerful person in the country, argued in a radio address at the beginning of the war that the socially amorphous Slavic masses and Bolshevism combined to present a threat to the old European races and ancient civilization.[10] An example of the racist Romanian line was a propaganda booklet from 1942 that provided nonflattering photographs of supposedly Soviet racial types: a Jew, a Central Asian ("Asiatic"), a Slav, and a Romani ("Gypsy").[11] Ion Antonescu told Transnistria's governor to treat the province "as if Romania will rule these territories for 2 million years.

What will happen afterward, we have yet to see."[12] Romanians engaged in systematic plunder, as well as widespread rape and violence, especially in the first six months of the occupation.[13]

Still, the Romanian occupational regime in Transnistria was less brutal than its German counterpart in other parts of Ukraine. Generally, as German victory became more doubtful, Bucharest's treatment of the subjugated people became less severe. Romanians reopened between 300 and 400 churches in Transnistria. The opening ceremonies for churches were often attended by important Romanian officials.[14] Antonescu eventually allowed Jews from Romania proper to send aid to their compatriots who had been deported to Transnistria. As a result, Transnistria had the largest proportion of Jews who survived the Axis occupation of Ukraine.[15] The Romanian administration even declared that all citizens in the province should enjoy civic rights, except for the right to engage in political activities.[16] Ultimately, Odesa experienced an economic and cultural revival under occupation from the nadir in 1941.[17] Although Romanian occupation was less brutal in Ukraine than the German occupation, Romanian authorities remained unpopular among residents of Transnistria, the majority of whom awaited the restoration of Soviet rule.[18]

Parts of the 2nd Ukrainian Front entered northeastern Romania during the Uman–Botoshany Operation from 5 March to 17 April 1944, in the first stage of the Red Army's occupation of the country. From April until late August, the frontline remained stable. During this period, the Soviet troops occupied a relatively small section of Romania, a 100 km deep into Romanian territory from the Soviet border, consisting of over 800 towns and villages.[19]

Red Army documents make it clear that there was an upsurge in military violations in the spring of 1944 in northern Romania. This is best illuminated by Colonel Zolotukhin's report cited in the introduction. For example, in Botoshany, the largest Romanian town under Soviet control at the time, the Soviet patrols detained 500 soldiers and officers in just three days from 17 May to 20 May, for "undignified conduct (*nedostoinoe povedenie*)."[20] In Soviet parlance, "undignified conduct" could refer to any number of military violations and criminal acts, including public drunkenness, robberies, murders, sexual assaults, straggling, and deserting. There was also a sharp increase in venereal infections among the troops in Romania. In April, the front's Sanitary Directorate recorded 2006 new cases of venereal diseases among the troops, including 540 among the officers.[21] This figure was probably only the tip of the iceberg, as the report conceded that many troops concealed their infections, using home remedies for treatment.[22] Filipp Zhmachenko, commander of the 40th Army of the 2nd Ukrainian Front, confirmed Zolutkhin's findings.

He recalled in his unpublished memoirs that the proliferation of venereal diseases among his troops in Romania forced him to open two new hospitals and to increase the number of physical examinations since the troops were hiding their infections.[23] The situation was similar in the 3rd Ukrainian Front, which was deployed in the Odesa region and Moldavia. According to the order issued by the army group's commander on 19 May 1944, there was a proliferation of acts of drunkenness, accompanied by serious crimes, such as murders, physical injuries, rapes, hooliganism, robberies, and resistance to civilian authorities. The order blamed the widespread availability of wine in the Odesa region and Moldavia for the upsurge in criminality.[24] These documents confirm that the two Front leaders believed that there was an upsurge in military violations when their soldiers entered Romania, Moldova, and the Odesa region.

After the Uman–Botoshany Operation ran its course, when the front stabilized, the commander of the 3rd Ukrainian Front created a front-line zone within 25 km of the line of contact on 25 April.[25] The order instructed all unit commanders and military councils to assume responsibility for organizing and safekeeping the property of evacuated civilians.[26] Despite the orders emphasizing that the commanders were required to guard the property of evacuated civilians, Zhmachenko wrote, with a tone that indicated his approval of looting, "It is understood that soldiers took the property to equip their dugouts."[27] This episode illustrates both the large-scale looting and the tacit approval it enjoyed from the leadership in the field, despite the orders on the level of the front to prevent the looting.

In June and July, the Red Army launched devastating offensives in Belarus and western Ukraine, reaching the borders of East Prussia and the river Vistula in central Poland. These developments compelled the Germans to shift eleven divisions, including six panzer divisions, from Romania, significantly weakening the Axis' position in the Balkans.[28] Taking advantage of these developments, the Stavka ordered the 2nd and 3rd Ukrainian Fronts to launch the Iasi–Kishinev Strategic Offensive Operation (20 August to 29 August), one of the most successful Soviet offensive operations of the war. The Red Army annihilated the entire Army Group South Ukraine, which included 900,000 German and Romanian troops. The crushing victory resulted in the overthrow of General Antonescu's military dictatorship on 23 August and Romania's declaration of war on Germany two days later.[29] The Soviet–Romanian negotiations began after the coup, culminating in the Armistice Convention on 12 September.

These monumental events enabled the Red Army to advance between 500 and 750 km westward – known as the exploitation phase of the operation – without encountering serious organized resistance, as the Germans

Figure 2.1 Start of the Iasi–Kishinev strategic offensive operation. Source: Universal History Archive/Universal Images Group via Getty Images.

desperately sought to reconstruct the frontline.[30] The total Soviet losses in the Iasi–Kishinev Operation were 67,130, including 13,197 irrecoverable losses.[31] In all the battles associated with the liberation of Romania, the Red Army suffered 286,000 casualties, including 69,000 irrecoverable losses.[32] This figure presumably includes the earlier attempts to invade the country in the spring of 1944 and the battles against Hungarians and Germans in the Debrecen Operation in Transylvania (Figure 2.1).

After the destruction of the Army Group South Ukraine, the 2nd and 3rd Ukrainian Fronts, which had operated jointly until then, split. The 2nd Ukrainian Front raced to Transylvania on the Romanian–Hungarian border to repel, with their newly minted Romanian allies, a joint German–Hungarian counteroffensive. It soon launched the Debrecen Operation, which was aimed at moving the frontline into Hungary proper. The Debrecen Operation was fought primarily in Hungary but also in Romania, which was entirely cleared of German and Hungarian troops by the end of October.[33] After the Iasi–Kishinev Operation, the 3rd Ukrainian Front headed south to Bulgaria and Yugoslavia, reaching the former in the middle of September and the latter at the end of the month.[34] Thus, the vast majority of the 3rd Ukrainian Front left Romania within less than a month, and the 2nd Ukrainian Front left within two months. Both army groups raced through the country to move into the space created by the collapse of the German front in southern Europe. Even the nonmechanized units marched at the speed of sixty to 65 km per day (Map 2.1).[35]

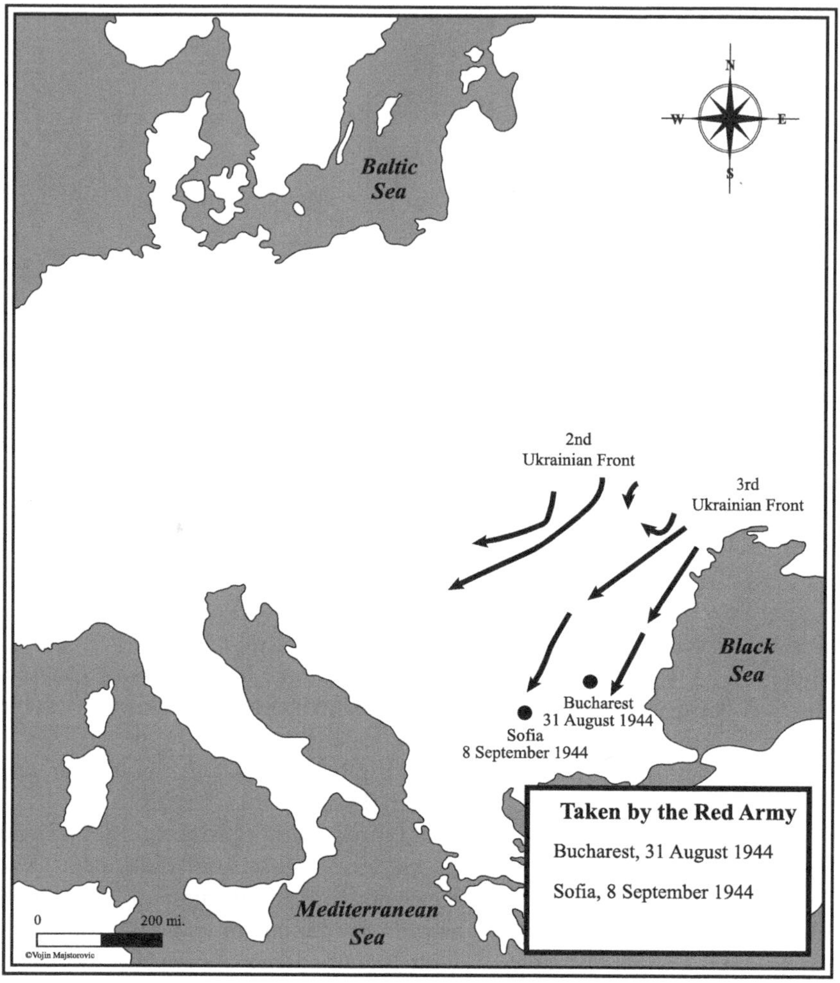

Map 2.1 2nd and 3rd Ukrainian Front movements in Bulgaria and Romania, 1944.

Following the Iasi–Kishinev Operation, around 1 million 2nd and 3rd Ukrainian Front troops fanned through Romania.[36] After the Armistice Convention on 12 September, the Soviets governed Romania through the Allied Control Commission (ACC). The ACC kept Romania's institutions intact, including the army, police, municipal, and national governments, to help with the war effort. Therefore, Romanian officials were able to receive complaints from victims and record the situation in the country as it was occupied by the Red Army. This was far from a perfect system. One can imagine that the victims of Soviet criminal conduct, especially sexual violence survivors, were reluctant to report the Red Army troops either to Romanian or Soviet authorities, as it invited unwelcomed scrutiny from the brutal occupiers. Nonetheless, the Romanian administration, even if weakened, left more reliable records of the Soviet rampage than was the case in the northwestern corner of Romania in the spring and summer of 1944, or Hungary and Austria later in the war, when state administration withdrew before the Soviet conquest. After the arrival of the Red Army, it took weeks or even months to rebuild the rudimentary state structures in these areas.

Constantin Sanatescu, the new Romanian prime minister of the recently formed pro-Allied Romanian government, wrote in his diary on 1 September, "the Russians are plundering each and every region. The behavior of Russian sailors who disembarked in Constanta is the worst. They have terrified the city; the people are running in all directions. Complaints from all areas devastated by Soviet troops have reached the presidency."[37]

A Romanian general sent to the region of Oltenia in the south of the country to investigate the state of affairs reported to Bucharest on 15 September that robberies, assaults, rapes, and even murders continued to be committed daily by troops and stragglers who flooded the area. According to him, people fled from the villages and were shocked and frightened.[38] The terror that spread among Romanian women was confirmed in Soviet reports. For example, the NKVD Army 134th Border Guard Regiment's report on its activities noted that in towns occupied by the Red Army in September, Romanian women and girls hid in fields and basements, afraid that Soviet soldiers would rape them. The report also noted the sharp proliferation of venereal diseases in the same regiment in September, indicating that Romanian women's fears were well justified.[39] Sergeant Pavel El'kinson, a scout in the 3rd Ukrainian Front, noted in his diary with some pleasure that young women were nowhere to be seen, correctly concluding that they were hiding from Soviet soldiers.[40] The widespread fear of the Red Army by women is indicative of the mass nature of sex crimes.

The Red Army lived off the land in Romania, and Moscow aggressively pursued war reparations from the country. From the perspective of Romanians, there was little difference between these official policies and the illegal looting by the rank and file during the exploitation phase of the Iasi–Kishinev Operation when the troops were racing through the country. However, the Soviet command did try to prevent illegal robberies, "categorically forbidding" soldiers from seizing Romanian property and allowing only the logistical departments to make official purchases for the needs of the army.[41] However, it was difficult to control the troops' conduct in the context of rapidly marching armies. Also, Romania had waged a brutal war of exploitation against the Soviet Union, and the Red Army troops could now repay their enemies in kind. Soldiers and officers of the 91st NKVD Regiment, carrying out duties in the southern city of Călărași, were outraged that Romanian military and police offices and homes were decorated with spoils from the Soviet Union. The troops, "seeing the looted Soviet property, express intensive hatred. Some are saying, 'Romanian scum is using our property, so why are we supposed to behave correctly towards them?'[42] Nonetheless, the magnitude of plundering by Soviet troops was truly astounding. According to Romanian authorities, from late August 1944 until 26 May 1945, Soviet soldiers illegally confiscated 254,465 horses, 810 heads of cattle, 743,530 sheep, and 210,324 swine.[43]

Soviet soldiers and officers took out their anger at symbols of Romanian statehood, and they reacted with particular fury at any attempt by its representatives to interfere with their activities. In the county of Arad, between 14 September and 5 October, the Red Army destroyed seventy-five headquarters of the Romanian authorities, both civil and military. Moreover, they disarmed 8 policemen and killed 1, as well as robbing 4,003 people, murdering 22, and seriously injuring 14. In the county of Iasi in the period from 10 October to 19 October, Soviet soldiers committed 42 aggressive acts against the gendarmes, 7,299 acts of vandalism, and 4,105 robberies.[44]

Most of these assaults occurred during the commissions of other crimes. However, some of the assaults against government agents were highly symbolic. A Soviet officer entered a courthouse in Chilia commune (a village or a small cluster of villages) and opened fire on the portraits of Romania's king and queen, "causing grave offense to their majesties," as the gendarme report put it.[45] Major Boris Slutskii, who served in the 3rd Ukrainian Front, recalled an illustrative episode in his mixture of diary and memoirs about the degree of disrespect that Soviet troops had for their Romanian counterparts. Junior Soviet officers were required to salute their more senior counterparts in the allied Romanian army after it had switched sides in the war, which they vehemently resisted and tried to avoid as much as possible. A Red Army sergeant encountered a Romanian colonel on a busy street in the city of Craiova, and instead of saluting him, he began to scream at him: "I won [the war]!" He then made the Romanian colonel walk by three times, each time demonstratively failing to salute him.[46] This episode revealed the sergeant's seething disrespect for the Romanian rank and the latter's utter powerlessness in the face of aggression by a theoretically allied soldier with a lower rank, reflecting Romania's wider subordination to the Soviet Union. According to Romanian authorities, in the village of Focșani in Vrancea County, seven Soviet soldiers led by a sublieutenant attacked a local Church. They desecrated icons, broke windows, damaged the altar and furniture, and stole tablecloths and napkins before escaping.[47] We do not know the precise motives of the perpetrators, but the desecration of icons indicates that they may have been motivated by Soviet anti-religious propaganda.

Rape was a frequent crime committed by the Soviet troops in Romania during the breakout phase of the Iasi–Kishinev Offensive, as was the case in other theaters of the war during the breakouts. Examining the official US Army figures, Madeline Morris argued that the US soldiers committed many more rapes during the breakout from Normandy than during the intensive combat preceding the breakout.[48] There are countless Soviet and Romanian reports testifying to these crimes, as well as numerous witness and survivor testimonies.

According to the statistics of the General Inspectorate of the Gendarmerie, the military police which continued to operate after Romania switched sides in the war, 231 women were raped in the county of Arad in western Romania from 14 September to 5 October. Thus, on an average day during this period, the Romanian authorities received reports about the rape of eleven women in the county of Arad. The document also noted that 213 women were victimized from 10 October to 19 October in the county of Iasi. On an average day, the authorities received reports about the rape of twenty-one women in the county of Iasi. According to the report, the situation was similar in Romania's other counties.[49] Another Romanian document maintained that in the county of Alba, the Romanian authorities received reports about rapes of thirty-seven women in just twenty-four hours on September 26–27.[50]

These figures are just the tip of the iceberg, of course. According to the 1948 census, the populations of the counties of Arad, Iasi, and Alba were 413,368, 276,942, and 54,914 of the country's total population of 15,872,624.[51] Although we cannot know for sure, the General Inspectorate of the Gendarmerie claim that the Soviet conduct in other countries was similar is credible based on the previously mentioned reports of mass rapes in Constanța, Oltenia, Călărași, and Vrancea. There are also Soviet and Romanian reports about outbreaks of rape in Bucharest, Craiova, and Timisoara.[52] These cities comprised all corners of Romania, indicating that sexual violence occurred everywhere.

The rampage in Arad is arguably more representative of Soviet conduct in Romania than what happened in Iasi, since the latter's proximity to the Soviet border and its role as a transportation hub meant that more troops passed through it than other parts of Romania. Regarding the intensive Soviet rampage in Alba, it is difficult to say that it was emblematic of Soviet troops' treatment of Romanian women since the available figures are available for only one day. If we were to take the average daily figure of women who reported rapes in Arad (11) to Romanian authorities, convert it to a percentage of Arad County's population (0.0026 percent), and apply it to Romania's population of 15,872,624, it can be estimated that on an average day, Romanian authorities received reports about the rape of 413 women by the Red Army personnel throughout the country. This figure would be generally accurate during the exploitation phase of the Iasi–Kishinev Strategic Offensive Operation on Romanian soil from 20 August to 30 September. According to this rough estimate, the Romanian authorities received reports about the rape of 16,933 women.

Reporting rape by Red Army soldiers under Soviet rule was extremely difficult and reports must have represented a very small minority of actual rapes. In addition to the widespread perception that victims were somehow responsible or brought shame on the family for their victimization, accusing soldiers of the so-called liberating army of rape could bring unwanted scrutiny from the occupiers. More specifically, accusations of rape in some instances were construed as slander by the Red Army command, a dangerous accusation in the context of an occupation by a vengeful enemy.[53] Historian Tudor Roșu described in greater detail what the Soviet rampage in Alba on 26–27 September looked like. In this period, in addition to rapes, the Soviet soldiers destroyed 87 shops and 1,559 homes throughout the Alba county, they stole 154 horses, killed 3 civilians, and seriously wounded 2. According to him, women hid wherever they could. One woman reported: "I hid for a while with the other tailors in a secret room … we only went out at night to get water and food. We were all trembling lest they find us."[54] The fact that an estimated 16,933 women reported rapes in 41 days despite these circumstances indicates that the Red Army personnel committed mass rapes in the country.

Even today rapes are seriously underreported to law enforcement.[55] As late as 1994–1995, FBI estimated that only about one-third of rape victims reported the crime to police, making rape the most underreported of all violent crimes.[56] A criminologist and sociologist, Robert Lilly, in his study of the sexual violence perpetrated by the American troops in Europe, multiplied reported cases of rape by twenty times to get a more accurate number of actual rapes.[57] Lilly's formula is more applicable to Soviet occupation, but even this approach underestimates the difficulties of reporting rape under Soviet rule, as the Soviet occupation of Romania was more brutal than the American occupation of France and Germany. If Lilly's formula were to be applied, it could be estimated that the Soviet army personnel raped 338,660 women in Romania from 20 August to 30 September 1944. The significance of this figure is not to give a precise number of victims, which is impossible to know, but to establish with certainty that the Soviet troops committed mass rapes in Romania.

After the bulk of combat units left Romania, the country remained crucial for the Red Army's war effort. Soviet troops remained in the country to carry out occupational duties. According to Western intelligence estimates, confirmed by Romanian information, the Red Army had 80,000 troops in Romania in May 1945 and half a million in November of the same year.[58] Also, given its large size and strategic location, Romania became a central point for the transfer of supplies and recruits to the frontlines further west and south. Finally, after the war, many Soviet soldiers who had fought in Czechoslovakia, Austria, Hungary, Yugoslavia, and Bulgaria had to pass through Romania on their way home. Some of these troops also committed acts of sexual violence in Romania. To cite just one example, the 4th Guards Army trained in Romania from September to November 1944, when it marched into Hungary. During this period, the troops, according to a report by the army's prosecutor, committed a great number of military violations in Romania, including murder, rape, robberies, and physical assaults.[59] As late as April 1946, the Soviet troops or deserters were committing rapes in Romania, although by then it had become a less frequent phenomenon.[60] The number of rapes committed by Soviet troops during the occupation of the country, after the exploitation phase of the Iasi Kishinev Operation after September 1944, was significant, but it is impossible to estimate.

It should also be noted that in the 1940s, the term "rape" referred to "sexual intercourse" (penetration) in the 1936 Romanian criminal code.[61] Thus, the term rape and the figures provided based on Romanian gendarme reports excluded a broader category of victims of sexual violence who experienced humiliation such as public strip searches, attempted rape, sexual torture, or sexual touching by hands, weapons, or other objects.[62] Thus, the number of victims of sexual violence in Romania, as elsewhere, was much higher than the number of rape victims, but the official data does not allow us to even begin to estimate their numbers.

2.2 Bulgaria and Yugoslavia

Bulgaria had been part of the Axis, benefitting substantially from its membership in the Berlin-led alliance. Namely, Germany forced Romania to cede the territory of southern Dobruja to Bulgaria in 1940.[63] After the German and Italian invasion of Yugoslavia and Greece in the spring of 1941, in which Bulgaria participated, Sofia annexed and helped administer parts of its neighbors' territories.[64] Moreover, Germany allowed Bulgaria to remain neutral in its war with the Soviet Union, although Sofia was in a state of war with the United States and the United Kingdom.

The main reason why Sofia managed to stay out of the Soviet–German war was the traditional Bulgarian sympathy for Russia, rooted in Russia's historical role as the liberator of Balkan Orthodox Slavs from Ottoman rule. Sofia's potential participation in the aggression against the Soviet Union was not feasible for the government.[65] The Bulgarian resistance movement, led by the Bulgarian Communist Party (BKP), numbered anywhere between 10,000 and 28,000 members at its peak.[66] However, considering that Bulgaria was a privileged German ally that did not have to fight against the Soviet Union, the very fact it had a sizable pro-Soviet resistance was impressive. Even though the Bulgarian army participated in anti-partisan campaigns in Yugoslavia, Greece, and Bulgaria proper, the country remained largely unscathed by war.

In contrast, Germany, Italy, Italian-run Albania, Hungary, and Bulgaria partitioned Yugoslavia in 1941. In addition, the Axis created the so-called Independent State of Croatia and a rump Serbian state under the Wehrmacht's control with a collaborationist regime. During the war, Yugoslavia was pulverized by a bloodbath featuring numerous insurgencies, intertwined civil wars, ethnic cleansing campaigns, and genocides perpetrated by the occupiers, their quislings, and competing nationalist or resistance movements. As a result, just over a million Yugoslavs were killed during the war.[67] Out of this chaos, by the autumn of 1944 when the Red Army reached Yugoslavia, the communist-led Yugoslav National Liberation Army (Partisans) was emerging as the clear winners against their domestic opponents, although they were unable to expel the Axis on their own. Josip Broz Tito, the leader of the Yugoslav Communist Party (KPJ) and the supreme commander of the Partisans, was recognized by the Allies as the head of the Yugoslav provisional government.

An estimated 275,000 soldiers and officers of the 3rd Ukrainian Front headed to Bulgaria from Romania. The first units reached the country in early September.[68] The Soviet forces did not encounter organized resistance in Bulgaria. There were no sizable German contingents in the country, and Bulgarian forces did not resist. As the Red Army was entering Bulgaria, the communist-dominated Fatherland Front seized power in an insurrection on 9 September. Sofia immediately declared war on Germany.[69] The Red Army movements through Bulgaria were, in essence, a continuation of the exploitation phase of the Iassko–Kishnev Operation. Unopposed, the Soviets continued their rapid advance until they reached the Turkish, Greek, and Yugoslav borders. The main difference between the Red Army's speedy movement through Romania and Bulgaria was that in Bulgaria the Soviet arrival resembled a triumphant march, with large crowds of Bulgarians meeting the Soviet troops with bread and salt (the traditional welcome in the Balkans), fruits, and other gifts (Figure 2.2).[70]

Figure 2.2 The Red Army enters Bulgaria. Source: Sovfoto/Universal Images Group via Getty Images.

As the 3rd Ukrainian Front marched south to Bulgaria, the 2nd Ukrainian Front raced to Romania's western frontiers with Hungary and Yugoslavia. The advance units of the 46th Army, the 2nd Ukrainian Front's left flank, reached the Yugoslav border on 6 September.[71] On that same day, guerrilla fighters from the Yugoslav National Liberation Army (The Partisans) lit huge fires on the mountain Fruška Gora, which dominates northern Serbia, to welcome the Soviet troops still more than 100 km away and to announce to the population that their hour of liberation had arrived.[72] The forces of the 3rd Ukrainian Front took positions along the Yugoslav–Bulgarian border throughout September. The Bulgarian 1st, 2nd, and parts of 4th armies (ten divisions in total), some of which were already stationed in the Bulgarian-occupied parts of Yugoslavia, came under the 3rd Ukrainian Front's operational command.[73]

With the defection of Romania and Bulgaria from the Axis, the German position was becoming untenable in southeastern Europe. The German forces in the Balkan Peninsula, especially in Albania, Macedonia, and Greece, were at risk of being completely cut off from the main body of German forces further north in central Europe.[74] German communications went through the Morava Valley in central Serbia.[75] To avoid their forces being split into two, the Germans began to move their troops further north while reinforcing their positions along the new Soviet–German frontline, the Romanian–Yugoslav and Romanian–Hungarian borders.[76]

The Soviet Belgrade Strategic Offensive Operation was aimed at seizing central Serbia and cutting off German forces in Albania, Macedonia, and Greece from central Europe while installing the Yugoslav communists in power in Belgrade. Three hundred thousand Soviet troops – 200,000 belonged to the 3rd Ukrainian Front, 93,500 troops to the parts of the 2nd Ukrainian Front, and 6,500 to the Danube Military Flotilla – attacked the Germans in Yugoslavia from Romania and Bulgaria on 28 September.[77] At the same time, some 40,000 fighters of the National Liberation Army of Yugoslavia (Partisans), who had recently penetrated Serbia from their bases in Bosnia and Montenegro, began attacking Germans from the west and south.[78]

After taking Belgrade, Soviet forces headed north to Hungary to participate in what was shaping up to be one of the fiercest battles of the war – the siege of Budapest – instead of moving west to Croatia and Bosnia. The task of liberating the so-called Independent State of Croatia was left to the Partisans, who were in the process of becoming a regular army heavily supplied with Soviet equipment.[79] To enter Hungary from Yugoslavia, the Soviet forces had to cross the fiercely defended Danube again. The Soviet exit from Yugoslavia became known as the Battle of Batina (7 November to 21 November). This was the most lethal Soviet–German engagement on Yugoslav territory, even though officially it was part of the Budapest Strategic Offensive Operation.[80]

The Soviet high command had every reason to be satisfied with their achievements in Yugoslavia. The Belgrade Strategic Offensive Operation had secured the southern flank of the Red Army fighting in Hungary. More significantly, it had managed to cut off a large number of German forces in the Balkans, which were now forced to move slowly through the poor mountain roads of Kosovo, Sandžak, Montenegro, Bosnia, and Dalmatia into the Independent State of Croatia.[81] The Soviets suffered 7,889 deaths during their operations in Yugoslavia, a low figure by the standards of the Eastern front.[82] The Germans suffered 13,000 losses just in October, a figure that excludes fighting in November, including the Battle of Batina.[83]

The Red Army servicemen and stragglers continued to commit many military violations and crimes in Bulgaria and Yugoslavia. One of the most frequent violations was the illegal consumption of alcohol by Soviet soldiers. Servicemen were entitled to 100 g of vodka per day, which they seem to have been issued fairly regularly.[84] The daily vodka ration, however, was not enough for a healthy adult to get heavily intoxicated. As long as the 2nd and 3rd Ukrainian Fronts operated in Russia and eastern Ukraine, illegal alcohol was relatively hard to come by for soldiers. The nature of vodka production made it harder for peasants to produce it for their consumption, while the extremely widespread destruction as a result of combat, ruthless scorched-earth policies pursued first by the Soviets and then by the Germans, and the brutal German exploitation of the economy meant that there was very little alcohol for Soviet troops to find in the newly liberated territories. However, according to the military leadership at the level of the front, the drinking escalated once the troops entered the wine-growing regions in Europe, which began in Moldavia and Odesa regions, where the civilians had large quantities of alcohol, especially wine.[85] More significantly, the countries of Southeastern Europe and Central Europe allowed private businesses, and the myriad number of taverns served the advancing troops. Meanwhile, many independent peasant households in the Balkans and central Europe produced wine or very potent fruit brandies, variously known as rakija in Yugoslavia and Bulgaria, pálinka in Hungary and Romania, and schnapps in Austria.

The Red Army command and local authorities repeatedly tried to curtail the drinking habits of the troops.[86] Red Army commandants and municipal authorities tried to ban the sale of alcohol to Soviet troops repeatedly.[87] These measures were ineffective. As historian Norman Naimark noted, the East Slavs had a culture of binge drinking, which greatly fuelled some troops' criminality.[88] Furthermore, alcohol was routinely offered to guests, a point most vividly illustrated by El'kinson, who wrote in his diary the following when he was in a village in the municipality of Razgrad in Bulgaria:

> We got eighteen liters of wine today, my head is spinning all day now there is no day that we don't drink, one can become a real alcoholic here. Every resident here has vodka [Russian speakers often refer to rakija as vodka, to the great annoyance of South Slavs] wherever you go they offer it to you. You walk on the street and they offer it to you.[89]

Refusing to be hospitable was extremely dangerous. A Soviet captain killed an elderly peasant in Yugoslavia who did not give him wine.[90] The captain was under investigation when the document was written, and his ultimate fate is unknown. He was likely executed or sent to a labor camp because when he committed the murder, he was serving a suspended sentence for looting in Romania.[91]

The magnitude of alcohol consumed by some soldiers was staggering. In the first nine months of 1944, 108 soldiers and officers from the 3rd Ukrainian Front died from alcohol poisoning, and many more went blind.[92] Soviet troops accidentally drank methyl alcohol from a depot in the Bulgarian city of Burgas, which led to forty-two deaths, and six soldiers went blind.[93] After the liberation of Belgrade, the Yugoslav authorities reported that Soviet troops seized 2,000 kg of sugar that they drank after mixing it with water, presumably after fermenting it with yeast.[94] When the forward troops of the 2nd Ukrainian Front liberated the Yugoslav town of Jaša Tomić near the Romanian border, the local citizens and Soviet troops celebrated by drinking in the local liquor factory. The troops opened large barrels of alcohol by firing bullets at them, flooding the basement floor. As the presence of alcohol threatened the fulfillment of the operational plans, one of the officers in charge set the alcohol ablaze, burning down the entire factory.[95] In one village near the city of Subotica, the Soviet troops stole 500 L of wine.[96] The drinking escalated to such a degree that the command of the 3rd Ukrainian Front believed that the number of accidents involving cars and trucks sharply increased during this period due to drunk driving.[97]

Consumption of alcohol beyond the daily norm issued by the command was itself a violation, probably the most frequent one committed by Soviet troops, but it also facilitated more serious crimes. Certainly, the majority of crimes committed by the Soviet troops, including robberies and sexual and physical assaults, were committed by heavily intoxicated troops. Drunken soldiers also turned on each other. On 5 September an argument between drunken members of the NKVD Army and a Red Army tank crew escalated into a firefight, leading to the death of a nearby civilian.[98] On 17 September, two junior officers belonging to the 46th Army Aviation Squadron got so drunk in a bar in the Bulgarian city of Rusa that they opened "aimless fire" inside the establishment. When the NKVD Army tried to detain them, they put up a fight and even threatened them with guns.[99] A soldier in the Yugoslav city of Mladenovac, in an intoxicated state, threw a grenade in the direction of the allied Yugoslav Partisans. Fortunately, nobody was injured in the incident.[100]

Josip Broz Tito, the leader of the Yugoslav Communist Party (KPJ) and the supreme commander of the Partisans, repeatedly ordered his officers to record the names of raped women and Soviet officers with whom his officers interacted as the Red Army units advanced through the country.[101] Thus, the Yugoslavs kept records of the Soviet troops' crimes. Vladimir Dedijer, an important Yugoslav official, published these figures in his postwar biography of Tito. According to Dedijer, the Soviet troops committed 1,219 rapes, 359 attempted rapes, 11 rape-murders, 248 attempted murders, 111 murders, and 1,204 robberies accompanied by physical violence during the war.[102] This document was subsequently added to Tito's files which were meant to prepare him for his meeting with Nikita Khrushchev in 1956.[103] This report indicates that compared to the partial information that is available about Romania, the Red Army personnel committed fewer rapes in Yugoslavia, even after applying Lilly's formula. The author did not find any estimates about the number of reported rapes in Bulgaria, but another scholar described Soviet behavior there as "exemplary."[104] Even if this characterization goes too far, there is little doubt that the Soviet behavior in Bulgaria was relatively restrained.

Some scholars of wartime sexual violence are skeptical about the use of numbers to measure the magnitude of sexual violence. They maintain that details about how those figures are obtained are often unclear, that some types of rapes and many women's experiences are not recorded in archives, and that focusing on data enables politization of rape, resulting in the loss of complexity of women's experiences.[105] There indeed is much that we do not know about the Romanian or Yugoslav investigations into reported rapes – we do not know the specific circumstances in which most of these reports were made and what kind of pressures both the victims and Romanian and Yugoslav authorities faced when making these reports. The archival sources that I have seen never say anything about the rape of boys and men, and they almost always refer to rapes at gunpoint, but overlook other rapes, such as when drunk soldiers took advantage of civilians' hospitality. Yet, limited as archival documents are, these figures contain enough information to illuminate the pattern of Soviet behavior in "enemy" and "friendly" countries.

Moreover, there is more evidence that the Red Army was more restrained in Yugoslavia and Bulgaria than in Romania, Hungary, and Austria. Sexual violence did not enter the Yugoslavs' or Bulgarians' social psychology, to borrow historian Norman Naimark's term to describe the widespread fear of rapes in Germany.[106] As in Germany, rapes came to dominate the lives of Romanians, Hungarians, and Austrians during this period.[107] Only a minority of Yugoslavs maintained that they or women in their lives were afraid of going outside their homes because they feared the Red Army.[108] Similarly, there is no evidence that Bulgarian or Yugoslav women concealed their gender by dressing as men or that they tried to avoid the Soviet troops' unwanted attention by smearing their faces with dirt or jam, as women in enemy countries were forced to do.[109] This is not to suggest that Yugoslavs and Bulgarians were not generally aware that the Red Army committed many rapes. However, available evidence suggests that they feared the Red Army far less than civilians from the enemy countries.

None of this means that the Red Army did not commit horrible crimes against civilians in the two countries. V. Kozhevnikov and M. Sivolobov, majors in the Red Army and correspondents for *the Pravda* newspaper, visited Bulgaria in September of 1944. They sent a confidential report to Red Army's political leadership in Moscow stating that the looting and rapes by some soldiers and officers led to disappointment among the local population toward the Soviets.[110] In Petrovgrad, Yugoslavia, the troops broke into the prison of The Department for People's Protection (the nascent Yugoslav secret police) and raped the imprisoned women.[111] Another Partisan report maintained that "soldiers and entire units around [the towns of] Mladenovac, Smederevo, S. Palanka, and in villages, in a drunken state attack civilians, especially women."[112] All of this archival evidence demonstrates that in Bulgaria and Yugoslavia, there were outbreaks of mass sexual violence, as well as other crimes against civilians such as robberies and murders, even if on a smaller scale than in Romania.

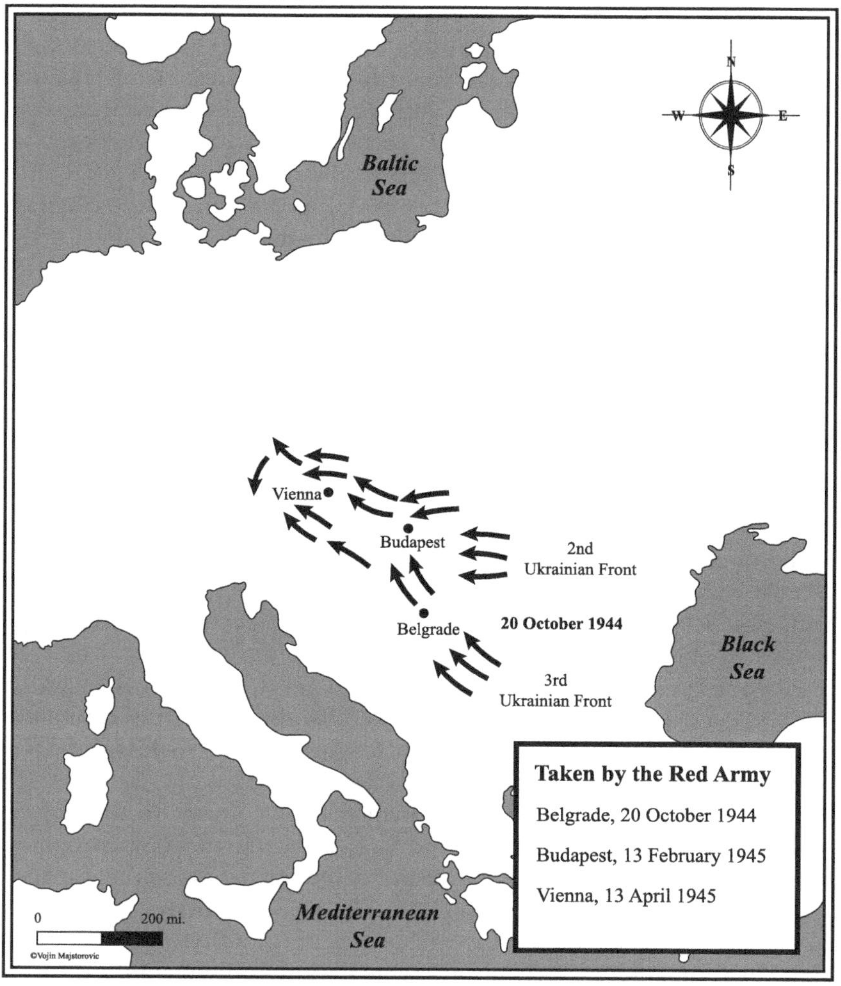

Map 2.2 2nd and 3rd Ukrainian Front movements in Yugoslavia, Hungary, and Austria, 1944–1945.

2.3 Hungary and Austria

Hungary was one of Europe's most determined revisionist states. After the First World War, it lost two-thirds of its territory and almost 60 percent of its population to Czechoslovakia, Yugoslavia, and Romania.[113] Hungary was ruled from 1920 by Regent Miklos Horthy, a reactionary conservative, who came to power after ruthlessly crushing a communist uprising. Even though Horthy was not an outright fascist in Mussolini's or Hitler's mold, he shared their virulent anti-communism. With the rise of fascism and Nazism in Italy and Germany in the 1930s, he aligned Hungary with the emerging Axis bloc.

Hitler rewarded Hungary for its loyalty with slices of Czechoslovak, Romanian, and Yugoslav territories. In return, Hungary participated in German aggression against Czechoslovakia, Yugoslavia, and the Soviet Union. However, its overall input to the German-led war against the Soviet Union was relatively small. In the first two years of the war, the Hungarian army's contribution ranged from 90,000 in the summer of 1941 to 207,000 in April 1942.[114] The Red Army wiped out most of the Hungarian frontline troops in the Soviet Union in January 1943 in the Voronezh–Kharkiv Strategic Offensive Operation. Otherwise, the Hungarian role on the Eastern front was limited to carrying out occupation duties in Ukraine with six light infantry divisions.[115]

Despite their marginal role in the war on the Eastern front, the Hungarian troops are on the record for behaving savagely in Soviet territories. Historian Krisztián Ungváry concluded that Hungarian occupation troops systematically committed war crimes against Soviet civilians, behaving with equal and sometimes more brutality than their German counterparts.[116] In addition, Hungarians and Germans murdered 18,000 so-called alien Jews from Hungary near Kamenets-Podolsk in occupied Soviet territories in 1941; Hungarians also killed 1,000 Jews in the Yugoslav region of Bačka in January and February 1942 together with some 2,000 Serbian civilians, while 42,000 Jews perished in labor battalions along the Soviet front.[117]

Hungary's Central European neighbor, Austria, had been annexed by Germany in 1938 with minimal resistance. From then on, Berlin treated Austria as part of Germany, while viewing Austrians as Germans, which carried substantial privileges in the Nazi system. Austrians benefited from the plunder of Jewish property and the Wehrmacht's systematic looting in the east, while the Austrian economy profited from German investments and hundreds of thousands of forced laborers. In return, some 1.3 million Austrians served in the German army between 1938 and 1945, of whom 242,000 were killed.[118] Austrian soldiers who served in the Wehrmacht were largely loyal fighters. They had an average desertion rate, they showed little resistance, and they were also involved in war crimes.[119] Thus, it is difficult to identify a specifically Austrian war experience different from Germany's experience.

Most Hungarians and Austrians began to question their close relationship with Germany once the Third Reich's defeat started to be seen as unavoidable. The majority of Hungarians during 1944 came to realize that the war would be lost and wanted it to end as soon as possible, even if it meant the Red Army's arrival.[120] In this context, scholars depict the Arrow Cross regime, imposed by the Germans, as enjoying minimal support from the population.[121] As one leading Hungarian novelist noted in his diary, Germans were magicians, since they contrived the miracle that all decent people looked forward to the arrival of the Soviets as liberators.[122] Austrian attitudes at the end of the war were similar. Soviet victories in Hungary, raids into southern Austria by Yugoslav Partisans, and Allied bombings led to a plummeting of morale. According to one historian, the last vestiges of support for the war in Vienna were gone by March 1945.[123] In sum, the Hungarians and Austrians began to contemplate their respective relationships with Berlin toward the end of the war, when they started fearing that the destruction they tolerated or endorsed as long as it was directed at others was about to be unleashed on them.

The 2nd and 3rd Ukrainian Fronts had encountered limited resistance from the Axis since leaving the Soviet Union. Bucharest and Sofia had capitulated, and the fighting in Yugoslavia was not very fierce. The Germans, however, decided to turn Hungary into a bastion and make their stand on the Eastern front there. The country was the last major source of oil and bauxite (necessary for the production of aluminum) badly needed by the Wehrmacht. Hungary was also the last major German ally in Europe, and if it went the way of Romania, the Red Army would have an open road into Austria.[124] After the Iasi–Kishinev Operation, the Germans and Hungarians managed to reestablish the frontline in Transylvania, some 650 km to the west of the site of the Army Group South's route.

As the Germans were building up their strength in Hungary, the Red Army was facing growing problems. The Soviet logistics were being increasingly strained, as the 2nd and 3rd Ukrainian Fronts' rapid advance into central Europe took them further away from their supply bases.[125] The Romanian railroad network's narrow gauge also added significant problems to Soviet logistics.[126] More problematically, the Stavka had prioritized the advance on Berlin, which meant that strategic reserves, replacements, and badly needed equipment went to armies advancing on the Third Reich's capital. The high command had taken two tank armies from the 2nd and 3rd Ukrainian fronts in the summer of 1944 and two all-arms armies after the Iasi–Kishinev Operation. In the words of historian Kamen Nevenkin, the advancing Soviet forces with only one tank army, "looked like a one-armed boxer: ferocious, but predictable."[127] Thus, the main reason why Soviet progress was so slow was that Berlin viewed Hungary as a top priority, whereas Moscow considered it to be of secondary importance.

The Germans were planning a major offensive operation in eastern Hungary to keep the country in their orbit in the autumn of 1944, when the forces of the 2nd Ukrainian Front struck first in the Debrecen Offensive Operation (6–28 October).[128] The Romanian 1st and 4th Armies fought under the 2nd Ukrainian Front's control, while the 4th Ukrainian Front, which operated further north in Carpathian Czechoslovakia and Ukraine, also went on the attack against Germans. The operation's first goal was to capture the cities of Szeged and Debrecen in southern and eastern Hungary, as gateways to the capital in the center of the country.[129] The second and more important goal was to encircle and destroy the Axis troops between the 2nd and 4th Ukrainian Fronts in eastern Hungary.[130] Foreshadowing the brutality of the combat in Hungary, the Germans launched a counterattack, frustrating the Soviet plans for encircling German troops in the east of the country.[131] However, the operation was not a total failure for the Soviets. The 2nd Ukrainian Front had taken Szeged and Debrecen, the future springboards for the attack on Budapest, and they liberated one-quarter of Hungary's population, and one-third of its territory was under Soviet control.[132]

As the Debrecen Operation was ongoing, the Soviet leaders were negotiating with the Hungarian government's representatives to get the country to abandon the Germans like the Romanians and Bulgarians did before them. After wavering, Horthy finally acted on 15 October, broadcasting Hungary's surrender to the Allies. The Germans promptly arrested him and forced him to renounce his surrender to the Allies. In his place, they installed in power Ferenc Szalasi, the leader of the pro-Nazi Arrow Cross.[133] Horthy's announcement on the radio that Hungary would surrender to the Allies on 15 October caused disarray in the Hungarian military, but the three Hungarian armies did not attack the Germans, switch sides, or disintegrate.[134]

The Budapest Strategic Offensive Operation lasted from 20 October 1944 to 13 February 1945. The operation was executed by the 2nd and 3rd Ukrainian Fronts, with Romanian, Bulgarian, and even Yugoslav auxiliaries under their control (the latter operating only during the Battle of Batina in November).[135] After heavy fighting, Budapest was encircled on 26 December.[136] What ensued was an extraordinarily brutal urban warfare, comparable perhaps only to Stalingrad.[137] Meanwhile, the Soviet forces holding the perimeter outside the city faced three determined but ultimately unsuccessful German counteroffensives aimed at breaking the siege and relieving the trapped Germans and Hungarians.[138]

Soon after the fall of Budapest, on 6 March, the Germans launched their last major offensive of the war around Lake Balaton, aimed at splitting and destroying parts of the 3rd Ukrainian Front. The German regime pinned such great hopes on the operation that they even transferred the 6th SS Panzer Army from Ardennes to Hungary.[139] Stavka, having learned about the German plans in advance, ordered Marshal Fedor Tolbukhin to organize defense and to prepare mobile forces for a counterattack. After absorbing the German attack, the 3rd Ukrainian Front struck on 16 March.[140] The Soviet counterattack developed into the Vienna Strategic Offensive Operation (16 March–15 April 1945). The 2nd Ukrainian Front's left flank fought alongside the 3rd Ukrainian Front in western Hungary and Austria. Its right flank moved north into Slovakia, then west into Moravia and Bohemia, where it assisted the 1st Ukrainian Front in the liberation of the Czechoslovak capital. After the Soviet troops took Vienna, they advanced toward Linz and Graz in early May.[141]

The fighting on the territory of Hungary lasted from 29 September 1944 to 4 April 1945. During this period, the 2nd and 3rd Ukrainian Fronts suffered a shocking 140,000 irrecoverable losses and 344,296 wounded, for total losses of 484,300.[142] More than half of the irrecoverable losses in Hungary were at the battle for Budapest.[143] The German and Hungarian casualties in Hungary are available only for separate battles. According to one rough estimate, the Axis' casualties in the siege of Budapest amounted to 60 percent of the Soviet losses.[144] In the Debrecen Operation, the Germans and Hungarians suffered 42,000 killed, wounded, and captured, compared to 84,010 total Soviet losses.[145] The fighting was less ferocious in Austria, with the Soviets suffering 94,185 overall casualties, 26,006 killed, and 68,179 wounded.[146]

The fighting in Hungary stood in stark contrast to the ideal of the Soviet operational art of deep operations. The 2nd and 3rd Ukrainian Fronts, unlike during the Iasi–Kishinev Operation, failed to maneuver, break through, encircle, and destroy a large number of enemy troops. Weakened by the transfers of two tank armies further north, just as the Axis were being reinforced, the Red Army got bogged down by stubborn resistance, ferocious counterattacks, and the conditions of urban warfare. The duration and brutality of the fighting greatly contributed to the growth of military violations, including outright war crimes such as illegal executions of prisoners of war, which in Hungary were relatively common.[147] For instance, a very gruesome incident prompted Colonel Sidorenko, commander of the 233rd Division, to remind the troops of the ban on executing captured enemy soldiers. Troops under his command had executed a group of over thirty Axis soldiers of various nationalities, including Czechs, Poles, Hungarians, and *Volksdeutsche* who had announced that they did not want to fight for the Germans.[148]

There was another contributing factor to the upsurge in military violations during the fighting in Hungary. At the height of the battle for Budapest, Stalin issued a decree on 23 December allowing Soviet troops to send packages with local goods to their families and friends in the Soviet Union.[149] This decree was issued to all of the fighting fronts, not just the Soviet troops in Hungary. As will be discussed later, this decree contributed to the troops seeking plunder, which in turn facilitated other crimes as well.

In discussing sexual violence that Soviet soldiers and officers committed in Romania and Yugoslavia, this study utilized reported instances of rape that women made to Romanian and Yugoslav authorities. However, the Red Army conquered Hungary and Austria and local authorities fled before the advancing Soviets, making it impossible to make similar projections. Thus, it is impossible to make direct comparisons between the number of rape victims in Austria and Hungary on the one hand, and Romania and Yugoslavia on the other.

However, other scholars who studied the Soviet criminal conduct in Hungary have indicated that the Soviet troops committed a large number of rapes in Hungary. Historian Catherine Merridale pointed out that Soviet behavior in Romania was more characterized by "marauding." In Hungary, in contrast, she found the cruelty and systematic nature of violence to be "something new."[150] Grant Harward also suggested that the scale of rape and murder in Romania was much more limited than in Hungary and Germany.[151] Andrea Peto, using medical and abortion records, claimed that the Soviet troops raped between 50,000 and 200,000 Hungarian women.[152] Krisztian Ungvary, based on the Wehrmacht's investigations into Soviet conduct following one of the Axis' counteroffensives in Hungary, maintained that in many towns the Soviet troops raped between 10 and 15 percent of the female population.[153] According to historian Horvath Attila, the Soviet troops raped up to 20 percent of the female population, or 800,000 Hungarian women in total, a figure which seems to be too high to be accurate.[154]

My research also strongly indicates that there was an upsurge in instances of sexual violence when the Red Army entered Hungary from Romania and Yugoslavia. Two Soviet diarists recorded for the first time that gang rapes, some in broad daylight, began to take place shortly after they entered Hungary.[155] Both diarists were surprised by the outbreak of sexual violence in public, indicating that they had not previously seen it. One of them, a doctor on the 2nd Ukrainian Front, wrote: "I've been at war for four years, but this is the first time that I have encountered such grandiose licentiousness."[156] Major Slutskii undoubtedly knew more about the magnitude of sexual violence than most other soldiers and officers in the Soviet army. He extensively wrote about the Soviet troops' aggressive pursuit of European women, and he even led an investigation into an outbreak of mass rapes in one Austrian village.[157] According to him, the 3rd Ukrainian Front began to commit many acts of sexual violence in Romania, and the discipline faltered further (*distsiplina drognula*) in Hungary, but the worst came in Austria.[158] Many Hungarian personal sources speak about sexual violence as a massive phenomenon, with gang rapes, repeated victimizations, and women being afraid to leave their houses for extended periods.[159]

Jeno Farkass lived through the siege of Budapest. He was an intellectual, writer, regular churchgoer, supporter of the Hungarian wartime dictator Admiral Horthy and Greater Hungary, and a nobleman with a large estate in the countryside. He began writing his diary just before the siege of Budapest started, and he stopped just after the war ended in May 1945 (the siege itself ended in late February). In the diary, he outlined how he, his wife, his mother, and their neighbors lived through the siege. Notably, they lived in Buda, where the fighting was fiercer than on the other side of the Danube in Pest.

Farkass and his neighbors experienced the full horrors of war only when the Red Army arrived in Hungary in the fall of 1944. As late as early January 1945, when the battle of Budapest had lasted for more than a month, they were enjoying cigarettes, and eating and drinking well.[160] His first encounter with Red Army soldiers who reached his street on 12 February was relatively positive. Some soldiers gave out cigarettes, and local women flirted with the occupiers and asked for cigarettes. More ominously, one Soviet soldier seized a watch from Farkass' neighbor. This is how he ended the entry for that day: "They didn't look bad – a little oriental and barbarian, but they smiled. They said that they wouldn't bother the Hungarians. They aren't mad at us. We were terribly excited."[161] His racist description of Soviet soldiers only worsened throughout the diary, as Soviet troops looted and raped.

The following day, however, all hell broke loose. On 13 February, Farkass reported rumors of rape from the neighborhood, as a Soviet soldier kept on shooting into the air in front of his house. The occupying troops came to his house on three occasions to rob them and drink their alcohol, using the excuse that they were searching for weapons.[162] The following day, numerous women in the neighborhood were raped, there were reports of gang rape of a girl of fifteen or sixteen, and some victims committed suicide. So many soldiers came to pillage their house that he stopped recording it unless they committed other horrifying crimes. On 16 February, two young soldiers tried to take women from the house to ostensibly peel potatoes, but it was obvious that they intended to rape them. The entire house resisted and said they would all go to peel potatoes, forcing the would-be rapists to leave.[163] However, the two soldiers returned with a backup of four or five additional soldiers. At gunpoint, they seized a woman from the neighborhood and raped her in a different room, as her husband went seemingly crazy and neighbors waited in horror for the rapists to leave.[164] Slowly, the Red Army managed to introduce some order in the city, although the looting and raping continued for weeks. Hungary's experience with the Red Army was more similar to Germany's than Yugoslavia's, even though the same troops fought in Yugoslavia and Hungary.

The Red Army's rampage in Austria was even more intense than in Hungary. According to historian Gunter Bischof, in Vienna alone, the Red Army victimized between 70,000 and 100,000 women, substantially more than the highest estimates for the number of rape victims in Budapest.[165] A Viennese Jewish woman, Mignon Langnas, wrote in her diary on 1 May 1945: "The Russians are in the house! During the whole 7 years, I didn't tremble with shock and desperation as much as I did in these hours."[166] That a Jewish woman who survived the Holocaust wrote this is indicative of the scale of terror the Soviet troops spread among the population.

It is unclear whether the Red Army's conduct in Austria was as terrible as in Germany. According to Bischof, it was.[167] Other historians have challenged this assumption, although none denied the massive scale of sexual violence.[168] Maria Mesner cited two studies, which revealed that in one Austrian district, 5.8 percent of all women between fifteen and sixty years of age were raped, whereas, in Berlin, the corresponding figure was 7.1 percent.[169] In her view, the significance of these numbers is that they contradicted a more popular version, reflected in some academic texts, that 100 percent of women were raped in some villages.[170] Historian Barbara Stelzl-Marx argued that the Red Army committed many rapes, but that the number was exaggerated for political and ideological reasons.[171] These findings indicate that sexual violence was also more widespread in these parts of Austria than in the Romanian counties of Iasi or Arad. It is difficult to tell with certainty the scale of sexual violence that the Soviet soldiers and officers committed in Austria. However, it does seem that it was worse than in Hungary.

2.4 Stragglers and Deserters

The Red Army had many service personnel who actively sought to avoid military service, one of the more frequent military violations committed by Soviet troops. Historian Mark Edele estimated that the Red Army had between 117,000 and 251,000 defectors, with the latter being probably closer to the real number.[172] The soldiers who risked their lives to defect to the enemy were on the extreme end of soldiers avoiding military service. They had no parallel in other contemporary armies. Estimates for the number of deserters (who fled from the army into the rear), draft dodgers (who avoided conscription), and stragglers (who lost contact with their units during marches or battles purposefully or not) ranged between 1.5 and 4.4 million.[173] For instance, during the heavy fighting around Stalingrad, the NKVD forces of Stalingrad and Don Fronts detained 140,755 Soviet stragglers between 1 August and 15 October.[174] Notably, major belligerents in the war had deserters, but not nearly as many as the Red Army. Almost 50,000 American and 100,000 British soldiers deserted during the war.[175] The exact number of German deserters is unknown, but it has been estimated to be at several hundred thousand, of which at least 15,000 were executed.[176]

The situation in the 2nd and 3rd Ukrainian Fronts reflected the broader trends in the Red Army. The NKVD Armies of the 2nd and 3rd Ukrainian Fronts and Command Posts, the rear area security services, were tasked with dealing with soldiers in the rear who fell behind their units. The two army groups' security forces caught tens of thousands of soldiers behind the frontline. They had to classify them according to various categories, such as deserters, soldiers who fell behind their units (stragglers), soldiers without proper documents, bandits, and so on. The distinction between these categories was often nebulous, but all soldiers detained by the rear area security forces were caught where they were not supposed to be. As such, they could all be called stragglers.

From the Red Army leadership perspective, the actions of stragglers represented the most serious military violation. Their actions directly sapped the Red Army's combat strength and undermined the morale of those soldiers who did not fall behind their units. Despite this, the number of stragglers was high. The NKVD Armies of the 2nd and 3rd Ukrainian Fronts detained 87,253 stragglers, an estimate that is grounded in solid evidence (Table 2.1). I estimate that the Command Posts of the 2nd and 3rd Ukrainian Fronts detained an additional 63,928 soldiers. This means that from 20 August until 9 May 1945, during the two fronts' operations in Europe, the security forces detained an estimated 151,181 stragglers (Table 2.2).

Table 2.1 *Detained Red Army servicemen by the NKVD Armies of the 2nd and 3rd Ukrainian Fronts in Europe, from 20 August 1944 until 9 May 1945.*

	The NKVD Army of the 2nd Ukrainian Front, 20 August–31 December 1944[a]	The NKVD Army of the 2nd Ukrainian Front, 1 January–9 May 1945[b]	The NKVD Army of the 3rd Ukrainian Front, 20 August–31 December 1944[c]	The NKVD Army of the 3rd Ukrainian Front, 1 January–9 May 1945[d]	Total
Left the field of battle in a disorganized way:			87	13,784	13,871
Deserters:	45	2,132	510	819	3,506
Left encirclement:	58			1,171	1,229
Marauders/robbers:	20	309	111	170	610
Fell behind their units:	8,306	6,662	3,842	7,193	26,003
Without proper documents:	5,740	4,866	3,152	4,411	18,169
Violators of the NKO Order 225 of 1942:	97		463	601	1,161
Violators of NKO Order 0860	1,483		1,076		2,559
Violators of general/ social order:		2,184	103	151	2,438
Suspicious individuals				1	1
Traitors/fought for the enemy			38	764	802
Spies/diversionists					
Former POWs:	2,163	5,379	3,270	6,092	16,904
Total	17,912	21,532	12,652	35,157	87,253

[a] "A note on results of operational activities of the NKVD Army for the Protection of the Rear of the 2nd Ukrainian Front, by Chief of Staff Colonel Zimin-Kovalev," RGVA, f. 32905, op. 1, d. 98, ll. 190–191. Zimin-Kovalev gave figures for all of 1944, without breaking down numbers by operation or month. However, the 2nd Ukrainian Front fought in Europe only for 133 days – from 20 August to 31 December, which represents 36.4 percent of the calendar year. Thus, the figures in this table represent 36.4 percent of the overall figures for 1944.

[b] Ibid., ll. 192–193. The document specified the dates given here, and the figures in this column are not estimates.

[c] "Report on operational activities of the NKVD Army for the Protection of the Rear of the 3rd Ukrainian Front, sent to the Military Council of the 3rd Ukrainian Front," RGVA, f. 32900, op. 1, d. 220, l. 88. This report divided the year 1944 into four operational phases, the last being from 20 August, when the Iassko–Kishinev Operation was launched, and Soviet armies entered Europe. Thus, these are actual figures and not estimates.

[d] I obtained the figures for the detained soldiers by the NKVD Army of the 3rd Ukrainian Front by combining numbers from two quarterly reports: one for January, February, and March (RGVA, f. 32900, op. 1, d. 220, ll. 141–142) and the other for April, May, and June 1945, (Ibid., l. 198). Both reports were authored by Major-General Pavlov, commander of the NKVD Army of the 3rd Ukrainian Front. He forwarded them to Colonel-General Zheltov, member of the Council of the 3rd Ukrainian Front. From the latter report, I left out figures for June and included only 30 percent for May, since the war ended on May 9.

Table 2.2 *Detained Red Army servicemen by Command Posts of the 2nd and 3rd Ukrainian Fronts in Europe, from 20 August 1944 until 9 May 1945.*

	Command Posts of the 2nd Ukrainian Front, 15 October 1944–20 February 1945[a]	Command Posts of the 2nd and 3rd Ukrainian Fronts, 20 August 1944–9 May 1945, estimated
Deserters:	2,127	8,698
Marauders/robbers:	2,018	8,280
Bandits:	319	1,310
Spies/diversionists	68	262
Rapists (*Nasilniki*):	229	944
Similar violators:	1,550	6,340
Without proper documents:	4,317	17,658
Violators of military order:	5,003	20,436
Total	15,631	63,928[b]

[a] RGVA, f. 32905, op. 1, d. 130, l. 172.

[b] The figures in the second column in Table 2 are projections based on the column 1 of Table 2. Column 1 indicates that in 128 days between 15 October 1944 and 20 February 1945, the Command Posts of the 2nd Ukrainian Front detained 15,631 troops or 122 troops on an average day. This means that on an average day during this period the Command Posts of the 2nd Ukrainian Front detained: 16.6 deserters, 15.8 marauders/robbers, 2.5 bandits, 1.8 rapists, 12.1 similar violators, 33.7 without proper documents, 39 violators of military order, and 0.5 spies/diversionists. There were 262 days between the two army groups entered Europe on 20 August 1944 and until the war ended on 9 May 1945. I obtained figures for the 2nd Ukrainian Front Command Posts in the second column by multiplying each daily category of detained soldiers with 262. I multiplied this number with two, assuming that the 3rd Ukrainian Front Command Posts caught same number of troops as 2nd Ukrainian Front Command Posts.

It must be mentioned that none of the soldiers caught by the NKVD Armies and Command Posts were easy to distinguish from deserters. As the NKVD Army's high command noted, many deserters were trying to pass themselves off as stragglers.[177] Other reports stressed that deserters posing as soldiers who fell behind their units engaged in banditry.[178] In any case, such soldiers had been detained behind the frontlines in places where they were not supposed to be, bringing them into close contact with the civilian population and beyond the oversight of control mechanisms. Stragglers, like deserters, had to confiscate food from civilians to survive. It must be assumed that once detained, in order to avoid sterner penalties, most marauders, rapists, and deserters would claim they had lost their documents or that they fell behind their units. Moreover, the various official categories were not mutually exclusive. Most soldiers committed more than one violation, but official documents classified them as belonging only to one of the categories. More obviously, soldiers also committed more than one crime of the same type. For instance, rapists were likely to have perpetrated many acts of rape before being caught.

It is impossible to understand the violence that the Soviet troops unleashed against civilians without considering the role of stragglers. Without a doubt, stragglers were the worst behaved toward European civilians among the Soviet troops. Likewise, they contributed a meaningful portion – although it is impossible to say how many exactly – of all the crimes in Europe that have been attributed to the Red Army personnel. The testimony of Hungarian and Yugoslav civilians, as well as the Romanian and Yugoslav authorities' reports, makes it clear that stragglers were particularly prone to abusing civilians.[179] The Red Army sources corroborate these claims.[180] Of course, not all stragglers were rapists or murderers, but at a minimum, they had to procure food on their own from the civilian population through violence or threat of violence. Moreover, they were beyond the sight of the Red Army's disciplinary institutions or the peer pressure of the majority of their frontline comrades, and thus, they were freer to engage in criminal conduct.

The work for rear-area security services was much harder in Europe than in the Soviet Union: They could not rely on the cooperation of the territorial-based NKVD and Communist Party activists, and they could not communicate as easily with witnesses in seeking out stragglers. In addition, each phase of the war in Europe presented its own challenges to the Soviet security forces in combating stragglers. In Romania, after the collapse of the Axis defenses in northern Romania in late August, around a million Soviet soldiers raced through the country to occupy the space that opened up to move the front as far west as possible before the Germans could reestablish their defenses. Behind them, chaos reigned. For instance, the 57th Army marched between 60 and 65 km per day during the same period.[181] Gabriel Temkin, a soldier in the 78th Division of the 2nd Ukrainian Front, wrote that during his unit's march through Romania, Soviet soldiers confiscated from Romanian soldiers and peasants' carts and any vehicles with strong wheels. They raced for up to 64 km per day, with only mounted Cossacks managing to outpace them.[182] In periods characterized by the army's rapid movements, such as the breakout phase of the Iasi–Kishinev Operation, supplies broke down, compelling many soldiers to search for food on their own, bringing them into contact with civilians, in violation of army regulations.

It is possible to reconstruct the NKVD Armies' daily activities in Romania to illustrate how difficult it was for them to carry out their duties under the conditions of rapidly moving frontlines. In Romania, the NKVD Army of the 3rd Ukrainian Front followed the regular Red Army units in two lines, approximately 30 and 60 km each. According to General Pavlov, the commander of the NKVD Army of the 3rd Ukrainian Front, the reason for such depth of the NKVD echelons was that criminal elements tried to enter deep behind the frontlines, and having two lines would increase the chances of catching them.[183] If we take into account that the average speed of movement for both the Red Army and NKVD through Romania was around 60 km per day, then the Red Army stragglers would simply have to remove themselves from the main road for one day until the second NKVD Army echelon passed. Thereafter, without effective security in the rear, they were free to roam the country.

In Yugoslavia, the stragglers and deserters utilized the friendliness of the local population and the eagerness of local authorities to appease supposed Soviet authorities to avoid the security forces. In December, the NKVD Army launched two separate operations against stragglers in northern Yugoslavia and Romanian regions near the Yugoslav border. These two actions netted 1,345 Soviet soldiers, most of whom were caught in Yugoslavia.[184] As late as August 1945, the NKVD Army carried out another operation in northern Yugoslavia, in which it detained 476 Soviet soldiers.[185] The NKVD identified two reasons for the high number of stragglers in Yugoslavia: the hospitality of the Serbian population, by which the NKVD meant that the local population was willing to provide the Soviets with food and lodging, and the absence of command posts.[186] The second reason was particularly important. Namely, the Red Army did not occupy Yugoslavia, and it did not have a system of command posts throughout the country except in the capital and a few other strategically located cities. In addition, the fact that northern Yugoslavia was in the rear of the large-scale fighting in Hungary also explains why there was such a large number of stragglers there. These factors also account for why there were relatively few stragglers in Bulgaria, and no comparable specific NKVD operations aimed at them. The General Prosecutor of the 3rd Ukrainian Front wrote to Tolbukhin that soldiers who were caught in the summer of 1945 "had been in a state of desertion for a long period. These individuals commit various crimes, robberies, thefts, murders, and rapes…."[187] Although precise numbers are impossible to establish, there is little doubt that 476 such troops who rampaged for up to ten months, as well as 1,345 soldiers who behaved likewise for up to three months until they were detained in December, committed a significant portion of all crimes attributed to the Red Army in Yugoslavia.

The absence of command posts in Yugoslavia placed tremendous pressure on the Red Army's otherwise overstretched control mechanisms. For example, Petrovaradin municipal authorities informed Belgrade on 14 November that passing Soviet soldiers had committed a series of robberies. They reported that the Soviet commandant did his best to alleviate the situation, but that his office was grossly understaffed.[188] Moreover, the lack of formal Soviet authority in Yugoslavia allowed for the emergence of usurpers who proclaimed themselves to be military commandants and became, in effect, rulers of several villages and towns.

A senior lieutenant and a captain deserted in late 1944 and declared themselves to be military commandants of a village near the Serbian city of Subotica. They recruited passing Soviet soldiers into their would-be command post. Their reign did not last long, ending by 30 January 1945, when the senior lieutenant killed the captain because the latter did not want to share his powers.[189] Similarly, Senior Lieutenant Stepan Burgelo declared himself to be the military commandant of the small Serbian town of Kladovo, and a group of soldiers posed as his garrison. The group systematically collected money, alcohol, and food from the local population, claiming that they were for the needs of the Red Army, but they used these foodstuffs to organize what investigators described as "drinking parties."[190] When the prosecutor of the Danube Military Flotilla opened an investigation into this case in early January 1945, Burgelo variously claimed that his command post belonged to the 2nd or 3rd Ukrainian Front. It took the prosecutor four months to establish that Burgelo was simply a usurper; meanwhile, he and his group continued to loot.[191]

In Hungary, the brutal combat produced even more stragglers and deserters. At a minimum, deserters had to loot to obtain food, but they often committed rapes and murders. According to a few reports, deserters merged into gangs that roamed in villages behind the frontlines, sometimes for months, before getting caught. They terrorized the civilian population and, in some instances, even attacked the Red Army. More creative groups forged official documents and sold them to other deserters.[192] Some deserters remained loyal to the Red Army, in their way. One gang punished an entire Hungarian village because the local peasants assaulted two Soviet soldiers, who were apparently not deserters, for trying to rape a local woman. When deserters heard about this incident, they burned down the house of the victimized woman and beat up all of the villagers.[193]

It must be mentioned that the Soviet command was aware of the worsening situation with stragglers in Hungary and tried to combat it. Major General Ankudinov, the military prosecutor of the 3rd Ukrainian

Front, reported to the military council of the 3rd Ukrainian Front on 31 January 1945 that the increasing number of stragglers and deserters came from the reserve regiments and other units in the rear.[194] He urged the command of the 3rd Ukrainian Front to order the NKVD Army to concentrate on the struggle against stragglers.[195] On 2 February, the 3rd Ukrainian Front command issued an order to Pavlov, which ordered him to instruct the NKVD troops to focus on securing towns along the railroad, where they were supposed to prevent the passing soldiers from seeking out alcohol and committing crimes.[196] On 11 February, the 3rd Ukrainian Front command issued a lengthy order aimed at curtailing stragglers and deserters. The series of measures were aimed at improving military rosters, and records of deserters, and regulating the movement of troops in the rear (in hospitals and reserve regiments); meanwhile, it reiterated the order to the NKVD Army to secure major towns along the railroads.[197] On 11 April, the 3rd Ukrainian Front command sent a circular to all units emphasizing the case of a junior lieutenant who was able to desert twice, returning to his unit briefly between two acts of desertion, because the unit's commanding officer failed to duly investigate his month-long absence after his first desertion.[198] The point of this circular was to stress the need for vigilance among commanding officers, a sure sign that the order from 11 February was not adhered to. However, the situation hardly improved, as can be inferred from the number of stragglers caught every month.

2.5 Conclusion

The Iasi–Kishinev Operation, one of the most successful Red Army offensives of the war, represented the height of Soviet operational art, enabling the Soviet forces to encircle and destroy Army Group South Ukraine. The 2nd and 3rd Ukrainian Fronts moved rapidly through Romania to take advantage of the success on the battlefield, leading to the overthrow of the pro-German Romanian and Bulgarian governments in Bucharest and Sofia. In the exploitation phase of the operation, the Red Army moved the frontline between 500 and 750 km to the west, occupying most of Romania and all of Bulgaria, reaching Transylvania in the north and Yugoslavia in the south. The fighting in Yugoslavia was not heavy. In Hungary, in contrast, the Nazis made a determined stand. The Soviet advances became much slower, as the fighting became more attritional and less mobile. The siege of Budapest was one of the bloodiest battles of the war. After the Germans launched their last offensive of the war at Lake Balaton in early March, which the 3rd Ukrainian Front absorbed, the Soviet forces went on an offensive that saw them drive across west Hungary deep into Austria, their advance ending when they encountered American and British forces pouring into Austria from southern Germany and northern Italy.

The 2nd and 3rd Ukrainian Fronts are conservatively estimated to have suffered 242,889 irrecoverable losses (killed or captured) in Romania, Bulgaria, Yugoslavia, Hungary, and Austria from late 20 August 1944 until 9 May 1945.[199]

In this context, the Soviet troops committed many military violations, which in the official Soviet jargon referred to both disciplinary and criminal code violations. The 2nd and 3rd Ukrainian Fronts soldiers and officers began to consume more alcohol in the spring of 1944, as they occupied the wine-growing Odesa region and Moldavia. They drank even more in Romania, Bulgaria, Yugoslavia, Hungary, and Austria, where not only wine was widely available but also the more potent fruit brandies. Alcohol fueled many other criminal robberies, assaults, and sexual assaults against the women of Europe.

The Red Army servicemen committed many acts of sexual violence wherever they went, but they did not commit sexual assaults with equal intensity everywhere. The number of rapes the Soviet troops committed increased during the exploitation phase of the Iasi–Kishinev Operation in late August and September in Romania. We know this based on Romanian and Soviet reports, as well as the snippets of available information about the number of reported rapes to Romanian authorities. In Bulgaria and Yugoslavia, the Soviet troops behaved with more restraint, evident in the fewer reported rapes in Yugoslavia, as well as testimonies and actions of Soviet soldiers and officers and Yugoslav and Bulgarian civilians. The number of women or their immediate family members who reported rapes in Hungary and Austria during the fighting is unknown, as the local authorities fled. However, it seems that the Soviet soldiers behaved more aggressively in Hungary than in Romania and that they committed more rapes in Austria than in Hungary. This assertion is based on Soviet archival and personal sources, and Hungarian and Austrian civilian testimonies, as well as the work of other scholars. The Soviet troops were more violent toward "enemy" women from countries who fought in the German genocidal war against the Soviet Union than in "neutral" Bulgaria and "friendly" Yugoslavia. The remainder of the book focuses on illuminating the reasons for some troops' violent conduct, with a focus on explaining the variation in the intensity of violence during various stages of the war.

Part II

The Leadership

3 The Kremlin's Policies

This chapter focuses on the Kremlin's policies in the countries of the Balkans and Central Europe in the last year of the war. By Kremlin, the author refers to Stalin and his immediate political and military underlings, including the leading officials in Stavka (the Main Command), the general staff, the Ministry of Defense, the State Defense Committee (GKO), and the Main Political Administration, and the NKVD Army. These officials and institutions were all based in Moscow and were distinct from the forces in the field. Moscow ultimately determined the policies and set the tone for how the 2nd and 3rd Ukrainian Fronts should behave in the Balkans and Central Europe (Figure 3.1).

3.1 Command Posts: The Mechanism of Control

A system of command posts (*komendatura*) led by military commandants helped govern the frontline zone (*prifrontovaia polosa*) from the earliest stages of the war in 1941. There were command posts near the frontlines, appointed by the local army commander, and NKVD command posts in larger cities further in the rear of the frontlines.[1] The command posts were responsible for securing the communications leading to the frontline, the food, and security in the rear areas of the front. The command posts gained importance beyond Soviet borders because the military commandants did not have to compete for influence with the local Communist Party, NKVD, or local government. Thus, the command posts in Europe were Moscow's primary tool in governing the occupied territories.

Stalin signed and circulated a document on 10 April 1944 entitled "GKO Resolution Related to the Red Army's Entry on the Territory of Romania" in his capacity as the chairman of the GKO.[2] This document specified Soviet policies in Romania and mechanisms for their implementation, and it served as a model for the 2nd and 3rd Ukrainian Fronts' policies in other countries. The most significant aspect of the GKO resolution was that it established command posts led by military

Figure 3.1 Red Army front commanders. Source: Sovfoto/Universal Images Group via Getty Images.

commandants in all district and county centers (*volostnii* and *uezdnii*) with military garrisons staffed with troops, to be appointed by the Military Council of the 2nd Ukrainian Front. Military councils, which included representatives from the Communist Party, the Red Army's political organs, the front commander, and commanders of different arms, helped the front commanders direct the war.[3]

Military commandants, furthermore, were instructed to determine policies based on the Red Army's needs and to implement their decisions through preexisting municipal authorities. In theory, this meant that the military units would inform commandants of their requirements for supplies and quartering and that the latter, acting through local Romanian authorities, would ensure that the Soviet military's needs were met. Commandants were made into virtual dictators, however, by being allowed to dismiss civil servants who opposed their policies. Stalin also instructed commandants to issue a decree stating that all personal (*lichnye*) and property rights of Romanian citizens were under their protection, effectively suspending these rights. Commandants were also responsible for maintaining order in territories under their control, which meant suppressing all activities that undermined Soviet rule in Romania, including the criminal conduct by Soviet troops and overt anti-Soviet activities by Romanians. The GKO resolution was sent to the entire wartime military, intelligence, police, and economic leadership of the country, indicating its significance.[4] In addition to the 2nd Ukrainian Front, the resolution was forwarded to the 1st and 3rd Ukrainian Fronts, Molotov, Malenkov, Beria, Antonov (the chief of general staff), Shcherbakov (head of the Main Political Administration), Anastas Mikoian (GKO member responsible for supplying the Red Army), Viktor Abakumov (head of SMERSH), Lazar Kaganovich (in charge of railways), and Andrei Vyshinskii (who played a key role in advising Stalin on Eastern Europe and forcing through political changes in Romania after 1944).

Between late May and early July, while the Red Army still occupied only a small corner of northeastern Romania, there were several changes to the system of command posts. The commander of the 2nd Ukrainian Front created the Directorate for the Utilization of Romania's Resources in May, simply called the Special Directorate in internal documents to conceal its true purpose, as the Soviets freely admitted in internal communication.[5] The Special Directorate's main objective was to study the Romanian economy, mobilize the local labor force, and exploit private and state resources for the short-term goal of supplying the Red Army and for the long-term objective of shipping valuables to the Soviet Union. By 7 July the Special Directorate assumed control over all command posts, now renamed special command posts, and it displaced the Military Council of the 2nd Ukrainian Front in appointing commandants.[6] The same person was placed in charge of exploiting Romanian resources and protecting Romanians from wanton violence, an obvious contradiction in a commandant's duties.

Soviet leaders were eager for the commandants, as representatives of the Soviet Union, to leave a positive impression on occupied populations. In the 2nd Ukrainian Front, Commandants and their deputies were appointed to their positions from the front reserves, from among convalescent officers released from hospitals. They were supposed to have experienced combat, and to be "developed in all regards, to be cultural and literate officers of the Red Army, with extensive life experience, never to have been caught in a drunken state or in a state of moral disintegration, and free of looting tendencies."[7] The Special Directorate appointed only ethnic Russian and Ukrainian officers to the position of commandants, strictly forbidding officers of any other nationality to hold the position, although the non-Slavs could become the commandants' deputies.[8] The commandants, their deputies, and translators were allowed to only speak Russian in front of Romanians, but the translators were to be recruited from among Soviet Moldavians (whose language was very similar to the Romanian).[9] Command posts were supposed to occupy the best (*luchshie*) buildings in the town, and commandants were supposed to receive visitors in classy (*shikarnye*) cabinets.[10]

These policies were about who the Soviet leadership thought was most capable of running command posts, which meant experienced officers with a proven track record of frontline service. However, these instructions were also about how the Kremlin wanted the Soviet power to be perceived by foreigners. Moscow sought the Red Army to appear powerful, perhaps even imperial, hence the stress on extravagant cabinets and the best buildings. This is also why only Russians and Ukrainians were permitted to be commandants. It is extremely rare to find examples of official discrimination in Red Army documents, but clearly, the high command wanted the Europeans to know that the Slavs were in charge. The Kremlin's insistence on the use of the Russian language in communication between the authorities and occupied populations had the rationale of forcing the population to adapt to Soviet rule while demonstrating the Soviet state's power.

In addition to special command posts, military units maintained the right to appoint military commandants near the frontlines as in the Soviet Union, which were sometimes referred to as battle command posts. The special commandants also carried out more traditional duties, such as administering the region, quartering Soviet armies, and struggling against deserters, marauders, and other illegal activities of Soviet soldiers. After the formation of the Allied Control Commission (ACC) after the armistice in Romania, which was headed by Marshal Malinovskii, the commander of the 2nd Ukrainian Front, the special command posts were taken over by the ACC, but they did not lose their mandate to exploit Romania's economy. In essence, Soviet policy placed the same person in charge of systematically pillaging Romania and protecting Romanian civilians from Soviet soldiers who did the same thing on their initiative.

3.2 Romania

After the Armistice Agreement was signed, the Soviets plundered Romania through official channels, the ACC. In September and October, 828 town halls were stripped of their property.[11] From 13 September 1944 to 1 March 1945, Romania delivered to the Soviet military authorities 202,397 cattle, 221,949 sheep, 76,209 swine, 88,746 tons of wheat, 72,110 tons of oats, 486 tons of rice, and 48 billion lei worth of other products.[12] Between 23 August 1944 and 31 May 1945, Romania supplied the Red Army with 15,357 train wagons of cereals and derivatives, 10,407 wagons of vegetables, 1,885 wagons of meat, 387 wagons of tinned meat, 163 wagons of fats, 124 wagons of dairy products, 88 wagons of fish, 27 wagons of delicacy, 20 wagons of fruits and derivatives, 155 wagons of alcoholic drinks, 4,061 wagons of fuel, 4,942 wagons of fodder, 1,023 wagons of salt, and 279 wagons of tobacco.[13] The Soviets appropriated sixty-seven industrial units and plants.[14] As a result of years of war and Soviet occupation, the standard of living in Romania sharply dropped. In the first three months of 1945, compared to the same period in 1944, Romanians consumed 33.1 percent less flour, 50.09 percent less sugar, and 86.3 percent less cooking oil. Due to shortages of oxen, in the spring of 1945, only 30 percent of arable land was sown.[15]

After the royal coup in Bucharest on 23 August, which brought to power a pro-Allied government, Moscow waited until 13 September to sign the armistice. The delay was caused by Moscow's wish to occupy as much of Romania as possible and to seize as much war booty while Romania was formally an enemy, including prisoners of war who were used as forced labor in the Soviet Union. According to Romanian military sources, between 23 August and 13 September, the Soviet Army captured 12,000 officers and noncommissioned officers, 150,000 soldiers, 20,000 carts, 3,000 cars, 150,000 weapons, 8,000 machine guns, and 800 cannons.[16] On 9 September the Soviets seized all ships in Danube ports Oltenita and Kalarasi and sent them to the Soviet Union by way of the Black Sea.[17] Moscow could have signed the armistice right after the royal coup that brought a pro-allied government to power, but then it could not have legally seized so many troops and so much property.

While the Soviet Union systematically exploited Romania's economy for its war effort and recovery, it ruthlessly forced political changes in the country. The post-armistice political arrangement was contradictory. The Romanian state continued to be dominated by the military apparatus headed by people whom the Soviets viewed as irreconcilable enemies and war criminals. The first prime minister of allied Romania was Constantin Sanatescu, who had fought as a high-ranking officer against the Soviet Union during the war. His security chief had held the same position under Antonescu.[18] The army, the most important institution in the country, remained staunchly conservative and anti-Soviet, and its leadership was left largely intact. In the early stages of the occupation, the political parties that offered support to the new government were largely non-fascist conservatives oriented toward Britain and the United States and, as such, were inimical to Soviet interests. The Kremlin did its best to prop up the small Romanian Communist Party, which grew in influence until it seized power on 6 March 1945.[19]

The main obstacle to Soviet political control of Romania was the country's military, which had been the Antonescu regime's most important base of support and Germany's steadfast ally in Romania. Moscow steadily eroded the Romanian army's power by limiting its size and taking away Romanian soldiers' right to self-defense. The Soviet command had full operational control over Romanian units fighting on the frontlines, eventually even forbidding them from communicating with their headquarters in Bucharest, effectively transforming the Romanian army into Soviet auxiliaries.[20] Even though the Armistice Agreement called for Romania to commit twelve divisions against the Axis, Bucharest at different times deployed fourteen to nineteen divisions on the frontlines.[21] At the same time, in Romania proper, the ACC forced extreme cuts to Romanian security forces, so that they could not maintain order, which then justified Moscow's decision to station more troops in Romania.[22]

Soviet authorities in Romania simultaneously strove to limit the right of self-defense to the steadily decreasing number of Romanian forces. The ACC blocked several attempts by the Romanian general staff to clarify the rights of Romanian police and soldiers when faced with transgressions by Red Army soldiers and officers. Meanwhile, under Soviet pressure, the king issued a decree stating that he would not pardon anyone who attacked Soviet soldiers.[23] On 2 February 1945, the Romanian Army submitted a report to the ACC, lamenting the absence of clear directives regarding the right of the Romanian security forces to self-defense and the atmosphere created by the law that stipulated the death penalty for those who attacked allied (Soviet) soldiers. The report maintained that Romanian police and soldiers no longer dared to carry out their orders, allowing themselves to be disarmed and maltreated.[24]

Soviet monetary policies were also subordinated to Moscow's goal of exploiting the Romanian economy. The lei, the Romanian currency, was allowed to circulate, but an artificial exchange rate was established with the Soviet ruble, whereby a hundred lei were equal to one ruble.[25] The Soviets established a third currency, the Soviet military lei, which seems to have been printed and distributed by the Red Army. Twenty lei were equal to one Soviet military lei. All prices were fixed at levels before the occupation of the Red Army. With the ability to print currency, which could only damage the Romanian economy (Soviet military lei), and the absurd exchange rates between the ruble and lei, Stalin ensured that Soviet military authorities would be able to legally purchase anything their armies needed (or requisition it, also legally, if Romanians refused to sell it at the fixed low prices). The Armistice Agreement stipulated that the Romanian government would regularly pay the Soviet high command in lei the funds it required to carry out occupational duties and wage war.[26] Subsequently, on 26 September, the ruble and the Soviet military lei were banned from circulation in Romania, while Soviet troops serving in the country started to receive salaries in lei.[27] Thus, with the takeover of central institutions in Bucharest, including the central bank, Moscow obtained unrestricted access to the Romanian currency and no longer required the use of military lei.

3.3 Bulgaria

The Kremlin's immediate political goal was to install friendly governments in Sofia like elsewhere in Eastern Europe. However, in contrast to other countries occupied by the Soviets, except Yugoslavia, the transition to communist rule in Bulgaria occurred rapidly and, from Moscow's perspective, smoothly. The Fatherland Front government, which took power on 9 September in Sofia, consisted of a broad coalition. The communists dominated it, holding the key positions of the Ministry of Justice and the Ministry of the Interior, while the other left-leaning pro-Allied parties played a more minor role. The government soon dismissed the parliament and banned all parties outside of the Fatherland Front.[28] The communist-dominated revolutionary committees took power throughout the country, in the words of one historian, "with astonishing and comical ease."[29]

Moscow's policies in Bulgaria were fair considering that Sofia had been a Nazi ally. According to the Armistice Agreement, Bulgaria assumed responsibility for maintaining the Allied (Soviet) occupational troops. Approximately one-sixth of the Bulgarian budget was spent on maintaining the Soviet contingent.[30] Although Bulgaria was not required to pay any damages to the Soviet Union, it was obliged to hand over to the Soviets as war booty all German and Hungarian war materials, property, businesses, and debts. In addition, the Soviets assumed control over all vessels in Bulgarian ports for the duration of the war.[31] Bulgaria was the only Axis country that enlarged its territory during the war since the Soviets permitted Sofia to retain the region of Dobruja, which it seized from Romania in 1940. Moscow also supported the Bulgarian armed forces, a unique situation for a former member of the Axis.[32] Historian David Stone rightly concluded that the Soviet occupation weighed more heavily on the Romanians than the Bulgarians because Bulgaria did not wage war against the Soviet Union.[33]

3.4 Yugoslavia

The Communist Party of Yugoslavia assumed power formally once the Red Army and Partisans liberated Belgrade in October, although it had already established its authority in territories under its control, including large parts of Dalmatia, Bosnia, Montenegro, and Serbia. Moscow's policies toward Yugoslavia were among the most benign in Europe. In fact, Stalin and the Soviet leadership put in a large effort to woo the Yugoslav Communists once it became clear that the Red Army would liberate the Balkans.[34] For example, when the Yugoslav delegation told Stalin in the summer of 1944 that Yugoslavia would repay the Soviet Union after the war for its assistance, Milovan Đilas, one of the highest-ranking Yugoslav communists at the time, reported that the Soviet leader "became sincerely angry: 'you insult me. You are shedding your blood, and you expect me to charge you for the weapons! I am not a merchant…you are fighting for the same cause as we. We are duty bound to share with you whatever we have.'"[35] Just before the Red Army entered Yugoslavia, Tito flew to Moscow to plan and coordinate Partisan and Red Army operations. During his visit, Tito received full diplomatic, economic, and military aid from the Soviet Union.[36] Stalin did not treat any other leader of a European country as well.

The Soviets provided the Yugoslavs with a large number of weapons, significantly eclipsing even their support for the Bulgarian military.[37] The Yugoslav leaders were ideologically zealous, but they were also highly nationalistic. Tito a pursued expansionist policies against all of Yugoslavia's neighbors, trying to aggrandize Yugoslavia's borders at the expense of Italy, Austria, Hungary, Romania, Bulgaria, Greece, and Albania.[38] The Soviet leadership was unhappy about the boldness and scale of Tito's demands.[39] Nonetheless, throughout the war, Moscow became Belgrade's chief supporter in its territorial claims against Austria and Italy; for several months, it even allowed Yugoslavs to occupy parts of Hungary, and it backed Belgrade's moves to gradually incorporate Albania into the Yugoslav federation.

If Moscow's policies in Bulgaria were correct considering that the country was part of the Axis, then in Yugoslavia they could even be characterized as magnanimous. Moscow's fair treatment of Bulgaria and Yugoslavia was rooted in the fact that neither waged war against the Soviet Union and that communists were effectively controlled in both countries. The Kremlin's reasonable dealings with Bulgaria and Yugoslavia set the tone for the Red Army commanders in the field to follow.

This chapter makes the point that the war and the Kremlin's policies brought deprivation, including severe shortages of food, to Romania, Hungary, and Austria. Yugoslavia, however, had experienced a brutal and exploitative occupation, insurgency, counterinsurgency, and a series of ethnic and political civil wars since 1941. All of these led to the civilian population having suffered extreme food deprivation for over three years when the Red Army showed up on the country's borders.[40] Radmila Petković, a middle-class resident of Belgrade, was a fourteen-year-old girl when the war started in 1941. She described the war years as "chaos, horror, misfortune, famine."[41] Her father, a lawyer, had to sell his clothes, gold, and a little ancestral land he inherited for food. The family fled Belgrade and spent large parts of the war in a village near the city to escape hunger and violence.[42] In Serbia, much like in the German-occupied parts of the Soviet Union, food was more plentiful in rural areas.[43] Thus, for the civilian population of Yugoslavia, the Red Army's arrival did not herald in suffering. If anything, it meant that the end of the war was in sight.

3.5 Hungary

The Soviet leadership pursued punitive policies in Hungary, even harsher than in Romania. The Kremlin and Budapest intensified contacts as the Red Army neared Central Europe, and Moscow ardently hoped that Hungary would switch sides and hasten the Soviet advance in Europe. Soviet leaders were even willing to accept Horthy as a temporary ally, despite his virulent anti-communism, his participation in the war against the Soviet Union, indecisiveness, and obvious reluctance to reach a deal with the Soviets until late in the war.[44]

Horthy's announcement on the radio that Hungary would surrender to the Allies on 15 October caused confusion, but the three Hungarian armies remained in the field.[45] Instead, Germans brought the fanatical Arrow Cross to power, which hardened anti-Hungarian attitudes in the Kremlin. Stalin was angry at this turn of events. He told one commander on 23 October that the Red Army must not distinguish between Hungarian and German soldiers.[46] Four days later, he issued a decree that ordered the creation of special teams to systematically carry out plunder in Hungary.[47] Such teams operated in Romania but not in Bulgaria and Yugoslavia. Five days later, he told the commander of the 2nd Ukrainian Front to take Budapest in the next couple of days, despite the latter's protests that this goal was unrealistic.[48] Undoubtedly, Hungary's failure to come over to the Soviet side embittered the Soviet leadership and contributed to Moscow's harsh treatment of the country.

Subsequently, Stalin's direct involvement in the 2nd and 3rd Ukrainian Fronts was primarily concerned with the slow pace of their advance in Hungary and not with soldiers' proliferating crimes against the civilian population. On 23 November, Stalin converted the entire 214th Cavalry Regiment into a penal unit because the regimental commander lost the unit's banner. The commander was demoted from lieutenant colonel to major, while the rank-and-file troops were instructed that they would have to atone on the battlefield for their sins against the motherland.[49]

On 5 March, Stalin singled out Malinovskii and Tolbukhin for poor leadership and failure to report their casualties correctly in an order sent out to all front commanders.[50] Thus, Moscow repeatedly signaled to the Red Army's command in the field that their major concern should be military victory, without regard for the Red Army's casualties or the treatment of the civilian population.

The Soviets organized a provisional government in the city of Debrecen on 2 December 1945. The communist role in the new government was relatively minor, and the provisional government included even Horthy supporters.[51] Moscow did not view Hungary as a high priority for Soviet security, so it did not push for an immediate introduction of communism. Stalin even told Hungarian communists that they would have to wait ten to fifteen years before seizing power.[52] The provisional government signed the Armistice Agreement with the Allies on 20 January 1945, which created the Soviet-led ACC. Thereafter, the ACC controlled the provisional government, and the 800 members of the ACC were present in every government office, major factory, and even railroad station.[53]

The Soviets extracted reparations in several ways from Hungary, with the same impulse to transfer as much wealth as possible to the Soviet Union and to alleviate the poverty of the Soviet population. The first and most obvious method by which reparations were extracted was through official compensation that the Soviets forced upon their defeated enemies. According to the Armistice Agreement signed between the Hungarian provisional government and the Allies, Hungary was required to pay $200 million to the Soviet Union and $100 million to Yugoslavia and Czechoslovakia.[54] Moscow also claimed all German property, investments, debts, and even Hungarian companies in which Germans had a financial interest, regardless of how small it may have been. This practice raised Hungarian reparations to the Soviet Union by an additional $200 million.[55]

Military commandants alone, under the Directorate's control, confiscated the following materials throughout Hungary between 15 October and 20 February: 42,054 kg of gold, 212,325 kg of gold coins, 337 gold watches, 22,017 kg of silver, 1,267 metal watches (yes, it seems that proverbial Soviet obsession with watches was reflected in official policies), and 264 alarm clocks.[56] In addition, commandants seized 5,795 heads of cattle, 2,785 oxen, 29,156 pigs, 12,345 sheep, 2,568 horses, and 30,000 birds; 142,180 tons of wheat; 2,898 tons of rye; 14,470 tons of barley; 1,105 tons of rice; 6,284 tons of corn; and 8,204 tons of beans.[57] The Soviets also systematically plundered banks and valuable art.[58]

The Soviets also extracted reparations from Hungary by employing special teams of professional looters. In his broader order regarding the

Red Army's entry into Hungary, issued on 27 October, Stalin decreed that all valuable machinery from industrial enterprises, which was not used for supplying the Red Army, should be shipped to the Soviet Union. To this end, he ordered the creation of the Directorate for the Utilization of the Internal Resources of Hungary, which had a military and civilian staff of 2,000 and 20, respectively.[59] Two days later, the Military Council of the 2nd Ukrainian Front subordinated the command posts to the Directorate in matters relating to reparations.[60] As in Romania, military commandants were charged with the contradictory tasks of expropriating property for official reparations and protecting civilians from soldiers who did so on their own initiative.

Moscow also extracted reparations by allowing the troops to send packages to their families and friends to the Soviet Union. The Kremlin borrowed this policy from the Wehrmacht, which, as historian Brandon Schechter pointed out, permitted German soldiers to send home parcels for free and to take whatever plunder they could carry with them home on leave without paying customs.[61] This policy, introduced by Stalin in a decree on 23 December 1944, coincided with the siege of Budapest when all the combat troops of the 2nd and 3rd Ukrainian Fronts were deployed in Hungary. However, the policy also subsequently affected the Soviet soldiers' conduct in Austria, as well as the two army groups' reserves in Romania and the occupation troops in Romania and Bulgaria. Soldiers, officers, and generals' parcels were, respectively, limited to 5, 10, and 16 kg.[62] This permission did not mean that Moscow explicitly wanted the troops to commit illegal robberies. Soldiers and officers after 11 January 1945 were supposed to receive their salaries in local currencies.[63] In theory, they were expected to purchase local goods from *Voentorg*, the official Red Army supplier, which obtained European property through official confiscations.[64] Moreover, when Stalin's decree was announced, it was accompanied by a propaganda campaign emphasizing that looting and marauding were impermissible.[65]

Despite these efforts to limit the looting, Stalin's decree encouraged plundering. The war-torn areas, which had been ravaged by the Nazi scorched-earth policy, a near state of anarchy that lasted for weeks between the departure of the old and establishment of new authorities, and the Red Army's systematic plundering, had left few goods available for soldiers and officers to purchase. Even official Soviet reports acknowledged as much.[66] Therefore, it is unsurprising that soldiers tended to deposit their salaries into savings accounts instead of spending money in Europe. The Soviet command tried to persuade the troops, through a political campaign, to agree to receive their salaries in foreign currency and to spend it in countries of their location.[67] Meanwhile, political departments popularized Stalin's decree and encouraged soldiers to send packages to the Soviet Union.[68] The Soviet leadership's thinking was obvious: Goods purchased with local currency, which the Red Army could print and which did not harm the Soviet economy, would be sent back home for the benefit of the long-suffering Soviet civilian population. This line of reasoning, of course, collided with the reality that there were no goods available for purchase since the Soviet money in Europe was largely worthless.

It follows, then, that if the troops were going to send goods back home, then most of them would have to engage in theft and robbery. The Soviet command must have been aware of this, but it was a price it was willing to pay. A soldier recalled that his battalion stood in formation to salute their commanding general. As the general inspected his troops in Hungary, he asked them if they had sent parcels back home. When they gave a negative reply, the general instructed them, half-jokingly, that they had to loot more effectively (*nado luchshe khvatat*).[69] It is difficult to ascertain how often and how many troops managed to send packages. Roughly one-third of the NKVD Army's 25th Border Guard Regiment had shipped parcels by 25 March 1945.[70] It should be noted that the NKVD Army was more privileged because NKVD troops spent most of their time in the rear, and they had more opportunities to send packages. In my view, according to veterans' diaries, memoirs, and interviews, a large number of troops, certainly more than half, eventually sent at least one package back home, but many sent more.[71] Subsequently, the 3rd Ukrainian Front command's only complaint regarding parcels was that a significant number of packages exceeded the prescribed weight limits.[72]

Moscow also extracted war reparations through forced labor.[73] This was the rationale behind Stalin's order on 16 December for the transfer of Eastern Europe's *Volksdeutsche* men aged seventeen to forty-five and women aged eighteen to thirty to the Soviet Union.[74] As a result, 111,831 ethnic Germans were deported from Romania, Hungary, and Yugoslavia to the Soviet Union for forced labor.[75] The removal of the *Volksdeutsche* community was the major crime against humanity ordered by the Soviet regime during the war in the Balkans and Central Europe. It also reflected the broader trend, which intensified during the war, for the Kremlin to punish supposedly disloyal nations en masse, including Volga Germans, Chechens, and Crimean Tatars all of whom were collectively deported to remote parts of the country far away from their ancestral homelands. This policy invariably affected local Hungarians because ethnic Germans who identified as Hungarians were deported. Since the Soviets had quotas for deporting Germans, in some instances, they tended to fill them with Hungarians when there were not enough

Germans.[76] Many Hungarian prisoners of war, almost half a million, were also sent to the Soviet Union and used as forced labor.[77]

The Hungarian population suffered enormous economic and material deprivation. In Budapest, hundreds of people died from starvation during the siege.[78] Although there was no major famine after the Red Army entered the city, there were massive shortages. Before the war, Budapest consumed every day 300,000 liters of sour cream and, after, only 12,000 liters.[79] The Red Army consumed more food than what was left to feed approximately 9 million Hungarians.[80] The industry also suffered. In Hungary, in 1945, heavy industry produced 35 percent of prewar levels, while 15–22 percent of national income went into reparation payments.[81]

The Soviets were not the sole cause of Hungarian misery. The US and British air forces began the strategic bombing campaign of Hungary in April 1944, which did not cease until March of the following year. The Western allies dropped 28,062 tons of bombs on the country. They targeted airfields, factories, railways, bridges, refineries, and oil storage facilities. The Hungarian authorities estimated that the bombing campaign killed 16,000 civilians and wounded 25,000.[82] The Germans also carried away everything they could get their hands on as they retreated. They took with them Hungary's gold and silver reserves, ships, trucks, and railroad rolling stock, and they dismantled and carried away 500 factories. What they could not take away with them, they blew up, including bridges over the Danube River.[83] Meanwhile, the fighting itself throughout the country but especially in Budapest, the country's economic center, caused enormous damage. In the capital, 38,000 families were left homeless by the fighting during the long siege.[84] Finally, Hungarian criminals also played a role in looting during and after the siege.[85] It took weeks for the Red Army and local authorities to establish some semblance of order.

3.6 Austria

Britain, the United States, and the Soviet Union announced in the Moscow Declaration of 1943 that Austria was Germany's first victim, but it would also have to pay the price for its participation in Nazi aggression.[86] In the long run, this declaration meant that Austria would emerge as an independent state. The Red Army occupied only parts of Austria, including the capital, while the Anglo-American troops entered from the west. Thereafter, France, Great Britain, the United States, and the Soviet Union divided Austria into four occupation zones.

Although Moscow treated Austria as a defeated Axis power, it adhered to the general line that Austria was a victim of Germany. Therefore,

Austria avoided some of the worst aspects of Germany's fate. Namely, it did not lose any territory, despite Yugoslavia's claims to Carinthia, a province in the south of the country.[87] Austrians avoided the fate of the *Volksdeutsche*, who were rounded up and deported to the Soviet Union for forced labor. Likewise, Austrians did not become victims of ethnic cleansing like Germans from the Third Reich's territories incorporated into Poland, Czechoslovakia and the Soviet Union. The Western allies also successfully opposed the Kremlin's plans to impose burdensome war reparations on Austria that Germany, Romania, and Hungary had to pay.[88] Moreover, the fact that Moscow did not plan or try to impose communist dictatorship in Austria meant that the scale of political violence experienced by Austrians was more limited than in other countries that the 2nd and 3rd Ukrainian Fronts occupied.

In 1945, or the initial eight months of occupation, the Soviet military tribunals arrested around 800 Austrian civilians. For 400 of them, the charges are known: 191 were charged with belonging to the Nazi Werwolf resistance group, 61 with espionage, 55 with maltreatment of Soviet prisoners of war and forced laborers, 31 with weapons possession, 22 with war crimes, 24 with violent acts, 11 for selling bad alcohol to Soviet troops, 4 with criminal activities, and 1 for being a former Soviet citizen.[89] By the standards of the Soviet justice system, and given the significant Austrian contribution to Nazi war crimes, the Soviet repressive apparatus in the first months of occupation acted with considerable restraint in Austria. This restraint can be partly explained by the fact that Moscow did not fully control Austria and partly because Austria was far from the Soviet Union's frontiers. Consequently, it did not rank high on Moscow's list of geopolitical priorities. It was far more important for the Kremlin to have a friendly and preferably communist regime in a neighboring country, such as Romania, whose adjoining territory made it a potential military threat to the Soviet Union.

London and Washington, D.C., prevented Moscow from obtaining direct reparations from Austria, which they got from Romania, Hungary, and Germany. However, the Western Allies consented to Moscow's demand that the Soviets should be entitled to German assets in Austria in their zone of occupation.[90] Moscow considered German property to be all property that at the end of the war had German owners or investors.[91] As a result, Austria ended up paying more than five times what Stalin originally demanded.[92] In Austria, as in all the countries discussed in this book except Yugoslavia, local governments were obliged to feed and clothe the Red Army, which, given the number of troops, was a heavy burden on the war-ravaged countries.[93] The NKVD teams of professional looters also seized industrial plants, and production installations, while confiscating goods in the quantity of 31,200 freight cars.[94] The Soviets also seized valuable art. In April 1945, for instance, the Red Army transported six lorries of art, furniture, and rare books from the Esterházy family's castle in Eisenstadt in Burgenland.[95] Meanwhile, according to one estimate, within a month of their arrival in the city, the Soviets seized 3,960 motorized vehicles out of Vienna's stock of 4,000.[96] In June 1946, 30 percent of the national budget went into covering the occupation costs.[97]

The Austrian population suffered heavily due to war and occupation. The daily calorie rations for the urban Austrian population fell from 2,000 calories in 1944 to between 350 and 850 calories in the spring and summer of 1945.[98] The rations were raised to 1,550 calories in September.[99] Throughout 1946, the average Viennese was consuming 25 percent fewer fats and meat and 75 percent less bread than in 1937. Austrians survived, in part, due to Soviet assistance, largely in the form of dried peas.[100] In Austria, as in Hungary, the local criminals took advantage of the security vacuum. The Viennese took the lead in plundering the Austrian capital with Soviet troops and liberated forced laborers joining in afterward.[101]

3.7 Conclusion

The Soviet leadership's policies in Romania, Bulgaria, Yugoslavia, Hungary, and Austria had three main objectives: to win the war as soon as possible, to impose friendly governments to help the successful prosecution of the war and to assure future control, and to revive the ravaged Soviet economy by exploiting the areas occupied by the Red Army. The Red Army also lived off the land, as did German, Romanian, and Hungarian armies in the Soviet Union beforehand. For the Soviet political leadership, the safety and well-being of European civilians was completely subordinated to these three larger goals. This was best illustrated by the fact that the Kremlin relied on the command post commandants to both exploit enemy territories and protect the civilians from undisciplined soldiers.

Even though Bulgaria was a member of the Axis, it never participated in Germany's war against the Soviet Union. Thus, the Soviet Union did not need to extract reparations from the country. The situation was the same in Yugoslavia, which was part of the Allies. The communists assumed control relatively quickly in Bulgaria and Yugoslavia and were perceived as loyal allies of Moscow. Thus, the Kremlin supported the country's governments and militaries. Overall, the Kremlin's policies were less severe in Bulgaria and Yugoslavia than in Romania, Hungary, and Austria.

4 Propaganda

The Main Political Administration of the Red Army (GlavPURKKA) was responsible for propaganda, morale, and discipline in the military.[1] It acted through political departments headed by political officers from the fronts down to company levels. Aleksandr Shcherbakov, one of Stalin's closest wartime allies, headed GlavPURKKA. GlavPURKKA was the Communist Party of the Soviet Union in the Red Army. During the war, the Central Committee sent around 8,800 Communist Party workers to the Red Army as political officers.[2] The party cadres were particularly prevalent at the higher levels of political command.[3] For instance, Lieutenant-General Ivan Anoshin, the head of the political department of the 3rd Ukrainian Front, was the leading communist in Bashkiria until 1939.[4] Before October 1942, political officers were known as commissars and they held equal rank and authority to military officers. Subsequently, Stalin restored unified command and subordinated political officers and communists to military commanders.

Historian Karel Berkhoff argued that the purpose of Soviet wartime propaganda was to shape perceptions, mental states, and to achieve a response that furthered the propagandist's intent.[5] When historians discuss propaganda in the context of the Red Army's entry into Europe, they usually do so to connect the anti-German hate campaign with the atrocities committed by the troops. One historian, notably, borrowed the famed author Mikhail Shokholov's term "school of hate" to describe the Kremlin's anti-German indoctrination.[6] However, the content and purpose of propaganda in the army groups that did not fight in Germany remain relatively obscure. Was hate propaganda directed at allies of Germany? If hate was such an important feature of propaganda, what did propagandists tell the troops in Bulgaria and Yugoslavia, which never joined the German anti-Soviet crusade? What can propaganda tell us about how Soviet leadership wanted the troops to interact with and make sense of the world around them?

4.1 Romania

Romania and the Soviet Union were hostile to each other from before the war. Moscow coveted Bessarabia, which it seized from Bucharest after the Molotov-Ribbentrop Pact. Thereafter, Romania was a major German ally on the Eastern front. Thus, the Soviet hate propaganda from the outset of the war focused on Romania, which was not the case with any other country the 2nd and 3rd Ukrainian Fronts occupied.[7] For example, Soviet media reported the massacre of 25,000 Jews in Odesa by Romanians, describing it correctly as "one of the biggest mass murders of Jews in history."[8] In January 1944, three months before the Red Army entered Romania, Il'ya Ehrenburg, the talented and famous Soviet military journalist who wrote for the military newspaper *Red Star*, wrote an article, "Virtuous Antonescu." In it, he cited the journal of a captured Romanian soldier, who wrote: "Odesa, 24 October 1941. Women and children were forced into wooden barns ... barns were soaked in kerosene and set ablaze. Women took the burning clothes off and screamed. The children cried. But they all burnt."[9] Ehrenburg concluded the article by saying that there was justice in the world and that Antonescu would soon experience this pain on his skin.[10]

However, the ferocity of the anti-Romanian hate campaign was blunted by the propaganda's pragmatic focus on Germans. Since it was easier to stir up hate against the much more numerous and powerful German army than its relatively weak Romanian ally, Soviet propaganda sometimes even blamed the Germans for crimes that were perpetrated by Romanians. This tendency was most evident in the Red Army's propaganda that sometimes downplayed the Romanian role in the atrocities in Odesa, the largest Soviet city occupied and administered by Romanians. For example, a pamphlet issued by GlavPURKKA in 1944, most likely in the winter or spring of that year, prominently featured a photo of a murdered man with a butchered face. Next to the photograph, the author proclaimed:

> It is hard to look at this face, comrade ... [his] eyes have been gouged, cheeks cut out ... he was bestially tortured by Germans in Odesa in the courtyard of the German-Romanian prefecture. Here they tortured citizens, and then burned them alive. Soldier of the Red Army! Murder the murderer! Blood for blood, death for death! ... Don't let the German beast escape alive![11]

Probably this was a photo of a Jew murdered by Romanians in Odesa or perhaps a partisan, the two groups that Romanians subjected to death. Nonetheless, Soviet propaganda used this crime to hone soldiers' hatred of Germans.

Similarly, the political department of an unspecified unit of the 3rd Ukrainian Front distributed a leaflet comprised of statements supposedly made by soldiers who joined the Communist Party in March or April of 1944. The pamphlet opened with the following call:

> Death to the German occupiers! FORWARD! STORM ODESA! … Bursts of fire have announced to citizens of Odesa that the hour of liberation is near … the damned Krauts and [their] Romanian satraps are finished. Let vile fascists rage … In the large encirclement around Odesa, Hitlerite cutthroats will meet their graves. In front of us are new battles, new victories, new glory … we are proud that our task will be to chase the hated Hitlerite on the Romanian land … forward to the liberation of Odesa, to the liberation of wonderful Moldavia! Death to the German conquerors![12]

This pamphlet directed Soviet soldiers' hatred at Germans, whereas the Romanians ruled Odesa for most of the war, annexed Moldavia, and were the undisputed masters in Romania, where the German military presence was limited.

When the Red Army entered parts of Romania in the spring of 1944, as we saw in Chapter 2, there was a sharp increase in military violations. Shcherbakov sent lengthy instructions to the 2nd Ukrainian Front, regarding this issue, on 19 July 1944.[13] In the order, he blamed the political departments for the situation, criticizing them for concealing from GlavPURKKA the proliferation of different types of military violations. He also described propaganda in the army group as too formalistic and detached from the soldiers' lives. The gist of Shcherbakov's order was that the political departments, in order to reverse declining discipline, needed to raise the morale of the troops through more effective propaganda. Among the most tangible measures Shcherbakov ordered was for agitators to concentrate on stirring up hatred against the Romanians.[14] Days later, on 27 July, the head of the political department of the 3rd Ukrainian Front sent a circular to the entire front regarding its anticipated entry into Romania. Among other measures, Anoshin advised political officers to systematically drill into soldiers "the hatred towards German-Romanian conquerors for all their villainy and the suffering of the people."[15] Thus, the Red Army's political leadership believed that stirring up hate against the enemy would create a more disciplined and motivated fighting force.

The hate propaganda was officially aimed at the enemy army in Romania. Occasionally, however, the troops were reminded by propagandists that they needed to treat civilians correctly.[16] Despite such warnings, many troops interpreted the hate propaganda against Romanian soldiers as official encouragement of their hatred of Romanians in general, which in turn provided a justification for their mistreatment of civilians.

The hate campaign against Romanians ceased only once Bucharest abandoned the Axis. Thereafter, Soviet propaganda had two goals: to support disciplined conduct with a much greater emphasis on the correct treatment of civilians and to build up national pride among the Soviet troops to prevent unfavorable comparisons (from the Kremlin's perspective) between capitalist Romania and the socialist Soviet Union. To fulfill the first of these two goals, propaganda began emphasizing the Red Army's liberating role in Romania. For example, the 7th Border Guards Regiment of the NKVD Army of the 3rd Ukrainian Front organized for its officers in early September a discussion about "The conduct of officers on Romanian territory and tasks relating to imposing order and discipline in units." All units of the regiment were also required to discuss the NKVD Lieutenant-General Appolonov's directive about the "Struggle of the party and Komsomol organizations with sexual (*polovaia*) laxity."[17] Guards Lieutenant-Colonel Nekrasov, head of the Political Department of the Rear of the 3rd Ukrainian Front, reminded all political officers that the Red Army entered Romania to defeat the Germans and liberate Europe as a highly organized and disciplined army of the Soviet people, which was incompatible with arbitrary behavior toward the civilian population.[18]

Colonel Smoleev, head of the political department of the 4th Guards Mechanized Corps, submitted to his superiors a detailed report about his department's activities in September when the corps marched through Romania in the wake of the Iasi Kishinev Operation. Two high-ranking officers of the political department visited a regiment, in which there were cases of marauding, to deliver lectures on the following topics: "Marauding – crime against the Motherland," and "About the conduct of Soviet soldiers on the territory of Romania." In another regiment of the same corps, propagandists discussed the following topics with soldiers and officers: "Struggle against marauders," "Discipline while marching," and "Relations with the civilian population in Romania." Political officers delivered the following lecture in the same unit: "The Red Army – the most progressive, conscientious and disciplined military in the world" and "Discipline and vigilance during the march."[19] Clearly, the political department of the 4th Guards Mechanized Corps sought to influence Soviet soldiers to behave correctly in Romania.

The second goal of the Red Army's propaganda after Romania switched sides was to reaffirm the superiority of the Soviet system. To achieve this, the propagandists stressed the exploitative and feudal nature of Romanian society and emphasized the preeminence of the Red Army. In all units of the 4th Guards Mechanized Corps, the following topics were discussed with soldiers: "Romania – agrarian country, country of landowners and capitalists," "Servitude in Romania," and "Kishinev encirclement."[20] The military success at the Iasi Kishinev Operation became an obligatory topic of discussion for the entire front since it illustrated the Red Army's dominance over the Romanian military.[21] All of these lectures highlighted the superiority of the Soviet Union. To create distance between the Red Army troops and Romania, propaganda occasionally reminded Soviet soldiers that they should never forget past Romanian transgressions. Military journalist Aleksandr Krivitskii argued in the Red Army's newspaper *Krasnaia Zvezda* in May of 1945 that a Soviet officer should never forget about "the baseness and craftiness of his [Romanian] enemy, who is always prepared to put on a sheepskin over his wolfish hair."[22] Obviously, even when the official line about Romanians became more positive, the anger and bitterness against the former enemy nation crept into the official discourse.

4.2 Bulgaria

Soviet propaganda about Bulgaria was free of any hostility, even after Moscow declared war on Sofia in September 1944. On the contrary, the Soviet command's message to its frontline officers and soldiers was unambiguous; the troops needed to treat the civilian population humanely because they were fraternal nations and traditional allies from the nineteenth century when Russia helped liberate Bulgaria from the Ottoman Empire. In Bulgaria, a special pamphlet published by the 3rd Ukrainian Front appealed to troops, "The name Soviet Union, the name Russia is – for Bulgarians everywhere – a great and sacred name … you are surrounded by love and respect as a soldier-liberator. Carry with dignity the honorable name of a Soviet soldier! … Be strictly disciplined and cultured everywhere!"[23]

Political departments of various units organized lectures and conversations with soldiers around the following topics: the Red Army's relationship with the Bulgarian people, the liberating mission of the Red Army, the political situation in Bulgaria, historical links between the Bulgarian people and the Great Russian people, and discipline and soldiers' appearance while marching.[24] All of these lectures were aimed at creating a positive image of the Bulgarians and sustaining disciplined conduct among Soviet troops. The Soviet propaganda also needed to explain to soldiers why Moscow declared war on Sofia, even though Bulgaria never fought against the Soviet Union. Therefore, the political workers emphasized that Moscow's declaration of war against Bulgaria was meant to liberate the Bulgarian people from oppression while exposing "the hypocritical position of the monarchist-fascist Bulgarian government."[25] Thus, Soviet propaganda sought to make a clear distinction to the rank and file between the former Bulgarian regime and the Bulgarian people.

The Soviet command went to great lengths to collect and disseminate information that could be used to help Soviet troops behave respectfully toward the Bulgarians. One of the more unusual documents was an informational report produced by the NKVD Army of the 3rd Ukrainian Front. The report discussed different Bulgarian traditions, including customs surrounding death, hospitality, and how to politely greet and take leave from someone.[26] This report was used presumably to teach Soviet officers about proper social etiquette in Bulgaria.

Most central to the Soviet leadership's efforts to create a pro-Bulgarian atmosphere in the army's ranks were Bulgaria's sites of memory celebrating Russia's role in the liberation of Bulgaria during the Russo–Turkish War of 1877–1878. The Russian imperial army played a crucial role in the creation of an independent Bulgarian state, and Bulgarians erected many monuments to the Russian army. The Military Council of the 3rd Ukrainian Front issued a directive requiring all political officers to use such historical sites in propaganda.[27] To this end, the NKVD Army collected information about all places in Sofia devoted to the memory of prominent nineteenth-century Russian figures, including monuments, squares, parks, churches, and street names.[28] Anoshin, the head of the political department of the 3rd Ukrainian Front, discussed in his memoirs how officers under his control visited local Bulgarian libraries and bookstores to collect the necessary historical information.[29]

Based on this research, the 3rd Ukrainian Front's political departments organized gatherings with Soviet soldiers and Bulgarian civilians at these sites of memory, where the audiences were informed about the nineteenth-century battles and the traditional military valor of the Russian soldiers-liberators.[30] In some instances, Soviet propagandists organized events for the public and Soviet soldiers where elderly Bulgarians spoke about the liberation of Bulgaria by the Tsarist Russian army from the Ottoman Empire.[31] The 3rd Ukrainian Front newspaper *Sovetskii Voin* discussed Russian sacrifices in the Russo–Turkish War, concluding that the Red Army had sealed the Bulgarian–Russian brotherhood with blood for the second time. The article went on to urge Soviet soldiers to behave as Bulgarians remembered their ancestors.[32] The aim of this propaganda was twofold: to instill pride in soldiers as successors of their glorious imperial-era predecessors and to remind them that they needed to behave correctly toward the brotherly Bulgarian nation.

4.3 Yugoslavia

Yugoslavia was the only country that the two army groups occupied during the war that was not a member of the Axis. The basic premise of

Soviet propaganda in Yugoslavia was that Yugoslavs were long-suffering Slavic brethren, who, while awaiting liberation by the Red Army, heroically resisted the German fascists despite the terror perpetrated by the occupiers. Political workers from various units were instructed to discuss the following topics with the troops: "The Red Army's aims and tasks connected with its entrance in Yugoslavia," "The Red Army – the most organized, disciplined and cultured army," and "Germans are the sworn enemies of Russian and all Slavic people ...."[33] Other topics covered were more conventional such as "Comrade Stalin – the genius leader of the people of the USSR and the commander of the victorious Red Army."[34] Another report stated that Red Army agitators should discuss with Soviet soldiers Tito's political and military achievements.[35] According to another document, Soviet propagandists also discussed "immoral incidents and military violations," "the heroic fight of the Yugoslav people for their independence," and "the oath and military discipline in the Red Army."[36] Following the liberation of Belgrade, the 3rd Ukrainian Front newspaper *Sovetskii Voin* carried an article that proclaimed:

> the battle for Belgrade and the liberation of Yugoslavia from the fascist tyranny strengthened, even more, the friendship and brotherhood of the two heroic Slavic people. That friendship has been cemented with blood and pure (*luitoi*) hatred for the enemy, as well as uncompromising love for our fatherland. Love and hatred – these are the sources of our power and might, and they will lead to complete victory over the German conquerors. Glory to the Soviet army! Glory to the citizens of Belgrade![37]

All of these lectures and articles were aimed at installing respect for the Yugoslav people among the Soviet troops in order to encourage them to behave correctly in the country.

The Soviet propaganda also utilized the Serbs' warm reception of the Red Army to cultivate sympathy for them among the troops.[38] Marshal Tolbukhin, in his instruction (*pamiatka*) to the 3rd Ukrainian Front, read to all troops as they entered Yugoslavia, declared the country to be fraternal by blood and spirit and glorified the Partisans' resistance to the Germans. He ended the instruction with a warning and an emotional appeal: "Be merciless towards marauders, rapists, and the violators of order and discipline! Accept the love and respect of the Yugoslav people, whom you liberated. Respect their traditions, laws, and families!"[39] Thus, Tolbukhin directly appealed to his troops to take the initiative to punish rapists. His threat was not groundless. When two soldiers got drunk and raped a woman in Yugoslavia on 26 October, one of the culprits was executed and the other was given a ten-year prison sentence. The 57th army's command turned this into a teachable moment, ordering that the rapists' fate be read out to all soldiers of the army with the warning that "atrocities in the territory of Yugoslavia in future will be severely punished."[40] Soviet propaganda instructed the troops to behave properly toward the Yugoslav civilians, even threatening them with strong punishments. When rapists were punished, other troops were informed of the harsh sentences to dissuade them from committing similar offenses.

Soviet propaganda seldom exploited the Axis war crimes against civilians from other countries to drum up hate against the Germans and their allies, with the notable exception of the death camps in Poland.[41] Another exception was the German atrocities in Yugoslavia. A Soviet military newspaper, *Zvezda sovetov*, discussed the large-scale war crimes perpetrated by Germans against the Yugoslav fighters and civilians.[42] After the publication of these documents, political departments of all units organized assemblies at which the Soviet soldiers "swore to destroy the enemy and to honorably carry their battle banners on the soil of the Yugoslav people."[43] Just before entering Yugoslavia, the Komsomol cell of the 572nd Rifle Bucharest Regiment of the 233rd Division took an oath to fight bravely against the Germans. One soldier announced: "Our motherland ordered us to help our brothers – the Yugoslav people. We vow, comrades, that we will not spare our lives to fulfill that honorable task."[44] Guards Lieutenant-Colonel Nikolai Zav'ialov, commander of a motorized rifle brigade, recalled in his memoirs that he delivered a speech to one of the battalions under his control in which he called on his troops to fight together with the Yugoslav Partisans. After his speech, soldiers, and officers purportedly vowed "to take revenge against the German-fascist conquerors for the monstrous crimes that they committed in Yugoslavia."[45] The image of Yugoslavia that Soviet propaganda depicted to the troops was very simple. It almost entirely ignored Serbian collaborationist forces and the nationalist anti-communist guerillas.

4.4 Hungary

Before October 1944, when the Red Army reached Hungary's borders, Soviet propaganda seldom mentioned the country. When Horthy's announcement that Hungary would sever ties with Germany did not lead to the disintegration of the country's armed forces, the Soviet high command began planning for an offensive on Budapest. As part of the preparations for the assault, the political department of the 2nd Ukrainian Front launched, according to one experienced veteran, political indoctrination on a scale that he had never seen before. The hate campaign consisted of agitators telling the troops about Hungarian crimes in the Soviet Union while emphasizing that the country was Hitler's last and most stubborn ally.[46]

The brutal combat and Hungarians' hostility toward the Red Army, caused in part by Soviet soldiers' criminal conduct, further shaped official propaganda. When soldiers of the 233rd Division entered Hungary from Yugoslavia, joining the bitter fight that had started weeks earlier, their commander informed them that Hungary was Germany's "last satellite, fighting against our Soviet country even now. To a large degree, in contrast to Bulgaria and Yugoslavia, the population of Hungary is hostile towards our units."[47] Similarly, the political department of the 336th Border Guard Regiment of the NKVD Army instructed its officers to discuss with the rank-and-file a document that described in gruesome detail an assault by an axe-wielding Hungarian man on two female Soviet medics. The document went on to proclaim that Hungarians may sometimes welcome Soviet troops hospitably, but that was only because they feared the Red Army. Therefore, the document concluded, "You must not trust any of them! As Soviet author Il'ia Ehrenburg proclaimed, 'They appear to be sheep but they were wolves and they still are [wolves].'"[48] Thus, the proliferation of Hungarian resistance and supposed terrorist attacks led the command to view the entire population with hostility, while it encouraged political departments to depict all Hungarians as potentially dangerous enemies. Although the Soviets needed to be alert and increase vigilance in Hungary, such attitudes and propaganda gave official credence to the popular view among rank-and-file troops that all Hungarians were enemies.

The Axis counteroffensives also gave a powerful impetus to hate propaganda. One of the numerous short-lived German–Hungarian offensives to relieve the besieged troops in Budapest frustrated the Soviet propagandists. Lieutenant-General Shikin, deputy head of the Main Political Administration in Moscow, sent a letter to Anoshin, the head of the political department of the 3rd Ukrainian Front, which was written on 27 January 1945 by an old Bolshevik identified only as "frontline soldier Volkov."[49] Anoshin passed on the letter to the political departments of the front and asked them to report on measures that they implemented as a response to the letter.

Volkov sought to explain the temporary success of the Axis offensive by blaming, in part, the supposedly lenient Soviet treatment of Hungarian civilians. He declared that Hungarians were the Red Army's most bitter enemy. As evidence, he cited the fact that enemy agents secretly rang church bells in territories under Soviet control to send signals to the German and Hungarian armies. He also claimed that in the town of Dunaújváros, Hungarians threw wounded soldiers off the balconies and burned female medics who were trapped inside the building. Volkov implored his superiors to stop being so nice towards Hungarians (*nuzhno brosit' tseremonii*), urging them to expel the entire civilian population from the frontline areas.[50] Volkov also railed against the general fall in the discipline. In particular, he said that the troops were drinking too much and cited an example of a certain military unit that took 2 hours to organize for battle after an emergency was declared, and that so many soldiers were drunk that many companies assembled 15 to 50 soldiers (a rifle company in the Red Army was supposed to number 178 soldiers). He blamed excessive drinking for the slow and incomplete assembly of the troops in this unit, explaining that "drunk soldiers do not want to listen."[51] It is unclear what measures political departments took in response to this letter, but at a minimum, they discussed the letter's content with the rank-and-file troops, undoubtedly inflaming anti-Hungarian attitudes. Similarly, Anoshin recalled regarding the same Axis offensive, a meeting with military correspondents and political officers of the front, at which they agreed that the frontline troops needed to hear "more hate and contempt for the enemy ...."[52] Clearly, the brutality of the fighting encouraged hate propaganda.

Particularly important in spreading hate propaganda were the Axis' atrocities against Soviet prisoners of war in Hungary. The Red Army's military commission investigated these war crimes.[53] Anoshin recalled in his memoirs that the Red Army discovered thirty-four mutilated corpses of Soviet troops near the village of Bel'sheiuarand.[54] Anoshin reported to Shcherbakov, the head of the Main Political Administration, about the Axis treatment of Soviet prisoners of war on 5 February 1945.[55] Anoshin claimed that Soviet investigators believed that the Germans had the order to kill captured Red Army soldiers. His report enumerated numerous instances of the worst kind of abuse of Soviet prisoners, most of them in or near Budapest, involving at least dozens but probably hundreds of soldiers. According to this report, the Red Army's war crime commissions and medical teams documented cases of Axis soldiers variously gouging eyes out of the Soviet troops, smashing their skulls, breaking all of their fingers, crushing them to death with tanks, and cutting off their genitals and heads. Materials gathered by the commissions were popularized among the troops through oral agitation, the military press, and the meetings of revenge. In Anoshin's view, this propaganda "was fueling a fervent hatred among soldiers and officers for Hitlerite scoundrels, as well as desire to mercilessly exact revenge for the monstrous crimes committed against Soviet prisoners."[56] It is very hard to dispute Anoshin's assessment of the impact that German and Hungarian atrocities, as well as Soviet propaganda that popularized them, had on the rank-and-file troops in Hungary.

It is important to note that Soviet hate propaganda, theoretically at least, was always aimed at Hungarian troops and not civilians. However, most propaganda that called the enemy monsters, while describing in lurid detail their crimes against Soviet civilians and soldiers, did not explicitly make the important distinction between enemy soldiers and civilians. As a result, propaganda contributed to the demeaning of all Hungarians in the eyes of the troops. However, political departments and even military commanders never completely stopped emphasizing that the civilian population should be treated correctly. For instance, when Malinovskii issued the order that restated the punishment for violence against civilians and was read out to all the 2nd Ukrainian Front on 30 October, he declared, "The enemy should be beaten and annihilated with the utmost hatred, but the civilian population should be treated with justice, and in no cases are pillage, marauding, and violence to be tolerated. However, I receive reports on cases of marauding and raping women …."[57] Malinovskii's order shows that Soviet commanders were aware that hate propaganda contributed to the soldiers' rampage, and that they tried to limit this consequence of the hate propaganda. However, the Soviet leadership refused to stop utilizing hate in propaganda since they viewed it as a powerful tool in motivating the troops to fight.

4.5 Austria

The Red Army entered Austria as part of the counteroffensive that grew out of the defensive battles at Lake Balaton in Hungary. After the escalation of violence against civilians in Hungary, the Military Council of the 3rd Ukrainian Front issued an instruction to frontline troops as soon as the Soviet forces crossed into Austria on 4 April.[58] The instruction proclaimed that Austria was Hitler's first victim and that the Red Army entered the country to liberate it and destroy German forces. It stated that the Nazi propaganda for years had frightened the Austrians with tales of the Soviet soldiers committing atrocities. Calling the Nazi propaganda a lie, the instruction went on to appeal to troops not to confuse Austrian civilians with German occupiers. It ended with: "Be merciless towards German enslavers but don't offend the Austrian population. Respect their traditions, families, and private property. Proudly carry the glorious title of a Red Army warrior … let your conduct cause respect everywhere for the Red Army."[59] Again, the appeal to soldiers to respect families and properties was tantamount to telling them to refrain from looting and committing sexual assaults. Historians have noted that the Soviet high command claimed it distinguished between Germans and Austrians from the outset of the occupation of Austria.[60] It is clear that they also followed the same line with the frontline troops. It is difficult to imagine more positive pro-Austrian propaganda, as it embraced the doubtful claim about Austria being Germany's first victim to persuade soldiers that Austrians should be treated correctly.

Despite such propaganda that may be characterized as benevolent to Austrians, the anti-German hate propaganda did not cease. The Red Army liberated hundreds of thousands of forced laborers from the Soviet Union and other countries in Austria. The Soviet forces also started catching up to Jews on death marches in Central Europe.[61] Soviet propagandists could have hardly missed these golden opportunities to imbue the troops with hate. According to Anoshin, whenever possible, former forced laborers were brought to Red Army rallies, where they presumably spoke of their experiences in captivity. One newspaper printed a letter from a soldier's liberated sister, in which she urged him "to exact revenge on the monsters for her suffering, humiliation, and tears."[62] In this way, propaganda provided the troops with vivid evidence of their compatriots' suffering and humiliation. Also, since forced labor was used extensively in Austria, it must have reinforced the troops' suspicions about the claim that Austria was Germany's victim.

Even political officers, who were expected to transmit official policies to the rank and file, found it difficult to accept the new idea that Austrians were not Germans. Anoshin sent a directive to the 3rd Ukrainian Front's political departments on 11 April, only seven days after the Military Council's Instruction to the troops, in which he complained that many political officers did not take the instructions seriously. He noted that some units' political departments did not undertake sufficient measures to combat the atrocities perpetrated by the troops. He demanded the "most energetic political and organizational measures to overcome instances of marauding and violence towards the local Austrian population."[63] Although it is unclear how Red Army units responded to Anoshin's directive, the NKVD Army's political department ordered its officers to discuss with rank-and-file troops the impermissibility of harming Austrian civilians and the need to distinguish them from German occupiers, while instructing communists and Komsomol members to lead a decisive struggle against violators of discipline.[64]

4.6 Conclusion

Propaganda in the 2nd and 3rd Ukrainian Fronts had three goals: to motivate the troops to fight, to encourage disciplined conduct and correct treatment of civilians, and to instill patriotism and pride in the Soviet Union. The theme of hate was at the center of all of these efforts. There was an obvious contradiction between the first and second goals, as many political department officers understood. The indoctrination of hate was formally aimed at enemy armies. However, for some Soviet troops at least, hate propaganda legitimized violence against all representatives of enemy nations, including civilians. Soviet officials were aware of this problem, but they always prioritized morale and combat capacity over the well-being of civilians.

After an enemy was defeated, the propaganda tended to focus only on encouraging disciplined conduct. Thus, in Romania, the hate propaganda intensified in the months preceding Iasi Kishinev Operation, but almost completely stopped after the signing of the Armistice Convention between Moscow and Bucharest. Hungary stands out for the duration and intensity of the hate campaign but so did the duration and ferocity of combat in that country. The Hungarians were less known to Soviet troops than the Romanians, as historically Russia and Hungary did not have many interactions. Thus, Soviet propaganda was suddenly tasked with creating the image of Hungarians as enemies from September 1944 until February 1945. The hate campaign did not relax until after the fall of Budapest. In contrast, by the time the Red Army entered Austria, the war was all but over, and the Germans did not have the strength for any more offensive operations. Accordingly, from the outset of the Red Army's appearance in Austria, the official propaganda emphasized the difference between Germans and Austrians, encouraging more proper conduct.

In contrast, the Red Army's political departments mobilized their substantial resources to create a positive image of the Bulgarians and Yugoslavs among the front-line troops. As P. G. Kuznetsov, an officer in the 3rd Ukrainian Front and subsequently Tolbukhin's biographer, accurately summarized the activities of political departments: "If before we discussed cultivating hatred among Soviet troops for the German-fascist conquerors, now we talked only about the friendship of the Bulgarian and Russian people."[65] The Soviet line between Bulgaria and Yugoslavia was underpinned by the idea that they were fraternal and historically friendly countries. The propaganda exploited historical sites celebrating nineteenth-century Russians in Bulgaria, while in Yugoslavia it utilized the presence of a large resistance movement and German war crimes against the civilians to paint the local population in a positive light. Most significantly, from the outset of the Red Army's entry into both countries, propaganda made it clear that violence against civilians was impermissible.

It's noteworthy that the Red Army propaganda aimed at the troops was very focused on nations while marginalizing the issue of class. In 1944–1945, the propaganda said almost nothing about the Soviet domestic class enemies. When the propaganda discussed European countries, it rarely paid attention to political and social divisions within those countries, encouraging the troops to view entire nations in a binary way as enemies or allies. Most Soviet soldiers and officers taking in propaganda would have concluded that the world was divided into good and bad nations. The good nations were those who sympathized with the Soviet Union, suffered at the hands of the Germans, and fought alongside the Soviets, such as the Yugoslavs and to a lesser degree, the Bulgarians. Bad nations were those who fought against the Red Army.

5 Disciplinary Policies

Military leaders may have extensively relied on propaganda to shape the soldiers' perceptions of the capitalist world and to encourage disciplined conduct. However, the command also had at their disposal an impressive arsenal of coercive institutions, also known as control mechanisms, to get the soldiers to obey orders, fight against the enemy forces, and remain loyal in words and actions to the Soviet Union. There were several coercive institutions in the army responsible for enforcing discipline: the military leadership in the chain of command at the level of fronts, armies, divisions, brigades, regiments, battalions, companies, and platoons; the NKVD Armies for the Protection of the Rear of the 2nd and 3rd Ukrainian Fronts, the Command Posts, the military counterintelligence Death to Spies (SMERSH), and military tribunals.

This chapter assesses the role of these coercive institutions in controlling the soldiers' conduct. The first part outlines the military regulations. The chapter's second section discusses the orders issued to the rank and file by the military leadership in each country that the 2nd and 3rd Ukrainian Fronts occupied. The third part examines the conduct of officers who staffed control mechanisms. It considers how the policies from above were implemented in the field, pointing out the friction between orders and their execution. It also discusses how the control mechanisms operated with relatively more efficacy in pro-Soviet countries. The fourth part seeks to illuminate the frequency and severity of punishments meted out to criminals. The final part discusses "Order number 15/2-008063 Struggle with Immoral Events" in the NKVD Armies of the 2nd and 3rd Ukrainian Fronts, which also had echoes in the command post system.

5.1 Coercive Institutions and Military Regulations

The Red Army high command based in Moscow consisted of the Headquarters of the Supreme Command of the Armed Forces of the Union of Soviet Socialist Republics (Stavka), the State Defense Committee (GKO), the Commissariat of Defense (NKO), and the general staff. Stalin formally headed all of these institutions, and he staffed them with his close military and political underlings.[1] The high command was primarily preoccupied with Soviet strategy in the war, deciding when and where Soviet armies should attack, organizing the war economy, diplomacy, and determining policies in the territories occupied by the Red Army. Sometimes the high command dealt with more mundane issues, such as discipline and morale, usually when somebody brought attention to a major problem in the field or a significant military setback brought scrutiny from above.

The most important institution for disciplining the frontline troops was the military leadership in the regular chain of command. It consisted of front commanders who, from 1944, held the rank of marshals. From May 1944 until the end of the war in 1945, Marshals Malinovskii and Tolbukhin headed the 2nd and 3rd Ukrainian Fronts. The Marshals and their staff were primarily responsible for implementing Moscow's military and political instructions and enforcing existing regulations and laws. Below the level of fronts were armies, corps, divisions, regiments, battalions, companies, and platoons, each headed by an officer with various levels of authority over the troops. Depending on their rank, the officers could compel soldiers not only to fight but also to behave correctly from the leadership perspective.

A booklet called *Disciplinary Regulations of the Red Army*, published in 1940, dealt with the disciplinary regime. In it, Marshal Semen Timoshenko, the Commissar of Defense at the time, proclaimed that soldiers were required to "unquestioningly obey their commanders."[2] Further, the document stated that in instances of "disobedience, open opposition, or malicious violation of discipline and order, the commander has the right to take all coercive measures, up to the use of force and weapons."[3] The remainder of the *Disciplinary Regulations* dealt with the disciplinary tools available to officers (*distsiplinarnye vzyskaniia*), such as reprimands, reprimands in front of other soldiers, and detentions of up to 5 days.[4]

Russian historian Oleg Budnitskii estimated recently that as many as 130,000–150,000 Soviet soldiers may have been executed in extrajudicial killings by their commanders without a legal process, noting that the number of such executions greatly decreased in 1944 and 1945.[5] The vast majority of these executions were carried out against deserters, soldiers accused of cowardice, or by officers acting vengefully and arbitrarily. Extrajudicial killings of troops for violence against civilians were exceedingly rare, but not unheard of. A divisional commander of the Soviet forces in Germany personally shot a lieutenant who was arranging for his men to rape German women.[6] There is also evidence that

Marshal Malinovskii, Commander of the 2nd Ukrainian Front, personally shot a Soviet major for rape in Hungary.[7] The available archival records, however, almost never mention extrajudicial killings, although it is likely that there would be more information about these in the mostly inaccessible TsAMO RF.

In addition, commanders of frontline units, as well as units in the rear, were allowed to send soldiers and sergeants to penal units without following a legal process for crimes such as straggling, deserting, theft of military property, and other military violations. Heads of command posts who ran towns in the rear of the frontline had the same authority.[8] Officers could also arrest and transfer junior officers and soldiers to military tribunals.[9]

Military tribunals were at the heart of wartime justice. Most soldiers and officers who were executed, sentenced to labor camps, or terms in penal units were sentenced by the military tribunals. On the first day of the war, 22 June 1941, Stalin decreed the creation of military tribunals in areas of military activities, which was broadly defined.[10] For example, all of Moscow was considered an area of military activity and the capital city's civilian courts and prosecutors were converted to military tribunals.[11] The military tribunals were controlled by the Military Collegium of the Soviet Union, whose chairman Vasilii Ulrich played a prominent role in the Great Terror.[12] Also, like during the Great Terror, the military tribunals consisted of three judges, the accused were not allowed to participate in the process, verdicts were to be reached within 24 hours, sentences were carried out within 72 hours, and the appeal process was abolished.[13] The only practical hope for convicts was that the army commander would commute their sentences. There were more than 3,735 military judges in the Red Army.[14] Military tribunals operated in military districts, frontline areas, frontline zones, fronts, armies, divisions, and NKVD armies.

Embedded in the Red Army was SMERSH, the army's counter-intelligence, before April 1943 known as *Osobyi otdel* (OO or Special Section).[15] SMERSH was part of the Ministry of Defense, and its chief Viktor Abakumov reported directly to Stalin, bypassing the country's military and police leaderships.[16] SMERSH was completely outside the regular chain of command, as its officers were only under the control of higher-ranking counter-intelligence officers. According to one estimate, there were 18,000 to 20,000 SMERSH officers in the field and 648 in the headquarters in Moscow.[17] They had a wide variety of tasks, such as identifying enemy agents within the Red Army, traitors, criminals, and deserters.[18] SMERSH was also tasked with screening Soviet civilians in occupied territories, Soviet prisoners of war, liberated forced laborers, and Soviet officers serving in the occupation apparatus across Eastern

Europe.[19] Occasionally, SMERSH was also involved in suppressing other types of criminal behavior, including attacks against women.[20]

The Kremlin created the NKVD Army for the Protection of the Rear of the Red Army early in the war by combining the various forces of the Commissariat for Internal Affairs. Most of the NKVD Army came from the border guards, but there were also railroad troops, escort troops, and other NKVD paramilitary formations.[21] The NKVD Army followed the regular military in the rear and carried out a wide range of sensitive and important tasks, providing intelligence, combating the Axis' partisans or saboteurs, guarding strategic and important sites, transporting prisoners of war, and sometimes fighting on the frontlines. Most significantly, the NKVD Army also enforced discipline, clearing the rear of deserters, marauders, rapists, and other criminals that stayed behind the frontlines. The NKVD Armies of the 2nd and 3rd Ukrainian Fronts numbered around 12,000 soldiers and officers in May 1944 and 19,865 in June 1945.[22] The NKVD Army was under the Red Army's operational control, meaning that the army leadership on the level of fronts could assign it specific tasks, but it had a separate chain of command. It was subordinate to the Chief of the Main Directorate of the NKVD Army for the Protection of the Rear of the Red Army headed by Lieutenant-General Gorbatiuk.[23] Gorbatiuk's boss was Lavrenti Beria, the wartime NKVD leader and one of Stalin's most trusted and powerful deputies.

There was also a system of command posts (*komendatura*), as discussed in Chapter 3. Command posts, led by military commandants, helped govern the frontline zone (*prifrontovaia polosa*) from the earliest stages of the war in 1941. There were command posts near the frontlines, appointed by the local army commander, and NKVD command posts in larger cities further in the rear of the frontlines.[24] The command posts were responsible for securing the communications leading to the frontline, the food, and security in the rear areas of the front. The command posts gained importance beyond Soviet borders because the military commandants did not have to compete for influence with the local Communist Party, NKVD, or local government. Thus, the command posts in Europe were Moscow's primary tool in governing the region.

5.2 Orders Issued in Each Country

5.2.1 Ukraine and Moldavia, Spring of 1944

As has been noted in Chapter 2, there was a sharp growth of military violations in the two army groups in the spring of 1944, on the territory of Odesa, Moldavia, and the small corner of Romania occupied by

Soviet troops. To counter these phenomena, Soviet commanders needed to impose firm discipline by issuing specific and enforceable orders to reverse the situation. They also needed to regularly subject the violators of military regulations to severe punishments and announce the penalties to other troops as a warning. There is a lot of evidence that such orders were issued in the 3rd Ukrainian Front, then occupying parts of the Odesa region and Moldavia.

Malinovskii, still commander of the 3rd Ukrainian Front, issued an order on 19 May 1944, which was read out to all officers of the front. In it, Malinovskii cited several recent instances of murder, rape, violence, shootings between drunken officers, and cases of alcohol poisonings, all of which were punished with executions. He blamed the widespread availability of wine in Moldavia and Odesa, stating that in March and April, sixty-two soldiers of the front died from alcohol poisoning. In the same period, he went on, there were thirty-seven murders (he did not specify whether the victims were civilians or soldiers), and fifty-four troops were held criminally responsible. He concluded:

> My orders are to be fulfilled precisely ... it is categorically forbidden for officers to send soldiers to collect trophy property from the civilian population. Do not allow one act of drunkenness, hooliganism, violence, and illegal confiscation of property from the civilian population to go unpunished .... The military prosecutor and the chairman of the military tribunal are to promptly investigate criminal acts, committed in a drunken state ....[25]

Malinovskii sought to use the front's coercive institutions to restore discipline in the ranks.

On 21 May, six days after Malinovskii's order, the Commissariat of Defense issued Order No. 0131, which highlighted that in the area of Odesa, the troops committed "a series of disgraceful atrocities and arbitrary acts that discredit the Red Army among the population."[26] Evidently, this intervention from Moscow forced Tolbukhin, who had just replaced Malinovskii as the commander of the 3rd Ukrainian Front, to issue another order on 29 May. Tolbukhin listed recent atrocities committed by Soviet troops. Some of the crimes he described were terrifying. A commander of a penal battalion shot a woman who protested when he and his deputy sexually harassed her. In another instance, an argument resulted in a drunken lieutenant shooting dead a SMERSH officer and pistol-whipping his driver. Tolbukhin ordered the military prosecutor to conclude his investigation into these cases by 5 June. He also ordered the military tribunal to pass sentences within three days after the investigation was completed. Crucially, he decreed that these criminals' direct superiors should be "held severely responsible (*privlech' k surovoi otvestvennosti neposredstvennykh nachal'nikov*)."[27] His instructions were also aimed at improving the security in the rear areas. He instructed the NKVD Army of the 3rd Ukrainian Front to strengthen its patrols around the railway stations behind the front. He also ordered the creation of additional regular army officer patrols to beef up security along the railroad where servicemen deserted and committed other crimes. He further demanded that there should be a verification of command posts' personnel knowledge of their duties. Finally, Tolbukhin asked to be informed about how his order was implemented.[28]

Thus, the Soviet command issued orders in the Soviet Union that were concrete, easy to enforce, and acknowledged the harm that the Red Army was inflicting on the civilian population. It is also significant that Moscow intervened in the Front's affairs with Order No. 0131. Certainly, the military commanders did not want to attract Stalin's attention for the wrong reasons and had to react quickly to avert further Moscow's involvement. Also, one must assume that on the Soviet territory, the leadership in Moscow and the command at the level of fronts were more likely to promptly learn about the troops' conduct than abroad. In the Soviet Union, the party channels, territorial NKVD, civilian authorities, as well as civilians themselves, could inform the leadership about the problems that emerged.[29]

5.2.2 Romania

When the two Ukrainian fronts stormed into all of Romania in late August during the Iasi Kishinev Operation, the Red Army issued orders to the troops to behave correctly on the divisional and regimental levels. Guards Colonel Polovnikov, the Chief of Staff of the 233rd Division, the second most important man in the unit, issued an order on 22 August to the forces of the division. The order began with a preamble: "Entry into the territory of an enemy state, where all sorts of tales have been told about the Red Army, challenges us to refute these slanders."[30] He instructed the troops to behave correctly to each other and the civilians, and he ordered officers to set an example of polite behavior. Polovnikov also ordered that all the troops should take care of their appearance while in Romania, and he banned soldiers from riding on carts or horses without saddles. More substantively, Polovnikov emphasized that individual preparation of food was banned, presumably to minimize contact between soldiers and civilians.[31] Namely, if soldiers would prepare their food, they would be compelled to go into Romanian homes to obtain supplies. It is worth mentioning that this order was widely violated, as the troops effectively lived off the land as they fanned through Romania unopposed after the Axis forces were defeated in the north of the country.

On 31 August, Polovnikov reiterated that officers of the Division needed "to establish the strictest order, not allowing instances of marauding, drunkenness, banditry, and aimless shooting."[32] On 9 September, Polovnikov issued another order. He instructed commanders of the Division's units to create sentry posts at entries into villages and towns to prevent enemy agents from getting close to the Red Army, as well as to control the movement of Soviet soldiers. Polovnikov also stressed that it was categorically forbidden to seize property and produce from the local population. He added that violators of this order will be held responsible according to military laws.[33]

Similar orders were issued on regimental levels. Mikhail Ivanov, a scout in the 3rd Ukrainian Front, recalled that when his unit crossed into Romania on 27 August, his regimental commander assembled the entire regiment and told them:

> Comrade soldiers, sergeants, and officers! We are on enemy territory! But we did not come here to take revenge, but as liberators of the people from fascism! So I am ordering you – do not allow acts of marauding and violence towards the peaceful citizens. In case of violation of the order, we will judge without mercy according to military laws![34]

Every soldier was then required to sign a document stating that this order had been explained to them.[35] Nikolai Popov, a soldier in the 4th Guards Mechanized Corps of the 3rd Ukrainian Front, remembered being read out a similar order.[36] Ivanov's and Popov's recollections indicate that the troops were ordered to behave correctly when entering Romania.

The first documented intervention from Moscow in the troops' behavior in Romania came on 5 October, when most of the 2nd and 3rd Ukrainian Fronts had already left the country. General Antonov, the chief of the general staff in Moscow, informed Malinovskii about the improper conduct of Soviet soldiers in Bucharest. Antonov wrote that many soldiers were wandering around the city, filling up restaurants, and stores. Many of them were poorly dressed, unshaven, and intoxicated. Antonov said that they committed "drunken debaucheries with prostitutes."[37] He went on to say that all of these facts are indicative of the poor state of discipline. Antonov concluded that the city's commandant had not taken any measures against these phenomena, and he asked Malinovskii to instruct Bucharest's commandant to introduce firm order in the city.[38]

There are three plausible explanations for the absence of orders from Moscow or the level of fronts about the troops' conduct in Romania until October, which was not the case in other countries. First, as Romania was the first foreign country the Red Army reached, the leaders could have assumed that the existing orders and regulations, which commanders on the level of divisions and regiments continued to issue, would suffice in preventing the attacks on civilians. In this scenario, they simply did not anticipate a need to issue an order on higher levels that were already being issued on divisional and regimental levels. This is a plausible explanation. The second possible explanation is that Moscow and front commanders did not care about the troops' behavior in an enemy country until Bucharest signed an Armistice Convention on 12 September and switched sides in the war. The third explanation is that Moscow and front leaders did issue such orders, but that the author did not find them. We will not know for sure the answer to this question until TsAMO RF opens to researchers and we can see every order issued by the Front Commanders of 2nd and 3rd Ukrainian Fronts.

5.2.3 Bulgaria

Moscow expressed strong interest in the situation in Bulgaria from the early moments of the Red Army's occupation of the country. On 27 September, two Soviet military journalists, Majors Kozhevnikov and Sivolobov, sent a detailed report to the Central Committee of the Communist Party of the Soviet Union on the situation in Bulgaria, which included a discussion about how the "isolated instances of marauding and raping" and officers "compromising behavior" undermined the Bulgarian people's faith in the Soviet troops.[39] Further, Aleksandr Shcherbakov, the head of the Main Political Administration of the Red Army, ordered Lieutenant-General Ivan Anoshin, the head of the Political Department of the 3rd Ukrainian Front, in late September to fly to Moscow and report in person about the moral and political state of the troops.[40] On 30 September, Major-General Burtsev, a high-ranking official in the Main Political Administration, sent a report to Georgii Dimitrov, the de facto leader of Bulgarian Communists and in charge of the Soviet Communist Party Central Committee's Department of Foreign Affairs, about the situation in Bulgaria. Burtsov noted, among other things, that the Red Army's looting was on the increase and that there were instances of rapes of Bulgarian women.[41]

One of the Soviet command's first measures against the criminals and deserters in the Red Army's ranks came on 20 September, when the Red Army established block posts around Sofia to prevent the entry of troops into the capital without special permit. At the same time, the NKVD Army of the 3rd Ukrainian Front created a Supervisory Service (*sluzhba nadzora*), a special task force, that was charged with rooting out the so-called immoral events in the city, a Soviet euphemism for the troops' criminal activity that included sexual violence.[42] On 19 November, Tolbukhin issued an order entitled, indicatively, "Strengthening of the Struggle against Marauding and Atrocities Committed on the Territory of Bulgaria." Tolbukhin noted that the Soviet troops had recently committed a series of rapes, robberies, and murders against the civilian population. He blamed the disinterest of commanding officers, the Army's political institutions, and the judicial bodies for failing to counter the growing criminality. Tolbukhin instructed commanders and prosecutors to investigate every so-called immoral event and to undertake decisive measures in the next three days to combat criminality in the Red Army. He also called on commanders to punish the immediate supervisors of the soldiers who looted, raped, or murdered.[43]

The Bulgarian Communists had close contacts in Moscow, through Dimitrov, which could help explain the Soviet command's interest in the Red Army's conduct in that country. His diary testifies that in the autumn of 1944, he was in close contact with Bulgarian Communists in the country and the highest Soviet state and military leadership.[44] None of his entries specified that he discussed the Red Army's conduct in Bulgaria; Dimitrov knew that writing down such information in a private diary could be dangerous in Stalin's Soviet Union. However, he recorded that he discussed with Soviet and Bulgarian leaders other issues such as the formation of the Fatherland Front government, Yugoslav-Bulgarian relations, and the Soviet armistice with Bulgaria.[45] On separate occasions during this period, he also met Anoshin and Colonel-General Biriuzov, Chief of Staff of the 3rd Ukrainian Front and second in command after Marshal Tolbukhin.[46] It is difficult to imagine that Dimitrov would not have discussed with them the issue of Soviet troops' conduct given that Biriuzov and especially Anoshin dealt with morale and discipline.

5.2.4 Yugoslavia

An important reason why the Soviet troops behaved overall more correctly in Yugoslavia was that Yugoslav Communists had close contact with the Soviet high command and military leadership in the field. They utilized these contacts to complain about the Red Army's criminal conduct, which allowed the Soviet officers to undertake measures to curb crimes against civilians. The Yugoslav leader, Josip Broz Tito, flew to Moscow in September on the eve of the Red Army's entry into Yugoslavia. He had two meetings with Stalin and many more with lesser officials where they worked out a plan of joint operations in Serbia. Thereafter, Tito and the Supreme Command were relocated to the Soviet-held Romanian city of

Craiova near the Yugoslav border. Tito lived in a villa that Soviet authorities confiscated from a Romanian civil servant, and he was guarded by the Special Department of the Ministry of State Security of the USSR responsible for protecting Stalin.[47] These were all signs of the respect and importance that Moscow attached to its relationship with the Yugoslav ally. From Craiova, Tito had continuous contact with the 3rd Ukrainian Front's staff.[48] The Yugoslav leader also had access to the Red Army's general staff in Moscow, and he even communicated directly with Stalin during this period. He used all of these channels to protest the criminal conduct of Soviet troops, which he heard about from his commanders in Serbia. Meanwhile, Soviet and Partisan units operating in proximity or together tended to have liaison officers, allowing for direct communication that bypassed the Yugoslav and Soviet leaderships.[49] After the establishment of Tito's regime in Belgrade, communication between the Yugoslav and Soviet allies became even more routinized.

As the Red Army entered Yugoslavia, local Partisan commanders informed Tito and the Yugoslav Supreme Command of the raping and plundering committed by the Soviet troops.[50] Tito, in turn, repeatedly cabled Partisan commanders in the field to lodge complaints with Soviet commanding officers.[51] He also requested the names of victimized women and the names of Soviet officers with whom his officers interacted, and he insisted that Soviet officers must provide receipts before they were issued any supplies by the Partisans.[52] Clearly, the Yugoslav leader demanded that his commanders forward to him as much information as possible so that his complaints would be more specific and effective.

Tito energetically confronted Soviet officers and officials about the Red Army's conduct. A meeting took place after the liberation of Belgrade between Lieutenant General Nikolai Korneev, the head of the Soviet Military Mission to the Partisans, and Tito, Milovan Đilas (one of Tito's closest allies at the time, and subsequently, a liberal dissident), the head of the Yugoslav security forces, and two leading Yugoslav military commanders. Tito requested from Korneev to immediately undertake measures to at least minimize incidents of plunder, rape, and violence against the Yugoslavs.[53] Tito also confronted the head of the Red Army garrison in Belgrade about Soviet disorder and drunkenness in the city.[54] In another incident, the Yugoslav leader sardonically told a Soviet officer from the 3rd Ukrainian Front's Political Department, "Obviously, your political department is not working well, is it? I could strengthen your forces with our political workers."[55] Tito even complained to Stalin about the Red Army's seizure of German war booty that he wanted for the Partisans, as well as Soviet disrespect for the nascent Yugoslav authorities and the victimization of women. However, Tito was far humbler and apologetic with Stalin than with Soviet officers.[56] Although Stalin did not deny Tito's claims, he took issue with the Yugoslav leader's supposed insolence. The Soviet leader accused his Yugoslav counterpart of being ungrateful and reminded him of the massive support that Moscow was providing to the Yugoslav Partisans.[57]

Despite Stalin's apparent indifference in the face of Tito's pleas, there is ample evidence to suggest that Yugoslav protests compelled the Red Army command to take more decisive action against their marauding troops. On 13 October, the Red Army commanders were ordered not to refuse help to their Yugoslav comrades when they complained.[58] Certainly, the Yugoslav commanders in the field believed that Tito's involvement had an effect. On 17 October, they cabled him that after his intervention, there were no longer any complaints against the Red Army and that Soviet officers agreed to undertake the necessary measures to curtail such violations.[59] Yugoslav commanders reported from battle sites on October 29 that the so-called negative phenomena were alleviated when problems were explained to Soviet officers.[60] Đilas claimed that Soviet officers reacted more forcefully to their soldiers' transgressions after the meeting with Korneev and Stalin's subsequent involvement.[61]

Although the Red Army's mistreatment of the civilian population unpleasantly surprised the Yugoslav leadership, they were more concerned with the appropriation of German war booty by Soviet and Bulgarian armies. Evidently, during his visit to Moscow in September, Tito had struck an agreement with the Red Army's general staff that all German equipment and weapons captured in Yugoslavia would be transferred to the Partisans.[62] Partisan commanders in the field were particularly outraged by the Bulgarian army's seizure of war trophies. Bulgarians had been enemies of the Partisans but had now switched sides in the war and were under Soviet operational control. In some instances, arguments over the plunder led to firefights and deaths among the soldiers of both armies.[63] Revolted, Tito even demanded that the Red Army command withdraw Bulgarians from Yugoslavia. Writing at Stalin's behest, Molotov refused the Yugoslav demand, while adding that according to the laws of war, the loot belonged to the army that captured it, thus rebuking the Yugoslav claims.[64] Nonetheless, Yugoslav protests ultimately bore fruit, since it seems that by 23 October Stalin personally ordered the Soviet (and presumably Bulgarian) units not to seize anything, including motorized vehicles, from the captured German depots in Belgrade.[65]

The Red Army involved its highest-ranking members to address Yugoslav complaints. On 12 October, Antonov, Stalin's deputy in the general staff, passed an order from Stalin to commanders of the 2nd and 3rd Ukrainian Fronts to instruct their forces to treat the Yugoslavs well, "especially since … the Yugoslavs view the Red Army as their liberators."[66] Antonov also provided details of a specific incident where Soviet officers tried to rape a Partisan woman, and he ordered an investigation into this case, demanding that the culprits be firmly punished. Finally, he asked Malinovskii and Tolbukhin to inform him about their measures in response to Stalin's order.[67]

Moscow's involvement in this issue, not long after the Red Army began its operations in Yugoslavia, as well as its interest in a single case of attempted rape, indicates strongly that the Soviet leadership took seriously Yugoslav complaints about the Soviet soldiers' criminal conduct. Colonel-General Biriuzov, Chief of Staff of the 3rd Ukrainian Front and second in command after Marshal Tolbukhin, ordered the NKVD Army on 20 October to specifically investigate Soviet troops' criminal acts in the Serbian city of Niš.[68] Similarly, on 15 November, Colonel-General Zheltov, a member of the council of the 3rd Ukrainian Front, ordered the chief military prosecutor of the front, Major General Ankudinov, to carry out an investigation into the Red Army's behavior in Belgrade and to introduce order in the city.[69] Ankudinov reported back on 24 November that the order was established in Belgrade and that "not one more or less serious violation of military discipline was left unpunished."[70] As evidence, he cited that just on 17 November four soldiers were sent to penal units while investigations were initiated into more serious cases.[71]

Yugoslav protests also affected lower-ranking Soviet officers. On 1 November Colonel Sidirenko, commander of the 233rd Division, stated in an order to all units under his control that he had been receiving complaints from the Yugoslav Partisans and higher-ranking Soviet commanders that numerous soldiers and officers were engaging in drunkenness, plunder, and rape.[72] Sidirenko introduced bans on soldiers and officers to prevent them from leaving their units even temporarily. He also ordered headcounts of all soldiers and officers to be carried out three times a day, and the establishment of officer patrols. He instructed the divisional prosecutor to speed up investigations into criminal acts and to charge guilty parties, and he warned commanders that they would be held responsible for violations perpetrated by their soldiers unless they immediately introduced necessary measures.[73] These were specific and enforceable measures, which indicated the determination of the Soviet command to curtail the abuse of civilians.

5.2.5 Hungary

Due to the extent of the Red Army troops' rampage in Hungary, some scholars have assumed that the Soviets had a policy of permitting rapes and murders of prisoners of war. Hungarian historian Krisztián Ungváry argued that Malinovskii gave his troops three days to freely loot and rape in Budapest after the Red Army captured the city.[74] He also claimed that Soviet executions of enemy soldiers were common, while the command issued orders to its troops to treat Axis soldiers humanely only in January 1945.[75] Norman Naimark made several questionable claims in his book, *Russians in Germany*. He maintained that Malinovskii's troops were supposedly ill-disciplined, comparing them to the allegedly more disciplined forces of Marshal Konev's 1st Ukrainian Front. Naimark also praised the superior leadership of Marshal Tolbukhin and his 3rd Ukrainian Front.[76] All of these speculations were based in non-Soviet sources, but they penetrated the historiography and formed the basis of numerous studies.

Based on these claims, historian Peter Kenez maintained that Tolbukhin was better at disciplining his troops than Malinovskii in Hungary.[77] Historian Jill Lewis, in a discussion of Soviet conduct in Austria, argued that the troops of the 2nd Ukrainian Front, among the first to enter Vienna, were more ill-disciplined, based on Naimark's assertions about Malinovskii's poor leadership.[78] Meanwhile, Martin Mevius argued in his monograph about the Soviet occupation of Hungary that Malinovskii forbade the mistreatment of civilians and prisoners of war only in January 1945, thereby strongly implying that these were previously permitted.[79] He claimed that the Red Army troops frequently mowed down surrendering troops, while they regularly executed Vlasovites, the SS, Arrow Cross, and wounded soldiers.[80]

Given archival restrictions and the paucity of sources about the Red Army, it is understandable that historians made such speculations. At the same time, several facts need to be pointed out. There is no evidence that troops from one front were inherently more disciplined than soldiers from another army group. The Red Army fronts were enormous formations consisting of hundreds of thousands of soldiers, all of which had their penal units. Also, commanders had very little to do with choosing their troops. Supreme Command of the Armed Forces of the USSR (Stavka) moved commanders around occasionally at the level of fronts, as well as frequently transferring armies between fronts.[81] Thus, even if one commander cultivated more disciplined troops through harsher discipline, either the soldiers or the commander could be transferred to another front.

Ungváry's most damning claim that the Soviet command on the level of fronts gave the troops a three-day window to freely loot and rape is not supported with any evidence from the archives. Furthermore, the NKVD Army of the 2nd Ukrainian Front and command posts detained

Figure 5.1 Street fighting in Budapest. Source: Sovfoto/Universal Images Group via Getty Images.

a similar number of Soviet soldiers for looting, raping, and other crimes when the Red Army conquered Budapest, as they did after the fall of Hungary's capital city.[82] This strongly suggests that Malinovskii did not give his soldiers three days to freely loot and rape, as the soldiers continued being arrested at similar levels after the fall of the Hungarian capital (Figure 5.1).

More importantly, both 2nd and 3rd Ukrainian Front commands repeatedly issued orders banning looting and raping. There is no evidence that these orders were suspended or canceled in Budapest. As soon as the troops of the 2nd Ukrainian Front entered Hungary, Malinovskii issued an order to his forces that proclaimed that some soldiers were engaging in marauding. He ordered his officers to establish firm order in their ranks and military prosecutors to promptly investigate all cases of marauding.[83] On 30 October, he issued another order, in which he declared that he was continuing to receive reports about cases of marauding and raping of women.[84] He instructed prosecutors to urgently investigate instances of rape and to punish the culprits as well as their commanders who tolerated it. As a further deterrent, Malinovskii ordered military prosecutors to inform families and communities of the executed criminals of their fate.[85] The policy of shaming the perpetrators of violence back home was exceptional and it reflected the command's frustration for its failure to root out the attacks on civilians. Malinovskii issued another round of similar orders prohibiting the abuse of civilians and captured soldiers in January 1945.[86]

The situation was similar in the 3rd Ukrainian Front. On 24 November, soon after the units of the army group started entering Hungary from Yugoslavia, Major-General Pavlov, the head of the front's NKVD Army, informed all regimental commanders that one of the NKVD Army's main tasks was "to struggle with deserters from the Red Army, marauders, as well as [soldiers engaging in] all illegal activities that shame the Red Army and the Soviet people."[87] Tolbukhin ordered officers on 11 March 1945 to read out to all the troops of the 3rd Ukrainian Front a verdict by the Military Tribunal that sentenced to death two soldiers who raped and murdered a Hungarian woman.[88] Tolbukhin wanted to communicate to his troops that rapists and murderers would be severely punished.

The highest military leadership in the field kept on issuing orders to contain looting and rape. It was not the command's policy to encourage and allow frontline troops and officers to abuse the civilian population. Moreover, Soviet commanders made sure that their troops knew murder and rape were potentially punishable by death. Several veterans recalled that they witnessed such executions in Hungary, indicating that they were not so rare.[89] Finally, Malinovskii's order, which stated that the families of punished soldiers would be notified of their crimes, seems to have been a desperate measure to shame the soldiers into behaving correctly. Malinovskii and Tolbukhin issued orders banning violence against civilians as soon as the troops entered Hungary; these were reissued regularly to remind the soldiers of official policies. In sum, the Soviet command's policies were not the cause of the increased sexual violence in Hungary.

The issue of the Red Army's executions of POWs is more complex. On the one hand, there is no evidence that the Red Army's regulations banning executions of prisoners were ever suspended in Hungary. The Soviets understood, if nothing else, that the murder of prisoners stiffened the enemy's resistance. Ungváry based his claim that Malinovskii banned the mistreatment of prisoners only in January on Soviet documents captured by Germans, presumably during one of their counteroffensives, which ordered the correct treatment of prisoners.[90] However, similar orders were issued periodically, indicating that such orders were disregarded, but that it was not a Red Army policy to execute prisoners.[91] It is undeniable that Soviet troops did murder prisoners with alarming frequency, especially Soviet citizens in the service of the Third Reich. This was, however, a crime from below, which was stoked by hate propaganda, encouraged by vicious fighting, and spurred on by commanding officers' relative indifference to the fate of enemy prisoners.

Although the 2nd and 3rd Ukrainian Fronts' orders were correct from the outset of the Soviet entry into Hungary, the brutality of the fighting exacerbated the suffering of civilians. The fierce Hungarian and German resistance only encouraged the Soviet command to pursue increasingly more extreme policies that collapsed the differences between enemy soldiers and civilians. According to an NKVD report, after the German troops temporarily recaptured the town of N'ired'khaze, local Hungarian civilians brutally attacked the wounded and retreating Soviet troops, in numerous cases torturing and killing them.[92] Evidently, civilians sought to exact revenge for the Soviet troops' conduct during their town's occupation. However, the Axis success was short-lived, and when the Red Army returned, the Military Council of the 27th Army decreed that all of N'ired'khaze's boys and men aged 16 to 50, 1,500 in total, were to be classified as prisoners of war. They were sent to a prisoner-of-war camp and presumably deported to the Soviet Union for forced labor with other prisoners.[93] Although this wholesale deportation of men seems to have been rare, it is notable that it was ordered from the highest echelons of the Soviet command.

The Red Army also committed war crimes when they suspected that Hungarians killed one of their own, even if it was in self-defense. A woman identified only as Elza, born in northern Serbian city of Novi Sad but of Czech and Hungarian background, spent the war years in Hungary after she married into a family of Hungarian civil servants. She recalled that the Soviet army discovered the body of a murdered Soviet soldier in Budapest. In her words, the Soviets "decimated" the whole street: they lined up everybody on the street and shot every tenth person on the spot.[94]

In addition, by the end of December, the Soviet command issued orders that all civilians crossing the frontlines and digging trenches for German and Hungarian armies were to be treated as prisoners of war.[95] These orders, dictated by the heightened security concerns in hostile territory in the context of vicious fighting, targeted a large number of completely innocent civilians. These instructions also explain the presence of Hungarian women in Soviet prisoner-of-war camps.[96] It should also be noted that these orders impacted Hungarian Jews who had been forced to clear mines or perform physical labor along the frontlines, and presumably were most likely to flee to the Red Army's rear; there were up to 30,000 Hungarian Jewish prisoners of war in the Soviet Union.[97] Moreover, these orders gave enormous power to NKVD troops and Soviet officers over powerless civilians since they could accuse almost anybody of crossing the frontlines or having worked for Axis defenses at some point. By the end of the war, the Soviets held

425,000 Hungarians as prisoners of war.[98] Practically all Hungarian prisoners were captured during the fighting in Hungary, since before the Red Army's arrival into the country, the Soviets held only 6,897 Hungarian prisoners.[99]

5.2.6 Austria

The 3rd Ukrainian Front soldiers first reached Austria on 31 March 1945 and the 2nd Ukrainian Front did so on 2 April 1945, in the closing stages of the war.[100] By this point, the Third Reich's demise was imminent, and the high command in Moscow and the leadership of the 2nd and 3rd Ukrainian Fronts had plenty of time to see how their soldiers behaved in "enemy" countries. Thus, soon after the Red Army entered Austrian territory, on 2 April 1945, Chief of Staff General Antonov and Stalin instructed commanders of the 2nd and 3rd Ukrainian Fronts to issue orders to the troops to behave correctly, not to hurt (*obizhat'*) Austrian civilians, and not to conflate Austrians with German occupiers.[101] I did not find evidence of Moscow issuing similar orders with regards to any other country the 2nd and 3rd Ukrainian Fronts entered, indicating that Moscow proactively sought to prevent the violence against Austrian civilians from breaking out.

Two days after receiving Antonov's and Stalin's orders, on 4 April, Tolbukhin and the Military Council of the 3rd Ukrainian Front issued an appeal (*obrashchenie*) to all the troops of the front. The appeal emphasized that Austria was the first country occupied by Germans and that Austria was a gateway to southern Germany, where the leading Nazis had escaped from Berlin. Tolbukhin went on to say that the troops' goal was to defeat the German army so that the Austrian people could reclaim their liberty. The appeal highlighted in bold letters that "**Liberating Austria, the Red Army is at war with the German occupiers, not the population of Austria**."[102] The appeal emphasized again in the next paragraph: "Mercilessly crushing the German enslavers, **do not hurt peaceful Austrian population** [V. M.: bold in original]. Respect their way of life, families, personal property."[103] Although I have not found a similar order from Malinovskii's 2nd Ukrainian Front, it was undoubtedly issued given Stalin's instructions.

Subsequently, on 11 April, Lieutenant-General Ivan Anoshin, the head of the Political Department of the 3rd Ukrainian Front, issued a circular, indicating that the leadership was not content with the troops' conduct in Austria. In the document, Anoshin noted that the political leaders did not seriously approach Tolbukhin and the Military Council's orders to instruct the troops on how to behave in Austria and did not explain the essence of the order to the rank and file. Anoshin instructed political officers of the front to undertake energetic measures to eliminate instances of marauding and violence against Austrians.[104] Soviet command undertook other measures to protest the Austrian population. It ordered the NVKD Army to increase patrols in Vienna and detain every soldier without special permission to be in the city, and to report detained troops' names to the NKVD Army Headquarters and to the Military Council of the 3rd Ukrainian Front.[105]

Moscow and the leadership at the level of fronts issued orders to the frontline troops in Austria to behave correctly toward the civilian population from the earliest stages of the Red Army's entry into the country. The command issued further instructions to make sure that these orders were properly implemented in the ranks. Thus, the Soviet leadership issued correct orders to the frontline troops which were meant to protect the Austrian population and ensure disciplined conduct by the soldiers and officers.

5.3 A Closer Look at Discipline Enforcers

The orders and directives issued by the high command in Moscow and the leadership at the level of fronts, divisions, and regiments, make it clear that Soviet military leaders did not have a policy of allowing their soldiers to attack civilians. These orders were issued to officers in the field, lower-level commanders, their deputies, NKVD officers, and Command Post commandants. However, a series of factors hindered the officers who staffed coercive institutions from implementing a strict disciplinary regime ordered from above.

This may be an obvious point, but officers responsible for discipline tended to distrust civilians, especially those from enemy countries, and they frequently failed to investigate the reports of Soviet soldiers' criminality. For example, on 2 November it was reported to the Sibiu command post that two drunken lieutenants entered the home of two Romanian women and tried to rape them. An investigation conceded that the lieutenants committed "elements of hooliganism" in entering a private home.[106] However, it asserted that there was no rape attempt, a conclusion that seems highly unlikely given the victims' testimonies.[107] Soviet authorities were reluctant to investigate and possibly punish perpetrators in this situation, despite the obvious guilt of the two lieutenants.

Some officers also viewed suspiciously civilians who lodged complaints. On 8 September a group of Romanian villagers reported to the 91st Regiment of the NKVD Army that the Red Army soldiers had committed a robbery in their village. However, an NKVD patrol determined that this was not true. Instead, Soviet soldiers simply wanted to exchange their tired horses for rested horses. According to the report, this complaint illustrated Romanian hostility toward the Red Army, an assertion that seems nonsensical to neutral readers of the document.[108] In another instance, Major-General Pavlov, the head of the NKVD Army of the 3rd Ukrainian Front, forwarded a report to the Military Council of the 3rd Ukrainian Front about the NKVD Army's activities in Romania and Bulgaria in September.[109] Pavlov claimed in the report that Romanians were perfidious – appearing loyal around the Red Army but secretly harboring hostility toward it. His evidence for this broad claim was that there was an inaccurate report of pillage by Soviet soldiers in one village. Pavlov's hostility toward the Romanians, evident in his accusation that they were perfidious, was shared by other officers responsible for discipline, hindering them from seriously investigating complaints of victimization by Red Army troops.

Most Soviet officers' sympathies were with their soldiers, even when they had to implement orders from above. Gabriel Temkin, a soldier in the 78th Division of the 2nd Ukrainian Front, recalled that after his regiment was forced to observe the execution of a convicted rapist, the prosecutor wept openly, saying through tears: "Why did we execute him? For that indecent whore."[110] More will be said about sexual violence in Chapter 7. However, this example clearly illustrates how those tasked with enforcing discipline sometimes had no sympathy for victims. If they implemented high command's disciplinary policies at all, they often did so with reluctance.

After the Uman–Botoșani Offensive Operation ran its course, when the front stabilized on 25 April, the commander of the 3rd Ukrainian Front created a frontline zone within 25 km of the line of contact.[111] The order instructed all unit commanders and Army's Military Councils to assume responsibility for organizing and safekeeping the property of evacuated civilians.[112] Despite the orders emphasizing that the commanders were required to guard the property of evacuated civilians, General Zhmachenko, Commander of the 40th Army, wrote in his unpublished diary "It is understood that soldiers took the property to equip their dugouts."[113] Zhmachenko's tone indicated that he approved of his soldiers' looting, illustrating how marauding sometimes had the command's tacit approval.

Even in Yugoslavia, where the officers tended to sympathize with the local population to a greater degree than in enemy countries, officers, and soldiers often refused to come to civilians' assistance when they came under attack from another Soviet soldier. When a Serbian civilian pointed out to an officer a group of Soviet soldiers who robbed his business, the officer yelled at him, while telling his soldiers to return to the military column.[114] Similarly, the local authorities in one town noted that in most cases the Soviet officers, when notified that their troops were looting, did not take any measures.[115] A Soviet soldier in Yugoslavia refused to help a woman who was escaping from a Red Army soldier who tried to rape her. After she asked the soldier for help, she was killed by the soldier who tried to assault her. Both soldiers escaped from the site of the crime and hid.[116]

The height of the Soviet officials' refusal to consider complaints about their soldiers' conduct was when Lieutenant-General Vinogradov, the deputy chairman of the Allied Control Commission in Romania, practically forbade Romanians from complaining about the Red Army's conduct on 1 March 1945. He told the Romanian authorities to put an end to the avalanche of complaints which due to lack of details could not be investigated, asserting that the crimes were committed by Romanian fascists dressed in Red Army uniforms. He went on to say that those who gathered information (and by implication, those who complained about being abused) about the actions of the Red Army needed to be identified and held responsible.[117] Vinogradov was the de facto dictator of Romania, and after his angry response to Romanian complaints about Soviet terror, it is unlikely that Romanians would continue to register complaints with the Red Army.[118]

5.3.1 *Fear of Slandering the Red Army*

When Soviet officers reported up the chain of command about the looting and raping, their reports could be, in rare instances, construed as slander of the Red Army, landing their authors in trouble. It is arguably this fear of being accused of slandering the Red Army that officers reporting on the criminality of the troops usually added caveats that the criminal acts were occasional or limited to only a few troops. Lev Kopelev, a Major in the Political Department of the 2nd Belarusian Front and a dissident after the war, was famously accused of slandering the Red Army. One of the first officers from his unit into East Prussia, he repeatedly denounced in reports the looting, raping, the anti-German hate campaign, and the destruction that the Soviet army left in its wake. His immediate superior, who did not like or trust Kopelev, used these reports to orchestrate Kopelev's downfall. He had him expelled from the party and arranged for SMERSH officers to investigate and hand Kopelev over to the Military Tribunal, which eventually sentenced him to a ten-year prison term.[119]

I have not encountered any evidence of soldiers and officers of the 2nd and 3rd Ukrainian Fronts being prosecuted for criticizing the Soviet troops' criminal conduct. However, Boris Slutskii, who like Kopelev was also a true communist believer, a writer of Jewish background originally from Ukraine, and a Major in the political department, wrote in his mixture of diary and memoirs that he was tasked with investigating an outbreak of mass rapes in the Austrian province of Styria. In this context, he wrote that "generals were sitting down, attentive and serious, listening to every word [about rapes]. The time when my signals about rape attempts were interpreted as slander of the Red Army has passed."[120] Clearly, officers who reported on the troops' atrocities had to carefully craft their reports so as not to go too far, even if prosecutions for slandering the Red Army were rare.

The Soviet allies in Eastern Europe, the local communist parties, also had to walk a fine line. They had to acknowledge the criminal conduct so as not to lose all credibility with the local population, and they had to report it to the Red Army's leaders in the hope that they could end the attacks on civilians. However, the local communists had to be very careful when discussing looting and raping with the Soviets, so as not to upset their Soviet patrons. An illustrative example is how Bulgarian Communists tried to suppress discussion of the Soviet misconduct domestically. The Bulgarian Minister of Propaganda went on the radio on 2 October to address the issue of "slander surrounding the conduct of the Red Army in Bulgaria."[121] The Minister conceded that there were individual instances of soldiers stealing chickens and horses, and of excessively drinking. However, he claimed that such isolated cases were unfairly generalized to all "legendary Russian warriors."[122] Reducing the Soviet troops' criminal conduct to the theft of a few chickens, as if that was the worst the troops did, minimized the harm that the criminal acts had on the local population.

As we have seen in the previous section, the Yugoslav Communists did not shy away from confronting the Soviet leaders about their troops' behavior. But even the Titoists suppressed the Yugoslavs who publicly complained about Soviet soldiers' conduct. On 8 October during the height of the military campaign in Serbia against the Germans, the Yugoslav military command issued an order to civilian authorities in eastern Serbia that anybody who pointed out the strengths of the German army or weaknesses of its Soviet counterpart would be tried by military courts.[123] Meanwhile, the Chief of Staff of Serbia instructed all Partisan units, concerning sexual violence perpetrated by the Soviet army, to "explain to [Yugoslav] fighters that these are isolated incidents. Suppress incorrect discussions which could damage the reputation of the Red Army."[124] Cursing of Russian and even the allied Bulgarian mothers, a popular way to express dissatisfaction with somebody in the Serbian language, became a punishable offense.[125] Even high-ranking officials had their careers ruined by bringing to light Soviet transgressions.[126]

5.3.2 Corrupt Officers

Another important explanation as to why officers in charge of discipline failed to take more resolute action against the rampaging soldiers was that officers' behavior was scarcely better than that of frontline soldiers. If anything, it was even worse as officers had less supervision and more free time to get drunk, loot, and attack women. From the soldiers' perspective, their officers' actions blurred the line between legal and illegal. Moreover, officers were less likely to enforce rules that they routinely violated. Marshal Malinovskii issued an order in May 1944, in which he outlined the deteriorating discipline in armies under his control. After describing a series of incidents, he said that fifty-four individuals were held criminally responsible, out of whom fifty were officers.[127] Generals and high-ranking officers also lead the way in looting. The NKVD border guards reported that some army officers not only refused the NKVD to inspect their vehicles when entering the Soviet Union, as they were hiding their loot but that they used force to fight them off.[128]

A series of reports written by Colonel Prokhorov of the 233rd Division's Political Department, revealed corruption, ill-discipline, and proclivity for sexual violence, among the unit's SMERSH officers, prosecutors, and high-ranking officers in the regular chain of command. According to Prokhorov, two highly intoxicated SMERSH Officers, Major Golovanov and Captain Antipov, forced their way into a private home in the city of Roșiorii de Vede in Romania in September. They robbed the owner of the house, vandalized the furniture, and tried to rape the owner's wife and the couple's daughter. Golovanov and Antipov also abused Soviet Major Kochkin, an officer in the Division's Political Department, who was billeted at the house. They cursed him, ripped off his epaulets and decorations, and confiscated his driver's license and personal watch.[129]

Colonel Prokhorov was Kochkin's boss. Prokhorov made it clear in a report on 14 September to heads of the Political Department of the 75th Corps that Golovanov's and Antipov's conduct was symptomatic of the behavior of SMERSH. He maintained that the division's SMERSH had two automobiles, three trucks, and several wagons, all of which were loaded with plundered goods. Prokhorov wanted the SMERSH commander to hold a meeting with all officers under his command about their behavior. Prokhorov also asked for permission to hold Golovanov and Antipov responsible for their actions via party channels.[130]

It is important to note that the conduct by two high-ranking SMERSH officers would not have come to light had they not abused and humiliated a senior officer in the Political Department. In Prokhorov's view, the SMERSH officers' attempted rape of two women was a minor issue, less significant than their mistreatment of his subordinate. Moreover, it is unclear whether Prokhorov was allowed to punish Golovanov and Antipov via party channels. However, even if he was, this was hardly a suitable punishment for systematic plundering, violence against an officer of equal and higher rank, and attempted rape. A party reprimand (*vzyskanie*) did not have immediate consequences. Almost certainly, Golovanov and Antipov would have remained at their posts, though it would have been harder for them to be promoted.

Guards Colonel Polovnikov, the Chief of staff of the 233rd Division, was previously mentioned for ordering the Division's troops to behave correctly toward other army personnel and civilians while urging officers to lead by example when the Division entered Romania. It should be mentioned that in March 1942, Polovnikov was removed as Commander of the 84th Cavalry Regiment for "amoral behavior."[131] He was then moved around different posts until he ended up in the 233rd Division.

According to Prokhorov, Polovnikov was corrupt, a looter, a serial rapist, and a murderer. In a report sent to the 75th Rifle Corps Political Department on 25 September, Prokhorov claimed that Polovnikov sent Orderly Maleev Kanish from Romania to the Russian city of Ivanovo to take numerous objects to Polovnikov's wife.[132] Further, Prokhorov accused the Division's Prosecutor Major Taimanov of conspiring with Polovnikov to grant leave to Polovnikov's unofficial secretary S. N. Kaznina, and soldier Botomolov, to take goods to Polovnikov's wife. More damning was the charge of serial rape. During the Division's march in Romania, Polovnikov caught up with Anna Pugiasheva, a clerk in the Division, who fell behind her unit and was riding on a cart. He told her that riding on carts was not allowed, and took her into his motorized vehicle, where he "started to force her to cohabitate," which was one of the Soviet euphemisms for rape.[133] Prokhorov further alleged that Polovnikov frequently invited young women signalers to his residence, some of whom he tried to rape. Prokhorov also named five young servicewomen by name to whom Polovnikov "applied physical force to compel them into sexual relations."[134] Polovnikov also had Captain Kazakhov, who served under him, procure women for him for "cohabitation."[135] Prokhorov added that Polovnikov was previously held responsible by the Party and Military

Tribunals, which was probably a reference to his dismissal as Commander of the 84th Cavalry Regiment for amoral behavior.[136]

On 21 October, Prokhorov reported to the Head of the Political Department of the 57th Army that Polovnikov ordered or permitted the execution of over 300 prisoners of war, whose clothes seemed to have been given to the Yugoslav Partisans. Prokhorov seemed exasperated at this point, asking the Head of the 57th Army's Political Department how to behave, "because my personal involvement does not give visible results."[137] On 11 November 1944, the Commander of the 75th Corps issued an order in which he criticized Polovnikov and the Division's Commander Colonel Sidorenko for maintaining poor communications with the Staff of the 75th Corps, but this had nothing to do with Polovnikov's looting and raping.[138] Polovnikov ended the war in his role as the 233rd Division's Chief of Staff.[139]

Prokhorov's reports shed light on just how rotten the control mechanisms had become, at least in some units. The second most important man in the Division, the Chief of Staff Colonel Polovnikov, regularly harassed and raped servicewomen. He was also a mass murderer, either ordering or permitting the execution of more than 300 captured soldiers. He corrupted his subordinates, evident in that he had a captain procure women for him. The SMERSH officers, who could have put an end to the criminal acts, were themselves busy looting and raping. Polovnikov's superiors at the level of the Corps and Army were aware of his criminal behavior. Presumably, the Division's Commander must have known about his subordinate's conduct as well but did nothing. The Division's Prosecutor, who also could have done something to prevent the attacks, helped Polovnikov with the looting while turning a blind eye to raping and murdering. Yet, in this unit at least, there was Colonel Prokhorov who tried to put an end to Polovnikov's behavior, indicating that there were officers in responsible positions who were opposed to such conduct.

A conflict also erupted between the NKVD and Army officers over who could use an apartment. NKVD Lieutenant Nikolai Dement'ev, head of the 15th Outpost (*zastava*) of the 17th Border Guard Regiment of the NKVD Army of the 3rd Ukrainian Front, set up his headquarters in an apartment in the village of Klekh in Hungary. At midnight, drunken Lieutenant Colonel Ignat'ev, chief of staff of the rear services of the 64th Riffle Corps, entered the apartment. He demanded from Dement'ev an explanation as to why he was in the apartment. Ignat'ev proceeded to insult the NKVD Lieutenant and hit him three times with a stick, as a result of which Dement'ev lost consciousness. The Lieutenant Colonel took his handgun, and together with his submachine gunner put Dement'ev in his car, effectively kidnapping him. In the car, Ignat'ev threatened Dement'ev with the handgun and continued to hit him with the stick. Eventually, he took the unfortunate Lieutenant to the 64th Riffle Corps' SMERSH officer. The SMERSH officer had Ignat'ev release Dement'ev and return the handgun to him.[140]

Another example that illuminates how officers who comprised the Red Army's coercive institutions comported themselves as criminals comes from the system of command posts. Ivan Serov, Lavrentii Beria's deputy and the future head of the KGB and GRU, flew to the city of Craiova, on Stalin's orders, to introduce the "Chekist order" in the city.[141] Craiova's significance at the time was that it hosted the leadership of the Communist-led Yugoslav Partisans. The Yugoslav leader, Josip Broz Tito, and his Supreme Command were based in the relatively safe Craiova. After several days, from 7 October to 12 October, Serov arrested a series of alleged Red Army's Romanian opponents.[142] Before returning to Moscow, he appointed as the city's commandant Major Mordvinkin, the Chief of Staff of the 17th Border Guard Regiment of the NKVD Army of the 3rd Ukrainian Front, describing him as an efficient and demanding officer.[143] Serov was, however, famously rapacious. Although it is unknown whether he returned to Moscow from Romania with loot, when Serov worked in Germany in 1945, his command transported entire wagons of plundered goods, including antique furniture, crystals, paintings, guns, and silverware. He distributed the loot to the Soviet elite, although he kept much for himself including the diamond crown from the Belgian Royal House.[144]

Mordvinkin's actions were observed by the highest police and state leadership, since, from Craiova, Serov informed Beria of Mordvinkin's actions. Nonetheless, Mordvinkin engaged in widespread plundering, getting caught for distributing the illegally obtained goods to his comrades in the 17th Border Guard Regiment.[145] His superiors were mostly concerned that Mordvinkin's behavior undermined his authority with his subordinates and that it could encourage others to behave similarly. He was warned that if he did not change his behavior, he would be subjected to disciplinary or judicial sanction.[146] It seems that Mordvinkin did not suffer any serious consequences for his conduct.[147] The largest problem from the perspective of the Soviet command was that Mordvinkin's actions undermined his authority, and not the crimes he committed.

A complaint lodged by Avram Eksenasi, a Craiova resident, addressed to the city commandant (Mordvinkin) on 14 October offered a glimpse into life in the city at the time.[148] According to Eksenasi, a Soviet soldier and two officers forced their way into his home, under the pretext that they were searching for weapons. They got drunk in his house, robbing him of jewelry and money. When the Soviet patrol came, called by

Eksenasi's neighbor, they simply greeted the marauders after noticing that they were officers, and left. When another patrol arrived, well after the looters had left, they could do nothing more than acknowledge that Eksenasi had been robbed. Thus, it was up to Mordvinkin and his men to investigate the identity of the officers who robbed Eksenasi and the patrol that allowed it to happen. It is easy to see why Mordvinkin was not likely to take Eksenasi's complaint seriously, given his predilection for looting. In fact, the entire chain of command responsible for peace and order in Craiova was corrupt, including officers who ransacked Eksenasi's house, the patrol that let them go, as well as Mordvinkin, his boss Serov, and of course, Serov's boss Beria.

This is not to suggest that officers staffing coercive institutions never or even rarely worked efficiently. They frequently did work professionally, as witnessed by tens of thousands of arrests and prosecutions in the Red Army. Historians of Stalinism have noted that there was a gulf between directives as they were conceived by the leadership and their inconsistent implementation.[149] It is not surprising that the situation was similar in the Red Army in the context of the chaotic war.

Europeans were puzzled by this inconsistent behavior. Alaine Polcz, a young Hungarian woman, lived in close proximity for months with troops from different units. The Soviet soldiers raped her numerous times, but she also had more positive encounters with other troops. She also experienced how the Soviet military could, at times, efficiently handle accusations of rape.[150] Polcz recalled in her memoirs: "This is what the Russians were like. They hit me with one hand, petted me with the other. Sometimes they came to grips over me: one wanted to spare me, the other to rape me, one to beat me, the other to heal me. One to take something from me, the other to give me something."[151] Jeno Farkass, the Hungarian aristocrat, was similarly puzzled by the Soviet inconsistency. He wrote in his diary on 15 February 1945, shortly after the Red Army entered the part of Budapest where he lived: "The Russians are often jovial and try to put people at ease. At the same time, the street is filled with clothes, underwear [from widespread looting]. Russians load belongings onto trucks. One can't understand their system."[152] This contradictory picture painted by Polcz and Farkass of the Red Army's inconsistent attitude to raping and looting is a fitting description of the Army's coercive institutions.

5.4 Soviet Control Mechanisms in Bulgaria and Yugoslavia

The Soviet coercive institutions did not enforce the laws with equal vigor across Europe. Given the Soviet officers' widespread sympathy for Bulgarians and Yugoslavs, they seemed to have been more likely to help out the Yugoslav and Bulgarian civilians and soldiers when attacked by other Soviet troops. This assertion is impossible to prove with certainty without TsAMO RF completely opening up to researchers. However, there is enough evidence to suggest that the Soviet control mechanisms were on balance more effective in Bulgaria and Yugoslavia than in Romania, Hungary, and Austria.

When three Red Army soldiers confiscated a handgun from a Yugoslav Partisan, he reported the incident to a nearby Soviet officer. The officer slapped the offending soldier, arrested him, and returned the gun to its owner.[153] When Soviet soldiers tried to hijack a Yugoslav officer's car at gunpoint, a Soviet officer intervened, forcing one offender to flee while he struggled physically with the second one.[154] Three artillery officers were stationed with Bratislav Filipović's family. On the Day of Artillery, a Red Army holiday, they all got drunk and another officer who did not live with them came to visit. He wanted to dance with Filipović's mother. However, her husband did not allow it. Later on, the same drunken officer opened fire at Filipović's father, presumably because he was offended that he was not allowed to dance with his wife. He missed, and the other three officers immediately jumped on their offending comrade, confiscated his gun, punched him several times, and stripped him of his epaulets. In this instance, Soviet officers interfered to protect a Serbian civilian and reported the incident to relevant authorities.[155]

A group of NKVD Army troops and a Bulgarian soldier were drinking together on 20 September. A drunken NKVD Sergeant started accusing the Bulgarian of fighting against the Red Army; he hit him and demanded his watch. However, another NKVD Sergeant intervened and attacked his comrade who had assaulted the Bulgarian soldier. Eventually, the offending soldier was tied up and taken to his battalion.[156] When a group of drunken Soviet soldiers and officers began harassing young men and women who gathered at a dance in Yugoslavia, a Soviet major forcefully intervened against his aggressive compatriots. A massive brawl broke out between the drunken Soviets on the one hand and a group of Yugoslavs and the Soviet major on the other.[157]

The Red Army's punitive organs worked more efficiently in Yugoslavia and Bulgaria because the officers who staffed these institutions were more likely to be outraged by the mistreatment of their allies or at least were willing to take complaints from friendly people more seriously. When two Soviet soldiers robbed a Partisan of 10,600 dinars, they were detained and the money was returned to its rightful owner.[158] When a Red Army senior lieutenant seized a handgun from a Bulgarian soldier and tried to hide, the NKVD Army detained him and returned the gun to the Bulgaria soldier.[159] When two Soviet soldiers robbed three apartments, they were detained by the NKVD Army, handed over to the nearby command post, and the property was returned to its owners.[160]

Even nonviolent crimes, which occurred routinely in enemy European countries, were sometimes punished severely. A Soviet sergeant robbed a Partisan of his horse. The Yugoslav stubbornly followed the Soviet soldier imploring him to return the horse. After 15 km, they came upon Soviet officers to whom the Yugoslav complained. The offender was arrested, the horse returned to its owner, and subsequently, the soldier was executed for his transgression.[161] An NKVD soldier and a group of Red Army officers got drunk and robbed a house. The property was returned to its owner when the perpetrators were detained on the same day. Although it is unknown what happened to the officers, the NKVD soldier was sent to a penal company.[162] Another NKVD sergeant stole seven thousand dinars from a house in Yugoslavia. After an investigation carried out by SMERSH, he was charged and sentenced to serve a term in a penal company, while the money was returned to its owner.[163] When a group of Red Army soldiers stole food and alcohol from a store, they were arrested, and the ringleader was sent to a penal company.[164] However, in a similar situation, involving the theft of personal belongings, the culprits' punishment was to answer in front of the party and Komsomol for their misdeeds.[165] Such investigations into non-violent crimes and punishments of offenders reveal that the officers who staffed control mechanisms worked more effectively in Bulgaria and Yugoslavia.

5.5 Military Tribunals

Ultimately, the disciplinary policies were supposed to be implemented by the Military Tribunals. What percentage of all the perpetrators of crimes were investigated? What kind of punishments were meted out to those convicted by the Soviet military justice system? How many criminals were ever processed by the military tribunals? Answering these questions is vital to understanding the implementation of leadership policies in the field.

Regarding the last question, it can be said that the vast majority of deserters and stragglers in the last year of the war were eventually caught. The rear security forces, consisting of the NKVD Armies and Command Posts, pursued them relentlessly. Ultimately, where were deserters supposed to go? Unless they managed to escape to the West, which very few did, they were bound to be eventually caught by the local or Soviet occupation authorities.

If most deserters and stragglers were eventually caught, the situation was the opposite with soldiers who attacked civilians, the majority of whom were never prosecuted for their crimes. This is patently obvious from the fact that rapes and especially looting were so widespread, whereas the prosecutions were not nearly as prevalent. However, we do not even know with certainty the fate of the rapists and looters who were investigated. Records of the Military Tribunals, which sentenced soldiers and officers, are held in near-total secrecy in TsAMO RF. Even scholars who have been granted access to this depository are not able to examine the Military Tribunal records.[166] The limited information that we have about the work of Military Tribunals comes from research published by a few Russian legal scholars.

The Military Tribunals sentenced 2, 530, 683 Soviet citizens during the war on all fronts and rear areas, 994,300 of them military personnel and the rest civilians. 471,998 people were convicted for counterrevolutionary crimes, 792,192 for military crimes (*voinskie prestupleniia*), and 1,266,503 for criminal code violations (*obshcheugolovnye prestupleniia*). Of the military personnel, 376,000 were convicted of desertion, while the number of soldiers convicted for other types of crimes has not been published, but presumably for a mixture of military crimes and criminal code violations.[167] It is also notable that among the 994,300 sentenced servicemen, 422,700 had their sentences postponed until after the war, 436,600 were imprisoned, and 135,000 were executed.[168] The majority of soldiers and officers convicted of military crimes and criminal code violations who had their sentences postponed were sent to penal units for three months or until they were wounded, after which their records were expunged.[169]

In 1944 the Military Tribunals convicted 99,425 soldiers and civilians for counterrevolutionary (political) crimes, 88,432 for military crimes, and 355,888 for criminal code violations. In 1945, they convicted 13,506 people for counterrevolutionary crimes, 69,059 for military crimes, and 152,892 for criminal code violations.[170] There was a sharp decline in the application of capital punishment throughout the war from 33.8 percent of all cases in 1941 to 21 percent in 1942, 7–8 percent in 1943–1944, and 5.1 percent in 1945.[171] According to military historian and former military lawyer Viacheslav Zviagintsev, a considerable part of all counterrevolutionary cases were fabrications, whereas most prosecutions for military crimes and criminal code violations were justified.[172] Similarly, historian Lynne Viola argued that the trials of NKVD officers in the closing stages of the Great Terror in the late 1930s and trials of World War II collaborators and war criminals in the 1940s had little in common with the staged show trials or the mass terror.[173] Thus, records of the Soviet judicial system in non-overtly political cases have been effectively used by scholars to explore historical events.[174]

These statistics, limited as they are, allow us to draw several conclusions. First, the Military Tribunals prosecuted a large number of Red Army service personnel for a wide variety of crimes. Almost 3 percent of all the troops who served (994,300 out of 34 million) were tried and convicted. We do not know how many were punished for attacking civilians, but the numbers were significant. According to one of Russia's main military historians, Oleg Rzhevskii, the military tribunals in the first months of 1945 on all fronts in Europe convicted just 4,148 officers and a large number of soldiers for violence against civilians.[175] As with statistics cited in the previous paragraph, we do not know any more details about these cases. However, if we assume that a similar number of officers were also tried in the fall of 1944 when the Red Army first entered Europe, and that at least a similar number of soldiers were tried as were officers (if not more), then it becomes obvious that a large number of servicemen were prosecuted for attacking civilians. The second conclusion that can be made is that the sentences passed in the last year of the war were less harsh than in earlier years, considering that the number of executions precipitously dropped. Rzhevskii confirms this, by adding that of the thousands of convicted troops, only a few were executed.[176]

My research on the Soviet military justice system in the 2nd and 3rd Ukrainian Fronts is based on glimpses into the workings of military tribunals when they were mentioned in other military documents, such as communication between different levels of command, orders passed on from above, and reports sent to the higher levels of command. Thus, the study offers insights into the workings of military tribunals in the two army groups, but any definite conclusions must await the complete opening of the Ministry of Defense Archive in Podol'sk.

First, executing violators of discipline, as the highest form of punishment, would have sent the strongest message about the leadership's opposition to the troops' criminality. Consistent implementation of capital punishment would have also acted as a strong deterrent. Although there were relatively few executions, they were continuously implemented in the 2nd and 3rd Ukrainian Fronts. What made capital punishment more feared by soldiers is that the army practiced the so-called exemplary executions (*pokazatel'nye rasstrely*). Many soldiers and officers reported that they witnessed at least one such execution.[177] In a typical exemplary execution, comrades from the convicted soldier's unit were gathered to observe the punishment. Members of the court or the commanding officer read out the sentence, while guilty soldiers in some instances had to dig their graves. The execution was carried out after the order was issued: "Fire on the traitors of the motherland!"[178] After observing one such execution, Alexander Pyl'cyn, a penal company commander recalled: "The regiment [which was forced to observe the execution] stood, dumbfounded. I could hear either quiet weeping, or groaning, in the ranks. The regiment continued to stand dumbfounded, until the soldiers filled the grave, and covered it with turf that had been prepared in advance."[179] Pel'cyn's testimony showed that soldiers were shocked and scared at seeing their comrades executed by their side, which was the whole point of exemplary executions.

Second, my research confirms that the very unlucky murderers, rapists, and deserters were subjected to capital punishment in the closing stages of the war in the 2nd and 3rd Ukrainian Fronts. Chance was probably the most important factor in determining a criminal's fate. All exemplary executions were didactic, but occasionally high-ranking commanders ordered their more junior commanders to carry out exemplary executions on the spot to deter similar conduct. Just as the forces of the 3rd Ukrainian Front were entering Hungary from Yugoslavia, the army group's commander, Marshal Tolbukhin, permitted commanders of the 37th Army, 57th Army, and the 4th Guards Mechanized Corps to carry out exemplary executions on the site of the crime.[180] Soldiers caught committing crimes in the period after this order was issued were more likely to receive the death penalty.

Although chance was the most decisive factor in determining whether the convicted soldier would receive the death penalty, the heinousness of the crime and the victim's nationality also played a role. For instance, two deserters entered a house in Yugoslavia, got drunk, and raped a woman while kicking out her husband and mother-in-law from the house. One of the "bandits," as the army document described him, was subjected to exemplary execution, while the second criminal received a ten-year prison term.[181] The fact that they deserted and committed rape helps explain why they were shot, although many deserters committed sexual attacks but only a few were executed. A drunken sergeant major (*starshina*) was executed by a military tribunal because he entered a house in Bulgaria demanding that the owner give him vegetables, and when refused, he shot the homeowner.[182]

The military tribunals seem to have passed harsher sentences for crimes committed in pro-Soviet Yugoslavia and Bulgaria, where the commanding officers tended to be more sympathetic to the local population and where there was more pressure from the high command for the troops to behave correctly. These factors probably played a role in the case of the previously mentioned sergeant who was executed for stealing a horse from a Yugoslav Partisan. Little is known about this case or the perpetrator's background, but it also possible that the attack on an allied soldier justified the unusually harsh sentence he received for a non-violent crime. It should also be noted that the offending soldier was from the 4th Guards Army which marched from Romania to Hungary via Yugoslavia. Theft of horses was part of the routine in Romania, where Soviet troops illegally seized 254,465 horses during the war.[183] The situation was evidently different in Yugoslavia.

In another case, a SMERSH officer was executed for raping a young girl in Poland.[184] The significance of this case was that even the most privileged members of the Soviet military were liable to be executed for rape. Deserters who organized into gangs and set up illegal command posts and plundered, murdered, and raped were also executed by Military Tribunals.[185] Crimes against the Soviet soldiers could also lead to executions. In one instance, a truck driver was executed for reckless driving leading to the deaths of three soldiers that rode in the back of the truck.[186] In another instance, a soldier killed his comrades after a dispute, for which he was executed by the Military Tribunal.[187] In another instance, the ringleader of a group of Red Army personnel who committed large-scale theft of army supplies worth almost 6 million rubles was executed, while other participants were sentenced to ten-year prison terms.[188]

Executions seem to have been the exception rather than the rule, even in Yugoslavia and Bulgaria where the control mechanisms tended to be stricter. It seems that in the majority of cases convicted soldiers had their sentences postponed until after the war and were sent to penal units for three months. An indicative document that sheds light on the fate of detained deserters was a note sent by Major-General Pavlov, the commander of the NKVD Army of the 3rd Ukrainian Front, to Colonel-General Zheltov, member of the Council of the 3rd Ukrainian Front on 23 February 1945. According to Pavlov, in January 1945, 17 deserters of the Front were sentenced to various terms in labor camps, 11 were under continued investigation in the NKVD, 57 were under investigation in reserve regiments in the rear, and 173 were sent to penal units.[189] The overwhelming majority of deserters were sent to penal units as punishment.

Soldiers and officers found guilty of violent crimes were also sent to penal units. A drunk lieutenant fired his gun in a train and killed a rank-and-file soldier. He was sentenced to a ten-year prison term and had his rank stripped, but Tolbukhin postponed the punishment until after the war and sent the lieutenant to a penal unit.[190] A sentry in the 62nd Guards Rifle Division of the 3rd Ukrainian Front left his post and entered a house in a Romanian village, trying to steal a goose. When the owner confronted him, he shot her dead. Military Tribunal sentenced him to a ten-year prison term which was postponed until after the war and he was sent to a penal unit for three months.[191]

The Red Army's apparent preference for sending soldiers who committed serious crimes to penal units was mirrored in the disciplinary practices in the NKVD Armies of the 2nd and 3rd Ukrainian Fronts toward the NKVD troops. The NKVD Armies, as mentioned earlier, had a separate chain of command although they were under the regular Army's operational control. Commanders of the two NKVD Armies summarily sent their soldiers and officers to penal units for a wide range of military violations and criminal acts including insubordination, dereliction of duty, desertion, and repeated rape attempts.[192] In rare instances when NKVD soldiers were prosecuted and convicted, their sentences were usually commuted. The Military Tribunal sentenced an NKVD soldier to a six-year term in a labor camp for murdering a Hungarian civilian, but he had his sentence commuted by General Kuznetsov, commander of the NKVD Army of the 2nd Ukrainian Front, to a two-month stint in a penal battalion.[193]

Being sent to a penal unit, on the one hand, was a serious penalty. Death rates in these formations were higher than in the regular army, which suffered appalling casualties. A term in penal units possibly meant death, or almost certainly, an injury.[194] On the other hand, soldiers and officers in penal units, even though under stricter control than regular soldiers, continued to have opportunities to straggle, plunder, and rape as they remained in the field. Thus, the Soviet command's usual punishment of sending soldiers to penal units may have been deadly for the perpetrators, but it was not immediately effective in preventing repeat offenders from committing their crimes. Also, if soldiers survived their time in penal units unscathed, they were returned to the regular army, and after the war, their records were expunged.

Being sent to a penal unit could appear to be a harsh sentence given other options. In one instance, an NKVD lieutenant who attempted to rape a Hungarian woman was subjected to fifteen days of house arrest, and his salary during the period was cut by 50 percent.[195] Another NKVD lieutenant brought an arrested Hungarian woman to his house, under the pretense of wanting to question her, and raped her (the document states that he slept with her) for two nights. When a SMERSH officer was informed about this, instead of putting an end to this criminal conduct, he took the woman to his residence where he proceeded to rape her. Both rapists received party reprimands. At the time that the report was written, the investigation was ongoing, leaving the prospects of a harsher punishment.[196] A group of three drunken NKVD soldiers tried to rape a young Hungarian woman in the presence of her father and brother. When the latter two intervened to protect her, they seized a weapon from one of the NKVD soldiers who presumably threatened them with it. In the ensuing struggle, the NKVD men shot the brother of the attempted rape victim and escaped. The Soviets received a ten and a fifteen-day sentence of house arrest. Pavlov justified his decision by arguing that the NKVD soldiers had a clean record before the incident, whereas the Hungarians committed a serious violation by seizing a weapon from the NKVD.[197] Captain Zhukov, a battalion commander in the NKVD Army's 134th Regiment, and Senior Lieutenant Belikov, the unit's SMERSH officer, got drunk in an apartment in Austria. They demanded that the apartment owner bring two women to them. When the owner refused, they smashed the furniture, paintings, and dishes. The regimental commander wrote that Zhukov should be handed over to the Military Tribunal. However, given Zhukov's clean record and history of being a brave commander, he was placed under house arrest for ten days. For the ten-day period, his salary was cut by 50 percent. The regimental commander also stated that the Belikov would be punished through the SMERSH chain of command.[198]

5.6 Order Number 15/2-008063

Although the Soviet command in most cases did not execute or imprison deserters, rapists, looters, and other criminals in the ranks, they still tried to reverse these phenomena. General Lieutenant Gorbatiuk, the head of the NKVD Army for the Protection of the Rear of the Red Army, ordered from Moscow a large-scale and concentrated campaign on 1 November 1944 called "Order number 15/2-008063 Struggle with Immoral Events."[199] The campaign lasted for at least six months, from November to April, and it involved the NKVD Armies of all fronts. As such, it was Moscow's most decisive measure to rein in the increasingly out-of-control troops.

Although I did not find Gorbatiuk's order, I found considerable correspondence within the 3rd Ukrainian Front's NKVD Army about the campaign, as well as the Front's communication with the NKVD Army's headquarters in Moscow. The campaign for the struggle against immoral events was not only unusual for its duration and intensity, but also because it was ordered by the military command, and it involved military commanders in the field. Typically, political departments alone dealt with the issue of morale. By involving military commanders Gorbatiuk wanted to make it clear that the issue of falling discipline needed to be taken seriously.

Major-General Pavlov and Lieutenant-Colonel Naneishvili, the Commander and the head of the Political Department of the NKVD Army of the 3rd Ukrainian Front respectively, sent a threatening letter to all regimental commanders and heads of political departments on 28 November 1944. They announced that drunkenness and accompanying criminality, which included theft and attacks on civilians, had taken on dangerous proportions. They blamed commanders for this situation.[200] Pavlov and Naneishvili wrote that commanders had to lead by example, adding that those who did not introduce order into their units would be held personally responsible and sent back to the Soviet Union.[201] The campaign required political departments of NKVD regiments in November and the first part of December to report every ten days about measures to curb "immoral events."[202] Thereafter, each regiment's measures against "immoral events" were discussed in the regular annual quarterly reports.[203]

Pavlov and Naneishvili wrote to Gorbatiuk on 14 December about their initial responses to Order Number 15/2-008063. Political departments responded mostly through the tested method of conversations with officers, Communist Party and Komsomol meetings, and agitation with rank-and-file soldiers. Some of the topics discussed in this veritable wave of propaganda were: "Moral character of a Soviet officer and his role in strengthening military discipline," "The exemplary conduct of Communists and Komsomol members in the struggle to increase discipline and strengthen the political and moral state of the troops" and "Strictly fulfilling the military oath – the holy duty of a border-guard warrior."[204] These lectures aimed to encourage proper conduct among the NKVD troops.

More unusually, military prosecutors and judges from military tribunals participated in the campaign. They discussed with the troops the legal issues and potential consequences for "military violations, voluntary abandonment of posts, and illegal appropriation of property from the local population."[205] The involvement of judicial bodies in the campaign represented a significant escalation of the usual approach to improving discipline. Typically, political officers gave lectures about the significance of disciplined conduct, but they lacked the coercive powers of the prosecutors and judges. The NKVD command wanted to warn the troops that continuing undisciplined behavior could lead to serious consequences. Pavlov and Naneishvili also wrote to Gorbatiuk that the command identified individuals who drank repeatedly and that political workers worked with them individually. Some repeat offenders were demoted and received Party and Komsomol reprimands. In more exceptional circumstances, serious offenders were demoted and transferred to the regular army's reserves.[206]

Despite these efforts, the NKVD troops committed considerably more military violations in October, November, and December of 1944, than in July, August, and September of the same year. The situation did not improve in January and February 1945.[207] The proliferation of military violations in the NKVD Army mirrored the situation in the regular military. The NKVD Army headquarters in Moscow was not impressed with the results of the campaign. On 2 March 1945, Gorbatiuk wrote to commanders of all the NKVD Armies demanding a renewed effort at curbing immoral events. He singled out the NKVD Armies of the 2nd, 3rd, and 4th Ukrainian Fronts for having the most violations while adding that in the 3rd Ukrainian Front, there were even instances of commanders trying to conceal their subordinates' misconduct. He said that drunkenness was the most frequent immoral event, which was often accompanied by debaucheries, serious violations of state laws, and illegal use of weapons.[208] Gorbatiuk was dissatisfied with Pavlov's and Naneishvili's initial responses to his order.

Naneishvili wrote to Gorbatiuk on 23 March outlining his plan for a renewed campaign against immoral events. Naneishvili again turned to the trusted arsenal of lectures about the "Responsibility of the Party in strengthening discipline and liquidating immoral events."[209] However, Naneishvili also stated that there would be verifications (*proverka*), which was a new measure forcing officers to take the high command's orders more seriously. Namely, higher-ranking officers would verify the quality and authenticity of reports sent by political departments relating to immoral events, the measures they took to counter them, and the process by which political officers familiarized the troops with decisions made by the military tribunal.[210]

The NKVD Army's struggle against the increasingly ill-disciplined conduct of its forces was the most comprehensive documented attempt to curb military violations. What ultimately distinguished it from other similar campaigns was the fact that it was ordered from Moscow, as well as its intensity, duration, and the involvement of military commanders, prosecutors, and judges who threatened soldiers with firm punishments. Although the NKVD's high command failed to reverse the so-called immoral events, it does not follow that the campaign had no impact. It was launched because of declining discipline, and without it, the troops' out-of-control conduct could have escalated even further.

The leadership of the command post system displayed similar concerns regarding the fall of discipline in their ranks. Nonetheless, the attempts by this institution to introduce order into their ranks were not as systematic as the NKVD Army's Order Number 15/2-008063. When the NKVD Army of the 2nd Ukrainian Front took over control of the command posts from the regular army in Hungary and Northern Transylvania, it identified as one of the problems the supposed moral dissoluteness of some of the commandants.[211] Some of these so-called morally dissolute officers were dismissed by the new NKVD leadership, while others received lectures about the proper moral characteristics of a Soviet officer. Thereafter, the command post leadership sought to control commandants through a series of verifications (*proverka*). To deter other commandments from incorrect behavior, the command sometimes circulated the names of the most persistent violators and announced their punishments to other commandants.[212]

Verification reports revealed that improvements to the quality of commandants under the NKVD Army's leadership, if any, were minimal. Some commandants continued to abuse their power, marrying local women and Red Army servicewomen, while personally enriching themselves by stealing expropriated property.[213] One of the worst offenders was Senior Lieutenant Rudenko, Commandant of Hungary's Mezőkovácsháza district. According to one of the reports, Rudenko stopped fulfilling his duties, cohabitated with a woman, used state property for personal enrichment, and illegally appropriated the rank of captain and the coveted title of Hero of the Soviet Union.[214] Similarly, Captain Chimpuridze, commandant of the Kiskunfélegyháza district, married a Hungarian woman in the local municipality, announcing it in the local press even though it was illegal for Soviet citizens to marry foreigners.[215]

Most of these incidents were announced to all commandants in circulars, warning them how not to behave. Most punishments, however, tended to be lenient. Rudenko's case went to a Military Tribunal, although it is unclear what punishment he received.[216] Chimpuridze was sent to the Red Army's reserves, where he most likely assumed another position suitable for his rank.[217] In exceptional instances, the military tribunal's decisions against individual commandants were circulated to warn other commandants of possible punishments. The Military Tribunal of the Rear of the 2nd Ukrainian Front sentenced the commandant of the Hungarian town of Cegled to a ten-year sentence in a labor camp for the theft of state property. Kuznetsov, however, suspended the sentence and sent him to a penal unit until the end of the war.[218] Like other individuals sent to penal units, commandants who fulfilled their service successfully had their rank restored and the conviction expunged from the record.

There were echoes of the NKVD Army's campaign to root out the so-called immoral events in the regular military, but nothing as intensive as Order Number 15/2-008063. Political departments had to report on the moral state of the troops every ten days, but this was part of the bureaucratic routine and not a consequence of the leadership's reaction to escalating disciplinary problems. However, on 12 December, Lieutenant-General Ivan Anoshin, the head of the Political Department of the 3rd Ukrainian Front, sent a circular to the units of Front. In it, Anoshin required all political departments to organize meetings with officers to discuss how to improve the political and moral state of the troops. Political departments of the front were also required to report any instances that undermined the dignity of officers of political departments.[219]

No further information about Anoshin's circular was found in the archives, indicating that Anoshin's order was not comparable to the campaign in the NKVD. The Red Army's struggle against the so-called immoral events was much less intense than the NKVD's fight against these phenomena. NKVD viewed itself as an elite part of the Soviet military and the Kremlin depended on the NKVD forces to implement the leadership's policies in occupied parts of Eastern Europe. These factors explain why there was a more concentrated campaign in the NKVD to root out the so-called immoral events.

5.7 Conclusion

Officially, the Red Army had a strict disciplinary regime. A booklet *Disciplinary Regulations of the Red Army*, which should have been familiar to all troops, stressed the importance of discipline and it specified mechanisms and tools available to officers to enforce discipline. Moreover, Moscow and the leadership at the level of fronts regularly issued orders that demanded disciplined conduct from the troops in the field. The only exception may have been in Romania, where orders demanding the correct treatment of civilians came from divisional and regimental levels.

The existing regulations and a series of orders after the Red Army entered Europe make it clear that the attacks on civilians were not part of leadership policy. However, a number of factors prevented the implementation of a strict disciplinary regime. Officers who staffed coercive institutions did not empathize with civilians or viewed them suspiciously. Officers also did not behave any better than the soldiers. If anything, they were worse behaved since they had more opportunities to get drunk, plunder, and raped and they were more likely to get away with crimes. The situation in 233rd Division, where high ranking officers engaged in rape, corruption, and murder of prisoners, illustrates this point vividly. In some instances, they also had to perform a balancing act between acknowledging the violence against civilians to enforce rules while avoiding the accusation of slandering the Red Army. All of these factors discouraged officers from investigating soldiers accused of committing crimes and preventing future attacks, leading to the gap between official policies and their actual implementation in the field.

Military Tribunals were the final arbiters of military justice in the Red Army. Relatively few criminal acts were ever brought in front of them. A fraction of all criminals were executed for their crimes in 1944 and 1945; some were sentenced to terms in the Soviet Union, while the significant majority of all criminals were sent to penal units. Given the shortages of soldiers in the closing stages of the war, it made perfect sense for the command to punish deserters and criminals with service in penal units. There, they continued to fight the Germans, and they had a small chance of coming out of penal units unscathed. However, they continued to be in the field, where they were able to commit further atrocities against civilians, and if they survived the war, they had their records expunged.

Officers from the control organizations did not apply themselves with equal vigor in implementing policies across Europe. Although a definite answer can be given only when the former Soviet archives become completely open to researchers, there is strong evidence that the disciplinary regime was stricter in "friendly" Yugoslavia and "neutral" Bulgaria than in "enemy" Romania, Hungary, and Austria. The Soviet political and military leadership had strong connections to Bulgarian and Yugoslav leaders, which the latter utilized to lodge complaints about the Soviet troops' misconduct, enabling Soviet officers to undertake timely and specific measures to curb criminal activity. Also, officers from coercive institutions, like the Red Army service personnel in general, had more positive attitudes toward Bulgarians and Yugoslavs than toward Romanians, Hungarians, and Austrians. Consequently, they were more likely to undertake stronger measures against criminals who committed crimes against civilians in Bulgaria and Yugoslavia.

Part III

The Troops

6 Soviet Soldiers' Views of the Countries of the Balkans and Central Europe

The standard narrative of the Red Army's encounter with Europe, which focuses almost always on Germany, is well-known. Soviet soldiers, hailing from an impoverished and repressive society, and raised on the Marxist–Leninist propaganda, were shocked to discover that Germans enjoyed a high standard of life. The soldiers' destitution and envy of the enemy's affluence merged with the desire to punish the ordinary Germans for starting the war of extermination against the Soviet Union. Versions of this story have been retold by numerous historians.[1]

However, soldiers and officers of the 2nd and 3rd Ukrainian Fronts encountered five different European countries in less than nine months: Romania, Bulgaria, Yugoslavia, Hungary, and Austria. Yugoslavia was an ally, and the Yugoslav National Liberation Army, recognized by Washington, D.C., London, and Moscow, was led by the Yugoslav Communist Party. Bulgaria was neutral in relations to the Soviet Union until September 1944 when Moscow declared war on Sofia. Bulgarians and Serbs (the Red Army moved mostly through the Serbian part of Yugoslavia) shared the Orthodox religion with most Soviet troops. The Russian, Serbo-Croatian, and Bulgarian languages are distinct but somewhat mutually intelligible. Romanians, Hungarians, and Austrians spoke languages that were completely foreign to most Soviet troops. The socioeconomic situation in the five countries varied greatly, but the poverty in some areas, especially Romania, shocked the Soviet troops no less than the material comfort of the major wealthy cities such as Vienna. Although Romania, Hungary, and Austria fought against the Red Army from the beginning of Operation Barbarossa, the degree of their involvement in military operations and the brutal occupation of the Soviet Union varied considerably.

Although the soldiers from the 2nd and 3rd Ukrainian Fronts wanted revenge and a few were envious of how some Europeans lived, these sentiments were only a part of the larger story of how the troops perceived the European countries they occupied. As discussed in Chapter 2, the Soviet troops behaved with relative restraint in Bulgaria and Yugoslavia, whereas they went on a rampage in Romania and especially in Hungary and Austria. To understand the reasons for the variation in the intensity of crimes against civilians in the region, it is necessary to appreciate the troops' views toward each country. It should be kept in mind that the Soviet soldiers' attitudes toward these countries were born out of prejudices and the conditions of war. They were also shaped by official propaganda. The soldiers' views constitute what historian Anna Hajkova called an "ethnic gaze."[2] As such, the troops' views did not reflect reality or some objective truth about these countries. Instead, the troops' views reflected their stereotypes.

The Soviet soldiers had varied attitudes toward each country they encountered, but there were also fundamental commonalities that must not be overlooked. Historian Amir Weiner convincingly demonstrated that the war fundamentally transformed the Soviet Union, as it engendered a more assertive citizenry, while nation displaced class as the primary criteria by which the Soviet state determined citizens' sociopolitical status.[3] An important mechanism of this transformation was the encounter with the world beyond Soviet borders. When the Red Army marched across the international frontier, the troops, almost all of whom had never stepped outside their native "socialist motherland," were compelled willy-nilly to think about the alien world they had encountered and compare it to their country. Was life abroad worse or better? The answer was often the latter. To deal with this uncomfortable realization, in the words of Major Boris Slutskii, a perceptive and intelligent Red Army officer, thousands of Soviet soldiers deliberately exaggerated the positive aspects of life in the Soviet Union to foreigners.[4]

Lida was a Polish polyglot and intellectual from Warsaw who escaped to Hungary in 1940 as a refugee, marrying a Hungarian count during the war. She was on her husband's estate in the village of Mora, some 30 km southwest of Budapest when she encountered the Red Army in December 1944. After the war, she published a book based on her wartime notes about her experiences with the Red Army under the pseudonym of Alexandra Orme to protect her family still living in Stalinist Poland (her real name was Alice de Barcza).[5] During the war, she and her husband were repeatedly interrogated by the Soviet occupation authorities. Although her narrative was filled with stories of rape of other women, she maintained that she escaped several rape attempts. Scholars of sexual violence note that victims in their testimonies tend to assign their experiences to other women.[6] It is possible that Lida was raped by the Soviet soldiers but that she did not record it. After the war, Lida and her husband resided in Italy and the United Kingdom, before settling in the United States. She returned to live in her beloved Poland in 1975 after her husband died.[7]

According to Lida, all Red Army personnel presented themselves as engineers, directors of factories, and professors. At worst, soldiers and officers that she met claimed to have been drivers or mechanics, and none admitted to being a collective farmer or a worker.[8] Lida and her husband were coerced into having a lengthy discussion with a Soviet major, which appeared to have been an unofficial interrogation. The major was interested in her husband because he was vice president of the Federation of Hungarian Factory Industries.[9] For one hour, the major questioned the couple, while a lieutenant drew up columns of figures. The major was extremely proud to conclude that the Soviet workers were paid twice as much and engineers and directors five times as much as their European counterparts.[10] Obviously, the majority of Soviet soldiers were collective farmers, and the standard of life was lower in the Soviet Union than in Europe, but these were the lies that the Red Army servicemen told the foreigners either because they believed them or because of nationalism.[11]

A Soviet soldier's worldview tended to be not only nationalist but also insular. This is not something unique to the Red Army or the 2nd and 3rd Ukrainian Fronts. Soldiers engaged in intensive combat are disinterested in the outside world. The two army groups continued to suffer appalling casualties in the late stages of the war, and they faced mortal danger at every turn. The troops were exhausted by constant fighting and endless marching. What little free time they had, they spent with their comrades, eating or relaxing together. From the perspective of the troops, all civilians were always outsiders. Their well-being and safety, let alone their worldviews, were peripheral to most troops.

6.1 Soldiers' Attitudes toward Romania

The Soviet Union and Romania were neighbors with a history of entanglement. The Soviet Union annexed Bessarabia in 1940, which in the interwar period was part of Romania. Consequently, Bucharest joined Berlin's anti-Soviet crusade in June 1941. Germany rewarded Romania by returning Bessarabia to it and allowing it to occupy and administer Transnistria, a territory in southwestern Ukraine with a population of 3 million people.[12] The Romanians were closely implicated in Nazi atrocities. According to historian Grant Harward, "Romanian Army closely collaborated with the German Army in Adolf Hitler's 'war of annihilation' which included not only destroying the Red Army but also murdering Jews and communists while starving 'subhuman' Slavs."[13] The soldiers of the 2nd and 3rd Ukrainian Fronts knew Romania better than any other European country they encountered.

Like their Balkan neighbors, Romanian Europeanized political elites from the nineteenth century tried to modernize their largely rural country to catch up with Central and Western Europe.[14] Despite Romania's relative backwardness, the country's wartime leaders presented their country as part of the great European civilization engaged in a crusade against the Bolshevik-led oriental East Slavs.[15] Although less brutal than the Germans, Romanians pursued policies of "Romanianization" and "Aryanization" in Transnistria at the expense of the local population.[16] Despite Buchurest's claims of Romania's superiority, the country's elite was deeply insecure about their status in Europe. Ion Antonescu, the country's military dictator, complained that Romania was viewed as "an Abyssinia of Europe."[17]

Romania's relative poverty and military weakness on the one hand, and the leadership's anti-Slavic propaganda and policies accompanied by proclamations about Romania's preeminence on the other, forged a sense of superiority and profound resentment among the Soviet troops over the Romanians. They regularly referred to Romanians as "Gypsies," a clear sign that they viewed Romanians as inferior to themselves.[18] In doing so, the Red Army personnel were not alone, as Romania's other neighbors used the slur "Gypsies" to describe Romanians, perhaps deliberately playing on Romanian sensitivities over being viewed as not fully European.[19] It should be noted that Antonescu's regime brutally persecuted the Roma during the war, deporting 25,000 to Transnistria from Romania proper, approximately half of whom died or were murdered there.[20]

Soviet soldiers loved to point out Romania's economic and social backwardness. Evgenii Moniushko, a Lieutenant in the 9th Artillery Regiment of the 72nd Division, passed through Romania on his way back to the Soviet Union, after being stationed in Czechoslovakia, Austria, and Hungary, all wealthier countries. He described Romania's poverty as a pitiful sight, noting that houses had straw roofs and that unpaved dirt roads served as main village roads.[21] Gabriel Temkin, a soldier in the 78th Division of the 2nd Ukrainian Front, wrote that when his unit entered Romania, many soldiers expected to find a country better off than the Soviet Union because in their hearts they did not believe the official propaganda about Romania's feudal poverty. Instead, they were faced with houses without chimneys and people walking barefoot and subsisting on a diet of maize porridge instead of bread. Disappointed by the reality, they jokingly embraced and repeated the Russian proverb: it's good everywhere, where we are not.[22] Anton Romenskii, a Komsomol organizer, recalled that Romanian peasants walked around in ripped shoes or barefoot. He talked with one peasant, who barely survived on the diet of corn. The peasant was illiterate as were his wife and children.[23] Major Slutskii

Figure 6.1 Romanian peasants meet the Red Army. Source: Sovfoto/ Universal Images Group via Getty Images.

put it best when he noted that Soviet soldiers felt their superiority over Europeans most acutely in Romania (Figure 6.1).[24]

For Soviet troops, the Romanian peasant staple diet of maize porridge came to emblemize Romania's poverty and backwardness, and they derisively dubbed Romanians *mamalyzhniki* (maize porridge eaters).[25] Petr Mikhin, an artillery officer in the 57th Army, described in his memoirs how he was shocked by the extreme poverty of the common people. Their huts were squalid and shabby, with clay floors and no furniture. Worst of all was the food that the owners served him and his soldiers, which Mikhin described as dark brown porridge with bits of corn, without any butter or fat. According to him, they managed to have only enough so as not to offend their hosts. The situation was the same in other houses he entered.[26] Aleksandr Toptygin, a soldier in the 9th Guards Mortar Regiment of the 5th Don Cossack Corps, claimed that Hungarians lived much better than Romanians, citing as evidence the fact that they ate bread instead of maize porridge.[27]

The near-obsession with maize porridge entered even official documents. An NKVD report about the city of Calarași maintained that the poorest peasants near the city lived in dugouts and had to engage in small trade to support their families. Peasants did not eat bread, of course, but maize porridge. When a bread store opened in the city, the report stated, a massive brawl broke out, and Romanian soldiers beat the people and took all the bread.[28] As late as 1948, the Soviet Military Commandant of Iasi, undoubtedly a high-ranking officer, told the passing Yugoslav delegation: "Oh, this dirty Romanian Iasi! And these Romanian corn-pone eaters [another name for maize porridge]."[29] The Red Army's rank-and-file and high-ranking officers were united by anti-Romanian stereotypes.

The traditional Romanian peasant diet was indeed based on corn even before the war, which was deemed to be of insufficient nutritional value compared to other grains.[30] By the time the Red Army occupied the country, after years of war, the situation only deteriorated further.[31] However, it should not be forgotten that many Soviet soldiers were themselves the survivors of a vicious man-made famine in the early 1930s, which resulted in the deaths of anywhere between 5 and 9 million people, including 2.6–3.9 million in Ukraine.[32] Given that up to two-thirds of the 2nd and 3rd Ukrainian Fronts were from Ukraine in the summer of 1944, many of the troops' recent experiences were far worse than anything they could have seen in Romania in 1944. Some soldiers also experienced malnourishment and hunger in the early stages of the war, especially while undergoing training in the rear where food was frequently of low quality and insufficient quantity.[33] Thus, the Soviet troops' shock at how Romanians ate was contrived. Some troops could have been genuinely surprised at the prevalence of corn in the Romanian diet. However, the frequency and how they recalled this indicate that they concentrated on the corn-based diet to denigrate Romanians and establish their superiority. It should also be mentioned that the longer Soviet forces stayed in the country, living off the land, the more impoverished Romania became. Although the Soviet military and political leadership were well aware of this fact, it does not seem to have ever occurred to Soviet soldiers that they were adding to Romania's poverty.[34]

In reality, not all Romanians lived worse than the Soviets. Romania's modernization drive was partially successful, though it left major discrepancies between the majority (three-quarters) rural and agricultural populations on the one hand and urban and industrial on the other.[35] The wealthy landowners and the Europeanized middle classes of the larger modern cities had no parallel in the Soviet Union. Consequently, it is unsurprising that neither the popular stereotypes nor propaganda could entirely convince Soviet troops that Romania was completely inferior to their homeland.

Mstislav Ivanov, a deputy platoon commander in the 303rd Division, recalled that his strongest impression of the country was the contrast between luxury and poverty.[36] Mikhail Tsurkan, an infantryman in the 2nd Ukrainian Front, noted that he liked the city of Timisoara a lot, describing it as neat, clean, cultured, and beautiful.[37] Nina Ivanovna

Glotova, a medic, recalled that Romania appeared to her to be very clean.[38] Aleksandr Solov'ev, a scout, arranged all European countries, which he saw, according to their standard of living, placing Romania at the bottom of the list. Nonetheless, he concluded that some Romanians lived better than the Soviet people.[39] The realization by some soldiers and officers that life was better in Romania, at least in some ways, injured Soviet national pride and led to feelings of envy and humiliation that contributed to violence.

For example, Nikolai Nadtochii, a senior sergeant in the 3rd Ukrainian Front, did not like Romanians. In his view, they were unfriendly and cruel. Nadtochii claimed that, for Romanians, even a sergeant was a high rank, so they laughed at him because his shoes had holes.[40] Next, he explained that since many troops could not buy anything with the money they were issued, some soldiers committed robberies at night.[41] By discussing his humiliation and looting in the same context, he revealed how these two phenomena were linked in his mind.

Pavel El'kinson, a scout in the 3rd Ukrainian Front, clearly struggled with the realization that some Romanians lived better than the Soviets, finding consolation in official propaganda about how capitalism made people selfish. He wrote in his diary on 5 September 1944 that "every [Romanian] lives individually. Each one has pigs, geese, chickens, and horses. This individualism has made them so greedy that for a piece [of bread] they would hang themselves."[42] Therefore, even though he conceded that Romanians lived relatively well, he used this realization to vilify them by characterizing them as selfish and materialistic. Several weeks later, El'kinson recorded that the city of Petrosani was small but very beautiful, with many well-dressed youth and beautiful women. He went on to say that:

> As we look at them, involuntarily, envy arises. How are they better than us? Has it really been preordained for us not to live anymore? They started this war and they are again enjoying life. In general, it's really hard to write about this and I can't find the right words. One soldier said it correctly when a superior yelled at him for not responding to [to a Romanian soldiers'] salutes. When they killed my brother, I became ready to kill them.[43]

Thus, El'kinson went from noting how comfortable life was in Romania, to fatalistic sentiments about his likelihood of death, and finally to approving murderous violence against Romanians, indicating how these phenomena for him were connected.

Another widespread Soviet stereotype that reflected their disdain for Romanians was that they were poor soldiers. To question Romanians' martial abilities was tantamount to questioning their masculinity and worth as men. The Soviets overstated the weakness of the Romanian army to establish their superiority. Nonetheless, this prejudice against the Romanians was also rooted in reality. Most Soviet soldiers who fought in Romania in 1944 came from a generation of soldiers recruited into the Red Army after the disastrous first year of the war. Hence, their impressions of the Romanian army were based mostly on their experiences in the latter stages of the war when Romanians were demoralized by repeated routs and the seemingly inevitable Allied victory.[44] In contrast, many Red Army soldiers in 1941 had been unpleasantly surprised by Romanian courage and competence.[45] The Romanian army was also highly dependent on German assistance, especially in armor, which Berlin never delivered in sufficient quantities.[46] But whatever equipment, and overall effectiveness the Romanian army had in 1941, these were largely gone by 1944.

Temkin recalled in his memoirs an illustrative episode about the Red Army's attitudes toward Romanian soldiers. When his division reached the River Prut in the spring of 1944, he was sent with several Soviet soldiers across the river to capture a Romanian soldier for intelligence. Through sheer boldness, cunning, and the Romanian army's low morale, they managed to capture nineteen soldiers and a pig (to be roasted).[47] Temkin's unit came up with a song to celebrate this achievement and ridicule Romanians: "*Kak Russkye na-Prut, tak Rumyni na-Serut.*"[48] Joseph Lampart, a political officer in the Black Sea Fleet, recalled that after landing in Romania in the course of the Iasi Kishinev Operation, he rode on a motorcycle through fields in which groups of Romanian soldiers were wandering. He added that not one of these soldiers dared to pick up a rifle and shoot at them.[49] Lampart used this story not only to depict Romanians as cowards but to implicitly extoll his bravery evident in how he freely roamed around large numbers of armed Romanians.

Mstislav Ivanov said that Hungarians and Germans were true warriors and dealing with them was a challenge but that it was good to have Romanians as enemies.[50] Aleksei Ustimenko, who operated a mortar in the 2nd Ukrainian Front, recalled that Germans were better soldiers than Romanians. He went on to say that Romanians were "rotten soldiers, [they were only good at] guzzling food."[51] N. N. Voronov, Marshal of the Artillery Forces of the Red Army, most clearly highlighted how the Soviets dismissed Romanian troops as weak and feminine by mocking Romanian officers for their supposed use of powder, lipstick, and makeup.[52]

When Romania was compelled to switch sides and join the Allies, Soviet views of Romanian military prowess hardly improved. The Soviets clung to an image of their dominance over Romanian men even when they fought together against the Germans and Hungarians. Captain Sergei Otroshchenko, commander of a tank battalion in the 18th Tank Corps, fought side by side with Romanians in the town of Arad. According to him:

> They [Romanians] are, of course, bad soldiers. I had to urge them [to fight on] constantly. Several times I wanted to take a rod and hit their colonel on the head so that he would fulfill his orders. They are extremely cowardly. As soon as they [Germans] would fire on them, they would become depressed … They are not like us Russians, Ivans.[53]

The implication of his assertion was clear: Russians were true warriors, unlike Romanians. From this, it follows, according to Otroshchenko, that a Soviet officer could and should subject a Romanian officer of superior rank to corporal punishment.

The negative Soviet views of Romanian soldiers were so widespread that they penetrated official reports. Colonel Nikofirov, the Red Army's representative to the Romanian military, submitted a report to the Soviet command about the fighting capacity of the Romanian 4th Army on 28 December 1944. Nikofirov reported that as a rule, the 4th Army had been unable to fulfill tasks set by the Soviets, maintaining that it had a shortage of officers on company and platoon levels, that many officers showed low initiative, and that they tended to act cowardly during battles.[54] He also singled out the Romanian military for committing acts of violence and plunder against Hungarian civilians.[55] An NKVD Army of the 2nd Ukrainian Front report written on 11 November went even further. The report asserted, absurdly, that Romanian soldiers who served in the Soviet Union learned Russian and represented themselves to Hungarian civilians as Russians when they committed criminal acts against them. Hence, the local population blamed the Red Army for the crimes perpetrated by Romanians.[56]

These two documents reveal that high-ranking officers shared the anti-Romanian prejudices of the Soviet frontline troops of Romanians as weak men and poor soldiers. In general, Soviet soldiers and officers entirely neglected the sacrifices the Romanian military made to the defeat of the Axis, suffering 167,000 casualties on the side of the Allies after they switched sides.[57] Their focus on the Romanian mistreatment of Hungarian civilians suggests that they wanted to denigrate Romanians. Considering the magnitude of Soviet crimes in Hungary, it is extremely unlikely that these two Soviet officers were genuinely angry or surprised by Romanian conduct. It never occurred to the Soviets that their abuse of civilians accompanied by a profound arrogance could have sapped the Romanian will to fight side by side with them.

The Red Army soldiers and officers, denying supposedly masculine traits to Romanians such as loyalty and bravery, conceived of them as speculators and petty traders interested only in making a quick profit. This was an unmistakable insult in the mentality of the young Soviet men who came of age in the Stalinist Soviet Union where profit making was demonized. As Junior Lieutenant Vil' Sarychev, commander of a battery in the 92nd Guards Division put it: "They [Romanians] were a weak enemy, they did not want to fight, and they were not warriors, especially when compared to Germans. But in addition to all of this, they were also scoundrels."[58] Nadtochii characterized Romanians as "hopeless barterers (*barakhol'shiki*)."[59] Iaak Rabinovich, a medical officer in the 2nd Ukrainian Front, wrote to his wife that Soviet soldiers and officers swarmed one store that sold pencils and paper, buying huge quantities of writing material. He concluded: "Understandably, prices jumped radically."[60] Similarly, Major Slutskii claimed that Soviet soldiers bought so many pencils in the town of Cernavoda that the prices went up all over the town automatically, without peddlers even consulting each other.[61] Elsewhere, Slutskii compared Romanian merchants to reptiles.[62] Rabinovich and Slutksii derided Romanian storeowners. However, it is notable that other countries the 2nd and 3rd Ukrainian Fronts occupied also had small shopkeepers but the Soviet troops never discussed them or dwelled on their mercantilism.

In 1944, there was nothing that Romanians could do to improve their image among the Soviet troops. When Romanians fought on the side of the Germans, they were viewed as weak German sidekicks. After Bucharest switched sides in the war, the Soviets took this to be evidence of the Romanians' treacherous nature, although it did not negate the previous negative stereotypes. After years of war, Soviet soldiers found it hard to accept Romanians as their allies. El'kinson wrote in his diary that it was strange that Soviet soldiers exchanged salutes with Romanian troops, adding menacingly, "Not to worry. We will take from them more than they took from us."[63] Slutskii maintained that fewer than 20 percent of Soviet and Romanian officers saluted each other, with Romanians being three to four times more likely to first hail their Soviet comrades.[64] Lazar' Brontman, a *Pravda* journalist in Bucharest on the day when Soviet forces entered it after the royal coup, wrote in his diary: "Strange people – until now we beat them, they fought against us, and now they are shouting [with joy] and saluting us."[65] Upon his return to Moscow, he joked with Georgii Aleksandrov, the head of the Central Committee's Propaganda and Agitation Department, that Romanians traded everything – from apples to their country.[66]

Among the 2nd and 3rd Ukrainian Fronts, there was a large number of troops who had personal negative experiences with Romanians. The two army groups recruited around 200,000 troops from the territories that comprised Transnistria in the spring of 1944, who months later became the occupiers of Romania.[67] Many soldiers who experienced the Romanian venal, exploitative, and genocidal policies in the Soviet Union had personal reasons to hate Romanians.[68] Mikhail Tsurkan, an infantryman in the 2nd Ukrainian Front, recalled that when Romanians occupied his village near Odesa, they beat people and killed Jews. He recalled how as a sixteen-year-old boy, walking around with his friends, he was invited by Romanian soldiers to participate in a mass execution of Jews. He ran away with his group of friends. When they saw from a distance that Jews were being executed, he claimed they all broke into tears.[69] Aleksandr Solov'ev, also a soldier in the 2nd Ukrainian Front from the Balta district in Ukraine, saw how Romanians marched columns of starving Jews through his village.[70] He said that "it was impossible to look at them, it was so sad … especially women with little children."[71] On 11 April 1944, a Jewish soldier from Odesa sent a letter to his family who was in the country's interior. He described in the letter how their relatives and friends were placed in ghettoes and murdered, adding that he saw a ditch full of recently executed women and children.[72]

In addition to recruiting heavily in so-called Transnistria, the 2nd and 3rd Ukrainian Fronts also filled the ranks with around 200,000 *spetskontigent* (special contingent) between April and October 1944 in Romania. The *spetskontigent* consisted mostly of prisoners of war and forced laborers.[73] Slutskii wrote that the 75th Corps of the 3rd Ukrainian Front liberated gigantic prisoner-of-war camps in western Romania, containing more than 6,000 prisoners each.[74] This is how he described these soldiers and their treatment of Romanians, "so they went forward … defenders of Odesa and Sevastopol, warriors from 1941, too sturdy to have succumbed to the regime of Romanian camps, too hungry not to hate that [Romanian] regime with the entirety of their souls …. They advanced and before them Romanian villagers recoiled, fleeing away from the roads."[75]

Thus, around 400,000 troops of the 1 million soldiers of the two army groups consisted of former Romanian prisoners of war, forced laborers, and survivors of the Romanian occupation. It is impossible to understand the troops' attitudes toward Romanians and their behavior in the country, without considering that many of the around 40 percent of the Soviet soldiers in the country had experienced Romanian violence and misrule.

6.2 The Encounter between Soviet Soldiers and Bulgarians and Yugoslavs

There is almost nothing in the English-language scholarship on the encounter between the Red Army and Bulgarians and Yugoslavs, which is not the case with other countries that the 2nd and 3rd Ukrainian Fronts occupied. Hence, it is worth exploring this topic in greater detail, as the Soviet experience in the two South Slavic countries challenges the prevalent image in the historiography of the Red Army as violent and foreign conquerors in Europe.

Both countries, but especially Yugoslavia, had powerful communist movements, whose many supporters eagerly anticipated the Red Army's arrival. Furthermore, both Bulgarians and Yugoslavs were traditionally pro-Russian. These attitudes were deeply rooted in perceived historical, cultural, and religious links, which often overrode political affiliations. As Milovan Đilas, one of the leading Yugoslav Communists and subsequently a famous dissident, noted, the people of Montenegro had a mythical belief in Russia's might and greatness, a claim that also applied to Montenegro's Slavic Orthodox neighbors, the Serbs and Bulgarians.[76] Many Serbs and Bulgarians, even noncommunists, welcomed the Red Army and saw Russia as a desired big-power patron due to their shared Orthodox religion, Slavic background, and Russia's role in the destruction of the Ottoman Empire, the hated imperial overlord in the Balkans for centuries. Czechoslovakia was the only other country where the Red Army received a similarly positive welcome.[77]

When the Soviet forces reached Bulgaria's borders and Moscow declared war on Sofia, there was uncertainty in the Red Army ranks whether the Bulgarian forces would resist. The Soviet frontline officers and troops were unprepared for their joyous reception.[78] Slutskii wrote that entire Bulgarian villages, including priests, met the advancing Soviet tanks with bread and salt.[79] Reports from different Red Army formations spoke of jubilant Bulgarian crowds in many towns bringing bread, salt, and flowers to the Red Army troops while surrounding the military columns and shouting "Ura!"[80] El'kinson wrote in his diary that when his unit was passing through a village, the locals offered them so many watermelons that "it appeared that we are not going to war but returning from a watermelon plantation. We tried to refuse, saying that the vehicles can't carry them. But they refused to accept [this explanation] and took offense if you did not accept them. It is rare to meet such people."[81] El'kinson was obviously pleased with the Red Army's reception.

Similarly, as a result of the idealized representations of one another, the first encounters between the Soviet army and Yugoslav civilians and Partisans led to jubilant celebrations all over the country.[82] Đorđe Lobačev, a Belgrade resident and a child of Russian émigrés, most vividly described the scenes of liberation in his memoirs. He wrote that as the first Soviet soldiers appeared on his street, while the fighting was still taking place in other parts of Belgrade, ecstatic people including women and children came out of hiding in the basements of their half-destroyed homes. They had flasks and bottles in their hands, hugged soldiers, and invited them to their homes, "forgetting that the liberation of the city had only begun."[83]

Some evidence even suggests that the Red Army was received better in Bulgaria and Yugoslavia than in the Soviet Union, which would make sense since the Bulgarians and Yugoslavs did not have direct experience with Stalinist rule. V. Kozhevnikov and M. Sivolobov, majors in the Red Army and *Pravda* correspondents, implicitly conceded this point in their report to the Red Army's political leadership about the situation in Bulgaria, which had been mentioned in Chapter 5. They wrote on 27 September that they saw many magnificent and festive scenes as the Red Army entered newly liberated Soviet cities but that what they witnessed in Bulgaria exceeded their expectations and moved them deeply.[84] El'kinson wrote in his diary that Bulgarians welcomed the Red Army more warmly than the Soviet people.[85] Subsequently, he wrote that the Yugoslavs welcomed the Red Army with even more enthusiasm than the Bulgarians.[86] A Soviet scout, Mikhail Ivanov, also claimed that in Yugoslavia the people received the Red Army even more warmly and sincerely than in the Soviet Union, recalling that in one village the people insisted that his commander allow soldiers to stay at their houses.[87]

There were hundreds of thousands of Soviet troops in Yugoslavia and Bulgaria, and there were many instances when Soviet soldiers and officers looted and subjected civilians to sexual and physical violence, but the majority of soldiers in most encounters treated civilians properly. Soviet soldiers were often billeted with Yugoslav and Bulgarian civilians, leading for the most part to friendly and respectful relations.

Nadežda Đurišić, a civilian, recalled that the Red Army organized a field kitchen in her uncle's courtyard and that they shared their food with Yugoslav civilians.[88] Z. E. Sutrina, a signaler in the 71st Guards Division, was billeted with two other officers and soldiers in the Bulgarian village of Kaluger for one night. She recorded in her diary that the owners of the house were impoverished and had many children. Nonetheless, they happily offered her and two officers bread, grapes, and cheese in the morning, while in the evening, the Soviets decided to share their meager military rations with the family.[89]

Three Soviet artillery officers were billeted in Bratislav Filipović's house for several weeks when he was fifteen years old. He reported that "they respected us, all three of them were correct ... we lived like one family."[90] Živojin Ilić hid in forests and caves for days and nights with his fellow villagers while the Soviets and Germans battled over mountainous eastern Serbia. When they returned to their village after the fighting ended, Soviet soldiers embraced them warmly. They offered the hungry

Figure 6.2 Red Army triumphant in Belgrade. Source: Mondadori via Getty Images.

refugees food, and the civilians buried the fallen Red Army troops.[91] Like elsewhere in Europe, the Red Army troops often coddled and displayed paternal affection toward the children (Figure 6.2).[92]

Ivan Protić, a Belgrade resident and a teacher, struck up a deep friendship with a Soviet captain who saved his house from expropriation because his father was also an educator. The Soviet officer repeatedly visited his house throughout 1944 dining with Protić's family. Their friendship continued even after the captain left Yugoslavia.[93] They exchanged letters after the war, while the captain paid him a visit during one of the joint Soviet–Yugoslav celebrations on the anniversary of the liberation of Belgrade. Their children continued the relationship. The captain's daughter with her husband visited Protić and his daughter Divna. In 1972, Divna, who was eighteen in 1944, visited the captain and his daughter during her visit to Moscow. They lost contact after their fathers died.

An exceptional aspect of the Soviet encounter with Bulgarians and Yugoslavs was civilians who wanted to enlist in the Red Army. A military report sent to Aleksandr Shcherbakov, head of the Main Political Administration of the Red Army, noted that many Bulgarians, especially youth and workers, wanted to join the Soviet military, and Bulgarian soldiers purportedly wanted to be led by Russian officers.[94] Similarly, after the liberation of one village, overjoyed Serbs offered to join the ranks of the Red Army.[95] They were refused, in both instances, presumably because it was against Red Army regulations to take non-Soviet citizens into service. It appears that civilians served in the Red Army only in extraordinary circumstances. Danilo Voravotić was liberated by the Red Army from a Hungarian internment camp, where he joined the Soviet military. He served in the 57th Army and was released only after the war. He was sent home with a large sum of money and a letter of gratitude from SMERSH.[96] The Red Army officers sometimes accepted Yugoslav citizens into their service illegally as nonmilitary specialists, employing them as translators, drivers, and tailors, which reflected their high trust in them.[97]

During the lengthy street-to-street fighting in Belgrade, the line between civilians and soldiers became blurred, as there were many instances of civilians joining the fight to help the Red Army. N. I. Iashchenko, commander of the 214th Regiment of the 73rd Guards Rifle Division, recalled in his memoirs that during the liberation of Belgrade, dozens of local citizens – youths, old men, and women – showed to Soviet troops the buildings, courtyards, basements, and sewers where Germans hid. According to Iashchenko, even more, civilians helped treat and transport the wounded Soviet soldiers, while some opened fire at the Germans with whatever weapons they could muster.[98] According to a Soviet-era mixture of a memoir and a scholarly study, during the liberation of Belgrade, soldiers of the Soviet 4th Guards Mechanized Brigade and Partisans were joined by local citizens who took an active part in the fighting. The civilians opened fire at Germans from behind corners, windows, and basements, sometimes even attacking withdrawing Germans with sticks and batons.[99] Similarly, in the village of Mali Izvor, the Soviets were assisted in their assault on the Germans by a ragtag group of Partisans and civilians equipped only with stones that they threw at the enemy.[100]

In some instances, Serbian civilians risked their lives to save the lives of Red Army soldiers. A Soviet veteran, Nadezhda Vdovina, recalled that when German airplanes attacked a village in northern Serbia, she, her driver, a young local woman, and the latter's mother rushed into the basement of a house. As the Germans fired, the young Yugoslav woman held Vdovina by her shoulders and hugged her, covering her with her body. The woman was wounded, but Vdovina was left unscathed.[101] In the village of Jabukovac, near the Bulgarian border, Soviet forces were forced to retreat temporarily. An elderly Serbian man hid a Soviet soldier in his house for four days, while Germans were in the village, thereby risking his own life.[102]

One of the unique aspects of the Red Army's experience in Yugoslavia was the encounter with the large resistance movement and the camaraderie that emerged between Soviet and Yugoslav fighters. It should be noted that although the Soviets fought alongside other allied armies, including the Romanian and Bulgarian militaries after they switched sides, they went into battles in entirely separate units and came into limited contact with each other. In contrast, in Yugoslavia, the Soviets fought in many battles literally shoulder to shoulder with Partisans.

When the Soviets entered Yugoslavia, the German defenders were entrenched in the mountainous terrain where the Red Army found it hard to operate. Thus, the Partisans who knew the local area well helped the Soviet troops infiltrate eastern Serbia, bypassing the well-defended roads.[103] Soviet tanks were loaded with Yugoslav Partisans as they headed into the battle for Belgrade.[104] As they traveled together, the Red Army supplied food for their Yugoslav comrades.[105] In other instances, Yugoslav Partisans were instructed to provide food for their Soviet comrades and not to accept money from them.[106] Several key victories in the battle for the Yugoslav capital, such as the capture of the Belgrade citadel, the forcing of the Sava River, and the destruction of thousands of German troops near the Avala Mountain who tried to break into the city, were achieved by the Red Army and Yugoslav soldiers fighting shoulder to shoulder.[107] Soviet soldiers were buried in central Belgrade in a ceremony in the presence of thousands of Yugoslav soldiers and civilians.[108] Three days after the liberation of Belgrade, a joint Red Army and Yugoslav military parade was organized by Yugoslav and Soviet commanders.[109]

Soviet and Yugoslav soldiers bonded over more sinister activities, as well. A Soviet captain and two Partisans were arrested in Belgrade by a Yugoslav patrol on 16 January 1945 when they broke into a private apartment and tried to rape three women.[110] Two Soviet officers and several Yugoslav Partisans on 17 November 1944 stole a car from the Swiss embassy in Belgrade, and the following day, they returned and stole fuel.[111] Near the city of Subotica, in June 1945, three Soviet soldiers, a local police officer, and a Yugoslav civilian committed a robbery on a farm.[112] When two Soviet officers were beaten up and robbed of their clothes and weapons by Hungarian border guards at the Yugoslav–Hungarian border crossing on 24 February 1945, they escaped to Yugoslavia. There, they called for support from the People's Defense of Yugoslavia (KNOJ; Yugoslav security troops) to help them retrieve their belongings and punish the aggressors. KNOJ and the two Soviet officers illegally crossed the border into Hungary and arrested two Hungarians in Soviet officers' uniform, but they had to let them go when 150 Hungarians arrived and some of them opened fire on the Yugoslav–Soviet allies.[113] Similarly, Red Army officers and Yugoslav Partisans launched illegal cross-border raids into Romania where they disarmed

Romanian troops, ostensibly also Soviet allies at the time, to provide arms for the perennially underequipped Yugoslavs.[114]

The Yugoslav and Soviet fighters also bonded over the execution of German prisoners of war. According to the Yugoslav Partisan Dušan Novaković, at his first encounter with Soviet troops of the 4th Guards Mechanized Corps near Belgrade, Soviet and Yugoslav soldiers hugged each other, and a Soviet officer presented the Yugoslav commander with a bottle of vodka. Then, the Soviet soldiers took over German prisoners of war held by the Yugoslavs and executed all Russians who fought on the German side (the so-called Vlasovites). They left the Germans with the Yugoslavs, whom the Partisans proceeded to execute.[115]

None of this is to suggest that all Serbs and Bulgarians were happy that the Red Army had liberated them. Some were aware of the Stalinist regime's proclivity for extreme violence. Others had cooperated with or worked for Germans and pro-German authorities. They were rightly afraid of what Soviet arrival would mean for them and their families. There were probably even more people for whom the Red Army represented another source of problems to deal with in the context of ongoing war and deprivation.

Yet, it should be kept in mind that the Red Army fought overwhelmingly on the territory of present-day Serbia. The main Partisan rivals in Serbia were Četniks. They were also ostensibly an Allied formation oriented toward the Western Allies, but they were not anti-Russian. When the Red Army entered Serbia, Četniks tried unsuccessfully to cooperate with the Soviets, who typically used them in local military operations against the Germans before disarming them and handing them over to Partisans.[116] After such initial experiences, Četniks tried to stay out of the Red Army's way or to switch permanently to the Soviet side.[117] Slutskii, who worked with the Četniks closely, believed that their leadership would have been unable to turn its troops against the Red Army even if it wanted to because, among the peasant soldiers, "pure, Serbian Orthodox Russophilia was extremely widespread."[118] Instead, the Četnik command was forced to express solidarity with the Soviets in its propaganda.[119] Furthermore, according to historian Aleksej Timofejev, the forces of the collaborationist Serbian authorities, another Partisan rival, appear to have never engaged the Red Army on the battlefield, a contention that my research confirms.[120] Thus, Soviet soldiers and officers were not exposed to anti-communist or anti-Soviet Serbs or Bulgarians since such people stayed out of the Red Army's way.

Furthermore, the Soviets did commit violence in Bulgaria and Yugoslavia, perpetrating acts of plunder, rape, and murder, which disillusioned some Bulgarians and Yugoslavs. Although violence against civilians was on a smaller scale than elsewhere in Europe, it did not go unnoticed by the civilian population. The previously mentioned report by Kozhevnikov and Sivolobov asserted that, despite the scenes of jubilation that followed the Red Army's entry into Bulgaria, occasional acts of marauding and violence severely disappointed the civilian population.[121] Numerous regular army and NKVD reports noted that criminal conduct by Soviet troops "dishonored" the title of a Soviet warrior in the eyes of the Bulgarian and Yugoslav populations.[122] Thus, even the Soviet sources acknowledged that the Red Army's occasional criminal conduct undermined its image among Bulgarians and Yugoslavs.

6.3 Soviet Views of Bulgarians and Yugoslavs

Most frontline Soviet troops did not stay long enough in Bulgaria and Yugoslavia, nor did they spend enough time talking to the local populations, to understand the nuances of the two societies. Even if they did, it is unlikely that they would have cared. For Soviet troops, the warm welcome they received was central to creating a positive impression of Bulgaria and Yugoslavia, especially after their icy reception in Romania. Captain Vil Sarychev, a battery commander in the 3rd Ukrainian Front, recalled that in cafes and restaurants in Bulgaria, everybody wanted to join the tables where Soviet officers were sitting and buy them food and drinks.[123] Many Soviet soldiers and officers recalled that Bulgarians would address them as "bratushky" – brothers.[124] Nikolai Nadtochii, a Red Army senior sergeant, said that of all the European countries he saw, he liked only Bulgaria. He recalled an incident when a Bulgarian officer screamed at a tavern owner who wanted to charge the Soviets. The Bulgarian officer then stopped by a table where the Soviets were sitting and offered to buy them a round of drinks.[125] Aleksandr Sedoi, a platoon commander, alluding to the absence of combat, said that "waging war in Bulgaria was good."[126] He noted that Bulgarians lived poorly, adding that, nonetheless, they would share everything that they had with the Soviets.[127] We do not know how the impoverished Bulgarians who had to share their food felt about the Soviet army's voracious appetite for food and alcohol. Perhaps, they were coerced or pressured to act welcomingly, as was the case with the tavern owner, but their seeming hospitality created very positive impressions of Bulgarians on Nadotochi and Sedoi.

The diary of Pavel El'kinson is the most revealing source about Soviet attitudes toward the Bulgarians. Arriving from hostile Romania, he seems to have been genuinely surprised and touched by the friendly welcome that the Red Army received in Bulgaria. El'kinson wrote on 8 September, his first day in the country, that Bulgaria was very different from Romania, where they were afraid that the Red Army would exact revenge.[128] The following day, his surprise did not abate. He noted that in every village and town, crowds of people lined up the streets, throwing fruits, bread, cigarettes, and flowers into passing Soviet vehicles. Wherever the military column would stop, he went on to say, Bulgarians would swarm soldiers, bringing food and asking about life in the Soviet Union.[129] When his unit was leaving Bulgaria for Romania again, he wrote that he was sorry to leave, adding that their hospitality would forever live in his memory.[130]

Likewise, almost all Soviet soldiers who served in Yugoslavia spoke enthusiastically of the population's hospitality. There they were also impressed with the presence of a large and vehemently pro-Soviet communist movement, which they took to be representative of the wider Yugoslav attitude toward them. A Soviet officer, Fedor Mishurov, recalled that Yugoslav Partisans offered the Red Army significant support in many operations they undertook together and that everywhere they greeted Soviet soldiers like brothers.[131] The Red Army artillery officer, Petr Mikhin, wrote in his memoirs that Serbs greeted the Red Army enthusiastically and that Partisans particularly loved them because they fought side by side.[132] Aleksandr Tverdyshev from the 73rd Guards Division, rank unknown, wrote in a letter to his daughter in Kazakhstan:

> I am in Belgrade – the capital of Yugoslavia. The most wonderful city, in which street battles are taking place now … the local Yugoslav Partisans will enter the history of the Fatherland war as wonderful knights (*chudo-bogatyri*). If without our help for three years, they achieved surprising results, with our arrival, they are committing wonders. The entire population of the city, young women and men are fighting in real battles shoulder to shoulder with us … if God allows me to return home alive, I will be able to tell you so much about the Yugoslav Partisans! They all admire the Red Army, but we, in turn, admire their determination, selflessness, and patriotism…[133]

El'kinson also wrote that his unit was advancing together with Partisans, who kept on saying that they will chase the enemy to Berlin.[134] The following day, he wrote: "You will not meet anywhere else such freedom-loving, such patriotic, such loyal and such friendly people. One is not sorry to go into battle and sacrifice his life for such a people. You feel you are fighting for people who respect you."[135] The presence of a pro-Soviet resistance movement obviously left a strong impression on Soviet soldiers and officers.

It is important to note that high-ranking officers responsible for the conduct of the rank-and-file were also impressed by the Partisan resistance to the German occupiers. Nikolai Zav'ialov, commander of the 5th Independent Guards Motorized Brigade, recalled that after a difficult and victorious battle, the Soviets and Yugoslavs dined together. One Soviet fighter, amazed, asked his Yugoslav comrades how they managed to persevere in conditions of fascist terror and launch an armed struggle. The Yugoslavs then told the Soviets about their life.[136] Colonel-General Biriuzov, Chief of Staff of the 3rd Ukrainian Front and second in command after Marshal Tolbukhin, related the following episode in his memoirs. Following the liberation of Belgrade, he saw an old man embrace a Soviet tank crew member, telling him that five of his sons joined Tito's Partisans but that now he had thousands of sons near him – the Soviet soldiers. Biriuzov was intrigued and chatted with the old man afterward.[137] Lieutenant-General Korneev was the head of the Soviet Military Mission to the Partisans and subsequently de facto Soviet ambassador to Yugoslavia in the period following the liberation of Belgrade. On the day of his arrival at the Yugoslav Supreme Command in 1944, after the dinner was finished, he stayed up drinking with Tito, whom he drunkenly kissed and tenderly called "Iushka, Iushka" (informal Russian nickname for Josip, Tito's first name).[138]

One manifestation of the Soviet identification with the Yugoslav suffering at the hands of the Germans was the violence committed against enemy soldiers to avenge the Yugoslavs. Captain Mikhin wrote that after a battle, soldiers under his command searched the captured Germans. In the pocket of one SS prisoner, they found a picture of five hung people, all civilians including a woman and a youth. In the picture, two small boys were standing by the gallows, looking sadly at the victims, likely their relatives. As the Soviets demanded to know why the SS executed the Serbs, a Red Army soldier who was wounded in the battle that just ended ran up to him and shot him dead. Mikhin, fearing that he would have to answer to the NKVD, ordered his soldiers not to shoot the prisoners. But the Soviet soldiers started beating the captured Germans mercilessly. One soldier tried to shoot all of the prisoners, but his machine gun jammed, and the remaining captives survived.[139]

El'kinson wrote that, during his unit's advance through Serbia, they came upon four dead Partisans. Around them stood two other Yugoslav fighters. Both Partisans recognized close relatives among their killed comrades: one his brother and the other his son. El'kinson was moved by the scene, noting that his heart hurt, and he wondered when all the killing would stop. Nonetheless, soon his unit came upon three captured so-called Russian volunteers, very likely from one of the armed formations from the Soviet Union that the Germans used in anti-guerrilla operations in Yugoslavia. Consequently, El'kinson and his comrades asked permission from the regimental commander to beat the prisoners, a request that the commanding officer granted. El'kinson wrote: "We beat them cruelly. Scoundrels. That's what they deserve. We beat them for the murdered Partisans, for treachery [of the Soviet Union]. They are not going to make it alive to their headquarters."[140] Evidently, El'kinson and his comrades beat the prisoners to death.

Another indicator of Soviet sympathy for Yugoslavia was that they found almost everything to be beautiful. Artillery officer Captain Petr Mikhin wrote that Yugoslavia in October was like Russia in August: sunny and warm, with trees still green and flowers in bloom. He summed it up: "Nature at its finest ... it was extremely beautiful ... the locals lived in paradise."[141] El'kinson described the flat expanses of northern Serbia as beautiful.[142] A Soviet pilot wrote in his memoirs about eastern and southern Serbia: "What mountains! You cannot be amazed by them enough. From the heights that we flew at, they are indescribable, you must see them for yourself."[143] As a result of the Soviet admiration for Yugoslavia, numerous Red Army soldiers who were wounded in Europe but were convalescing in Yugoslav and in Soviet hospitals in Yugoslavia expressed their wish to be buried in "brotherly Yugoslavia."[144] These positive impressions of the country reflected Soviet soldiers' pleasant experiences there.

At the same time, the Soviet ethos was pervaded with a sense of superiority vis-à-vis Bulgarians and Yugoslavs, which led many Soviets to look down upon their allies. The haughty attitudes reflected Moscow's imperial outlook, and they also echoed propaganda among the rank-and-file troops, which stressed, accurately, the primacy of the Red Army in the liberation of the Balkans. The troops' sometimes arrogant attitude was shared by the Soviet political leadership. During an informal meeting of leading Yugoslav and Soviet Communists, which included Tito and Stalin, the Soviet dictator asserted the superiority of the Bulgarian army over the Partisans, praising the professionalism of the former tsarist officers.[145] Tito was outraged since Stalin not only insulted his pride, the Partisan army, but compared them unfavorably to a despised former enemy. This was pure provocation from Stalin, regardless of whether it was true, meant to put the assertive Yugoslav leadership in its place. Further down the chain of command, Partisan commanders had to appeal to the Red Army's political departments to include in their public statements the fact that Belgrade was liberated jointly by the Red Army and Partisans and not just by the Soviets. They also had to plead with the Soviets to stop treating the Partisans as an unknowledgeable second-rate army.[146]

Mikhin most vividly illustrated Soviet arrogance. Two Bulgarian officers visited his part of the front to make arrangements to assume control of the frontline. According to Mikhin, their meeting was warm.

Nonetheless, they were professional officers in their forties, and they expressed surprise that Mikhin, a commander of an artillery battalion, was only twenty-three. He interpreted this as an insult to his professionalism. This is how he comforted himself:

> He was twice my age, but in essence, who was he in comparison to me? We had fought all the way from Moscow to this place, while they hadn't even tasted battle yet ... I was a battle-hardened and experienced officer of a powerful army, while he was representing the armed forces of a rump government, whose tsar had fawningly served Hitler.[147]

Similarly, Mikhin described a Partisan leader he encountered in an explicitly patronizing manner as cunning, pathetically emotional, and excitable.[148] The fact that many Soviets looked down upon the Yugoslavs was disappointing, particularly to the Partisans, as one Partisan report ruefully conceded after describing the Red Army's conduct following the liberation of Belgrade.[149]

Soviet arrogance was not caused by anything that the Yugoslavs or Bulgarians did. Instead, the Red Army soldiers' and officers' dismissiveness of the Yugoslav contribution to their own liberation reflected the Soviet worldview according to which they were the dominant power. The denigration of their allies' contribution to the anti-German cause served the purpose of affirming their supremacy. The Soviet Union recognized Tito's nascent government, and the Red Army was not formally an occupying force in Yugoslavia. Nonetheless, some encounters between the Soviets and Partisans revealed that the former could not accept that the latter had any authority in their own country. One Red Army officer declared himself to be the commandant of the city of Novi Sad to General Kosta Nađ, the Partisan commander in northern Serbia. When Nađ retorted that Novi Sad was ruled by the Yugoslav military and civilian authorities, the Soviet officer responded that he did not care and he would shoot anybody who refused to obey his orders.[150] A drunk SMERSH major crashed an official gathering in the town of Aranđelovac, which was attended by Yugoslav and Soviet officers. The intruder ordered everyone to disperse. When the Yugoslavs refused to obey, he entered an argument with a Yugoslav colonel. Eventually, the Soviet major was escorted out but not before he managed to disperse part of the assembly.[151]

The Red Army's frontline soldiers and officers were constantly on the verge of death. Moreover, since they entered Romania in the summer of 1944, they felt an acute sense of isolation from the surrounding population whom they hated in any case. Their reception in Bulgaria and Yugoslavia as heroic liberators, as well as the Partisan struggle against the Axis, validated their views of the war. At the same time, Red Army personnel felt a sense of superiority given their major contribution to the defeat of the Nazis. Therefore, they were also dismissive of others as junior partners at best.

6.4 Soviet Troops' Views of Hungarians

As seen in Chapter 2, the Soviet rampage in Hungary was worse than in Romania in its intensity and duration. This outcome, however, was far from preordained. Hungary was a relatively distant country that historically had fewer interactions with Russia than its immediate neighbors. Although Budapest allied itself with Berlin in its aggression against the Soviet Union, its overall input in the war effort was relatively marginal. Consequently, when Soviet soldiers first reached Hungary in October, they did not have much to draw on for negative stereotypes about Hungarians, and few had personal reasons to exact vengeance.[152] The Red Army personnel identified Hungarians as German allies, but beyond this, there was little substance to their anti-Hungarian attitudes.[153]

As the Soviet forces massed along Hungary's borders with Romania and Yugoslavia, the frontline troops were informed of the ongoing peace negotiations between Moscow and Budapest and Horthy's aborted attempts to abandon the Axis.[154] Exhausted by endless marching and fighting, they fervently hoped that Hungary would abandon its German ally, as Romania and Bulgaria had, and thereby, shorten the war and increase their chances of survival. In the words of one veteran, "There was great disappointment and anger when we realized that the Hungarians decided – that is how Red Army soldiers saw it – to stick with their German allies."[155] The Soviet troops drew their own conclusions about Hungarians: "A crow will not take out a crow's eye."[156] This was an incorrect assessment. The majority of Hungarians during 1944 came to realize that the war would be lost and wanted it to end as soon as possible.[157] However, they were powerless to end the German occupation or overthrow the Arrow Cross regime.

Nonetheless, Soviet soldiers now more firmly identified Hungarians with Germans, increasing the possibility that Hungarian civilians would share their fate. Moreover, Hungarian's continued fidelity to the Axis led to a tsunami of anti-Hungarian hate propaganda. Considering the absence of preconceived negative notions about Hungary, it became necessary for the Soviet command to persuade the troops that Hungarians were a brutal enemy to mobilize and prepare them for a fight on Hungarian soil. The success of the hate campaign can be judged by the relative frequency with which veterans repeated the propaganda mantra that Hungary was Hitler's last ally.[158] Although this claim was repeated frequently, it was not even true since the Croatian Ustaša state collapsed weeks after Hungary.

In addition to hate propaganda, the extraordinarily brutal fighting in the country from October 1944 to March 1945 greatly embittered the troops and played a critical role in shaping the troops' attitudes toward Hungarians. Although the rank and file fervently hoped to easily pass through Hungary, the 2nd and 3rd Ukrainian Fronts encountered some of the fiercest combat of the war in the country, which they wrote about in letters and diaries at the time and recalled in memoirs and interviews after the war.[159] Experienced soldiers even compared the siege of Budapest with the epic Battle of Stalingrad.[160] As mentioned earlier, Stavka prioritized the advance on Berlin, sending the best reinforcements and supplies to army groups advancing on the German capital. Stavka even transferred north two all-tank armies from the 2nd and 3rd Ukrainian Fronts. In contrast, the German leadership viewed Hungary as essential for its war effort due to the country being a gateway to southern Germany and Hungary's important natural resources.[161] The Germans could not prevent a Soviet victory, but they turned Hungary into their bastion.

The two Red Army fronts suffered a total of almost half a million casualties in Hungary.[162] In these circumstances, Soviet troops became increasingly indifferent to the suffering of civilians. Moreover, the more Soviet soldiers subjected civilians to violence, naturally, the more Hungarians became fearful and hostile to the Red Army, leading to further embitterment by the troops. As Guards Senior Lieutenant Efim Romanov, a doctor in the 2nd Ukrainian Front, put it: "We had serious problems only with the local population in Hungary. Magyars hated us, and to be honest, they had a reason to. And 'ours,' by the way, responded in kind."[163] Soviet troops characterized Hungarians as bad people, hateful, and more perfidious than even the Germans.[164] Hate propaganda and the ferocious fighting transformed the Soviet attitude toward Hungarians from unfriendly when they entered the country to outright malicious by the time the fighting ended.

Pavel El'kinson brilliantly illuminated in his diary this transformation of views. His first diary entry in Hungary was in a town near the Yugoslav border, with a mixed Yugoslav–Hungarian population. On 11 October, he noted that the local Yugoslavs were well disposed to the Soviets, but not the Hungarians, many of whom had escaped before the Red Army arrived. The few Hungarians who remained were afraid.

He and his comrade were drunk while staying in a local house, and they were interested in pursuing the two young women living there. However, their grandmother guarded them all night, and nothing happened.[165] This entry revealed an escalation in aggression toward the local population. Although he expressed interest in women before, commenting on their appearance, he never suggested pursuing them or that they needed protection from Soviet soldiers. The troops' views of civilians were hardening as they entered Hungary, even before the heavy fighting erupted.

On 15 October, after noting that negotiations failed, El'kinson wrote that Hungary would offer resistance.[166] Two days later, he recorded that heavy battles were raging, while the local population was afraid of the Red Army. This entry also noted the first instance of rape in his diary, as he wondered what would happen in Germany if the troops were behaving so badly in Hungary.[167] The next day, on 18 October, he wrote with some surprise that soldiers were saying that gang rapes were taking place in the middle of the day. He repeated that the Hungarians were terrified. Although he was surprised at such conduct by the Soviet troops, he did not have compassion for Hungarians. To the contrary, he derided their feebleness, saying that the owner of the house walked into his own home as if on needles, asking permission to enter his room. He concluded this entry: "To hell with them. They are very rich."[168]

El'kinson's musings indicate the rapidity with which discipline was collapsing in the Red Army's ranks and the hardening of the views toward the civilians in Hungary. For the first time in the diary, he mentioned rapes, which escalated into gang rapes in broad daylight, just as heavy battles erupted, and soldiers realized that they would have to fight their way through Hungary. El'kinson, like other Soviet soldiers, blamed Hungarians for this turn of events, failing to distinguish between civilians and the country's leadership. He had no sympathy for ordinary Hungarians, mocking their subjugation and justifying it because they were supposedly rich. By referencing the living standard of Hungarians, El'kinson revealed how his attitude toward "enemy" nations was influenced by the Stalinist demonization of the wealthy and well-off classes, such as kulaks, landowners, and the bourgeoisie. It also confirms that some Soviet troops resented some of their enemies' affluence.

The ferocity of the fighting intensified further, accompanied by the brutalization of the troops. On 26 October, after days of heavy fighting during which he lost several close comrades, El'kinson seemed depressed and afraid. He wrote:

It seems again that the war will last a long time. I am in a bad mood. But there is only one source of pleasure: you get drunk from wine ... It is such a pity to die on foreign soil. I am so sorry for the killed guys ... they went from the Caucasus to Hungary and died here. Such a pity. I want to go back home to my country. I want to live so much. Although I am a bit drunk now I understand what I am writing. We just need to move forward. Forward to Berlin. Forward to victory, closer to home.[169]

Successive diary entries continued to highlight the escalating viciousness of the war, accompanied by an ever-gloomier mood. For instance, on 9 November, he again reported the deaths of several close comrades, while he barely survived an explosion. In contrast to when the brutal fighting started, he now said that he could not even muster compassion for his friends.[170] Between 17 October 1944 and 3 January 1945, he made no references to civilians.[171] When he was transferred to a somewhat safer position further in the rear in early January, El'kinson reported that he lived well and that every night he had fun with women (*khodim po babam*) with the chief of reconnaissance.[172] The term *khodim po babam* has no equivalent in English, but it implies having sexual relations with women while characterizing them with the vulgar term *baby*.[173] We do not know who these women were. They could have been Red Army servicewomen, but more likely they were local women coerced into these supposed parties by desperation or outright threats of violence. Either way, it is clear that El'kinson believed that access to women offered a well-deserved respite from war and fighting.

It is worth considering how El'kinson's terse statement that he visited women every night with his commanding officer looked from the perspective of civilians caught up in the ravages of the war. Alaine Polcz was a twenty-one-year-old in January 1945. As the daughter of an important official in occupied Transylvania and a wife of a Hungarian deserter who previously served on the Eastern front, she escaped with her husband and mother-in-law to Hungary proper before the arrival of the Soviet and Romanian armies to Transylvania. The Soviet troops overtook them in the Vertes Mountains, some 70 km to the west of Budapest. Her husband was arrested and taken away by the Soviet forces.

The Vertes Mountains were an area of heavy fighting, and numerous Red Army units passed the house where she stayed. According to Polcz, many soldiers did not bother her and even behaved correctly. Nonetheless, numerous troops attacked her physically and sexually.[174] Polcz was raped so frequently and so violently that she was not sure how many times she was assaulted. On one occasion, she was gang raped by a group of eight to ten soldiers, one of whom almost broke her back.[175] For weeks, she was caught in the crossfire, while the Soviet troops repeatedly assaulted her. She was also isolated, as she was far away from her home and relatives, while the local inhabitants were fearful of taking in the wife of an arrested soldier and of sheltering a young woman, both of which could invite unwanted attention from the occupiers. Additionally, Polcz felt responsible for taking care of her aging mother-in-law, who was also raped. Her mother-in-law was bedridden and rapidly losing weight. To improve her health and alleviate her suffering, Polcz slept with a soldier for a cup of milk and with an officer for a mattress for her mother-in-law as she slept on the floor. The officer then had his orderly sleep with Polcz as well, before helping her carry away the mattress.[176] It should be mentioned that although Polcz wondered on one occasion if she would be killed during the gang rape, she did not die. She went on to live a fulfilled life, both professionally and personally. She had a very successful career as a child psychologist and a writer in Hungary. Her mother-in-law also seemed to have lived a long life after the war.[177]

It is extremely unlikely that El'kinson and Polcz's paths ever crossed, but her experiences were not unusual in Hungary in the winter of 1945. It can be assumed that the women El'kinson visited every night were, if not physically forced into attending these parties, then at least compelled by their desperate situation. Polcz's experience of being gang raped and then sleeping with other soldiers to get warm milk and a comfortable mattress for her relative was far from exceptional; they resemble the better-known story told by the anonymous author of *A Woman in Berlin: Eight Weeks in the Conquered City: A Diary*.[178] The situation was not too different in the West. As historian Atina Grossmann noted in her discussion of the interaction between the Americans and German women in the postwar period, given the unequal balance of power, it was often difficult to disentangle coercive, pragmatic, and consensual sex.[179]

Another illustrative episode of how heavy combat brutalized the troops leading to the proliferation of war crimes was shared by Lieutenant Romanov. During the storming of Vienna, at the end of the war, a German sniper shot the commander of an artillery regiment. The dead commander's gunners caught the sniper and shot him on the spot. Unsatisfied with their revenge, they seized a nearby column of German prisoners. The gunners announced that they would shoot the prisoners until they filled a nearby explosion crater with their bodies. When Romanov tried to stop the massacre, the gunners pointed the submachine gun at him and asked: "Comrade officer, do you really want to join the Germans in the pit?"[180] Romanov desisted, and the German soldiers were executed. The fighting was so savage that the Soviet soldiers threatened to murder their officer for trying to prevent the illegal execution of enemy soldiers.

In addition to ferocious fighting contributing to the hardening of attitudes against civilians and enemy soldiers, Hungary and then Austria were the first unambiguously wealthier enemy countries with a higher standard of living that the troops of the 2nd and 3rd Ukrainian Fronts encountered. Medic Aleksandra Aleksandrova (Petrova) grew up very poor in Dedovichi in Russia's Pskov Oblast. She recalled in an interview that it was almost impossible to survive in her village, saying "May God forbid people from living like that" (*tam ne dovedi Bog kak liudi zhivut*).[181] She said that she tried to find somebody in Hungary as destitute as she was in her childhood but that nobody was as impoverished.[182] Another soldier recalled his inability to understand what changing booths were on the beaches along Lake Balaton, asserting, "That is culture for you."[183] Signaler Anna Skorobogatova said that she entered a completely empty store in Hungary, without explaining how she got into it. There, she saw underclothes (*bel'e*) that she could not even dream of finding back home. She stole the goods, but then, she claimed, she confessed to her commander who made her return the stolen merchandise.[184] An officer wrote in his diary that houses in Hungary were tidy, beautiful, and large, emphasizing that most villages had electricity.[185] According to another source, Soviet soldiers were envious of mechanized agriculture in Austria.[186] Meanwhile, simple Austrian cottages appeared to Soviet soldiers to be like castles.[187] The troops also found Vienna, quite understandably, to be beautiful.[188] Others noted how clean the city was and the complete absence of garbage.[189]

Yet not all Soviet troops were completely impressed with Central Europe, noting the absence of heavy industry and skyscrapers, signs of modernity for the young men who came of age in Stalin's Soviet Union.[190] Mariia Kuz'minichina Rist, a signaler in the 66th Guards Rifle Division, found Vienna to be beautiful, but the citizens were very impoverished and on the verge of starvation. She recalled feeling sorry for the civilians. According to her, Soviet military personnel sometimes gave Austrians their bread.[191] Rist's recollections of hunger in Austria were true, as the daily calorie ratio for the urban Austrian population fell from 2,000 calories in 1944 to between 350 and 850 calories in the spring and summer of 1945.[192]

Despite some reservations, the higher living standard fueled anger at the local population. However, the effect of the higher living standard on Soviet conduct should not be exaggerated. After all, the Soviets saw in Sofia and Belgrade modern European cities, but it did not lead them to rampage on a similar scale. Envy became relevant when it was fused with hate generated by propaganda and intensive combat, as was the case with Pavel El'kinson. As Temkin, a soldier in the 78th Division, put it, envy and resentment justified looting as moral and even an act of social justice.[193] However, these factors did not cause violence.

6.5 The Soviet Troops' Views of Austrians

When the Red Army entered Austria in April 1945, the forces of the 2nd and 3rd Ukrainian Fronts finally fulfilled the long-held goal of catching up to and finishing off the wounded fascist beast in its lair, as propaganda had urged them to do since they first left the Soviet Union in the summer of 1944.[194] For years, the Soviet troops fought in the most brutal war in modern European history, including the genocidal occupation of the Soviet Union, which they either experienced or witnessed firsthand. There was scarcely a soldier in the 2nd and 3rd Ukrainian Fronts who did not personally suffer at the hands of the Germans by being wounded, having a close comrade killed, or having a relative or a friend murdered, starved, or taken to Germany into forced labor.

Vladimir Arkhipov, a signaler in the 3rd Ukrainian Front, sent to his family a letter on 19 March that illuminated the prevailing mood of Soviet soldiers on the eve of their entry into the Third Reich. After a long battle during which the Soviets stopped the last German offensive of the war at Lake Balaton, he wrote that he had been listening to music on Radio Moscow with his comrade Stepan. Arkhipov related that Stepan, before falling asleep, sadly looked into his eyes and wondered when they would finally destroy the so-called German filth so that they could go back home and listen to a live orchestra, without being interrupted by explosions. Two days earlier, Arkhipov reported, Stepan had received a letter from home, informing him that his father and two cousins had been murdered by the Germans, his wife taken to Germany for forced labor, and his younger brother beaten so badly that he was still unwell. Arkhipov felt his friend's pain. He asked his parents: "Can we really forgive the [German] scum for the villainy they inflicted?"[195] He answered his question: "No, we will not forgive them. We will get to them as well. Thousands [of soldiers] like Stepan will exact revenge. There will be a holiday on our street!"[196] Soviet troops understood their arrival into the Third Reich as their victory and the time to inflict their justice. This is what Arkhipov had in mind when he wrote that there would be a holiday on their street.

As Major Slutskii wrote, "justice" reigned in the Austrian province of Styria, where he was stationed, and every soldier felt he was the enforcer and guardian of this so-called system of justice.[197] Slutskii's sentiment that soldiers had a right to mete out their form of "justice" was not unique among the officer corps. For instance, Marshal Vasilevskii, the commander of the 3rd Belorussian Front, responded with the following when told that his soldiers were attacking civilians in East Prussia: "I don't give a fuck. It is now time for our soldiers to issue their own justice."[198] Obviously, the idea that soldiers had a right to vent fury against the Germans, Austrians, and their property was present among ordinary soldiers as well as the middle- and high-ranking commanders.

Suddenly, the high command changed the official line on revenge, as well as the very definition of the enemy. Once the Red Army reached Austria, Soviet leadership appealed to soldiers to treat Austrians not as Germans but as the fascists' first victims.[199] Many soldiers and officers viewed the changing line as an attempt to rob them of their hard-earned right to punish the hated Germans and to loot and rape. The always perceptive Slutskii called these soldiers the "left opposition" to the official line.[200] In his words, the troops did not believe agitators "a single iota" when they told them about the differences between Germans and Austrians.[201] For soldiers, "German was a German. And one had to give it to them."[202] Just what "giving it to Germans" meant was clear: subjecting women to sexual violence.[203]

Undoubtedly, the majority of troops rejected the differentiation between Austrians and Germans. One soldier referred to Austrians as "pure-blooded Aryan degenerates."[204] El'kinson stuck to more classical "fritzes."[205] Another soldier maintained that Austrians were the same as Germans.[206] Generally, the Soviets were cynical of Austrian claims that they were distinct from Germans or that they were loyal to the Red Army. Some soldiers would provocatively tell the Austrians "German, come here," just to hear them profess how they were Austrians and not Germans.[207] Evidently, Soviet soldiers enjoyed hearing frightened Austrians renounce their connection to Germany. The troops joked that it was easy for Austrians to put up Soviet red flags upon the Red Army's arrival. They simply removed the swastika from the Third Reich's flag. "Adaptable people," El'kinson concluded unapprovingly.[208]

Additionally, the profile of the troops partially changed toward the end of the war, as a large number of liberated forced laborers in Austria, Germany, and the so-called Protectorate of Bohemia and Moravia, partially liberated by the 2nd Ukrainian Front's right wing, were enlisted into ranks. Historian Filip Slaveski found that the influx of former forced laborers and prisoners of war into the Red Army added to the wave of violence at the end of the war in Germany proper.[209] The situation was similar in Austria. Although precise figures are hard to come by, at a minimum, the two fronts were each reinforced by tens of thousands of former prisoners of war and forced laborers in the winter and spring of 1945.[210] Soviet officials believed that recent recruits were even less disciplined and particularly prone to desert.[211] Some of these soldiers had been treated terribly by their Austrian overlords. Those who were freed from the prisoner-of-war camps were survivors of the Nazi genocide against Soviet prisoners of war. Consequently, these soldiers, more than others, had a personal account to settle with Germans and their allies.

6.6 Conclusion

As the 2nd and 3rd Ukrainian Fronts moved across numerous countries of the Balkans and Central Europe, they developed a series of stereotypes. These views were mostly independent of the official line; they were extremely widespread among the frontline troops and high-ranking officers alike. The Soviet soldiers' behavior reflected how they viewed a given country. Thus, the troops were dismissive of Romanians as culturally and economically inferior, considering them to be a nation of traitors, weak men, and petty merchants. In contrast, Soviet soldiers were sympathetic to Bulgarians and Yugoslavs because many welcomed them as liberators, while they also respected the Yugoslavs for their resistance to the common enemy. Although the Soviets viewed the two South Slavic countries positively, they also considered them to be junior partners at best indebted to the Red Army for their liberation. The troops knew very little about Hungary before entering the country, but Budapest's failure to abandon the Third Reich as Bucharest and Sofia had embittered the troops. Furthermore, the prolonged and brutal fighting that took place in the country contributed to the feeling of growing indifference to the suffering of civilians. The troops also blamed Hungarian civilians for the country's continued partnership with Germany. Finally, soldiers and officers of the 2nd and 3rd Ukrainian Fronts considered Austrians to be Germans, and they behaved there similarly to Soviet armies elsewhere on the territory of the Third Reich. When these stereotypes about each nation are considered, it becomes easier to understand why Soviet soldiers acted with more restraint in Bulgaria and Yugoslavia than in Romania, Hungary, and Austria.

7 Sexual Violence

Soviet soldier Nikolai Nikulin recalled in his memoirs that the main topics of discussion for soldiers were death, food, and sex.[1] Indeed, the troops of the 2nd and 3rd Ukrainian Fronts thought and talked about women and sex a lot. Historian Regina Mühlhäuser in her influential study of the Nazi soldiers and sex on the Eastern front argued that the boundaries between consensual and forced sex and between nonviolent and violent sex were fluid. She used the term "sexual encounters" to describe the range of sexual acts that occurred between German troops and women in occupied territories, which ranged from outright rapes to what she called nonviolent encounters. In her scheme, some nonviolent encounters were consensual, but they were largely asymmetrical and often developed due to fears, specific needs, and pragmatic choices.[2] Although the Soviet troops committed many acts of rape, as discussed in Chapter 2, they also engaged in sex that was in the gray area identified by Mühlhäuser.

The Soviet troops were equally interested in obtaining sex when the fighting was on Soviet soil or enemy territory. However, the intensity of coercion they applied to get sex varied considerably between individual soldiers. Furthermore, what soldiers were willing to do to women to get sex and what they could get away with fluctuated in different contexts. This chapter seeks to illuminate these contexts, as well as Soviet troops' mentality – assumptions about women and sex, attitudes toward foreign women, and their ideas about soldiering.

7.1 Attitudes toward Soviet Women

7.1.1 Attitudes toward Soviet Women in the Rear

The war radicalized Soviet troops' views of women and sex by encouraging them to be more violent to obtain sex. The definition of martial masculinity, first developed by historian of the American Empire Aaron Belkin but also utilized by the Russianist Erika Fraser, explains the Soviet troops' attitudes toward women and sex. Belkin defined martial masculinity as the "beliefs, practices and attributes that often have enabled individuals to claim a great deal of authority, perhaps more than any other form of masculinity, based on their relationships with military institutions and ideas."[3] In other words, the war encouraged sexual aggression of Soviet soldiers and officers based on their sacrifices and services, allowing them to pursue women sexually with fewer restraints than was the case in peacetime as civilians.

A widespread view held by the Soviet troops was that soldiering was masculine, while the home front belonged to the feminine sphere.[4] They viewed their role as vital, whereas they judged the role of the home front to be of secondary importance. Propaganda encouraged these sentiments by emphasizing that the troops fought for their women who were violated by the Germans and by linking liberation with the protection of women.[5]

However, many frontline troops continued being emotionally involved in their families' problems back home, which were considerable. The home front was devastated, most obviously by millions of deaths and widespread destruction of property. There was also a massive famine in the interior of the country, which, according to one estimate, took the lives of 1.5 million Soviet civilians, a figure that excluded the people who starved in besieged Leningrad.[6] The famine continued into the late stages of the war. As late as 1944, malnutrition was the leading cause of death of adult civilians.[7] There were 16.5 million refugees in the country, who had fled or were evacuated by the authorities to the east of the country.[8] Stalinist repressions continued during the war, targeting entire nationalities for deportation, most notably ethnic Germans, Crimean Tartars, and Chechens.[9] Although service in the military was undoubtedly more dangerous, civilians were also subjected to militarized labor, where long and grueling work hours were accompanied by the criminalization of shirking or switching jobs.[10]

Soviet soldiers and officers were keenly aware of their family's suffering in the rear. Some of them helped out by having their salaries paid to their family members.[11] How soldiers and officers felt when their families faced these grave difficulties was movingly illustrated by an orphaned 2nd Ukrainian Front Sergeant Ivan Kuz'mich Parshikov in letters from Hungary to his younger sisters in southern Russia in the fall of 1944. Their father had been killed during the war, and their mother appears to have died before it. One of his sisters was being sent to Grozny, probably as part of a group of colonists from Russia sent there to replace the deported Chechens. His youngest sister was going to live in an orphanage, and the third sister would be employed in the same orphanage. Parshikov wrote:

> Hello my dear little sister Nadia! … I received your letter and the letter made me very sad. I found out from that letter that you will be separating … That letter made me extremely upset that my heart started beating and hurting terribly. Life is not dear to me nothing is dear to me now my friends now went to a concert but here I am sitting in tears writing this letter to you. Nadia I miss you so much if I could only spend with you one day and see how you are living and see how you are doing now. I am even angrier at Germans at Hitler for doing this. If it wasn't for the war: I would be at home, father would be alive and none of this would be happening … Behave well, don't be like many other girls, be modest, be reserved, and be just. You cannot do anything if somebody hurts you now, keep quiet, and after the war, I will come back and talk to them in a different way … Nadia, be careful, don't trust people because only few of them wish you well and most will wish you ill … That's it for now … your brother IK Parshikov.[12]

Parshikov was crushed by the loss of his father during the war and the breakup of his remaining family. As the elder brother, he felt responsible for the well-being of his younger sisters, but being in the army, he was aware of his powerlessness to help them. It is also noteworthy that he outwardly blamed the Nazis for creating this situation, mimicking Soviet hate propaganda, and not the Soviet authorities who had ethnically cleansed the Chechens and separated his family to populate the territories they had emptied of its original residents. His preoccupation with Nadia's sexual purity is also notable. Parshikov's advice to her not to be like "other girls" was likely an appeal for her to avoid the company of men and to remain modest. He could not have failed to see the widespread sexual violence in Hungary perpetrated by the Red Army, which likely explains his advice that she should suffer in silence until he returns to settle the score and protect her.[13] Unfortunately, Parshikov was killed not long after sending this letter.

As historian Matthew Lenoe argued, as early as 1941 and 1942, soldiers' fears that their romantic partners may betray them were among the most corrosive emotions they felt.[14] As the war dragged on, these feelings only hardened. The troops held that the people back home had an easy life or were ungrateful, overlooking the extreme hardships and sacrifices made by civilians. Semen Mostov, head of a regimental political department, shared these concerns in his diary after visiting Moscow. According to him, the troops were being forgotten by the civilians, which was why they had to win the war as soon as possible. In Mostov's view, since the Red Army had liberated Soviet territories, the war had become more distant for civilians, and they had lost a sense of its difficulty. Furthermore, he believed that corruption had become widespread, and all women, as he put it, "had become obviously licentious [*razlozhilis'*]."[15] This diary entry revealed Mostov's sense of alienation from the home front and his condemnation of it. The entry also revealed his anxieties about the supposed sexual laxity of Soviet women. The latter sentiment was also shared by Parshikov, despite the vast differences in their ranks.

At the same time, as the political departments responsible for the soldiers' morale understood well, the troops' alienation from the home front was undermining the army's morale. Soldiers needed support from the rear to sustain their fighting spirit. The soldiers' relationships with their girlfriends and wives were a vital part of their sense of connection to the home front, a theme that Soviet propaganda rigorously dwelled on. Konstantin Simonov, a poet and writer, was one of the main Soviet voices of the era.[16] He was central in cementing the image of Soviet women as objects in the war, with little agency of their own, in the service of building morale among the troops. His 1942 poem "Kill Him!," published in *Pravda*, was a classic of Soviet popular culture during the war.[17] The poem enumerated all the reasons why the Soviet soldier must kill a German. Simonov stated that the Soviet soldiers must kill Germans for the Russian national identity, for the house where they were born, for their mother, father, and the elderly teacher, and for everything dear to them. Among these reasons, why the Soviet soldier should kill the enemy is a stanza that says that killing a German is the only way to prevent him from raping the Russian soldier's wife.[18] The women in this poem are a source of anxiety for soldiers, as people that the enemy may violate, as well as an inspiration for the soldier to fight.

Simonov also wrote the poem "Wait for Me." The poem, written from a soldier's perspective, appeals to his wife to wait for him to come back home alive, regardless of how difficult and long the wait became, to wait for him longer than even the soldier's mother. It ends with lines: "You saved me, how I survived only the two of us will know, you simply knew how to wait, like nobody else."[19] "Wait for Me," published in *Pravda* in early 1942 and then reprinted in newspapers throughout the country, was very popular among the troops. Soldiers would cut the poem out of military newspapers and send it home, while the newspapers would publish responses with titles such as "I am Waiting for You" (*Zhdu tebia*).[20] "Wait for Me" and the ensuing propaganda reinforced the image of an ideal woman as almost blindly devoted to her husband. In this poem, women matter only as objects in a soldier's fantasy, but there is no thought as to how they survived the war in the rear or under German occupation or the necessary compromises they may have had to make to survive.

In the poem "To the Woman from the City of Vichuga," written in 1943 upon the request of officers of an unidentified regiment, Simonov reveals how soldiers felt when one of their comrades was left for another man by his wife. In the poem, a woman writes coldly to her husband, a lieutenant who has been killed before the letter reached him, that she found a new man and that she no longer needed him or his salary. The lieutenant's fellow officers opened their dead comrade's letters and wrote back to her shaming her for not being able to love him, for not finding the right words to leave him gently, for causing her former husband's death (as per the superstition that the only soldiers who survive are those for whom a woman waits back home), and for the fact that other soldiers now await the letters from home with trepidation. The officers also said that it was not a soldier's fault that there was no leave in the Soviet army and that they all went into battle and died on her behalf, asking her rhetorically, how did she become so heartless. The poem ended with lines: "Accept our contempt but not forgiveness, Disrespecting you, The deceased's regimental comrades."[21] Wives in "To the Woman from the City of Vichuga" are depicted as potentially treacherous and responsible for their husband's lives.

As scholar Sergei Strashnov noted, the poem was an invitation to society to condemn women who left their husbands during the war.[22] However, did these women really love their husbands in the first place? How long were they together before they were separated by mobilization? Did the husbands love their wives? Did they live happily before the war? Were their husbands abusive? How did women survive on the home front or under occupation? Did they or their children starve? Was the new man, if there was one, able to take care of them and keep them alive? All of these questions were relevant when women made decisions to end their relationships during the war, but Simonov and most soldiers never considered them.

The frontline troops' perspective was easy to understand. They were doing the hard part, fighting the enemy, to defend their country and women, and the least their women could do was remain loyal. Yet, as historian Catherine Merridale noted, male soldiers' marriages and relationships with their girlfriends and wives in the interior came under increasing strain as the war dragged on, resulting in many divorces, which in turn increased the male troops' antagonism toward all women.[23]

The soldiers left by their wives felt devastated. This was dramatically illustrated by the example of Major Khudiakin. Days after the German capitulation, he received a cold letter from his wife, Alevtina, living in the city of Chita during the war. She wrote to him that as a patriot, she waited for the end of the war to deliver him the bad news. Alevtina told Khudiakin that she never loved him, that she found a new husband who held a higher rank, was wounded three times, and had numerous medals. She also said that the new husband was significantly taller than Khudiakin, and she alluded to the fact that he had a bigger penis. She admitted to cheating on him before the war started. Alevtina added that Khudiakin's daughter now refers to her stepfather as father. She ended the letter with a statement that he, Khudiakin, no longer existed for her and their daughter and that he should never appear in their lives again or even write to them. She attached a photo of herself with her new husband, supposedly to show Khudiakin how they were a good fit.[24] On 26 May 1945, Khudiakin, an officer in the political department of a frontline unit since 1942, committed suicide. His boss, Colonel Frolov, petitioned his superiors to permit him to bury Khudiakin as a hero, and not as a coward who committed suicide. He called Alevtina "scum" (*svoloch'*) and asked, "How can such a rear whore-patriot even live on this planet" (*i kak tol'ko takuiu tylovuiu bliadopatriotku zemlia nosit*)![25] It is unknown whether his petition was approved, but I have never seen officers use such language in official documents, indicating Frolov's extreme anger at Alevtina and his sympathy for Khudiakin. His invective also revealed a hatred of a broader category of women, those who were supposedly disloyal to their husbands.

7.1.2 Attitudes toward Servicewomen

If Soviet soldiers and officers saw women during the war, it was mostly their comrades in the Red Army. The Red Army's relationship with its female troops was riddled with profound contradictions. The Soviet Union was officially committed to the equality of women.[26] Throughout the 1930s, official discourse encouraged women to participate in martial activities in anticipation of war with the capitalist countries, despite the Soviet regime's turn to more conservative values. A large number of women were called up only in 1942, after the disastrous first year of the war.[27] Eventually, hundreds of thousands of Soviet women volunteered for the front, believing that their sense of "womanhood" was compatible with their desire for "soldierhood."[28] Ultimately, over 900,000 women served in the Red Army throughout the war, out of a total of 34 million Soviet citizens who at one time or another served in the military from 1941 to 1945.[29] As historians Roger Markwick and Euridice Cardona noted, mass participation by women in warfare on such a scale was historically unique.[30] A combination of ideology and the desperate need for human resources resulted in a large influx of women into the Red Army.

Although women served in large numbers, they faced a hostile environment among their male comrades and officers, many of whom found it difficult to accept women as soldiers or their superiors. At best, women had to overcome the widespread attitudes among officers who wanted to "protect" them from the frontline service. The author Svetlana Alexievich interviewed Second Lieutenant Stanislava Petrovna Volkova. She had a university education and had finished a specialized officer course for sappers. When Volkova arrived at the front, however, she was assigned to clerical duties at the headquarters, despite her training and skills. Outraged, Volkova and another female officer in a similar situation went to speak to Malinovskii, the army group commander. Eventually, after a lot of insistence and argument with officers at the headquarters, Volkova was sent to the front as a commander of a sapper platoon. The officers who let her go, however, warned her that she would likely have only two months to live, the lifespan of an average sapper platoon commander.[31] Other women combatants had similar experiences of having to overcome the men's desire to protect them from violence before they would be allowed to go to frontline positions.[32]

Even worse than the paternalistic desire to protect women from the horrors of war was the fact that many officers sexually pursued women in the ranks. In many situations, Red Army servicewomen were able to reject the officers' approaches, although sometimes they suffered for their principled stance. Lidiia Glushcenko, from Chelyabinsk province, was twenty-two or twenty-three years old in 1944. She was a car and truck driver when she rejected the advances of her Captain in the rear. Consequently, she was sent to a frontline unit.[33] A regimental commander tried to turn Seargant Mariia Bondarenko (Kataeva), a sniper, into his lover. According to Bondarenko (Kataeva), she told him that she did not volunteer for the front for romance, adding, "You are over fifty, and I am eighteen."[34] Her career was not impacted by the rejection of his advances. Nina Demesheva (Skvortsova), a nurse and later a dancer in the 3rd Guard Army's Dance and Song Ensemble, recalled that when she was a nurse, the Chief of Medical Service offered her to become his lover and to become his orderly in the rear.[35] She refused, but her career developed without apparent problems.

It should be noted that the so-called Field Mobile Wives (*Polevaia pokhodnaia zhena* or PPZh), as female lovers of officers were derisively known, were viewed negatively by society. Tat'iana Pugacheva (Chertova) recalled that she and other women were afraid to admit that they had served in the military during the war because of the fear of being perceived as having had many sexual partners. She said women even hid their medals. According to her, the societal attitude only changed in the

1970s.[36] Bondarenko (Kataeva) the young sniper, said that in her village in Kirov Oblast in Russia after the war, the people told her husband not to marry her because she was in the army. Two days after the wedding, her husband showed the villagers the bloodied bedsheets, proving that he had married a virgin.[37] Her husband's actions indicate how some Red Army personnel were deeply steeped in the conservative peasant culture. These negative views of women in service in general and PPZh in particular may help explain some of these veterans' narratives that stress their willingness and ability to reject officers' advances. However, many such testimonies exist, indicating that Red Army servicewomen often were in a position to reject officers' approaches, arguably, in part at least because their own experience of military service emboldened them to stand up for themselves.

Soviet soldiers' identity was linked to their sexual prowess, and many believed that they were entitled to intercourse.[38] According to one scholar, male soldiers did not view the Red Army women primarily as comrades, but as sex objects in uniforms.[39] Although there were officers who pursued women but were capable of accepting a rejection, there were also those who harassed and assaulted women. There were also serial rapists of servicewomen in the ranks. Major Semen Geft, head of an armored service of a guard's mechanized division, utilized his authority to coerce female soldiers into sex when they delivered food to him. Geft threatened the women that he would dispatch them to penal units if they refused him or if they told other officers. Geft, a serial abuser, was eventually sentenced to a ten-year prison sentence, which he avoided by serving a three-month sentence in a penal battalion, where he earned the nickname "fucker major" (*ebar' maior*).[40] Guards Colonel Polovnikov, who was discussed in Chapter 5, was a prolific rapist of servicewomen in the 233rd Division. According to a report by the Division's Political Department, he had raped at least six women, but the real number was probably much higher.[41]

A Medical Assistant Sofiia, who wanted to remain anonymous and thus concealed her surname and the unit where she served, illuminated well the position of having to navigate the threat of rape, sexual harassment, and genuine feelings and desire. She admitted to Svetlana Alexievich, who interviewed her, that she was a field campaign wife to two officers. Sofiia explained that it was better to find a protector than to be afraid of all the soldiers, conceding that regular harassment and the threat of rape on the frontline were a dangerous reality. She recalled that wounded soldiers would depend on her on the battlefield as the nurse, but that after the battle, they would sexually assault her. She also said that she entered relationships with senior officers because she wanted to survive the war, saying that many other women had similar arrangements but were ashamed to admit them after the war. She was the sole woman in the battalion. She did not love the first battalion commander but was genuinely in love with the second commander. She gave birth to a daughter by him. After the war, he returned to his legal wife, never contacting Sofiia or their daughter again.[42] Sofiia's story illuminates how the Red Army could be a predatory environment for many women. It is also notable that Sofiia, like some civilians in Europe, was also forced to choose to be with one man who held a rank so that he could protect her from the rank and file.[43] This indicates that there were continuities in how some Red Army officers treated foreign and Soviet women, and how women everywhere, including servicewomen, experienced interactions with male Soviet officers.

Red Army men pursued servicewomen with such aggression that some women claimed that friendships between sexes were impossible to establish. Vera Lebedova, a political officer, told a military correspondent that she sometimes just wanted to talk with somebody and laugh together with them. At the beginning of the war, she tried doing so, but she quickly stopped because men would interpret such behavior as an invitation to make sexual advances.[44] For Lebedeva, even ordinary friendships with men, possible before the war, were no longer viable.

Even men who were not directly violent could contribute to the hostile atmosphere toward women in the military that Lebedeva referred to. Boris Komskii, born in 1924 in Kyiv, fought at Kursk. After being wounded and hospitalized, he was appointed Komsomol organizer in units in the rear where he spent most of the war. As his diary revealed, he pursued servicewomen persistently but also held them in contempt when they expressed sexual interest in him. He was a romantic who wrote poetry but was also a womanizer. He had a girlfriend back home called Tamara. He also fell in love and had a lengthy relationship with another girl in the army Rimma (whom he described as a slut because she agreed to sleep with him), and he pursued servicewomen Katya, Rimma's best friend. With regard to Katya, Komskii was convinced that she was "a pure soul" and "one in a thousand."[45] He vented his contempt for frontline women to Katya, which made her cry. This did not prevent him from trying to kiss her, but Katya rejected his advances, which is why he viewed her as a pure soul.[46] Komskii did not directly apply force to obtain sex from women, according to his diary. His relationship with Rimma seems to have been consensual and based on mutual desire. However, his attitudes to and treatment of women, like that of many of his comrades, made it very difficult for Red Army women to experience a sense of camaraderie with male soldiers and to receive recognition for their professionalism.

Although many soldiers were interested in pursuing romantic relations with women, apart from troops in the rear, only higher-ranking officers tended to be able to find mistresses in the military. There were simply too many men and too few women. More critically, only officers held the power to pressure and reward servicewomen for sexual liaisons. As a woman sniper in an all-women squadron told her male commander during the Battle of Stalingrad: "We are here in the army to fight, but they [officers] view us as if we were ladies or girls! We are not girls! All of us have higher or incomplete higher education. But they approach us with dubious proposals. It is impossible to get rid of them..."[47] When recovering from a wound in a hospital near Kyiv, Boris Baklanov, a SMERSH officer, pursued a doctor called Rosa. He pressured her relentlessly to give in to his sexual advances.[48] She refused to have anything to do with him in the hospital, her workplace, presumably because it would tarnish her professional reputation. He utilized his connections in SMERSH to facilitate the relationship with Rosa; he obtained information about her through the security agency and procured a room in Kyiv for their rendezvous.[49] Based on his account of their affair, thereafter they had a mutually fulfilling sexual and emotional relationship.

Officers, soldiers, and even some female combatants in many instances tended to despise the so-called PPZh.[50] One illuminating and popular wartime *chastushka* (ditty) proclaimed: "Now everybody is gentle with you, You have success everywhere, But I with my soldierly soul, Despise you, PPZh."[51] Another, even cruder *chastushka*, proclaimed: "Our Vaniushka (endearing nickname for Ivan) for the war received one medal, but Tatyana for her cunt got two medals and a Star!"[52] Contempt for women who became officers' lovers became particularly noxious if they received the highly coveted medals and awards from the leadership based on faulty reports written by their commanders and lovers, who were sometimes the same man.

Although some women entered into relations with officers seemingly voluntarily, many were compelled. For instance, general forced servicewomen to attend parties with male officers, punishing them if they refused.[53] A young male soldier wrote in a letter: "In the army, they regard women like gramophone records, you play it and play it and then throw it away."[54] Another soldier essentially conceded that officers forced Red Army servicewomen into sex. He said that two women in his unit were PPZh, "The command pulled them into dugouts, one cannot refuse commanders' pretensions."[55] One soldier recalled that all women arriving at the unit had to report to the regimental commander, his deputy, and the chief of staff, after which the trio decided who would bed the newly arrived servicewomen. Historian Oleg Budnitskii described this situation as an informal harem.[56] Veteran I. S. Posylaev recalled that the majority of women on the front became officers' lovers, explaining this phenomenon by the following: "How could it be otherwise? If a woman would be alone – there would be no end to the harassment."[57] Another soldier noted that women in his unit were mostly the so-called PPZh. He claimed that they received many medals for "battle results" (*boevye zaslugi*) but that the soldiers called them medals for "sexual efforts" (*polovye potugi*).[58] Sexual coercion in the Red Army was widespread, but so were the prevailing attitudes that justified it.

However, despite the fact that it was obvious to many that the PPZh were frequently forced into relationships with officers, it is rare to find the troops, male or female, who sympathized with them. Even Major Slutskii, a well-educated member of the intelligentsia, claimed that PPZh were an embarrassment for the Red Army in Europe.[59] A front-line medic wrote in her diary that she sang a derisive song with other wounded female soldiers about "PPZh scum" while recovering in a hospital.[60] The SMERSH Officer Baklanov considered Soviet nurses and doctors who previously had sexual relations with men as undesirable partners because they were "pretty well-soiled."[61] Lieutenant Vladimir Kagarlitskii, commander of an Air Defense Battery Squadron, unapprovingly wrote that one of his comrades had turned An'ka, a woman he knew from the training in the rear, into his PPZh. He described their relationship as her "downfall," indicating that he viewed her role in the relationship as her defeat.[62] He also noted that many PPZh were proud of their status, saying that when he asked two military women where they served, they responded that PPZh was their unit.[63] In many cases, soldiers were suspicious of all women in the Red Army, viewing them only as actual or potential officers' lovers. Likewise, the troops who condemned PPZh, such as Slutskii, did not condemn officers who initiated or coerced women into sexual relationships. In the troops' mentality, it was normal for officers to want to have sexual partners, but women in these relationships were to be judged harshly.

Tati'iana Repina's (Atabek) wartime experience, which she recorded in her diary, illustrates how women had agency and made a significant military contribution but were also subjected to disrespect, harassment, and violence from their comrades and superiors. Repina was born in Moscow in 1923 to a family of middle-class professionals. After several attempts to enlist, she was sent by the army to study at Kyiv Military Medical School (*uchilishche*) in Sverdlovsk in 1942, after which she was sent to the front as a medical assistant. She received two medals for bravery and heroism in battles with the enemy and was promoted to the rank of lieutenant. She served in the 154th Rifle Division, first in Medical

Battalion and then in the 212th Independent Sapper Battalion. She was seriously wounded toward the end of the war in East Prussia and was relocated to a hospital in Kaunas.[64]

Repina was devoted to her prewar boyfriend Alesha, who served in another unit in the army. On 1 January 1944, she wrote in the diary: "Oh, I want to do my job so well. I would remove my own skin to get good results ... even if I have to hear a thousand ridicules and rough jokes that make my heart ache and make life bitter."[65] She added that nobody knew that in her pocket she carried the letter from her "one and only, and it is very unlikely that a handsome suitor will confuse my soul with his compliments."[66] By a "thousand ridicules" and "rough jokes," she was referring to unwanted advances and vulgar comments, to judge by the context.

Repina was pursued by numerous men, including the battalion commander and the guards divisional engineer who sang her songs in an attempt to seduce her. Also, a man named Dunin, whose rank she did not state but must have been high, had numerous officers try to organize a mock wedding for him and Repina, with a proper banquet that she ran away from. There were at least two more unidentified suitors that she wrote about. It seems that most of these men accepted when she rejected their advances, although some were more stubborn in pursuing her than others.[67] On 20 January 1945, however, she was either sexually assaulted or raped by the Chief of Staff Major Satarov.[68] Her account, understandably, is not very specific. She said that the incident happened at night and seemed to her to be "an insane dream."[69] She did not scream because other people slept in the same room. She confided in the diary that she never felt so insulted or wronged in her life. She ran outside and cried inconsolably.

Her closest friend, with whom she seemed to have had a profound emotional and intellectual connection, was a man in his late thirties or early forties. She referred to him with formal Lev Nikolaevich. He appears to have been a political officer. Others in their collective spread rumors about them, but in the diary she maintained that their relationship was platonic.[70] After the war, however, she claimed that until a female soldier chose a man at the front, she would never be left alone and that Lev Nikolaevich was her shield.[71] It is possible that Lev Nikolaevich became her lover, but she did not admit it in the diary or she removed it from the published version. It should be mentioned that after the war, Repina had a successful personal and professional life, raising three daughters and pursuing a brilliant career in Soviet academia as a psychologist.[72]

Many women served in dangerous positions and contributed to the war effort.[73] As scholar Anna Krylova put it, female combatants managed to synthesize their identities of being a soldier and a woman.[74] In the words of Alexander Hill, one of the foremost military historians of the Red Army, the Soviets gained significantly from the mobilization of substantial numbers of women.[75] However, it was a struggle for women to have their contribution, professionalism, and skills recognized in the Red Army. If the soldiers and officers subjected their comrades risking their lives alongside them to dehumanizing objectification, harassment, and even sexual violence, then they were always likely to treat foreign women with even more aggression.

7.1.3 Attitudes toward Women in Occupied Territories

Historian Regina Kazyulina argued that Soviet propaganda in the occupied territories created three tropes of women. First were the ideal women, those who selflessly resisted Germans, usually to their death. Then, there were those merely tainted with the occupation who could be forgiven if they joined the armed fight against the Nazis. However, the third category was irredeemable – those who survived the occupation by betraying their homeland and husbands in the Red Army by actively collaborating with the Germans and having sex with them in exchange for luxury goods.[76] Although the Soviet regime vilified women who had sexual relations with Germans, it did not prosecute them unless they committed other crimes.[77] The Soviet state and society viewed any sexual encounters between women and German soldiers with suspicion and hostility. Even women who were forced by the Germans to work in brothels, aptly described as sexual slaves by historian Maris Rowe-McCulloch, could not discuss their experiences after the war for fear of societal and even legal censure (Figure 7.1).[78]

Thus, the official propaganda contributed to the Soviet troops, who were already hostile to women, to view with particular venom the women they accused of having sexual relations with Germans. The troops did not care about the circumstances that led to women's relations with occupying soldiers. A popular wartime ditty, sung to the tune of the popular song "Katiusha," proclaimed:

> Apple and pear trees bloomed,
> River mists appeared above the river,
> In the green garden,
> Katiusha was kissed by the elderly sergeant-major
> Katiusha forgot the past,
> She burnt Vania's letters in the oven,
> In the neighboring kitchen, she found an old cook,
> The cook brought her every day, crusts of bread, lard, and sausage,
> In exchange, Katiusha gave herself up to him.[79]

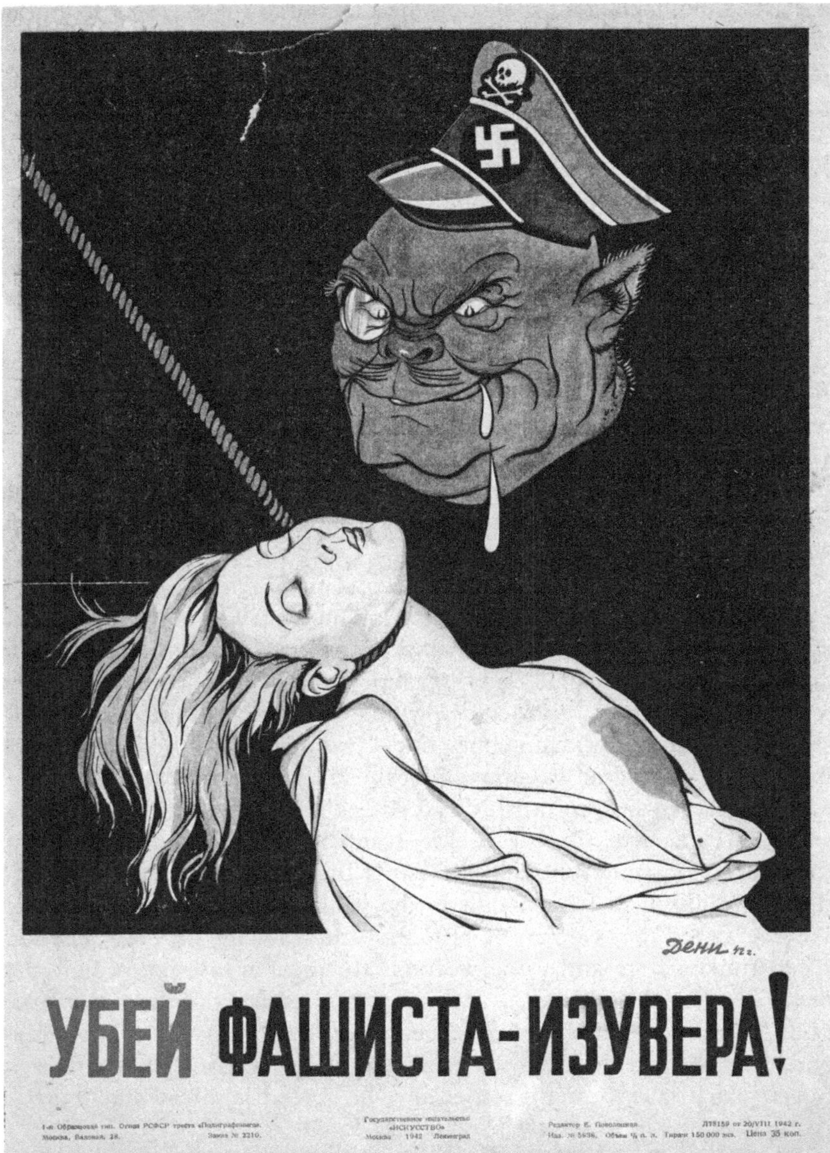

Figure 7.1 Kill the fascist fanatic. Source: Fine Art Images/Heritage Images via Getty Images.

It is notable that in the original, the hero of the song, Katiusha, treasured the soldier's letters and protected their love, as long as he protected their homeland. Clearly, this *chastushka* revealed the soldiers' fears about their wives and girlfriends' faithfulness under the occupation.

Pavel Luknitskii, a journalist on the Leningrad Front, recorded in his diary after visiting the liberated town of Lug in Northwest Russia that many women had worked for Germans and had clearly cohabitated with them. According to him, these women were easy to recognize: They had German clothes and shoes, and some were pregnant, while others had already given birth. He concluded that "Everybody expresses sharp contempt for them. The societal condemnation of their amorality and anti-patriotism is just and necessary."[80] The Central Committee of the CPSU sent agitators to the liberated territories in late 1943. Agitators reported back to Moscow that the civilians confronted them with questions such as why Red Army service personnel despised women who stayed in occupied territories and whether the Soviets shot all women in Kyiv who had cohabitated with Germans.[81] The Red Army did not have a policy of executing Kyivites who had sexual relations with Germans. However, the fact that this rumor was widespread, as well as the fact that the Red Army's contempt for women from occupied territories was well known, is indicative of the hostile attitude of Soviet troops toward women from occupied territories.

The condemnation of women from occupied territories, especially those who were accused of having relations with Germans, could easily turn into a murderous rage when fused with alcohol. According to an order issued by Tolbukhin, a group of 3rd Ukrainian Front officers heading to the front, murdered a woman in the Odesa region because she was wearing German rubber boots.[82] Apparently, the fact that she had German footwear was enough for the killers to conclude that she was a collaborator who presumably had sexual relations with the occupiers. In another instance, Captain Aleksei Ivanovich Stepanov, commander of the 3rd Ukrainian Front's 38th Guards Independent Sapper battalion, declared himself to be a doctor in the village of Retikhino in Ukraine. He demanded that women be brought to him for medical examination. In a drunken state and using weapons to threaten his victim, he raped citizen A. D. Panteshenko.[83] Murderers and rapists did not need much of an excuse to accuse women of betraying the country by collaborating and sleeping with the enemy. Particularly vulnerable in this regard were Soviet expatriate women – especially the forced laborers that the Red Army liberated in its westward march.[84]

Some Red Army soldiers and officers viewed all Soviet women as objects that they had to fight for, to protect them and liberate them from the enemy. The women conceived in the imagination of the troops were not fully human: They did not have needs, preferences, ambitions, or interests. The troops viewed women who stepped beyond the traditional roles by seeking new partners in the rear, joining the military, or sleeping with the enemy with hostility. Here, the male troops' attitudes and behavior mirrored what happened in the 1930s when largely male peasant migrant workers in the growing cities pushed back against the entry of women into the industrial workplace.[85] It did not matter much to Soviet troops if the extreme circumstances of war forced women into deviating from their traditional roles. Arguably, the Red Army personnel should have treated their female comrades most correctly since they fought shoulder to shoulder together. However, Red Army servicewomen most openly violated gender roles by joining the fight against the Nazis. This is one reason why the Soviet servicewomen faced considerable hostility from their male comrades and superiors. These reactionary attitudes by the Soviet troops toward sex and women in their lives were a part of the ideological mix that drove widespread sexual violence in Europe, but they were just part of the story.

7.2 In Europe: "Spoils of War"

When the 2nd and 3rd Ukrainian Fronts crossed the international border and entered Romania, several factors came together that made it more likely for the troops to extract sex through violence. The Red Army's trophy teams, tasked with systematic looting of enemy territories, focused on material goods. As seen in Chapter 3, the trophy teams seized goods such as gold, watches, silver, foodstuffs, livestock, industrial machinery, and art. As historian Brandon Schechter argued, trophies had an aura around them: They were things that had belonged to people now dead or in captivity and, for Soviet soldiers, the things came from an alien world.[86]

Some Soviet soldiers and officers held the idea that women from conquered countries were also legitimate spoils of war. Major Boris Slutskii recorded how he and other Soviet troops reacted to encountering Constanța, the first major European city, after more than three years of brutal combat and deprivation on the Eastern front:

> Suddenly, almost colliding with the [Black] Sea, Constanta appeared in front of us. It almost corresponded to our regular dream of happiness and "after-war." Restaurants. Showers. Beds with clean bed linen. Stores with reptilian merchants. And women, elegant urban women – the girls of Europe – the first tribute that we took from the defeated [enemy].[87]

Slutskii may not have been a typical Red Army soldier – he started the war as an ordinary soldier and ended it with the rank of a major, and he was a poet with legal training and a representative of Soviet intelligentsia more at home in a literary salon in Moscow than on the frontline. However, his determination to extract tribute from the enemy and his adherence to the atavistic view of women as legitimate spoils of war made him a typical Red Army serviceman as any of the peasant soldiers.

Slutskii, with the rank of major, had power as well as access to the best housing and food in Romania. However, the rank and file could not offer protection to Romanian women from other troops, nor could they consistently provide them with food or other life necessities. Instead, ordinary soldiers only had brute force to obtain the bodies of women, which they viewed as legitimate war booty.

In addition to some troops believing that they were entitled to a tribute, there was an ironclad conviction among soldiers and officers that enemy nations were the aggressors and that nothing Soviet soldiers did could compare to their suffering or the plight of Soviet civilians under the Axis. This notion could be used to justify the most outrageous behavior. The two Soviet attitudes, that the winner was entitled to the spoils of victory and that the enemy nations were the aggressors who deserved unjust treatment, were captured by Sergeant Pavel El'kinson, a scout in the 2nd Ukrainian Front.

El'kinson wrote in his diary on 5 September 1944 in a Romanian village that women deliberately dressed badly and painted over their faces, adding that they were afraid of Soviet troops.[88] On 15 September, he recorded: "When you enter their [Romanian] home, they start crying like you are getting ready to butcher them. In general, they are disgusting people…"[89] The following day, he noted rumors circulated among Soviet troops that the Romanian press was reporting the Red Army was pillaging, adding, "They are such scum [*gadye*]. What would they do if we behaved towards them like they behaved towards us?"[90] Obviously, El'kinson had all the evidence to conclude that Romanian civilians were terrified of Soviet soldiers. However, he did not raise any objections to the Soviet soldiers' conduct, which caused Romanians to fear the Red Army. To the contrary, he seemed upset that Romanian women tried to make themselves less attractive, that Romanians screamed out of fear in their own homes, or that Romanian newspapers reported the Soviet abuses. What bothered El'kinson was when Romanians offered resistance – even passive resistance – to the Soviet troops. Condemning the Romanian reactions to Soviet abuses, without condemning the abuses, implicitly justified the troops' behavior.

It did not matter how heinous the crime was; it could always be justified by the argument that the Germans had done worse. Alice de Barcza writing under the pseudonym Alexandra Orme was a Polish woman living in Hungary who could communicate with Soviet soldiers in a mixture of Polish, Ukrainian, and Russian languages. Along with her Hungarian aristocratic husband, she was subjected to lengthy interrogations in the winter of 1945. During one of those interrogations, they were placed in a hut with a ten-year-old Hungarian child who had been raped by a drunk Soviet officer. Waska, her guard who was on friendly terms with de Barcza and her husband, justified this heinous crime with the following: "with us, in the Ukraine, the Germans raped young girls and then shot them, that's what they did. And our fools saw them and learned what to do, but they never shoot them, not even when they're drunk. The German raped, then out with his revolver, and that was the girl finished. That, you see, is the difference."[91]

Thus, the sympathetic Soviet soldier could not simply condemn the rape of a child, which he understood was reprehensible. Instead, he had to contextualize it, justify it, and minimize it by saying that Germans were the first to rape children as if that made this atrocity any more tolerable.

The Soviet troops had positive views of Yugoslavia. However, these attitudes that liberators were entitled to sex were ingrained in the troops' ethos and invariably shaped their interactions with local women, whom they harassed and pursued brazenly, though often without resorting to outright violence. Mitra Mitrović, a high-ranking official in the Yugoslav Partisans and Milovan Đilas' wife, proclaimed: "A fat tank crew member approaches me and tells me, 'So, darkie [she had a dark complexion], will you come with me or what?'"[92] Even high ranking Yugoslav Communist women were pursued by Soviet soldiers. Women were not safe from soldiers' approaches and harassment even in their own homes.[93] Soviet soldiers and officers solicited prostitutes and went on crime sprees together.[94]

In friendly countries such as Yugoslavia, where the Soviet troops could not plausibly claim that the local population was the aggressors, some Red Army personnel justified their demands for tribute on the grounds that they had liberated them from the Germans. On 25 October, a Soviet officer entered a Partisan encampment in Belgrade seeking Yugoslav women. When asked what he wanted, he said that the Soviets sacrificed during the liberation of the Yugoslav capital and that they had the right to do as they pleased.[95] On that same day, in a different part of the city, three Soviet officers tried to rape a Partisan woman, with one of them shouting, "bitch, you will sleep with me."[96] Subsequently, they seized three young civilian women from their mothers, explaining: "We fought for Belgrade."[97] These actions and quotes by rapists directly reveal that some Red Army soldiers and officers believed that they were entitled to sex, and they were willing to commit violence to exercise the perceived privilege.

7.2.1 *Permissive Attitude toward Rape*

Closely linked with the idea that women were legitimate war booty was the permissive attitude to rape among the Soviet leaders, as well as officers responsible for enforcing discipline. The leader's role is vital in setting the tone in an authoritarian state such as the Soviet Union, and Stalin led the way in being dismissive of sexual violence. It is hardly surprising that a murderous tyrant did not care about crimes against foreign women. It is still noteworthy that Stalin repeatedly dismissed sexual violence committed by his troops as understandable and inconsequential for the victims. Illustrative of the Soviet leader's attitudes was his discussion of rapes with the delegation from Czechoslovakia in March 1945. He explained the rapes to the Czechoslovaks by arguing that every Soviet soldier felt that he was a hero, and as such, he believed that he was permitted to do anything that he pleased since all would be forgiven to heroes. He went on to ask forgiveness from the Czechoslovak delegation.[98]

Only a month later, in April, Stalin met the Yugoslav Communist Milovan Đilas, whose wife was harassed by the Soviet troops and who had previously complained about the Red Army's conduct resulting in a diplomatic spat between Moscow and Belgrade. This was Đilas' first meeting with Stalin since the majority of the Red Army had left Yugoslavia. Stalin returned to the topic of sexual violence. According to Đilas, Stalin told him that Soviet soldiers had suffered terribly, concluding: "And what is so awful in his having fun with a woman, after such horrors?"[99] The Soviet dictator went on to tell the Yugoslav Communist that he had spared an air force major from the firing squad and sent him to the frontlines (presumably to a penal unit) for trying to rape a woman and then killing an army engineer who had tried to protect her. Stalin was critical of the engineer, dismissing him as "chivalrous," and approvingly citing the rapist's description of the engineer as a "mole from the rear." The Soviet leader concluded, "now he [the major] is one of our heroes. One has to understand the soldier. The Red Army is not ideal. The important thing is that it fights Germans – and it is fighting them well, while the rest doesn't matter."[100]

Obviously, Stalin viewed sexual violence as a minor issue, reducing rape to "having fun with women." By mocking the man who tried to prevent rape as "chivalrous" and using the murderer and rapist's description of the conscientious officer as a "mole from the rear" revealed that his sympathies were actually with the major, not his victims.

The Soviet dictator was not alone in being dismissive of rape. Many lower-ranking officers shared similar views, including those directly responsible for preventing attacks on civilians. When Slutskii was investigating an instance of mass rape in an Austrian village, he gathered a group of soldiers stationed in the village, among them the perpetrators. He did not threaten them with punishment but appealed to their humanity, telling them that they should be ashamed of their behavior. He professed certainty that he was successful in dissuading further violence.[101]

Slutskii believed that appealing to rapists' sense of decency was enough for them to snap out of committing sexual violence as if they were mischievous children who misbehaved a little. At least, he could have threatened them with martial law, if not subject them to it, but he did not, because at some level he sympathized with the rapists.

It is possible to infer a similar reluctance to condemn the rampaging troops by high-ranking officers in the language that they employed in official documents. There were a number of terms that high commanding officers used to describe sexual violence. "Rape" was the most accurate term of course, and it should be noted that officers used it regularly. Often, however, they could not bring themselves to use such words to describe Soviet troops' conduct. To avoid the word "rape," they employed several euphemisms such as "immoral events." "Immoral events" could mean almost any military violation, such as excessive consumption of alcohol, suicides, simulating injuries, self-inflicted wounds, or theft of socialist property.[102] However, this expression was also a euphemism for rape and to a lesser degree looting. For instance, Lieutenant-General Ivan Anoshin, the head of the political department of the 3rd Ukrainian Front, castigated political officers for not struggling against "immoral events in relation to the local Austrian population."[103] From the context, it was obvious that he criticized his subordinates for not doing more to prevent rape. Other euphemistic terms for sexual violence were "extraordinary events" and "negative phenomena," which also included almost any military violation including rape.[104]

The term "cohabitation" was the most pernicious and cynical euphemism for rape. It most vividly illustrated the failure of officers to hold the troops responsible for inflicting harm on women. Thus, Major-General Kuznetsov, commander of the NKVD Army of the 2nd Ukrainian Front and head of the command post system in the country, described in one document a clear case of attempted gang rape. According to him, three drunken NKVD officers entered a home in Hungary in the middle of the night and tried to force the female owner of the home and her sister to come to their apartment. The two women escaped and reported the assault to the local command post. Kuznetsov described the attempted gang rape as an "attempt at cohabitation."[105] Clearly, by conflating rape with "cohabitation," Kuznetsov created room for the perpetrators to get off with a relatively light punishment. The problem was not necessarily that Soviet officers who employed euphemisms for rape found sexual violence completely acceptable. They did not, and that is why they wrote these reports. At the same time, much like Stalin, Slutskii, and undoubtedly many officers, it was difficult for them to harshly judge their soldiers who committed crimes because they identified with them.

The idea that the troops needed to have sex to perform effectively in combat was widespread in the 1940s. Men in authority in various armies believed that the troops needed to release stress from combat through sex or that, without regulated sex in brothels, they would become unruly, commit rapes, contract venereal disease, and thereby undermine military effectiveness.[106] These notions tied into the permissive attitude to rape by Soviet political and military leaders and, as such, were not unique to the Soviet leadership. Hitler said that "if the German man as a soldier is to be ready to die unconditionally he must have the freedom to love unconditionally."[107] As historian Elizabeth Heineman argued, Wehrmacht's underlying assumption was that men needed sex and that occupied populations could be compelled to provide sex, just as they provided food and labor.[108] This was the rationale for Wehrmacht creating the brothel system in the Soviet Union. The Japanese military also ran brothels, employing 50,000–200,000 sex slaves.[109]

The American General George Patton said of his soldiers: "If they don't fuck, they don't fight."[110] It is estimated that twelve American divisions set up their own brothels, which went against the instructions from the high command that the use of brothels was impermissible.[111] The Americans, unlike the Japanese and the Germans in the East, employed prostitutes in brothels, and these women were seemingly free to leave.[112] The commander of the famous 101st Airborne Division, was informed that his troops were committing rapes at the end of the war. He responded that his men had just returned from France and that "it was necessary for a little fun" before he took extraordinary measures.[113] Thus, the belief prevalent among some Soviet political and military leaders that soldiers needed sex and were entitled to it was shared with officers in other armies.

7.2.2 Attitudes toward Foreign Women

To appreciate why the troops subjected more women from enemy countries to sexual violence than from neutral or allied countries, it is important to appreciate how the troops' views of women in general intersected with their views of countries discussed in the previous chapter. The troops' dismissive attitudes toward Romanians as a nation of weak soldiers, traitors, and petty traders interested only in a quick profit were discussed in Chapter 6. In addition, some troops even claimed that Romanian men were willing to haggle over their women, whom they depicted as sexually depraved.

Romania had a higher rate of venereal diseases and more brothels than the Soviet Union, at least according to the Soviet commanders who often expressed concern about the sexual health of their troops.[114] If one analyzes Soviet first-hand sources, it appears that some Soviets believed that prostitution in Romania was a national trait. Nikolai Aleksandrov, who served in an automobile company in the 3rd Ukrainian Front, stated that "Romanians are authentic speculators, unusual sell-outs."[115] In the subsequent sentence, he claimed that there were thirty-three brothels in Constanta when the Red Army occupied the city. Next, he asserted that the owner of the apartment where he was billeted traded his wife to Soviet troops for financial compensation.[116] Aleksandrov linked the supposed Romanian willingness to engage in trade to Romanian women being prostitutes who traded sex for money. In his worldview, even married Romanian women, who appear as mere objects in the schemes of their greedy husbands, could be purchased.

Slutskii recalled that many soldiers took pride in a story that circulated widely, according to which a Romanian husband purportedly complained to the Soviet military commandant that a Red Army officer did not pay him 1,500 lei for having sex with his wife, as they had agreed. Illustrating how Soviet troops linked the domination of Romanian women with national pride, Slutskii asserted that Soviet soldiers took pride in the fact that in their country this was an impossible scenario.[117] Slutskii went further, however, construing Romania as one large brothel. He claimed that syphilis was so widespread that it was not held to be a moral but a financial problem. According to him, all doctors treated it, even dentists and ophthalmologists. He predicted that Soviet soldiers would remember Romanians as "the people of syphilis" (*sifilistikov*).[118] In another part of his memoirs, he described the attitude of Romanian women toward the Soviets as depraved.[119] By doing so, he blamed women for the violence that Soviet men committed.

The presence of Soviet troops placed Romanian women in an impossible position. The longer the Red Army troops stayed in Romania, the more they contributed to the country's impoverishment, forcing more women to become prostitutes to survive. Likewise, the widespread sexual violence perpetrated by the Soviet troops scared more women into seeking Soviet officers who could offer them protection from other rampaging troops. The Soviets then concluded that Romanian women were "depraved," as Slutskii asserted. Moreover, as Soviet soldiers engaged in more sexual violence against Romanian women, venereal diseases became more widespread, cementing their view of Romanians as "the people of syphilis."

Slutskii, as a trained lawyer and a poet, was a true intellectual. He was a keen observer of the events around him, and at times, he was upfront about the criminal Soviet conduct. However, concerning Soviet behavior in Romania, he never acknowledged the large-scale Soviet sexual violence and how it shaped Romanian interaction with the Soviet troops. Instead, he proffered stories the essence of which was that the Romanian men were so avaricious that they traded their wives, who were in any case depraved. The ideas contained in Slutskii's pronouncements about Romanian women were simultaneously causes of the abuse since they provided sufficient denigration to justify the inhumane Soviet conduct, as well as the justification for the large-scale abuse, which was meant to obscure Soviet responsibility for the violence by blaming the victims.

Soviet soldiers and officers also developed extremely pernicious ideas about Hungarian women. The troops' stories of how Hungarian women betrayed their husbands, fathers, and sons, while aggressively pursuing Soviet soldiers and officers, is a frequent trope in Soviet accounts of their encounter with Hungarian women. Slutskii, who viewed European women as licentious, judged Hungarian women for surrendering so easily, in his words, to their husbands' killers.[120] He viewed Hungarian women as less approachable than their Romanian counterparts, but still, in his view, "they gave in with shameful ease."[121] It is notable that for Slutskii, a woman consenting to sexual relations was "shameful." Petr Mikhin, an artillery officer, described how he supposedly broke up a drunken party between local women and soldiers under his command. He clearly blamed the women, claiming that pursuing and seducing men were in their nature:

> Hungarian women always found some opportunities and ways to have a bit of fun with our men ... I rebuked the Hungarian girls "What are you doing? Your husbands are fighting against us, spilling blood, and you are amusing yourselves with Russian soldiers!" "Let them fight," was the playful answer, "but we want to have fun with your soldiers. They're so handsome..."[122]

Mikhin presented himself as a paternal-like figure who took care of his soldiers and their love interests. His story also emphasizes that Hungarian women aggressively pursued Soviet troops, not the other way around, while betraying the men in their lives. It is also likely that Hungarian women who slept with Soviet soldiers reminded them of their own wives' potential betrayal back home, feeding a cycle of fear and resentment against all women.

Other veterans had similar unlikely stories of Hungarian women actively trying to seduce them.[123] However, the most self-serving, the most ridiculous, and the least credible story was told by Grigorii Chukhrai, an officer and a well-known postwar Ukrainian filmmaker. He claimed that a Hungarian couple, at whose house he spent the night, hid their daughter from him in the attic. Subsequently, she came out of hiding and joined them at the table because he was getting along well with her parents. After the supper ended, when he went to sleep, the parents supposedly sent their daughter to his bed to have sex with him, which he indignantly refused. He asserted that he found afterward from his Hungarian translator that it was a Hungarian custom for parents to encourage their daughters to have premarital sex with multiple partners.[124]

Almost certainly, none of these stories told by Soviet soldiers and officers were true. They were myths that the veterans appropriated as their own experiences. As such, they served the purpose of presenting Hungarian society in general, and women in particular, as immoral and sexually deviant, compared to the upstanding Soviets. At the same time, none of the Soviets who advanced these stories, except Slutskii, mentioned rapes committed by Soviet troops. Their emphasis on the supposed degeneracy of enemy women, while overlooking the sexual violence perpetrated by the Red Army personnel, represented a silent justification of rape. This narrative held victims responsible for the nature of relations between the Red Army troops and civilians, and the stories also served the purpose of those who told them to establish their own supposed moral superiority. Slutskii, Mikhin, Chukhrai, and others clearly sought to depict themselves as morally superior to the perverse Hungarian society, where wives betrayed their husbands, while parents sent their children to have sex with their conquerors.

The Soviet narratives about sexual encounters between the Red Army troops and Hungarian women were far removed from the brutal reality, as revealed by Hungarians in many personal sources. Palotaine Kali Gabi, from the village of Baracs, Hungary, described her family's horrific experiences with the rapists from the Red Army in a 2013 documentary film *Silenced Shame*. In one incident, a group of Soviet troops, at least one of whom was an officer, took her mother from their house. When her mother came back, Gabi, thirteen years old at the time, could not understand why her mother was bloodied, had her clothes torn, and why the Soviets would have beaten her. Gabi's mother was obviously raped, but they never talked about it in the family.

In another incident, about which Gabi said she still doesn't really understand what happened, a group of Soviet soldiers' motorbikes broke down next to their house. They entered Gabi's house to eat and drink, while they fixed the motorbike. After the officer finished his supper, he began to harass Gabi, who was, in her words, "nothing more than a skinny child."[125] Her grandma pulled her away and took the soldier to the bedroom of Gabi's mother. While the mother was in the bedroom, the grandma took the rosary in her hands and held Gabi close, and they prayed. Gabi's grandmother, effectively, sacrificed her daughter to save her young granddaughter, and the mother went along with it. Neither Gabi nor her mother or grandmother ever mentioned this incident again.[126] The sexual assaults by Soviet officers obviously represented a lifelong trauma for Gabi and her family, in which older women did what they could to protect the child in impossible conditions. Although Soviet soldiers usually described sexual encounters in Hungary and elsewhere as entirely voluntary or initiated by women, Gabi's account illustrates the degree of violence that accompanied these acts.

These poisonous views of women from enemy countries, adhered to by many Soviet soldiers and officers, did not have an equivalent when it came to Soviet, Bulgarian, and Yugoslav women. This is one reason why the same troops committed fewer sexual assaults in Bulgaria and Yugoslavia. The overwhelming majority of personal Soviet sources revealed that they were thrilled with the two South Slavic countries, but they practically never mentioned Bulgarian and Yugoslav women in any type of sexual context. The only exception was Slutskii who wrote that "after Romanian depravities (*posle rumynskogo razvrata*)," the Soviet troops were shocked by the "brutal" inaccessibility of Bulgarian women.[127] He also claimed that almost no Soviet officer could boast of sexual conquest in Bulgaria and that it was the only country where men accompanied Soviet officers to parties and not women.[128] With regard to Yugoslavia, Slutskii noted that the widespread sympathy for Yugoslavs led the Red Army collective to condemn rapists in its ranks.[129] This was his explanation for why there were relatively few rapes in Yugoslavia.

This is not to suggest that the Soviet troops did not assault Bulgarian and Yugoslav women. Obviously, there were thousands of rapes in the two South Slavic countries. However, with the articulated hatred of Bulgarian and Yugoslav women absent, which existed in Romania and Hungary, and the greater willingness of the army collective to condemn rapists, fewer Soviet soldiers and officers acted with aggression. In turn, Bulgarian and Yugoslav women and societies more generally, facing less overall violence from the Soviet side, felt freer to resist aggressive soldiers' sexual advances, as it was less likely that the occupying troops would react with extreme brutality than in the so-called enemy countries.

Early feminist authors, such as Susan Brownmiller and Gerda Lerner, argued that conquering soldiers who raped women also meant to target men in victims' lives. Brownmiller and Lerner argued that in traditional societies, rape bought dishonor on wives and daughters of enemy soldiers, as men who could not protect their womenfolk were seen by victorious and defeated soldiers as emasculated and humiliated.[130] Thus, acts of rape also communicated to the defeated enemy soldiers that they had been emasculated and disgraced. Historian Norman Naimark found a similar motivation to humiliate the enemy among Soviet soldiers who raped German women.[131] Consequently, it is not surprising that the troops of the 2nd and 3rd Ukrainian Fronts were more likely to subject "enemy" women to sexual violence; they had a lesser need to humiliate men from friendly countries.

The Soviet troops' views of European women intersected with their views of women's nationality, which shaped the troops' treatment of women. Again, this phenomenon was not unique to the Red Army. For instance, an official Japanese military report acknowledged that the Japanese troops' widespread raping in China was caused by the fact that soldiers felt "free to do things to enemy women that would never be permitted at home."[132] Historian Mary Louise Roberts also discussed how stories from World War I and the official propaganda that eroticized French women, meant to motivate the troops to fight in 1944, resulted in many GIs viewing France as "a playground of easy women and loose morals."[133] Consequently, according to her, the American forces brought to France an extraordinary amount of sex, and the GIs came into contact with prostitutes more than with any other type of French person.[134] The Nazis were obsessed with so-called racial hygiene and regulating sex based on perceived ethnic and racial groups. Historian Doris Bergen argued that the Nazi ideology helped determine what the authorities permitted, encouraged, and rewarded, and the ideology also shaped what the soldiers, officers, and camp guards on the ground could do.[135] Obviously, Soviet troops were not the only soldiers whose treatment of women was partially shaped by the women's nationality (Figure 7.2).

Figure 7.2 Soviet soldiers in Budapest. Source: Ullstein Bild via Getty Images.

7.2.3 Gang Rapes

A Romani woman, Ruža, who was a twelve-year-old child in 1944, recollected in an interview that Soviet soldiers came into her village in Yugoslavia and instituted a veritable system of terror. She recalled that they roamed the streets and opened every door, raping any women they could find, not caring if they were young or old. She recalled that one day the Red Army sounded a siren, after which "they went to the center to a gathering. On the second and third day, they raped us."[136] Ruža's account indicates that the entire unit, or at least a large part, went on a raping spree, after being ordered to do so or as a minimum after they received approval from their commanders after the siren was sounded. Ruža's description of the two-day-long rampage by the troops is an extreme example of a mass rape, but it is far from only one. Most accounts of rape that have been referenced in this study, whether from personal or official sources, involve at least two perpetrators, making them by definition gang rapes. The Soviet rapists rarely acted alone. To understand the Soviet-perpetrated sexual violence in Europe, it is necessary to try and illuminate the group dynamics of the crimes such as those elucidated by Ruža.

The standard military theory holds that peer bonding between soldiers at the level of the platoon and their bonding with platoon leaders, bred through training and combat, creates primary group cohesion.[137] The primary group cohesion is a vital part of morale that allows the soldiers to endure combat, which is central to the military accomplishing its goals on a tactical level. Scholars have noted that the Red Army had relatively low primary group cohesion compared to the Wehrmacht.[138]

Scholar of gender Joshua S. Goldstein claimed that gang rapes facilitate bonding and a sense of allegiance in small units between soldiers. In his view, men who would not rape individually do so as part of a display within the male group, to avoid becoming an outcast.[139] In this view, gang rapes served the purpose of strengthening primary group cohesion. In wartime, being an outcast increased the chances of death in combat situations, and thus, soldiers had a lot to lose if they were seen as outsiders. Historian Yuki Tanaka persuasively argued that in the Japanese military during World War II wartime, gang rapes were not only a byproduct of existing soldierly bonds but also helped create and reaffirm such bonds in noncombat situations.[140] Historian Catherine Merridale, writing on the Red Army's rampage in East Prussia, also pointed out that Soviet troops used gang rapes to express their hatred for women, affirm their love for each other, and cement their bonds through mass sexual violence.[141] Thus, it makes sense that in the Red Army, which suffered high casualties that made the creation of durable primary group bonds difficult, group sexual violence was common, as it strengthened primary unit cohesion.

7.3 Nonviolent Encounters in Europe

Although the sex the Soviet troops had with European women was more likely violent and nonconsensual, some sex was in the gray area. Mühlhäuser stressed that under the Nazi occupation, the boundary between consensual and nonconsensual sex was fluid. This did not mean that the nonviolent encounters were consensual as we understand consent today. Instead, she stressed that such relationships, although excluding outright physical violence, were asymmetrical in that they were based on fears, specific needs (such as food), pragmatic choices, sexual desire, and wish to flee for a moment at least from the brutalities of war.[142] As such, these relationships may have been transactional from the perspective of women. These relationships between the Soviet troops and European women in the gray area, especially those freer of coercion and with some mutual desire, were rare for several reasons.

First, the Stalinist military, concerned with undue foreign influence on its troops and paranoid about security, discouraged its officers and soldiers from getting close to non-Soviet citizens. In general, the men in leadership positions were more likely to have opportunities to get to know European citizens and to get away with developing closer relationships with them. Boris Baklanov, an extremely privileged SMERSH officer, recalled that his superior told him to "watch out" when he saw Baklanov on the street with an Austrian woman who was Baklanov's German-language tutor and a lover.[143] Baklanov interpreted this advice to mean, "Well, go ahead if you want to, but just see you don't land up in trouble."[144] Obviously, Baklanov's boss signaled to him that he would look the other way at his romantic liaisons, a treatment that not all Soviet officers could expect, let alone ordinary soldiers.

Usually, terse military documents discussed sexual relationships between the troops and foreigners only when they led to larger violations such as the spreading of military secrets or desertion. European women also rarely discussed such relationships, as their societies condemned them. Second, it was illegal for Soviet soldiers to marry foreign citizens, a regulation that European women were generally aware of.[145] Ultimately, the ban on marriages to foreigners meant that soldiers and officers who intended to stay with a European citizen or marry them had to plan on deserting, an option that must have discouraged some from pursuing serious relationships.

Despite these significant factors that restrained the development of longer-term intimate relations between Soviet troops and European women, there were numerous instances of such relationships. It seems that nonviolent relationships were more common in Bulgaria and Yugoslavia than in other countries. Slavic origins of Bulgarians and

Serbs on the one hand, and most Soviet soldiers on the other, enabled at least some communication between the Red Army and host populations. In Slutskii's view, the Red Army soldiers who knew local languages were more fortunate in facilitating romantic liaisons with women.[146] Thus, it can be presumed that Soviet soldiers found it easier in Bulgaria and Yugoslavia to court the local women than elsewhere in Europe. Also, it is likely that in the two countries where Russians were viewed by large segments of the population as close allies with a shared religious and ethnic background, it was less of a taboo for local women to enter relationships with the Soviet troops than in enemy European countries where such women were viewed as traitors.

There is sufficient evidence to conclude that some young women displayed interest in Soviet soldiers and officers. Soviet Z. E. Sutrina, a signaler in the 71st Guards Division, recorded in her diary on 14 September 1944 that during a stroll with two other signalers in the Bulgarian town of Iankovo, several high school girls approached Sutrina's group, inviting them to their dance. When Sutrina asked the girls whether they liked the Soviet soldiers, they confirmed it, adding that they all wanted to see Moscow.[147] In a different village, when Sutrina was walking with two male soldiers, a group of young women approached them and invited them to their house as guests. The Soviets refused, asking them instead to join them for a walk.[148] A woman related in an interview that her neighbor in Belgrade was romantically interested in a Soviet soldier but that he was brazenly interested in one thing only, by which she presumably meant sex, so her neighbor's mother ordered her to stop seeing him.[149] The fact that the young woman was interested in pursuing a relationship with a Soviet soldier and that her mother could put an end to it is illustrative of the freedom this Yugoslav family had in how they interacted with the Soviets.

There were also social events where Soviet men and European women could meet. The Soviet Air Force reported that Serbian peasants met its crews, who delivered aid to Yugoslav Partisans at the airstrip every night, and that large groups of local youths organized dances in their honor and invited the crews for dinner.[150] El'kinson wrote in his diary that upon the liberation of a Serbian village at ten o'clock at night, the entire village came out to celebrate. The civilians celebrated with soldiers all night, singing and dancing.[151] It should be noted that almost certainly at all of these parties, there was alcohol involved.

On 17 November 1944, the Corps of the People's Defense of Yugoslavia (KNOJ), the Yugoslav version of the NKVD that carried out daily patrols in Belgrade, complained that Soviet officers and soldiers often walked around the city with Yugoslav women after the curfew.[152] It is impossible to tell who these Yugoslav women are. Some were possibly prostitutes. Either way, the NKVD report implied that they were with Soviet officers voluntarily. A Red Army lieutenant met a nurse in the Yugoslav hospital in Romania, and instead of returning to his unit after recuperating, he relocated with her to the Serbian city of Vršac where the hospital also moved. They lived together in Vršac for several weeks before he was arrested by the NKVD.[153]

Links between the Soviet soldiers and European civilians continued even after the Red Army left a particular area, indicating that Soviet soldiers attached meaning to these relationships. In December, the head of the Political Department of the 233rd Division, stationed in Hungary at the time, complained that a soldier revealed military secrets in a letter to a woman whom he had met in Yugoslavia.[154] Troops of the 3rd Ukrainian Front sent more than 30,000 letters to European civilians during the fifteen days of October, even though it was illegal for the Red Army members to use civilian postal services in Europe.[155] Sometimes, Soviet soldiers added their photographs to the letters to be remembered.[156] Given the differences between the Romanian and Russian languages and alphabets, it can be assumed that most of these letters were addressed to Bulgarians and Yugoslavs. It is impossible to tell how many of these letters were meant for soldiers' romantic interests, to friends or mere acquaintances, but it seems logical to assume that in many cases young soldiers would tend to write to women who interested them. Either way, this evidence indicates that Soviet soldiers thought that they had formed relationships with civilians.

Baklanov claimed that he fell in love with Hungary as a country and its people, but he also began seeing a young woman called Maryjka after the war.[157] It seems that he liked her more than any of the other women he claimed to have had sexual encounters with during the war, describing her "as a kind, open-hearted person" and "very chic, with light brown hair, a slim waist and wonderful legs."[158] He was stationed in Vienna, and he saw her during his frequent business trips to Hungary, concealing his true professional identity by representing himself as a military journalist. She left him when she realized that he was connected with security services.[159] Baklanov's account indicates that his relationship with Maryjka was free of outright coercion and that she was able to end it at will.

In rarer instances, Soviet soldiers and officers even married local women. As rare as marriages were, since they were illegal, I have found documented evidence for numerous such cases. Slutskii wrote that some Soviet soldiers who were reenlisted in the army following their liberation from the prisoner-of-war camps tried to stay with their new wives by deserting.[160] Similarly, an NKVD analysis of the Soviet soldiers' conduct during their march from Austria to Romania in the summer of 1945 found that many of the documented 181 deserters were former forced laborers or prisoners of war in Germany, Austria, or Hungary. During their captivity, and before their enlistment into the Red Army, some of them married local women or had children with them. When their units were supposed to be relocated to different areas, they deserted.[161] Similarly, a senior sergeant deserted in September 1944 and married a Bulgarian woman in a religious ceremony.[162] In an action aimed at deserters in Yugoslavia in the summer of 1945, the NKVD reported, that in some instances, Soviet soldiers who deserted months earlier lived with and even married local Yugoslav women, trying to pass themselves off as Yugoslav citizens.[163] Again, the nature of these sources tells us little about the actual relationships, but it is safe to presume that at least some of these relationships were reciprocal.

Historian Sterzl-Marx, who examined the sexual and romantic encounters in the gray area between Soviet officers and Austrian women, suggested that such relationships were partially made possible by the fact that, due to war and prolonged captivity, there was a great imbalance in postwar Austria. For every 70 men, there were 100 women.[164] She suggested that Soviet officers could not offer luxury goods to the women, as their American counterparts, but that they could offer basic food, cigarettes, and coveted travel permits and passes.[165] She argued that given their youth, for women, these relationships represented "the great love of their lives."[166] She cited several examples of Austrian women to illuminate this point.[167] The opposition to these relationships came not only from the Soviet authorities but also from women's families. In one case, the father of Ingeborg Walla-Grom destroyed her relationship with a young Soviet soldier by telling him, incorrectly, that she suffered from venereal diseases.[168]

7.4 Conclusion

The Red Army's troops prized sexual prowess, proven through sexual activity, as one of the defining characteristics of strong manhood. They tended to view all women – Soviet civilians, their female comrades, and European women – through this prism, as potential sexual partners or conquests in their jargon. Although many Soviet soldiers and officers viewed all women as sex objects, how much violence they were willing to employ to obtain sex, and what they could get away with, varied considerably between different groups of women.

The troops wanted "their" Soviet women to be grateful and faithful girlfriends and wives. Women who stepped outside of these bounds tended to be despised, whether it was women who had sexual relations with the enemy soldiers or with other Soviet men in the rear. Red Army servicewomen by their very presence in the military had also stepped beyond the traditional norms that most soldiers and officers subscribed to. If Soviet soldiers had opportunities to encounter Soviet women, then it was mostly likely their comrades in the Red Army. The overall atmosphere made it hard for women to serve in the military, as they frequently faced unwanted propositions, harassment, and direct sexual coercion, usually from senior officers who held power over them.

The Soviet soldiers and officers' attitudes toward women and sex intersected with their ideas about nationality. In the "enemy" countries that had waged war against the Soviet Union, the Red Army servicemen went on a veritable rampage that exceeded in magnitude and brutality anything they had done on Soviet soil or to Red Army women. The Soviet troops tended to view European women as legitimate spoils of war deserving of rape. They told ridiculous stories about the corrupt nature of Romanian and Hungarian women that justified the violence. In victimizing the enemy women, they were also dishonoring their menfolk – husbands, fathers, and brothers who had fought against the Red Army. The terrible gang rapes bonded the perpetrators to each other. The significance of the nationality factor in the Soviet-perpetrated sexual violence is also evident in the Soviet troops' relatively more restrained behavior in Bulgaria and Yugoslavia, two countries that did not wage war against the Soviet Union and whose population spoke languages that were intelligible to the troops.

The Soviet troops also engaged in nonviolent sexual encounters with European women. These relationships were relatively rare because the Soviet regulations effectively banned fraternization with all foreigners. Furthermore, some Soviet soldiers and especially officers held power over European women, but they were not better off materially, as was the case with Americans in Western Europe and the Germans in the Soviet Union. Thus, it was harder for them to "buy" favors from European women.

8 After the War

Gabriel Temkin, a soldier in the 78th Division of the 2nd Ukrainian Front, was one of the few soldiers who served in the Red Army since the beginning of the war and survived. Temkin, a Jew, not only survived the carnage in the trenches but also escaped from Nazi captivity and made it back to the Red Army lines with the help of generous Ukrainian and Russian villagers. Temkin noted that in the last days of the war, soldiers became more contemplative of life and death, a topic that was previously taboo due to widely held superstition that talking about death would bring it on. When the Third Reich capitulated on 8 May local time and on 9 May Moscow time, this is how Temkin and his comrades celebrated: "We were embracing, touching each other as if to make sure that we were not daydreaming, that we had indeed survived! We were firing salvos, having a jolly good time, drinking wine, and celebrating victory."[1]

The end of armed hostilities gave rise to new circumstances. The situation on the ground changed profoundly for the 2nd and 3rd Ukrainian Fronts after the fighting ended, as soldiers and officers were no longer at risk of imminent death. Furthermore, the political and military leaderships were no longer focused on winning the war and could devote more of their attention to governing the conquered territories. This chapter examines the leadership policies and soldiers' attitudes to Europeans in the new postwar context.

8.1 New Context

Each defeated Axis country was formally administered by the Allied Control Commission (ACC) after the war. The ACCs for Romania, Bulgaria, and Hungary were effectively run by the Soviet Union, although they also had representatives from the United States and Great Britain. The ACC for Austria, however, was jointly controlled by the Soviet Union and the Western Allies, while the Red Army was tasked with occupying only one part of Austria. The ACCs came into existence after the Red Army occupied a part or whole of an enemy country and after the Kremlin signed an armistice agreement with its provisional government. The Soviets either appointed or had great influence over the composition of provisional governments. The ACCs were run by the Red Army's high-ranking officers.[2] Acting through the ACCs, the Kremlin sought to extract war reparations and to increase its influence, which it did in part by strengthening local communist parties. The ACC ceased to exist after the Allies signed permanent peace treaties in 1947 with Hungary, Romania, and Bulgaria, and in 1955 with Austria. By then, however, local communists were in power everywhere except in Austria, assuring that the Soviets would continue to exercise control over the nascent Eastern bloc. The Red Army and especially the NKVD troops in Central Europe and the Balkans acted as enforcers of ACC decisions.

There was a major reorganization of the Red Army fronts in Europe after the war ended. The Supreme Command of the Armed Forces of the USSR (Stavka) created two new army groups on 29 May: the Central and Southern Groups of Armies. The Central Group of Armies was forged on the basis of the command and units of the 1st Ukrainian Front, but it also included units of the 2nd Ukrainian Front and the much smaller 4th Ukrainian Front (1st and 4th Ukrainian Fronts operated mainly in Czechoslovakia, although the latter had a limited presence in Hungary in late 1944). The Central Group of Armies was headed by Marshal Konev, and it was responsible for occupation troops in Czechoslovakia, Austria, and Hungary. The Southern Group of Armies was forged on the basis of the command and units of the 3rd Ukrainian Front and was headed by Marshal Tolbukhin; it was responsible for Romania and Bulgaria.

The four Ukrainian fronts, which became the Central and Southern Groups of Armies and formed the occupational troops in Czechoslovakia, Austria, Hungary, Romania, and Bulgaria, numbered under 3 million troops in the war's final days.[3] After Germany capitulated, there was a swift decline in Soviet troops in the region due to demobilization and transfers to the Far East to fight the Japanese. The Kremlin transferred the highest leadership of the 2nd Ukrainian Front (Marshal Malinovskii and his immediate subordinates) to the Far East.[4] In addition, between May and July 1945, 565,000 troops were transferred from the western Soviet Union and Eastern Europe to the Far East; among them were the 53rd Army and the 6th Guards Tank Army, which previously belonged to the 2nd and 3rd Ukrainian Fronts.[5] Demobilization, based on age, was a slow and loosely organized process.[6] Demobilization started in late June 1945 and ended in 1948.[7]

According to partially available data, the Red Army's garrisons in Europe diminished rapidly after the war, and most of the troops were transferred to bases in the Soviet Union before their final demobilization.

The precise number of Soviet troops after the war in each country that this study focuses on is difficult to estimate because the size of Soviet occupational garrisons was a secret during the Cold War. After the fall of the Soviet Union, historians were largely content with establishing that the Red Army had a presence in a certain country, without investigating the occupying garrison's precise size. Thus, all figures are speculative, but combined, they indicate a sharp decline in the number of Soviet troops in Europe after the war.

Yugoslavia was the only allied country in this study that was neither occupied nor administered by the Red Army. Nonetheless, a large number of troops transferred in the summer of 1945 through the northern Serbian province of Vojvodina on their way from Austria and Hungary to the Soviet Union, Romania, and Bulgaria.[8] According to contemporary Western diplomatic estimates, there were 130,000 Soviet troops in Bulgaria in April 1946.[9] Soviet troops left Bulgaria in 1947 after Sofia signed a peace treaty with the Allies.[10] In 1946, according to one scholar, the number of Soviet troops in Austria peaked at 150,000, while the last Soviet soldier left the country in 1955.[11] Western intelligence agencies estimated that in November 1945, there were half a million Soviet soldiers in Romania.[12] A Romanian estimate of the number of Soviet troops in the country from May 1945 until the Peace Treaty was signed in September 1947, based on the average rations required by the Soviet high command, was also half a million.[13] I have not found the exact figure for the number of troops in Hungary; however, they remained in the country well after the Axis capitulated, ostensibly, to maintain communication between the Soviet occupation troops in Austria and the Soviet Union.[14] Thus, within less than a year after the war ended, the number of Soviet troops diminished from less than 3 million to a couple of hundreds of thousands.

8.2 The High Command's Policies

Two important factors encouraged the Kremlin and the Red Army's high command to make a determined effort to rein in the rampaging troops in the postwar period. First, officers could devote more of their attention to disciplinary issues after the war when their top priority was not to defeat the enemy forces. Second, Moscow planned to control the areas that the Red Army occupied in Europe first through ACCs and then through local communist parties, which required the local communists to participate in elections. Yet, Soviet soldiers' acts of looting, rape, and murder were strongly undermining the popularity of the Soviet Union and, by extension, of local communists. From the Kremlin's perspective, the troops' conduct was making the occupied territories less governable.

It should be noted that other major factors harmed how civilians viewed the Red Army. Reparations were hugely unpopular and led to the plummeting of Soviet and local communists' reputations in the region, as the Kremlin was well aware.[15] Also, citizens from defeated countries were dissatisfied with their countries' postwar borders, for which they blamed the occupying allied power. For instance, some Austrians held the Soviet Union responsible for postwar Austrian borders that did not include German-speaking parts of Italy and Yugoslavia (Southern Tyrol and the Maribor region).[16] Similarly, Hungarians were widely outraged that northern Transylvania became part of Romania. To a lesser extent, they were anxious about the fate of the Bačka region, which the Hungarians had seized from Yugoslavia in 1941 but then had to relinquish in the autumn of 1944.[17] In contrast, it could be presumed that Romanians became at least less hostile to the Soviets once Bucharest was allowed to fully assert its sovereignty over Transylvania in the spring of 1945, a territory it contested with Budapest.[18] Furthermore, Europeans, especially those from the countries that were part of Germany or in alliance with the Third Reich, had been subjected for years to Nazi anti-Russian propaganda. It surely left a mark on how local populations viewed the Soviet Union (Figure 8.1).

The Kremlin was unwilling to forsake reparations, and there was very little that it could do to resolve the conflicting national territorial claims. However, compared to these larger economic and geopolitical issues, the question of violence was more pressing for Europe's civilians, and it was something the Kremlin could influence without incurring a cost to its interests. A series of reports written by high-ranking NKVD and Red Army officers, as well as pro-Soviet Europeans, made it clear to the Soviet military and political leaderships that the troops' criminal conduct was seriously undermining the Red Army's image in the region and damaging the prospects of local communists.[19] It was also significant that the highest Soviet leadership paid attention when the Western press began to report widely on the Red Army's behavior in 1945. Soviet leaders feared that media attention to this issue would further discredit the Soviet Union.[20]

High command relied on propaganda to change soldiers' conduct. As the Military Council of the Southern Group of Armies (the front's governing body) stated in a circular, it was necessary to imbue the soldiers with attitudes that would make them intolerant of comrades who dishonored the calling of a Soviet warrior with their conduct.[21] In other words, the high command now expected propaganda to encourage the correct treatment of civilians. With this goal in mind, the official line toward Germans started to change in the early spring of 1945 when Soviet propaganda began stressing the difference between the so-called Hitlerites

Figure 8.1 Soviet soldier regulates traffic in Vienna. Source: Imagno/Getty Images.

(German soldiers and Nazi party members) and ordinary Germans. Thus, the new propaganda theme started shortly before the end of the war but strengthened after 9 May.

Il'ia Ehrenburg lost members of his family in the Holocaust and was one of the first chroniclers of the Holocaust through the Jewish Anti-Fascist Committee.[22] As a journalist for the main army newspaper *Red Star*, he was also one of the most prominent voices of Soviet anti-German propaganda. During this period, he lost official favor. Geoergi Aleksandrov, the head of the Central Committee's Propaganda and Agitation Department, and one of Stalin's top wartime ideologues, sharply criticized Ehrenburg for his anti-German rants. Writing in *Pravda* on 14 April 1945, Aleksandrov charged Ehrenburg with incorrectly accusing all Germans of being supporters of Hitler, while asserting, "… comrade Ehrenburg does not represent Soviet public opinion. The Red Army, in fulfilling its great liberating mission, is struggling to liquidate the Hitlerite army, Hitlerite state, and Hitlerite government, but it never aimed to and it never will aim to exterminate German people. That would be stupid and pointless."[23]

Ehrenburg's anti-German writing had made him extremely popular among the army's rank and file throughout the war. Thus, political departments made a determined effort to change the frontline troops' positive impressions of Ehrenburg. The 2nd and 3rd Ukrainian Fronts' political departments discussed Aleksandrov's critique of Ehrenburg with the soldiers and officers even though they did not fight in Germany proper.[24] The attacks on Ehrenburg and his ideas were meant to undermine a man who symbolized the unchecked hate and thirst for revenge that had fueled the Soviet rampage on enemy soil.

In addition, the new propaganda line also tried to disassociate other Axis nations from Germans. In Austria, this trend began as soon as the Red Army stepped on the territory of the old republic in March 1945.[25] By 15 January 1946, Colonel Mikhailov, the deputy commander of the NKVD Army of the Central Group of Armies, described Austria, in an internal document that was sent to the highest NKVD leadership in Moscow, as Nazi Germany's first victim.[26] In Austria, agitators discussed with the rank and file the following topics: "The proper way for a warrior to carry himself in Austria" and "the moral character of a soldier-victor," and "There is no room in our ranks for drunks and marauders."[27] Soviet propagandists instructed the troops to treat the civilians correctly while the war lasted; however, what was new was the total absence of hate propaganda in the postwar period.

Similarly, the official propaganda and discourse reinvented Romanians after the war. Marshal Tolbukhin and Lieutenant-General Ivan Anoshin, commander of the Southern Group of Armies and the head of its political department, respectively, sent a letter to all generals and higher-ranking officers of the front on 28 July. The authors' main point was that officers had to rein in the ill-disciplined troops. Tolbukhin and Anoshin praised Romania in this document for being the first country to have broken off from the Germans when it was supposedly not yet obvious that the Third Reich would lose the war; they commended the so-called democratic reforms in Romania (communization of the country) as an expression of the will of the Romanian people; and they acclaimed the Romanian contribution to the defeat of Nazi Germany after Bucharest switched sides in the war. For these reasons, Tolbukhin and Anoshin asserted, it was the responsibility of Soviet officers to educate soldiers to treat Romanians decently and to be intolerant of those who abused civilians.[28] Tolbukhin reiterated in another order, which he issued on 18 August, that the Soviet Union had a new approach to Romania and the Romanian people and that officers needed to acknowledge it by cultivating among their troops' sympathetic attitudes to Romanians.[29]

Prior to Bucharest's surrender in September 1944, Anoshin often heaped abuse against Romanians, in one instance calling Romanian soldiers "monsters" (*izvergy*).[30] Thus, the new line on Romanians represented a 180-degree turn. According to the Soviets, Romanians went from being the principal Nazi collaborators to the first Soviet ally who abandoned the Germans and made an important contribution to their defeat and whose people were democratically inclined. This reinvention of Romanians in Soviet propaganda reflected the Red Army's high command's determination to stamp out the abuse of civilians in that country.

The propaganda campaign amounted to a new Kremlin-backed narrative of the war. According to this version of events, the Red Army were not conquerors; they were liberators of people from the fascist yoke. The only Soviet enemies were the Nazi soldiers. Soviet soldiers and officers should appreciate the differences between Nazis and Germans and between Germans and other Axis nations, which were even less responsible for the war than the Germans. The new line held that soldiers should also acknowledge the changes that had taken place in Central Europe and the Balkans since the Soviet arrival and recognize the Romanian contribution to the defeat of the Nazis. The aim of the new narrative of the war, which originated in Moscow, was to create more positive views among soldiers and officers of their former enemies and, thereby, to make acts of plunder and violence less justifiable and indeed unacceptable from within the Red Army.

Another important tool that the military leadership used to try to restore order in the ranks was to implore and threaten troops to behave correctly. Indicative of the leadership's resolve to end the violence, one officer described telegrams from Moscow that ordered the commanders in the field to put an end to rapes as "brutal and decisive."[31] The command on the level of the front also issued a wave of orders to commanders in the field that called for increased discipline while stressing the impermissibility of mistreating civilians. According to my count, Marshal Tolbukhin and the Military Council of the Southern Group of Armies issued at least eight such orders or circulars.[32] In addition, the NKVD Army, lower-ranking regular army commanders, and command post commandants issued their own similar orders to troops under their control.[33]

Often the command reiterated in these orders existing rules and policies against looting and rape, by naming the guilty officers and emphasizing their punishment. For example, Tolbukhin issued a circular on 13 September in which he stated that the Red Army Major Aldoshin beat and raped a Bulgarian woman in the dormitory of the Red Cross in Sofia. Tolbukhin announced that the Military Tribunal was in the process of prosecuting Aldoshin, adding that his conduct was unbecoming of an officer and that he tarnished the reputation of all Soviet officers. Tolbukhin's instruction was read to all the officers of the Southern Group of Armies.[34] Similarly, in orders circulated to all the officers of the front, Tolbukhin highlighted the names of the most undisciplined units and their commanding officers, while stressing the demotions and other reprimands the officers had received.[35]

Soviet commanders also introduced more proactive measures to improve soldiers and officers' behavior. On 26 May, the 3rd Ukrainian Front banned soldiers and officers with venereal diseases from leaving their units and required them to be sent to hospitals only "in an organized manner" (under guard).[36] The aim of this policy was twofold: to more effectively control the soldiers who had a record of undisciplined conduct and to prevent the proliferation of venereal diseases. The high command also tried to produce more accurate rosters of soldiers in each unit to better control their movements and have a clearer understanding of who deserted.[37] Commanders were responsible for discipline set up roadblocks near major cities in an attempt to restrict and control the movement of the rank and file into large urban areas where soldiers could commit atrocities or go into hiding.[38] The Red Army also carried out random inspections of units that had a reputation for being ill-disciplined. Inspectors' findings were sent to Tolbukhin so that he could follow up regarding how and whether the situation subsequently improved in these units.[39] More significantly, there was a substantial increase in the number of NKVD troops responsible for discipline. Between May 1944 and

June 1945, the NKVD Armies of the two fronts increased from an estimated 15,010 to 19,865 troops.[40]

Some officers responsible for the protection of civilians went to great lengths to fulfill their duties. Major Rumiantsev, the commandant of the Austrian city Feldbach, instructed the city's residents in the summer of 1945 not to open the doors of their homes to any Soviet soldier except employees from the command post. He told them to call patrols as soon as an unauthorized soldier entered their backyards. He also instructed civilians in Feldbach that they should not hand over material goods or provide services (such as laundry services and shoe repair) to the Red Army and NKVD troops without his written consent.[41] Major Rumiantsev evidently took seriously his duty to protect civilians and tried to assure that there was order in the city.

The Soviet leadership also tried to change the troops' conduct by introducing tougher disciplinary policies. It did so by applying pressure on the Red Army's officers responsible for discipline and the judiciary to work more effectively to stamp out the abuses of civilians. For instance, on 28 July, Tolbukhin "demanded from all generals and senior officers to put an end to criminal practices by some soldiers who violated the rights and interests of Romanian civilians....and not to leave one fact [of looting and rape] uninvestigated, and to hold the guilty [soldiers and officers] strictly responsible."[42] On 24 August, the Military Council reiterated this demand.[43]

In the last months of the war, Soviet soldiers who committed rapes and other crimes were typically sent to penal units. Those sentenced to stiffer punishments such as the death penalty or terms in labor camps often had their sentences suspended until the end of the war. After the German capitulation, neither penal units nor suspended sentences existed as possible punishments. As a result, and in combination with numerous orders calling for the severe punishment of rapists and murderers, military tribunals became involved in an increasing number of cases, and the sentences they handed out were more severe. On 10 October, the Commander of the Southern Group of Armies issued a circular that approved of harsh sentences such as prison terms against nonviolent recidivists, rapists, murderers, and embezzlers of state property, but he condemned the involvement of military tribunals against nonviolent violators of discipline – those who lost secret documents or drank prodigiously but did not commit violent crimes. The motive behind this order was that the judicial authorities' increased activities were undermining the high command's attempts to form an effective officer corps, by punishing officers who committed relatively minor infractions instead of instructing them how to behave correctly.[44] This order shows that the Red Army's control mechanisms started operating more effectively after the war.

Despite these improvements, most perpetrators of violent crimes remained unpunished. In his study of the Red Army's conduct in postwar Germany, historian Filip Slaveski argued that commanding officers faced a dilemma when having to discipline their troops. On the one hand, Slaveski contended, officers would have been killed by their men had they punished every act of rape, murder, and looting. On the other hand, officers would have lost control of their units if they did nothing. The officers tried to overcome this dilemma by punishing the worst offenders while allowing themselves and their men to act like conquerors.[45] Slaveski's explanation is important in understanding why the tough measures ordered from above were mostly ineffective in rooting out violence.

Notwithstanding the high command's efforts to curtail the looting, rapes, and murders, according to historians who have worked mostly with non-Soviet local sources, the situation for civilians did not improve for months and in some places for years after the war ended. In Norman Naimark's view, German women were freed from the persistent threat of rape only in the winter of 1947–1948 when Soviet troops were stationed in strictly guarded camps.[46] In Austria, in the words of one scholar, the worst of the Soviet rape epidemic ended in late 1945, which was more than six months after the war ended.[47] This does not mean that Soviet criminal conduct ceased entirely in that country. Austrian police analysis of criminal cases for 1946 revealed that well over 90 percent of perpetrators of rape were Soviet soldiers, or in politically correct contemporary jargon, they were men in Russian uniforms.[48] Although scholars who study Hungary and Romania have not specifically addressed the issue of when Soviet conduct improved, they leave little doubt that, as in Austria, the situation changed slowly.[49]

My research confirms the excruciatingly slow speed with which the Soviet troops' conduct improved after the war. The reason why the high command issued so many instructions proscribing the mistreatment of civilians was that these orders were not being followed, as soldiers continued to commit acts of plunder, rape, and murder. Partially available official statistics on the proliferation of venereal diseases in the army's ranks are highly illustrative. Between 1 June 1945 and 1 March 1946, 133,359 Soviet soldiers and officers contracted venereal diseases in European countries, including Germany, Czechoslovakia, Poland, Austria, Hungary, Romania, and Bulgaria.[50] In an average month, therefore, it can be calculated that 14,817 Soviet troops reported venereal disease infections. The significance of the available statistics is that the drop in new infections was gradual: in December 1945, there were 15,774 new infections; in January

1946, 14,362 cases; and in February, 13,730.[51] This data should not be misinterpreted. The Red Army's sanitary authorities did not register all infections, and not all or perhaps even most diseases were a result of rapes. What these statistics do tell us, however, is that the pattern of interaction between Soviet troops and European civilians was changing very slowly, especially when it is considered that the number of troops stationed in Europe during this period was diminishing rapidly.

When all of the evidence is taken into account, it must be concluded that civilians in countries occupied by the Red Army got a break only when large numbers of troops left the area. The high command's determined effort to change the troops' conduct was largely unsuccessful in ending the atrocities. Nonetheless, such efforts should not be entirely dismissed. Without these attempts to rein in the troops, it is possible that the frontline soldiers' and officers' conduct would have continued to escalate after the war, as it did in the months before the German capitulation.

The fact order was reintroduced so gradually is surprising, considering that several circumstantial factors favored a lowering of violence. Without vicious fighting, the post-combat fury at the enemy, fueled by hate propaganda, began to dissipate. Moreover, there were no longer mass rampages like those that occurred after the capture of large enemy cities such as Budapest and Vienna. There was also a sharp decrease in the number of deserters after the war.

The NKVD Army of the 2nd Ukrainian Front detained 2,132 deserters between 1 January and 9 May 1945, whereas the NKVD Army of the Central Group of Armies caught only 314 deserters from 10 May to 31 December.[52] The situation was similar to that of the NKVD Army of the 3rd Ukrainian Front, which detained 121 deserters in April and 118 in May but only 23 in June.[53] In September, the next month for which the figures are available, the NKVD Army of the Southern Group of Armies caught only thirteen deserters.[54] Although there were more deserters who were caught by command posts and by the Red Army, these numbers reveal an unmistakable trend – there were far fewer deserters in peacetime when soldiers did not face the daily prospect of death. Since deserters were most prone to engage in criminal activity, the drop in their numbers meant that European civilians got a respite in this sense after the war.

8.3 Frontline Soldiers and Officers in the Postwar Period

Although the factors discussed above should have minimized the violent acts against the local population, there were numerous reasons why soldiers and officers continued to commit atrocities. First, without having to fight a war, soldiers were bored, and they had a lot more free time to spend

Figure 8.2 Soviet soldiers in Vienna. Source: Alexander Ustinov/Slava Katamidze Collection via Getty Images.

with their comrades and to consume alcohol, which invariably fueled military violations. The command tried to keep the troops busy by holding regular exercises and quartering the troops in camps, but these measures were not entirely effective.[55] If the soldiers did not stay put in the camps, they were on the march. Soldiers on the march were more ill-disciplined, and after the war, millions of Soviet troops were on the move – relocating to their new bases across Eastern Europe and the Soviet Union; or they were demobilized and heading home (Figure 8.2).[56]

After the Southern Group of Armies marched from Austria to Romania in the summer of 1945, the front's high command analyzed the Soviet troops' behavior. The report's main findings were that there was a significant number of instances of marauding and violence against civilians and that during the march there was an increase in instances of desertion, in comparison to when the troops were stationed in camps or barracks after the hostilities ended.[57] Even a group of NKVD troops, who were responsible for the discipline of the rank and file, deserted during this march.[58] There were several reasons why soldiers on the move behaved worse than the troops who were stationed in the camps. They were often stuck for a long time on overcrowded trains, they were bored, and, with easy access to alcohol, they drank a lot, brawled, and committed other acts of violence. Furthermore, the troops knew that they were in any locale briefly. Therefore, some troops must have concluded that they were less likely to be caught and punished. Finally, the cohesion of units disintegrated more easily during marches, making it easier for troublemakers and criminals to slip beyond the oversight of disciplinary institutions.

The disturbances caused by Soviet troops on the move resembled more riotous behavior than the seemingly targeted violence to which they subjected enemy populations after battles. In these circumstances, it seemed to have mattered little to Soviet soldiers whether they were in friendly or enemy countries. Historian Mark Edele, for instance, documented how returning veterans often engaged in drunken violence on Soviet soil against property, civilians, and even authorities as they made their way home.[59] If the troops behaved in such a manner in the Soviet Union, it is not a surprise that they acted even worse in European countries. For example, one Romanian official complained to Marshal Tolbukhin that there were instances of Soviet troops throwing Romanians out of moving trains in order to take their seats.[60]

Furthermore, some of the troops who had fought a brutal war for years generally found it difficult to adjust to peacetime. One soldier wrote in his diary when he learned of the ceasefire on 8 May: "I simply cannot believe it ... the silence is striking. Not one shot. It is strange that we ever got used to it all [war], but now it is hard to unlearn it."[61] Similarly, Lieutenant Evgenii Moniushko, who was stationed in Hungary after the war, wrote that nobody could forget the war, adding that soldiers never parted with their weapons, with most sleeping with carbines and submachine guns.[62]

The widespread thirst for revenge could not be turned off as easily as hate propaganda. There is very little evidence that soldiers from the former 2nd and 3rd Ukrainian Fronts accepted the new official line, which stressed that they should view civilians from formerly enemy countries as victims of German Nazism or accept them as their allies. Pavel El'kinson, a scout in the 46th army, complained about the increasingly relaxed Soviet attitudes toward Austrians. Noting that some "Fritzes" (Austrians) were hitching rides on Soviet trucks and wagons, he complained in his diary: "how quickly people are forgetting what must not be forgotten."[63] Subsequently, when he marched with his unit through Hungary, El'kinson noted that Hungarian attitudes changed toward the Soviets: "Hungarians ... are now very brave and they feel powerful. They are already not the slave-like compliant Magyars who were here at the time of our offensive."[64] El'kinson pined for the time when Austrian and Hungarian civilians were servile and terrified of Soviet soldiers, as in the initial period of the Red Army's occupation.

Soviet troops resisted the new line that they should accept the Romanian army as their ally. Major Boris Slutskii's insights into the issue are significant since he was stationed in the staff of the Southern Group of Armies, which was headquartered in the Romanian city of Constanta, where the Soviet and Romanian troops came into close contact. He described relations between the two ostensibly allied armies as cold and even hostile. He stated that Soviet troops habitually refused to salute senior Romanian officers, as they were required to do by the Red Army's regulations. According to him, all troops sympathized with a Red Army sergeant who shot dead a Romanian colonel, after the Romanian slapped the Soviet sergeant for refusing to salute him as his rank demanded.[65] He also described another incident where a Soviet soldier walked by a Romanian colonel, refusing to greet him. The Soviet soldier then made the colonel stop, and he walked by him twice more, stressing his disrespect for the Romanian rank by refusing to greet him each time he walked by.[66] Romanian archival sources confirm that Soviet troops regularly disrespected senior Romanian officers, sometimes assaulting them and even murdering them. Two notes from the Romanian military delegation to the ACC, dated 11 March and 25 May 1946, listed well over a dozen violent incidents committed by Soviet soldiers and officers against their Romanian counterparts.[67]

The widespread rejection by the Red Army's frontline soldiers and officers of the Kremlin's postwar line, which stressed that not all Germans were enemies, that Austrians were Germany's first victims, and that all civilians should be treated correctly, is unsurprising. Soldiers fought a brutal war for four years against a genocidal enemy. Throughout this period, military officials encouraged hate and occasionally tolerated illegal violence against civilians. Predictably, Soviet troops refused to accept the Romanian army as their ally. Romania was a traditional Russian and Soviet adversary; the anti-Romanian hate propaganda was strong throughout the war and Romania had been an important German ally for most of the war. The always perceptive Slutskii described how the troops clung to the ideas of Il'ia Ehrenburg, the most prominent proponent of the anti-German hate propaganda, even after they were criticized by the Main Political Administration of the Red Army. In his words, "Ehrenburg did not leave us, he merely retreated, leaving behind 'moral left opposition' to our occupational authorities' peaceful policies."[68] Clearly, this so-called moral left opposition represented a significant chunk of the troops, and they were principally and even viscerally opposed to the Kremlin's new narrative that the Red Army liberated the former Axis countries and that the only Soviet enemies were Axis soldiers and officials.

Even though the war ended officially on 9 May, violence against Soviet soldiers, albeit on a much smaller scale, persisted after the German capitulation. In Austria, Hungary, and Romania, there were instances of attacks on Soviet soldiers, either by opponents of the nascent pro-communist regimes, by former Axis soldiers trying to return to their homes while avoiding capture, or, more often, by desperate civilians and local police who acted in self-defense.[69] In particular, it seems that such attacks were prevalent in Hungary.[70] Overall, these assaults were not frequent, and they were often justifiable since they were in self-defense or in response to Soviet acts of aggression. Nonetheless, they further poisoned the troops' perceptions of the local population.[71] The significance of such incidents is that they justified for Soviet troops the hostility with which they viewed civilians and made it more difficult for the rank and file to accept the new official line.

Additionally, the profile of the troops partially changed after the war. Filip Slaveski found that the influx of former forced laborers and prisoners of war into the Red Army added to the wave of violence at the end of the war.[72] The situation was similar with the 2nd and 3rd Ukrainian Fronts. Although precise figures are hard to come by, at a minimum, the two fronts were each reinforced by tens of thousands of former prisoners of war and slave laborers.[73] Soviet officials believed that recent recruits were even less disciplined and particularly prone to deserting.[74] Many of these soldiers had been treated terribly by their German overlords, and those who were freed from prisoner-of-war camps were survivors of the Nazi genocide against Soviet prisoners of war. Consequently, these soldiers, more than others, had a personal account to settle with Germans and their allies. One such soldier, Aleksandr Levin, survived captivity for four years while concealing his Jewish identity. Freed from a camp in late April, he joined the 2nd Ukrainian Front, fighting briefly in Czechoslovakia and Austria. In his first letter to his family, on 12 May, he wrote:

> (It is) terrible when I recall the hopelessness of existence in captivity, especially during the last two months which I spent in a stone torture chamber (*zastenka*). All, all, all of that is behind me! I am again a soldier of the Worker-Peasant Red Army. I now only regret that I wasn't able to show in the battles for our Motherland that which I thought about the entire time that I was in captivity. Admittedly, I must say that I relieved part of my hatred on the heads of the "pure-blooded" Aryan degenerates.[75]

Considering that the fighting was almost over by the time Levin rejoined the Red Army, it is likely that he vented his hatred either against civilians or German prisoners of war.

The Red Army troops' rampage in Europe was always accompanied by a sense that as members of a victorious army, they were entitled to compensation in the form of loot and even women's bodies. The German capitulation only encouraged these sentiments, despite the official propaganda's pronouncements. When the Soviet-appointed chancellor of the Austrian provisional government complained to Marshal Tolbukhin about the conduct of Soviet soldiers, the commander of the 3rd Ukrainian Front supposedly responded that the Soviet plundering was based on an ancient law of war that to the victor belonged the spoils.[76] The veracity of the Austrian chancellor's claims are uncertain since there is some doubt whether a Soviet marshal would admit as much to a foreigner. Nonetheless, they at least reveal how Austrians perceived Soviet policies based on the Red Army's behavior.

Moscow's policies did indirectly encourage plundering. Soviet troops were freed from customs control on 14 June 1945.[77] Undoubtedly, this policy shift invigorated their impulse to commit acts of looting in order to take the plunder with them home as they anticipated demobilization or transfer to the Soviet Union. Considering that according to some sources, only about half of the troops were fully uniformed, impoverished soldiers would have had a strong incentive at least to put clothes on their backs before they returned to the Soviet Union.[78]

The desire to enjoy the spoils of war and to take loot with them to the Soviet Union was not limited to the rank and file. Officers of higher rank had more opportunities to loot the most valuable goods, and they had better chances of transporting these across the border.[79] The corruption and greed of leading Soviet generals in Europe after the war have been well documented, with the author Anthony Beevor comparing the behavior of Soviet generals in postwar Germany to venal Ottoman pashas.[80] The situation was similar among officers of the Southern and Central Groups of Armies. For instance, the Commander of the 58th Dnepropetrovsk Mortar Regiment co-opted the unit's car for his family, which he brought over from the Soviet Union, assigning one soldier to be his wife's driver and another soldier to be the child's babysitter. He then tried to personally take possession of the car.[81] NKVD Major Afans'ev, a battalion commander in the NKVD Army's 34th Border Guard Regiment of the 2nd Ukrainian Front, seized 300–400 grams of gold items that had belonged to a Jewish family persecuted by Romanian authorities. The gold was stored in the battalion's vault for nine months, but Afans'ev did not register it with the regimental financial department.

Afans'ev was clearly planning to take the gold for himself.[82] One veterinarian's luggage weighed 983 kilograms when he arrived in Tashkent from Vienna. Obviously, most of the luggage consisted of loot.[83]

Among the most prized assets for higher-ranking officers were motorized vehicles, which they were allowed to bring with them to the Soviet Union.[84] In theory, officers could privately purchase vehicles in Europe and take the cars back home. In practice, however, there were not many cars left after the Red Army systematically confiscated motorized vehicles for official purposes. Therefore, according to a report by the military prosecutor, a series of officers bribed Romanian citizens to sign fictitious contracts stating that these officers had bought their cars from Romanians. In this way, the officers illegally privatized army cars.[85] Although none of these officers mentioned in the prosecutor's report managed to legally take control of cars, evidently, many did. To avoid detection of their ill-gotten goods when crossing the border, several generals clashed with the NKVD border guards when the latter wanted to check their documents and cars. In the most extreme case, the commander of the 59th Guards Division had his men disarm and beat up the NKVD border guards who tried to check the drivers' documents at the Soviet–Romanian border.[86] The value of cars must have been great to Soviet officers if they risked a conflict with the NKVD in order to keep the vehicles.

The widespread desire for loot can also, in part, be explained by the fact that Soviet soldiers and even higher-ranking officers came from a society that was much poorer than the European countries in which they were stationed after the war. Even the relatively privileged Soviet generals simply could not have obtained private cars in the Soviet Union. These needs were reinforced by the strong belief that they were entitled to goods and, to a lesser degree, to women as members of the conquering army. The change in the official line did nothing to challenge Soviet troops' needs and assumptions that had fueled their criminality in the first place.

8.4 Conclusion

The Kremlin and the Red Army's highest military leadership made their most determined effort to stamp out the frontline troops' abuse of civilians after the Third Reich's capitulation. Without having to fight a war, the command could focus more of its attention on reigning in the troops, whose conduct was undermining the Red Army's attempts to govern conquered territories. To this end, the Soviet leadership tried to change the narrative of the war. The new propaganda hammered home the message that the Red Army were liberators, and their sole enemies were Axis soldiers, officials, and members of the local far-right parties. Since the 2nd and 3rd Ukrainian Fronts did not fight in Germany proper, it was easy for the propagandists from the two fronts to emphasize the differences between the more inveterate German enemy and their Austrian, Hungarian, and Romanian allies, without inadvertently encouraging hate against Germans.

The results of these measures were limited, at best. New policies were too late to change the popular assumptions about the victorious army's rights and privileges with regard to conquered civilians, assumptions shared by the frontline troops and middle-ranking commanders. Likewise, the Soviet troops' hatred of the enemy was too deeply entrenched in their worldview and experiences to have been overturned by a propaganda campaign. None of the new policies that emanated from the Kremlin did anything to change the dynamics of relations between Soviet soldiers and European civilians. Finally, the new line did nothing to interfere with the dynamics between soldiers that fueled the violence: martial masculinity and the need for soldiers to bond with each other through attacks on women.

Conclusion

Historian Alexander Prusin, when talking about the Russian Empire's anti-Jewish violence in Eastern Galicia during World War I, argued that there were two modes of violence: the "authorized" violence by the state and the "wild" violence by the troops and civilian mobs. "Authorized" violence aimed to achieve the specific objective of impoverishing Jews while enriching the so-called Russian part of the population (as Imperial authorities viewed Galicians who largely considered themselves to be Ukrainians) through legal restrictions, reprisals, expulsions, and deportations. "Authorized" violence, Prusin continued, often degenerated into "wild" violence, examples of which included riots, pogroms, and looting.[1] He argued that both modes of violence advanced the Russian authorities' goal of nationalizing Eastern Galicia by impoverishing Jews and diminishing their numbers. Prusin's discussion of violence from above and below helps us think about the reasons for the Red Army's conduct in Europe.

The command structure was complex in the Red Army, but there were two layers of leadership. First, there was the leadership in Moscow. It consisted of Stalin, his immediate political underlings, and the Red Army's high command (Stavka, general staff, and the Main Political Administration). The second leadership component was in the field, with the forces. It consisted of the 2nd and 3rd Ukrainian Fronts commanders, as well as army, corps, divisional, regimental, battalion, and squadron commanders. Political departments, whose heads were deputy commanders in the army but who also reported to the Main Political Administration in Moscow, were responsible for propaganda and the morale of the troops.

When the Red Army marched into the Balkans and Central Europe, links existed between "authorized" and some forms of "wild" violence, but these connections should not be overstated. Moscow wanted, above all, to win the war as quickly as possible, regardless of material and human costs. Next, it sought substantial compensation from Romania, Hungary, and Austria, which it extracted through the systematic looting of these countries' wealth, the exploitation of former Axis soldiers and *Volksdeutsche* civilians as forced labor, and the imposition of burdensome reparations. Furthermore, the Kremlin was determined to replace the governing elites in all countries with neutral and then pro-Soviet politicians. To achieve these military and political goals, the Soviet leadership had to employ "authorized" violence.

Moscow's internationalist plans for controlling the region were different from the ethnic-based tsarist plans to "nationalize" borderlands that Prusin talked about. Soviet war aims contrasted even more starkly with Axis genocidal goals in the Soviet Union during World War II. Stalin wanted to strengthen the political forces loyal to the Soviet Union (communists) and eventually bring them to power. Through local communists, the Kremlin sought initially to have influence and then to rule the people who lived in the region, after some of the minorities such as the *Volksdeutsche* had been ethnically cleansed. Very illustrative of the divergence between Soviet and Nazis occupational regimes are their food policies in major cities. For instance, as soon as the Germans occupied Kyiv in 1941, they deliberately starved the city's population, killing hundreds of thousands in the famine as part of a wider plan to depopulate the Soviet Union's urban centers.[2] In contrast, one of the Soviet occupational regime's first moves in Vienna and Berlin was to feed the local population to prevent the outbreak of famines, even as it seized food for the Red Army.[3] Ultimately, the highest Soviet leadership planned to treat civilians in occupied territories, after the war ended and compensation was paid, as badly as they treated their population. Therefore, violence against civilians from below undermined the larger Soviet objective of governing the area.

What can be said at most about the Kremlin's complicity in "wild" violence was that it sent mixed signals to the frontline troops. For instance, the Kremlin's goal of feeding the Red Army and transferring wealth to the Soviet Union was advanced by the looting from below of soldiers and officers. The most obvious way in which Moscow encouraged this type of "wild" violence was Stavka's decision of December 1944 to allow soldiers and officers to send parcels to the Soviet Union. However, even this decision did not mean a blank check for soldiers to loot freely. The troops were formally required to purchase goods from *Voentorg* (the official Red Army supplier). Furthermore, when the decree was announced, it was accompanied by a propaganda campaign reminding soldiers that looting was a punishable offense in the Soviet armed forces. Therefore, soldiers and officers were placed in a peculiar predicament: They were told to purchase and send goods to their suffering relatives in the Soviet Union; however, goods were often unavailable in sufficient quantities.

The only obvious way out of this dilemma for soldiers was to loot. Yet, they were also instructed that looting was impermissible in propaganda campaigns, launched in parallel with the Stavka decision permitting them to send parcels to the Soviet Union.

Furthermore, the high command was always concerned with discipline, which was central to maintaining the army's fighting capacity. The Soviet leadership understood that armies preoccupied with looting and raping were less effective on the battlefield. The NKVD Army's campaign called "Order number 15/2-008063 Struggle with Immoral Events" was the foremost example of the leadership's struggle with undisciplined conduct. The campaign lasted for six months, from November 1944 to April 1945, and it involved officers on the level of the front threatening their subordinates with severe punishments for undisciplined behavior such as straggling, excessive drinking, plundering, and sexual assaults against women. Order number 15/2-008063 also committing an intense and prolonged propaganda campaign against such behavior, while criminals were demoted, transferred to the reserves as ordinary soldiers, or transferred to the Soviet Union. Undoubtedly, some NKVD Army soldiers and officers exposed to this campaign understood that criminal conduct was impermissible. There were other such campaigns in the Red Army, albeit on a smaller scale.

Links between "authorized" violence and "wild" violence are even weaker when it comes to sexual violence. Sexual violence did not advance Moscow's interests in the Balkans and Central Europe. Instead, leaders' permissive attitudes toward wartime rape as an incorrect but unavoidable feature of war played a role in allowing mass sexual violence to occur. This attitude was personified in Stalin's statements to Czechoslovak and Yugoslav leaders about rapes being an unavoidable part of the war.[4] The Soviet leader did not view rape as a serious problem. For him, the main thing was that the Red Army was victorious. Many Soviet men (and not only Soviet), ranging from high-ranking officers to ordinary infantrymen, shared the view that men in general and soldiers in particular needed sex. Thus, they may be excused if they obtained it by force. These popular attitudes to rape, when fused with hatred of the enemy and brutalization, led to a weakening of opposition to sexual violence within the Red Army and contributed to the normalization of rape.

In assessing "signals" that frontline troops received from above, it is critical to consider the role of the second layer of Soviet leadership (officers in positions of authority in the field) because they were in close contact with the rank-and-file. Marshals Malinovskii and Tolbukhin, commanders of the 2nd and 3rd Ukrainian Fronts, communicated with the rank and file through orders that were read to all of the troops of their respective fronts. In these orders, the two marshals regularly warned their troops against committing robberies, assaults, and rapes, while reminding them of the severe punishments that criminals could expect.

Soviet leadership, in Moscow and at the level of fronts, also instructed the rank and file on how they should behave toward civilians through propaganda, which was disseminated by the army's political departments. Propaganda sent even more mixed signals to the frontline soldiers and officers about the acceptability of "wild" violence than orders that came from Marshals Malinovskii and Tolbukhin or lower-level commanders. Officials in the Main Political Administration and officers of political departments believed that Soviet soldiers needed to hate the enemy and desire revenge to be motivated to fight. Therefore, propaganda agitators went to great lengths to exacerbate the desire for revenge against Germans, Romanians, and Hungarians by discussing Axis crimes against Soviet civilians and prisoners of war.

The vicious hate propaganda undoubtedly encouraged the blurring of the line between enemy soldiers and civilians, inciting Soviet soldiers to subject civilians to violence. The hate propaganda, however, was officially always aimed at German, Romanian, and Hungarian troops, and not at civilians. In some instances, agitators made it clear that soldiers ought to direct violence at the resisting enemy and not troops who surrendered. Furthermore, the hate propaganda stopped by the time the Red Army entered Austria, as it stressed that Austrians were the Nazis' first victims. Yet this change in the official line did not seem to bring relief to Austrian civilians. Overall, there is little doubt that the indoctrination campaign against the Germans, Romanians, and Hungarians signaled to frontline troops that all representatives of the "enemy" nations were valid targets and that their rage was justified given Axis crimes.

Furthermore, representatives of the Soviet leadership in the field engaged in "authorized" violence, insofar as they enforced orders that arrived from Moscow. For these individuals, the line between "authorized" and "wild" violence was very thin. As shown repeatedly in the study, officers, heads of command posts, intelligence officers, and others in positions of authority often engaged in "wild" violence while fulfilling their official tasks. They looted regularly (even before they were allowed to send parcels back home), they drank excessively, and they committed sexual violence. Such conduct must have also signaled to some of the rank and file that "wild" violence would be tolerated by the Red Army's control mechanisms.

The Red Army's disciplinary policies were the most important way in which the Soviet leadership communicated to soldiers the limits of permissible conduct in relation to civilians. Disciplinary policies, unlike propaganda that set the tone and instructed the troops on how to view the wider world around them, had a direct and potentially serious impact on soldiers. Thus, if the control mechanisms could have investigated reports of violence against civilians consistently, and if they would have punished all criminals severely, then the leadership would have sent a clear signal to the frontline troops that the abuse of the civilian population was impermissible.

It is impossible to draw definite conclusions about the Red Army's disciplinary policies while military tribunal records remain inaccessible.[5] However, some information on the workings of the Soviet military judicial system can be found in broader analytical reports that summarize the activities of military tribunals and to a lesser degree in personal accounts. These sources allow us to make some conclusions about the signals that the leadership sent to the frontline troops through disciplinary policies. The military tribunals in the first months of 1945 for all of the Red Army convicted 4,148 officers and a large number of soldiers for violence against civilians. The military tribunals executed only a few of these criminals.[6] Presumably, in the Red Army in general, as in the 2nd and 3rd Ukrainian Fronts, the vast majority of convicted soldiers and officers were sent to penal units.

The Red Army's control mechanisms processed and punished a large number of soldiers and officers for crimes against civilians in Europe. Certainly, most soldiers testified that they witnessed at least one so-called exemplary execution when officers had a deserter or a rapist executed in front of their comrades. The Soviet leadership, therefore, did not completely ignore the issue of rape. At the same time, given the size of the Red Army, and more importantly, the magnitude of violence that the troops committed, these measures were inadequate to prevent continued abuses. Furthermore, the overwhelming majority of convicted robbers and rapists were sent to penal units, where some continued to be in close contact with the civilian population even if under stricter control.

There was more that Moscow and the Red Army command in the field could have done to send clearer signals that "wild" violence against civilians was unacceptable in general. The Soviet leadership could have ceased hate propaganda once the Red Army entered Europe, and they could have ordered more executions of soldiers who committed violence instead of sending them to penal units. Even though the Soviet leadership did undertake measures to curtail violence, given its intensity and scale, it is highly improbable that either the Kremlin or officers in the field could have prevented it entirely.

Although the sexual violence and looting were facilitated by authorities at the top and middle levels, they ultimately originated from below. There is no single answer as to why soldiers embarked on the rampage in the Balkans and Central Europe. As the Red Army's 2nd and 3rd Ukrainian Fronts moved across numerous countries of the Balkans and Central Europe, they developed a series of stereotypes. These extremely widespread views were shaped by the official line, although they were independent of it. The Soviet soldiers' behavior largely reflected how they viewed a given country. Thus, the troops were dismissive of Romanians as culturally and economically inferior, considering them to be a nation of small traders. In contrast, Soviet soldiers were sympathetic to Bulgarians and Yugoslavs because many welcomed them as liberators, while they also respected the Yugoslavs for their resistance to the common enemy. Soviet soldiers viewed Hungarians as German allies, and they were angered that people who lived so well would invade a poor country such as the Soviet Union. Finally, they considered Austrians to be Germans, and they behaved there similarly to other Soviet armies on the territory of the Third Reich. These stereotypes help explain why Soviet soldiers acted with more restraint in Bulgaria and Yugoslavia than in Romania, Hungary, and Austria.

The Soviet troops' desire for revenge against the "enemy" for their misery on the frontline and the suffering of their families and friends under the occupation played a role in mass rapes. However, explanations that stress this motive can only go so far since the magnitude of Soviet violence in Hungary did not match the Hungarian role in Axis crimes in the Soviet Union or the Hungarian army's contribution to the German war effort. Similarly, the argument that intense combat fueled violence against civilians, as was the case in Hungary, can only go so far in explaining the rapes. There were many intense battles on Soviet soil, such as Stalingrad and Kursk, but the heavy fighting did not result in violence against civilians in Stalingrad and Kursk areas on a scale anywhere near to what happened in Budapest.

The common thread in many Soviet male troops' interactions with all women – Soviet servicewomen, the women of "neutral" Bulgaria and "allied" Yugoslavia, as well as "enemy" Romanian, Hungarian, and Austrian women – is that they viewed them primarily as potential sex partners. Many Red Army soldiers and officers viewed sex to be a legitimate reward for risking their lives and fighting successfully against the enemy. To get what the troops fervently believed was their entitlement, men could court women, harass them, or sexually assault them. This did not mean that in the soldiers' worldview violence was acceptable against all women all of the time. They were more likely to court servicewomen and, in the case of officers who held power in the army, to bribe them with gifts or offer them protection from dangerous tasks or other men in the Red Army. Soviet soldiers were also, overall, more restrained with regard to Soviet, Bulgarian, and Yugoslav women.

There was less restraint in Romania, Hungary, and Austria. Soviet troops were more likely to employ outright violence to obtain sex there, explaining why there were more rape victims in these three countries. Furthermore, the Soviet view of "enemy" women specifically justified the violence. Most notably, the Red Army troops told stories of how Romanian men regularly traded their wives for financial gain or how Hungarian women aggressively pursued Soviet soldiers. These narratives, which are not credible, served the purpose of implicitly justifying sexual violence by blaming the victims. The reason that in "enemy" countries the Soviet soldiers committed mass sexual violence was that their negative views of nations, also known as the ethnic gaze, fed into the misogynist worldview in which women were deemed the legitimate spoils of war.

This study has paid close attention to the issue of the extremely large number of stragglers that the Red Army produced as it entered the Balkans and Central Europe. From August 1944 to May 1945, more than a hundred and fifty thousand soldiers were detained by NKVD armies and command posts, behind the frontlines. Among them were tens of thousands of deserters, stragglers, and outright criminals, who avoided the frontlines and terrorized the civilian population in the rear. European witness testimony and Soviet reports make it clear that stragglers were the worst behaved toward civilians, and there is no doubt that they contributed heavily to the overall violence that has been attributed to the Red Army.

The presence of so many stragglers also reflected the limits of the command's control of the frontline troops. The stragglers and deserters represented an ideological and military threat to the Soviet regime. Their existence undermined the myth of a unified people fighting in the Great Patriotic War, but more practically, they also sapped the Red Army's combat strength. Yet, the leadership was unable to eliminate stragglers and deserters. If the military and political leadership could not prevent this threat, then they were certainly incapable of preventing crimes against civilians that were of far lesser concern.

In sum, there is no single explanation that can account for the proliferation of military violations in the two army groups in 1944 and 1945. Instead, a multitude of continuously evolving and mutually interacting factors must be considered. The troops' desire for revenge against "enemy" nations that waged the genocidal war against the Soviet Union, fueled by hate propaganda and extraordinarily brutal fighting, was an important reason for the violence against civilians. Furthermore, the attitude prevalent among many Soviet men – commanders responsible for discipline as well as the rank and file – that all men, and especially soldiers, were entitled to sex, led to the normalization of wartime rape. Consequently, the men, even those who seemingly did not engage in sexual violence, were understanding of those who did, allowing for the proliferation of sexual violence in the army's ranks. Moreover, the leadership, which could have stopped or lessened the sexual violence by pursuing stricter disciplinary policies, was focused overwhelmingly on winning the war and not the violence against civilians. Finally, the Red Army was an ill-disciplined force. The high command was unable to control their soldiers. This is most evident in the proliferation of a large number of deserters and stragglers, among whom were criminals who terrorized the civilians. All of these factors together help explain the Red Army's behavior in the Balkans and Central Europe.

C.1 The Red Army's Atrocities in Comparative Perspective

Although the global history of atrocities in general and sexual violence in particular during World War II remains to be written, this book has offered numerous comparisons between the Red Army and its peers. The narratives about the Red Army's mass sexual violence that dominate the English-speaking world, which come largely from Germany's experience were fused with the postwar fears of Communist and Soviet/oriental expansionism.[7] Although these narratives depict the Soviet army as a historically unique horde of rapists and looters, was the Red Army exceptional, both in its troops' conduct and the command's reactions to it?

C.1.1 Brothels

The underlying assumption about sex, shared by many decision-makers during World War II in various armies, was that men needed to have sex to perform well in battle and that rape was an unfortunate but necessary part of war. Otherwise, officers feared that discipline would break down as soldiers' sexual frustrations built up, the rank and file would pursue civilians, leading to the proliferation of venereal diseases, or homosexuality would spread among the troops.[8] Although these assumptions were shared by individuals in Soviet, American, and Axis armies, they were enshrined into policy by German, Japanese, and Italian high commands.

The German army used existing brothels across Europe to provide sex to its soldiers. In the Soviet Union, where the Stalinist state did not permit the existence of a prostitution infrastructure, the German army set up an elaborate system of brothels. The women working in brothels were usually not prostitutes before the war. They were coerced into brothels through threats of deportation to Germany, some were kidnapped at gunpoint, while others entered brothels "voluntarily" because they or their family members were starving.[9] As Regina Mühlhäuser noted, many women were sexually enslaved, but even for women who reported to brothels of their own volition, the line between voluntary action and coercion was blurry given the prevailing conditions in occupied territories.[10] Although little is known about Wehrmacht brothels, the newest research indicates that women forced to work in brothels had to serve eighteen men per day, and their communication with the outside world was curtailed.[11] When the German army was pushed westward, there was evidence that some women were evacuated, while others were shot.[12] No other military in the European theater of World War II developed such an exploitative system of sexual slavery, which was inseparable from the wider racial war of conquest that Berlin waged in the East.

Italians followed the German example by creating brothels for their soldiers on the Eastern front. The Italian system appears to have been less coercive. Although famine also compelled some women to work in Italian brothels as in German brothels, the Italians dismissed girls and women after becoming infected with venereal diseases, and the women deployed in brothels were not forcefully kidnapped and held against their will.[13] It should also be mentioned that the Japanese created a similar system of sexual slavery in the Far East as the Germans, enslaving tens or hundreds of thousands of girls and women across their Co-Prosperity Sphere in the so-called comfort stations.[14] The institutions that the Germans and Japanese created, which confined girls and women and compelled them to sexually serve millions of Axis soldiers, had no parallel to the Allied armies, but especially the Red Army.

The United States had an official ban on the use of brothels.[15] Nonetheless, numerous generals tried to organize for their troops to visit brothels, as they believed that access to regulated sex would solve the problem of rape while providing a safer environment for their soldiers to avoid venereal diseases. These brothels were not operated by the Allied militaries directly, and they typically employed women who were prostitutes before the Allied occupation. For instance, General Patton in Palermo established a medical team for the six largest brothels for exclusive use by his soldiers. The brothels existed before the Americans occupied the city.[16] The American high command tended to shut down brothels in France and Italy once it learned of generals regulating them or sending their troops there.[17] In Paris, however, despite the Chief

Surgeon declaring brothels off limits, the unofficial policy prevailed, with brothels organized by race and rank for American troops.[18]

The American unofficial reliance on brothels was inspired by similar ideas about soldiering and sex that animated the Germans: Soldiers needed to have sex to maintain their military performance and to prevent rape, and sex needed to be regulated to prevent the spread of venereal diseases in the ranks.[19] However, lacking the murderous Nazi racial ideology, the brothels that operated in American occupation zones were different. The women seem to have been less coerced into working there, and they were freer to leave, although near-famine-like conditions also drove women into prostitution in war-ravaged impoverished areas such as southern Italy.[20] The Red Army personnel sometimes utilized brothels. However, unlike the Americans, there is no evidence that Soviet generals in the field regulated brothels or encouraged their soldiers to visit them. Also, unlike their German or Italian enemies, Soviet officers did not go into the pimping business of creating brothels where none existed.

C.1.2 Sexual Violence Outside of Brothels

The patterns of American soldiers' (GIs) behavior were similar to those of the Red Army, even though it was far less violent overall; their treatment of women was shaped by their views of various nations and the wider military context. They committed few rapes in the United Kingdom, more in France, and they committed most acts of sexual violence in Germany. Even according to the official Judge Advocate General's Corps report, the American soldiers viewed French women to be "attractive and free with their love," while in Germany the Americans were conquerors leading to the proliferation of rapes.[21] Furthermore, most rapes were reported at the tip of the spear during the offensives, among combat troops, resembling the Soviet rampage in Romania during the breakthrough after Iasi Kishinev Operation.[22] When the breakthrough occurred on enemy soil, the number of reported rapes increased considerably, as American generals acknowledged.[23] In April 1945, Judge Advocate General was receiving 500 reports of rape per week.[24]

The American military leaders, like their Soviet counterparts, intended to govern Germany after the war and, ultimately, needed their troops to behave correctly. General Omar Bradley, commander of the US Twelfth Army Group, stated that the Allies needed to impress upon Germans that they were morally superior, which required "the maintenance of discipline throughout the occupying forces at the highest possible level."[25] The US commanders were also worried about the spread of venereal diseases undermining the Army's combat capacity, in some instances equating infections with betrayal.[26] Despite these concerns, it is estimated that 50 percent of all married troops and 80 percent of all single American soldiers had sex during the war.[27] In Italy in 1945, it has been estimated that 80 percent of American troops had sex, 75 percent of whom said they paid for it and 25 percent claimed that they paid nothing at all.[28] In Italy, like in France, brothels were legal before the US occupation.[29]

According to Ruth Lawlor, 904 American soldiers were tried for rape in the European Theater of Operations from 1942 to 1945, just over half of whom were convicted. Of these, ninety-six men were executed for crimes of rape or rape and murder. Almost 90 percent of those ultimately executed for rape were African Americans, even though they comprised only 10 percent of the American troop strength. Lawlor explained this phenomenon with reference to the centrality of the Jim Crow system of racial segregation to the US Army's disciplinary regime, which was also used to shield combat troops and elite units from prosecution. Unlike the Red Army, the US Army never prosecuted officers for sex crimes, further illustrating the fact that the US military justice system was used to shield the privileged from prosecution.[30] Cases of rape were usually brought to trial when they were necessary to preserve relations between the occupation Army and the host country, and then, only when doing so would not bring unfavorable attention to the American war effort.

When the Nazi leaders issued the infamous criminal orders in the Soviet Union before Operation Barbarossa, one of the decrees, The Military Jurisdiction Decree, stipulated that prosecution of soldiers who committed crimes against civilians was not obligatory and should be undertaken only to maintain discipline. The Decree also invested divisional commanders with the authority to take disciplinary action.[31] As Mühlhäuser noted, even though the Soviet Union was turned into an extralegal territory, not everything was permitted. Some divisional officers interpreted the Decree strictly, while others were much more lenient.[32] However, the German military justice system stands out for officially applying different standards to prosecuting rape in the Soviet Union. The Red Army, officially at least, applied the same regulation wherever it operated.

There is no comprehensive data available on how Wehrmacht dealt with rapists. David Raub Snyder, who examined documents from the 6th and 253rd Infantry Divisions, which fought on the Eastern front, found that there were only a handful of prosecutions of sex offenders, primarily for homosexuality between soldiers.[33] He also examined 418 prosecutions from dozens of military courts throughout the army, but only 40 percent of the sample were from the Eastern front, even though the majority of Wehrmacht was deployed in the East.[34] Snyder's figures indicate that the Wehrmacht gave a freer hand to soldiers to rape in the East. Furthermore, Snyder found that Wehrmacht's system of justice was primarily concerned with maintaining discipline, pacification of the partisan threat, and preserving Wehrmacht's "usable human material," which meant that most soldiers were sent to penal battalions, especially from 1942.[35] The Wehrmacht, like the Red Army, was concerned with continuing to utilize the soldiers, regardless of the crimes they committed, by sending them to penal units.

Systematic statistics for the Red Army prosecutions are not accessible to researchers, but based on partially available information, several comparisons can be made with the situation in the American Army. First, the Soviet military justice did not single out Asian troops from Russia's Far East or Central Asia for prosecution, even though the Germans, Austrians, and Hungarians in their narratives focused on Asian troops as leading the way in raping.[36] The majority of troops prosecuted for rape, as far as can be inferred from archival materials based on their names, were East Slavs.[37] Second, throughout 1944 and 1945, hundreds of thousands of Red Army troops were prosecuted for military crimes and criminal code violations.[38] The number of troops prosecuted for rape or abuse of civilians was a minority of all cases, but it was still significant, certainly more so than in the Wehrmacht. We know that just in the first months of 1945, 4,148 officers and a large number of soldiers were prosecuted for committing crimes against civilians.[39] If we were to assume that a similar number of officers were prosecuted in the last four months of 1944, then it could be concluded that over 8,000 officers were prosecuted during the war. If we were to add the prosecutions of soldiers, many more of whom were prosecuted, as well as the prosecution of soldiers and officers after the war, then it could be conservatively estimated that well over 20,000 Red Army personnel were prosecuted for crimes against European civilians. However, it should be kept in mind that these are estimates and that we will know the exact number of official prosecutions only after the Soviet-era archives are completely opened to researchers. The vast majority of those convicted were sent to penal units but some were executed or sent to labor camps.

Unlike the American justice system, which seemed to have protected officers, the Stalinist state had a history of brutality toward its elites and managers. The Red Army was not an exception, both during the Great Terror when it was one of the regime's targets and during the war. Indicative of this approach, the Soviet state executed fifty-two generals during the war, mostly for incompetence in the early stages of the war.[40]

Historian Oleg Budnitskii highlighted many instances of extrajudicial violence against lower-ranking officers by their superiors, which largely went unpunished.[41] The Red Army, unlike the US Army, had no compunction in punishing its officers for a wide array of crimes, including rapes.[42]

When it comes to sexual violence outside of brothels, it is difficult to estimate the scale of rape the Germans committed in the Soviet Union. By numerous accounts, sexual violence committed by the German troops against Soviet civilian women was widespread across the vast occupied space.[43] The German soldiers also engaged in "occasional sexual bartering," usually offering Soviet women food for sex.[44]

Because of underreporting everywhere, and the difficulty in comparing vastly different regions of the war theater, it is impossible to get a truly accurate picture of the prevalence of sexual violence committed by American troops in Europe. The best estimates we have, including Robert Lilly's claim that the American soldiers raped around 14,000 women in Western Europe, are still partial: Lilly obtained his figure based on the number of rapes reported by the US military, which he then multiplied twenty times to get what he thought to be a more accurate number.[45] There are no comparable figures for the Soviet case, as it is not known how many rapes were reported by the Red Army's prosecutors and judges.

The French figures about the number of rapes committed by American soldiers, to the degree that they are available, indicate more instances of rapes. According to French information, the US troops committed 208 rapes and 30 murders in the Department of Manche during the war.[46] Applying Lilly's formula, it would appear that the Americans raped 4,160 women in 1944 and 1945 in the Department of Manche, which had a population of 435,468 in 1946.[47] These figures indicate that the GIs committed many rapes. If we compare the American conduct in Manche with the Soviet behavior in the county of Arad, which had a similar population of 413,368 and where the Romanian authorities received reports about 22 murders and the rape of 213 women in 21 days (4,260 according to Lilly's formula), it becomes clear that the Soviet conduct was incomparably worse.

Manche was not representative of all of France, as it was located in Normandy, where many of the US troops deployed in Europe passed on their way to the front and back home. Presumably, in other parts of France, there were far fewer rapes. In contrast, only the 2nd Ukrainian Front operated in Arad. Furthermore, the Soviet figures are for twenty-one days, but American for the entirety of the war and the postwar period. Finally, the Soviet occupation of Romania was punitive and much more brutal. Thus, it must have been harder for women there to lodge complaints with the authorities than in France. All of these factors further indicate that the GI behavior in Manche was much more restrained than the Soviet conduct in Arad.

In Germany, the Soviet rampage was much more violent than the American conduct. According to German historian Miriam Gebhardt, the Western Allies raped 190,000 German women from 1944 to the end of the occupation, 55 percent of whom (104,500) were raped by American soldiers.[48] Gebhardt's estimate is based on mothers' postwar claims to German authorities that 5 percent of illegitimate children with foreign fathers were born as a result of rape. Gebhardt also utilized studies that suggest that one in ten rapes result in pregnancy and that one in ten such pregnancies were brought to term. She did not have reliable figures for the Soviet zone, but Gebhardt still estimated that Soviet military personnel raped 670,000 German women.[49] Thus, her figures for the Soviet number of rapes in Germany are more speculative. Another problem with Gebhardt's methodology, which she admitted, was that her study failed to account for rapes of boys, men, and girls, as well as women too young or too old to give birth.[50] Some women were killed during the rape, so these victims were also excluded from her statistics. Other scholars have estimated that Soviet soldiers raped up to 2 million German women.[51] Gebhardt's estimates suggest that the American soldiers committed mass rapes in Germany but far fewer than Soviet troops. While these figures are estimates, they do allow us to speculate about the broader dynamics that characterize wartime sexual violence.

Returning to the question of Soviet exceptionalism when it comes to the issue of rapes, the Red Army was the only major belligerent in the war that eschewed brothels, as a result of Marxist–Leninist–Stalinist determination to root out institutionalized prostitution. Soviet commanders neither encouraged their soldiers to visit brothels like some of their American counterparts did nor did they create a system of sexual slavery like the German and Japanese armies. This is not to suggest that there was a link between the availability of brothels and rape of women outside of brothels. After all, there were no brothels in the Soviet Union, but the Red Army troops did not commit mass rapes of Russian and Ukrainian women. The Wehrmacht's use of sexual slavery and official discouragement of prosecution of soldiers who committed crimes against Soviet civilians, rooted in the racial war the Nazis waged, put the German military in a different category than the Red Army, even if German soldiers may have committed fewer rapes outside of brothels.

Similar dynamics shaped Soviet and American soldiers' conduct. Soldiers in both armies felt a sense of entitlement to women and shared the assumption that men needed sex to increase their combat effectiveness. Both armies banned sexual fraternization and sexual violence, the Soviets more vigorously.[52] Both armies prosecuted a minority of all rapists, but the Red Army did so more energetically. Yet, the Red Army committed by far more rapes. The fact the Red Army had 1 million soldiers more in Germany than the US Army partially explains this.[53]

Other factors that help explain why the Soviet troops committed more rapes include the fact that the Kremlin's occupation policies were more punitive. The Stalinist Soviet Union was one of the most violent and brutal dictatorships, and so was the regime's treatment of its military personnel. Killings of its own soldiers and officers, whether in extrajudicial attacks or more formal prosecutions, were without parallel among the Allies. The reserve regiments that most soldiers from 1944 and 1945 experienced resembled forced labor camps more than the army. Furthermore, the Red Army was a less effective and disciplined force, evident also in the number of deserters and stragglers that it produced. The fighting was also more ferocious on the Eastern front than in the West, while the American homeland was spared the genocidal occupation. The Soviet casualties, both military and civilian, could not compare with the losses experienced by their Western Allies. The Eastern front was much more brutal and so was the Soviet soldiers' conduct.

Notes

Introduction

1. RGASPI, f. 17, op. 125, d. 241, ll. 86–97.
2. Semen Timoshenko, *Distsiplinarnyi Ustav Krasnoi Armii* (Leningrad: Voenizdat, 1941), 3.
3. Jochen Hellbeck, *Stalingrad: The City that Defeated the Third Reich*, trans. Christopher Tauchen and Dominic Bonfiglio (New York: Public Affairs, 2015), 115.
4. G. F. Krivosheev, ed., *Rossiia i SSSR v voinakh XX veka: Poteri vooruzhennykh sil* (Moscow: Olma-Press, 2001), 261. This figure is the average size of the Red Army in the third quarter of the year.
5. Ibid., 298.
6. Miriam Gebhardt, *Crimes Unspoken. The Rape of German Women at the End of the Second World War*, trans. Nick Somers (Malden: Polity Press, 2017), 17.
7. Anna Hajkova, *The Last Ghetto: An Everyday History of Theresienstadt* (Oxford: Oxford University Press, 2020), 12.
8. The website address is iremember.ru. Numerous scholars have based their studies in part on the interviews conducted by the administrators of the site. For more information on this source, see Roger Reese, *Why Stalin's Soldiers Fought* (Lawrence: University Kansas Press, 2011), x; Roger Markwick and Euridice Cardona, *Soviet Women on the Frontline in the Second World War* (New York: Palgrave Macmillan, 2012), 5–6.
9. Aleksej Timofejev, *Rusi i drugi svetski rat u Jugoslaviji: Uticaj SSSR-a i ruskih emigranata na događaje u Jugoslaviji 1941–1945* (Belgrade: Institut za noviju istoriju Srbije, 2011), 216.
10. For Romania, see Constantin Hlihor and Ion Scurtu, *The Red Army in Romania* (Iasi, Oxford, Portland: The Center for Romanian Studies, 2000). For Hungary, see Krisztian Ungvary, *The Siege of Budapest: 100 days in World War II*, trans. Ladislaus Lob (New Haven: Yale University Press, 2005); for Austria, see Barbara Stelzl-Marx, *Stalins Soldaten in Österreich Die Innensicht der sowjetischen Besatzung 1945–1955* (Vienna: Böhlau Wien, 2011).
11. David Glantz, *Colossus Reborn: The Red Army at War, 1941–1943* (Lawrence: University Press of Kansas, 2005), 378. Glantz included in control organs the state security, political departments, and judicial institutions.

1 On the Eve of the Balkan Offensive

1. Petr Mikhin, *Guns against the Reich: Memoirs of a Soviet Artillery Officer on the Eastern Front* (Mechanicsburg: Stackpole Books, 2011).
2. Richard Overy, *Russia's War* (New York: Penguin Books, 1998), 242.
3. Glantz, *Colossus Reborn*, 141.
4. Chris Bellamy, *Absolute War: Soviet Russia in the Second World War: A Modern History* (London: Macmillan, 2007), 600.
5. Krivosheev, *Rossiia i SSSR v voinakh XX veka: Poteri vooruzhennykh sil; staticheskoe issledovanie* (Moscow: OLMA-Press, 2001), 290–291.
6. RGASPI, f. 17, op. 125, d. 241, l. 90.
7. Iuri Mukhin, *Po povetske i po prizyvu. Nekadrovye Soldaty Velikoi Otechestvennoi Voine* (Moscow: Iuaza/Eksmo, 2005), 9.
8. David Glantz, *Colossus Reborn*, 595.
9. Krivosheev, *Rossiia i SSSR*, 292.
10. TsDAGO, f. 57, op. 4, d. 314, l. 95.
11. Lieutenant Colonel V. A. Matsulenko, "Combat Activities by the Forces of the Third Ukrainian Front's 37th Army in the Iasi-Kishinev Operation (August 1944)" (Candidate Dissertation [Soviet equivalent of doctoral dissertation], Frunze Military Academy, 1951), reproduced in Richard Harrison, ed., *The Iasi-Kishinev Operation: The Red Army's Summer Offensive into the Balkans (20–20 August 1944): Soviet General Staff*, trans. Richard Harrison (Solihull: Helion & Company, 2017), 223.
12. David Glantz, *When Titans Clashed: How the Red Army Stopped Hitler* (Lawrence: University Press of Kansas, 1995), 179–180. For rifle division, see TsAMO RF, f. 4, op. 11, d. 62, ll. 130, document reproduced in V. A. Zolatarev ed., *Russkii Arkhiv: Velikaia* Otechestvennaia: Prikazy *Narodnogo Komissara Oborony SSSR 22 iunia 1941 g.–1942 g.* (T. 13 2–2) (Moscow: Terra, 1997), 176–177.
13. IAN RAN, f. 2, op. 31, d. 30, l. 106.
14. A. P. Artem'ev, *Bratskii boevoi soiuz narodov SSSR v Velikoi Otechestvennoi voine* (Moscow: Mysl, 1975), 58.
15. Mansur Abdulin, *Red Road From Stalingrad: Recollections of a Soviet Infantryman* (Mechanicsburg: Stackpole Books, 2004), 144.
16. Ibid., 144.
17. Mikhin, *Guns against the Reich*, 127.
18. Spetarul Milesku et al., eds., *Istoriia Respubliki Moldova. S drevneishikh vremen do nashikh dnei* (Kishinev: Elan-Poligraf, 2002), 240.
19. Alexander Hill, *The Red Army and the Second World War* (Cambridge: Cambridge University Press, 2017), 515.
20. For the 59th Army, see Glantz, *Colossus Reborn*, 591; for the 60th Army, see No author, "Auschwitz Holocaust Memorial Ceremonies Begin without Putin, Obama," RT, accessed May 27, 2016, www.rt.com/news/226543-poland-auschwitz-commemoration-putin/. The article features a picture of a document from TsAMO RF, which the Ministry of Defense released in 2015.
21. Hill, *The Red Army*, 516.
22. Alexandra Orme, *Comes the Comrade* (New York: William Morrow & Company, 1950), 61.

23. Timofejev, *Rusi*, 216.
24. Glantz, *Colossus Reborn*, 471.
25. Timofejev, *Rusi*, 216; see also Antony Beevor, *The Fall of Berlin 1945* (London: Viking, 2002), 14.
26. RGVA, f. 32905, op. 1, d. 198, l. 302.
27. RGVA, f. 32900, op. 1, d. 484, l. 74.
28. For Malinovskii, see Boris Sokolov, *Marshal Malinovskii: Hero of the Soviet Union: Architect of the Modern Soviet Army*, trans. Richward W. Harrison (Solihull: Helion & Company, 2017), 13–14; for Timoshenko, see R. M. Portugal'skii, A. S. Domank, and A. P. Kovalenko, *Marshal S. K. Timoshenko* (Moscow: Izdatel'stvo MOF "Pobeda-1945 god," 1994), 12.
29. N. V. Petrov, *Kto rukovodil organami gosbezopasnosti, 1941–1954: Spravochnik* (Moscow: Zven'ia, 2010), 298.
30. Gennadii Krivozhin, Aleksei Nosov, and Dmitrii Romanov, *Zolotye Zvezdy Poles'ia. Ocherki o Geroiakh Sovetskogo Soiuza* (Kiev: Izdatel'stvo Politicheskoi literatury Ukrainy, 1978), 131.
31. V. A. Zhilin, *Tankisty-geroi 1943–1945 gg* (Moscow: Iauza i Eksmo, 2008), Chapter "Zhizn – sluzhenie Rodine."
32. No author, "Kuz'ma Nikolaevich Derevianko," *Pamiat' Naroda*, accessed May 23, 2020, https://pamyat-naroda.ru/commander/340/.
33. No author, "Aleksei Sergeevich Zheltov," *Pamiat' Naroda*, accessed May 23, 2020, https://pamyat-naroda.ru.
34. M. G. Vozhakin et al., eds., *Velikaia Otechestvennaia. Komandarmy. Voenni biograficheskii slovar'* (Moscow: Kuchkovo Pole, 2005), 153–154.
35. David R. Marples, Eduard Baidaus, and Mariya Melentyeva, "Causes of the 1932 Famine in Soviet Ukraine: Debates at the Third All-Ukrainian Party Conference,"*Canadian Slavonic Papers* 56.3–56.4 (2014): 295.
36. On eating rook's eggs, see Interview with Nikolai Zubko, *Ia pomniu*, accessed May 27, 2016, http://iremember.ru/memoirs/pekhotintsi/zubko-nikolay-yakovlevich/. On eating beets, see Interview with Vasilii Marin, *Ia pomniu*, accessed May 27, 2016, http://iremember.ru/memoirs/pulemetchiki/marin-vasiliy-vladimirovich/. On earing leaves, see Interview with Aleksandr Solov'ev, *Ia pomniu*, accessed May 27, 2016, http://iremember.ru/memoirs/razvedchiki/solovev-aleksandr-ivanovich/. On the assistance from the West, see L. A. Gurvits, *Vospominaniia frontovogo radista. Ot KV-radiostantsii – do morskikh krylatykh raket* (St. Petersburg: Ku't Inform Press, 2008), 29.
37. On cannibalism, see Interview with Zubko, *Ia pomniu*. On bloated stomachs, see Interview with Aleksandr Solov'ev, *Ia pomniu*.
38. Interview with Grigorii Russkikh, *Ia pomniu*, 2010, accessed November 28, 2024, https://iremember.ru/memoirs/pekhotintsi/russkikh-grigoriy-antonovich/.
39. Interview with Mariia Rist (Fedorko), *Ia pomniu*, accessed November 28, 2024, https://iremember.ru/memoirs/svyazisti/rist-fedorko-mariya-kuzminichna/.
40. Ibid., 86.
41. TsDAGO, f. 57, op. 4, d. 347, l. 92.
42. IAN RAN, f. 2, op. 101, d. 2, l. 3.
43. Gurvits, V*ospominaniia*, 74; N. A. Kirsanov and S. I. Drobiazko, "Velikaia Otechestvennaia voina 1941–1945 gg: natsional'nye i dobrovol'cheskie

formirovaniia po raznye storony fronta," *Otechestvennaia Istoriia* 6 (2001): 60–75, accessed May 27, 2016, http://militera.lib.ru/research/1/art/card 41557.html.
44. Karel Berkhoff, *Harvest of Despair: Life and Death in Ukraine under Nazi Rule* (Cambridge: Belknap Press of Harvard University Press, 2004), 90–91.
45. Christian Streit, "Soviet Prisoners of War in the Hands of the Wehrmacht" in Hannes Heer and Klaus Naumann, eds., *War of Extermination: The German Military in World War II, 1941–1944* (New York: Berghahn Books, 2000), 80.
46. Ibid.
47. Ibid., 81.
48. Mark Edele, "Take (No) Prisoners! The Red Army and German POWs, 1941–1943," *The Journal of Modern History* 88:2 (2016): 347–348.
49. Doris L. Bergen, *War & Genocide: A Concise History of the Holocaust 3rd Edition* (Lanham: Rowman & Littlefield, 2016), 186–187.
50. Ibid., 129.
51. Alex Kay, "'The Purpose of the Russian Campaign Is the Decimation of the Slavic Population by Thirty Million,' the Radicalization of German Food Policy in Early 1941," in Alex J. Kay, Jeff Rutherford, and David Stahel, Nazi Policy on the Eastern Front eds., *1941: Total War, Genocide, and Radicalization* (Rochester: University of Rochester Press, 2012), 111.
52. Quoted in Berkhoff, *Harvest*, 89.
53. Ibid., 309.
54. For less brutal, see Vladimir Solonari, *A Satellite Empire: Romanian Rule in Southwestern Ukraine, 1941–1944* (Ithaca: Cornell University Press, 2019), 235–237, and for exploitation, see Ibid., Chapter 7.
55. Jeff Rutherford, *Combat and Genocide on the Eastern Front: The German Infantry's War, 1941–1944* (Cambridge: Cambridge University Press, 2014), 7.
56. Oleksandr Melnyk, *World War II as an Identity Project: Historicism, Legitimacy Contests, and the (Re-) Construction of Political Communities in Ukraine, 1939–1946* (New York: Columbia University Press, 2023), 336.
57. Yitzhak Arad, *The Holocaust in the Soviet Union* (Lincoln: University of Nebraska Press, 2009), 525.
58. Krivosheev, *Rossiia i SSSR*, 232.
59. Yury Boshyk ed., *Ukraine during World War II: History and Its Aftermath: A Symposium* (Edmonton: Canadian Institute of Ukrainian Studies, 1986), 28.
60. For 26.6 million, see Krivosheev, *Rossia i SSSR*, 227. Krivosheev estimated that the military deaths amounted to 11.3 million, Ibid., 250. Lopukhovsky and Kavalerchik, probably more accurately, estimated military losses to be 14,546,000. Lev Lopukhovsky and Boris Kavalerchik, *The Price of Victory: The Red Army's Casualties in the Great Patriotic War*, trans. by Harold Orenstein (Barnsley: Pen and Sword Military, 2017), 94.
61. Keith Loew, *Savage Continent: Europe in the Aftermath of World War II* (New York: St. Martin's Press, 2012), 13–16.
62. Regina Mühlhäuser, *Sex and the Nazi Soldier: Violent, Commercial and Consensual Encounters during the War in the Soviet Union, 1941–1945*, trans. Jessica Spengler (Edinburgh: Edinburgh University Press, 2021), 7.
63. Ibid., 149–150.

64. Maris Rowe-McCulloch, "Sexual Violence under Occupation during World War II: Soviet Women's Experiences inside a German Military Brothel and Beyond," *Journal of the History of Sexuality* 31.1. (2022): 10 and 14.
65. Ibid., 15–18.
66. Mühlhäuser, *Sex and the Nazi Soldier*, 155.
67. Wendy Jo Gertjejanssen, "Victims, Heroes, Survivors: Sexual Violence on the Eastern Front during World War II" (PhD diss., University of Minnesota, 2004), 154.
68. Raffaello Pannacci, "Sex, Military Brothels and Gender Violence during the Italian Campaign in the USSR, 1941–3," *Journal of Contemporary History* 55.1. (2020): 89.
69. Regina Mühlhäuser, "The Unquestioned Crime: Sexual Violence by German Soldiers during the War of Annihilation in the Soviet Union, 1941–1945," in Raphaëlle Branche and Fabrice Virgili, eds., *Rape in Wartime* (New York: Palgrave Macmillan, 2012), 37–38.
70. For Italian, Hungarian, and Romanian officers, see testimony by Golda Vasserman, "Iz getto – v Partizany," in Boris Zaborko, ed. *Zhivymi ostalis' tol'ko my. Svidetel'stva i dokumenty* (Kiev: Biblioteka instituta iudaiki, 1999), 25. For SS see Gertjejanssen, "Victims," 301.
71. For lower estimate, see Krivosheev, *Rossiia i SSSR*, 250; for the higher estimate, see Lopukhovsky and Kavalerchik, *The Price of Victory*, 133.
72. Krivosheev, *Rossiia i SSSR, 250*; Lopukhovsky and Kavalerchik, *The Price of Victory*, 133.
73. John Chambers ed., *The Oxford Companion to American Military History* (Oxford University Press, 1999), 849; "France" in I. C. Dear ed. *The Oxford Companion to World War II* (Oxford: Oxford University Press, 2001), accessed May 27, 2016, www.oxfordreference.com.myaccess.library.utoronto.ca/view/10.1093/acref/9780198604464.001.0001/acref-9780198604464-e-637?rskey=dnviOy&result=643; I "United Kingdom" in Ibid., accessed May 27, 2016, www.oxfordreference.com.myaccess.library.utoronto.ca/view/10.1093/acref/9780198604464.001.0001/acref-9780198604464-e-1692?rskey=CCpoZH&result=1701.
74. Krivoshev, *Rossiia i SSSR*, 285–293.
75. Ibid., 288–293.
76. David Glantz, *Red Storm over the Balkans* (Kansas: University Press of Kansas, 2007), 37.
77. Ibid., 379.
78. For August and September 1943, see Krivosheev, *Rossiia i SSSR*, 288–289. For August 1944 Ibid., 297–298.
79. For the lower estimate, see Lopukhovsky and Kavalerchik, *The Price of Victory*, 133. For higher figure, see Krivosheev, *Rossiia i SSSR*, 518.
80. For 1,3:1 see Krivosheev, *Rossiia i SSSR*, 518. For 2,5:1 see Lopukhovsky and Kavalerchik, *The Price of Victory*, 133.
81. Roberto J. Carmack, *Kazakhstan in World War II: Mobilization and Ethnicity in the Soviet Empire* (Lawrence: University Press of Kansas, 2019), 16.
82. TsAMO RF, f. 148a, op. 3763, d. 126, ll. 33–34, document reproduced in V. A. Zolotarev et al., eds. *Russkii Arkhiv: Velikaia Otechestvennaia Stavka VGK. Dokumenty i materialy 1944–1945*, t.16.5(4) (Moscow: Terra, 1999), Document No. 91.

83. Vladislav Grinevich, “Voennye mobilizatsii v Ukraine v 1943–1944 godah. ‘Vy dolzhny smyt’ svoei krov’iu vinu pered Rodinoi i ee velikim vozhdem tovarishcem Stalinym,” *Zerklo nedeli*, 2 September 2005, https://zn.ua/SOCIUM/voennye_mobilizatsii_v_ukraine_v_19431944_godah_vy_dolzhny_smyt_svoey_krovyu_vinu_pered_rodinoy_i_ee.html.
84. Interview with Iurii Favorov, *Ia pomniu*, accessed 27 May 2016, http://iremember.ru/minometchiki/favorov-uriy-leonidovich.html.
85. Antony Beevor, *Berlin: The Downfall* (New York: Viking, 2002), 228.
86. RGASPI, f. 17, op. 125, d. 241, l. 90. For punishment of offenders, see TsAMO, f. 1512 (233sd), op. 1, d. 93; RGVA, f. 32900, op. 1, d. 348, l. 71; l. 234; RGVA, f. 32900, op. 1, d. 178, l. 10; RGVA, f. 32900, op. 1, d. 413, l. 177. For instances of violence against underlings, see RGVA, f. 32900, op. 1, d. 178, l. 10; RGVA, f. 32900, op. 1, d. 348, l. 71.
87. Mark Edele and Michael Geyer, “States of Exception: The Nazi-Soviet War as a System of Violence, 1939–1945,” in Sheila Fitzpatrick and Michael Geyer, eds., *Beyond Totalitarianism: Stalinism and Nazism Compared* (Cambridge, Eng., 2009), 345–395.
88. Interview with Mikhail Tsurkan, *Ia pomniu*, accessed 27 May 2016, http://iremember.ru/saperi/tsurkan-mikhail-antonovich.html; Interview with Georgii Siniavskii, *Ia pomniu*, accessed 7 February 2023; https://iremember.ru/memoirs/drugie-voyska/sinyavskiy-georgiy-evtikhievich/; Interview with Nikolai Nadtochii, *Ia pomniu*, accessed 7 February 2023, https://iremember.ru/memoirs/razvedchiki/nadtochiy-nikolay-danilovich/.
89. TsDAGO, f. 57, op. 4, d. 314, l. 81.
90. I. G. Popov, *Batal’ony idut na zapad* (Moscow: Izdatel’stvo Moskovskogo universiteta, 1985), 157–158.
91. Ibid., 158.
92. TsDAGO, f. 59, op. 1, d. 1614, l. 175.
93. Ibid., 175–176.
94. RGASPI, f. 17, op. 125, d. 241, l. 92.
95. TsDAGO, f. 59, op. 1, d. 1614, l. 175.
96. IAN RAN, f. 2, op. 101, d. 2, l. 7.
97. Daniil Vladimirovich Fibikh, “Frontovye dnevniki 1942–1943 gg.” *Novyi mir* no. 5 (2010), accessed May 31, 2016, http://magazines.russ.ru/novyi_mi/2010/5/fi2.html.
98. Rebecca Manley, *To the Tashkent Station: Evacuation and Survival in the Soviet Union at War* (Ithaca: Cornell University Press, 2009), 43.
99. Interview with Mark Papish, *Ia pomniu*, accessed May 27, 2016, http://iremember.ru/memoirs/pekhotintsi/papish-mark-abramovich/.
100. Interview with Grigorii Rabinovich, *Ia pomniu*, accessed May 27, 2016, http://iremember.ru/pekhotintsi/rabinovich-grigoriy-alekseevich.html.
101. Abdulin, *Red Road*, 142.
102. Interview with Grigorii Rabinovich, *Ia pomniu.*
103. Milovan Đilas, *Conversations with Stalin* (New York: Harcourt, Brace & World), 48.
104. Grinevich, “Voennye mobilizatsii v Ukraine v 1943–1944 godah.”
105. IAN RAN, f. 2 razdel 2, op. 17, d. 6, l. 4; IAN RAN, f. 2 razdel 2, op. 17, d. 15, l. 2.

106. Arhiva Organizatiilor Social Politice din Republica Moldova, Fond 51, inventar 3, dosar 45, ll. 5–12, 28–29, 48–49. I am grateful to Diana Dumitru for sharing this information with me.
107. RGVA, f. 32900, op. 1, d.341, l. 53.
108. IAN RAN, f. 2 razdel 2, op. 17, d. 12, l. 8.
109. Arhiva Organizaiilor Social Politice din Republica Moldova, 80–81, 107–111, 114–116. I am grateful to Diana Dumitru for sharing this source with me. This report related to the immediate postwar period.
110. Gurvits, *Vospominaniia*, 78.
111. Interview with Mikhail Ivanov, *Ia pomniu*, accessed May 27, 2016, http://iremember.ru/artilleristi/ivanov-mikhail-nikolaevich.html.
112. Ibid.
113. Interview with Aleksandr Solov'ev, *Ia pomniu.*
114. Abdulin, *Red Road*, 109.
115. Catherine Merridale, "Culture, Ideology and Combat in the Red Army, 1939–1945," *Journal of Contemporary History* 41.2 (2006): 322.
116. Mikhin, *Guns*, 88.
117. Reese, *Why*, 217–218.
118. Antony Beevor, *Ardennes 1944: The Battle of the Bulge* (New York: Penguin, 2016), 50–54.
119. Mark Edele, *Stalin's Defectors: How Red Army Soldiers became Hitler's Collaborators* (Oxford: Oxford University Press, 2017), 36.
120. Timothy Johnston, *Being Soviet. Identity, Rumour and Everyday Life under Stalin 1939–1953* (Oxford: Oxford University Press, 2011), xxv.
121. Reese, *Why*, 103–104.
122. Ibid., 223–224.
123. Merridale, "Culture, Ideology and Combat," 317.
124. Matt E. Lenoe, "Emotions and Psychological Survival in the Red Army, 1941–42" *Kritika: Explorations in Russian and Eurasian History* 22.1. (Spring 2021): 341.
125. Reese, *Why*, 103–104.
126. Anna Shternshis, *Soviet and Kosher: Jewish Popular Culture in the Soviet Union, 1923–1939* (Bloomington: Indiana University Press, 2006), xiv.
127. Letter from Vul'f Zelenyi, reproduced in Il'ia Altman i Leonid Terushkin, eds., *Sokhrani moi pis'ma. Sbornik pisem I dnevnikov evreev perioda velikoi otechestvennoi voiny* (Moscow: Tsentr i Fond 'Khookost' i izdatel'stvo MIK, 2007), 187.
128. Boris Slutskii, *Zapiski o Voine. Stikhotvoreniia i ballady* (St. Petersburg: Logos, 2000), 313.
129. Ibid., 319.
130. For achievements, see Ibid., 199. For atrocities against German prisoners, Ibid., 28. For rape, see Ibid., 57.
131. Oleksandr Melnyk, "Political Identity under Invasion: Kherson Oblast in Summer 1941," *Journal of Ukrainian Studies* 30.1 (2005): 72.
132. Solonari, *A Satellite Empire*, 221–222.
133. Berkhoff, *Harvest*, 206.
134. Gertjejanssen, *Victims*, 50.
135. Sergy Yekelchyk, *Stalin's Empire of Memory: Russian-Ukrainian Relations in the Soviet Historical Imagination* (Toronto: University of Toronto Press, 2004), 25.

136. Mark Edele, "'What Are We Fighting for?' Loyalty in the Soviet War Effort, 1941–1945," *International Labor and Working-Class History* 84 (2013): 258.
137. Melnyk, *World War II*, 66.
138. Amir Weiner, *Making Sense of War* (Princeton: Princeton University Press, 2001), 250.
139. Berkhoff, *Harvest*, 223 and Solonari, *A Satellite Empire*, 224.
140. Karel Berkhoff, *Motherland in Danger: Soviet Propaganda during World War II* (Cambridge: Harvard University Press, 2012), 211.
141. Vladislav Grinevich, "Z istorii formuvannia ukrains'kogo radians'koi patriotizmu u roki radians'ko-nimets'koi viinii 1941–1945 rr," *Problemi istorii Ukraini: fakti, suzhdennia, poshuki*, 13 (2005): 419.
142. TsDAGO, f. 1, op. 70, d. 221, l. 28.
143. IAN RAN, f. 2, op. 31, d. 30, l. 199,
144. IAN RAN, f. 2, op. 31, d. 14, l. 28.
145. Berkhoff, *Motherland in Danger*, 211–212.
146. Carmack, *Kazakhstan in World War*, 35 and 12.
147. Interview with Sergei Otroshcenkov, *Ia pomniu*, accessed May 27, 2016, http://iremember.ru/memoirs/tankisti/otroschenkov-sergey-andreevich/.
148. Lenoe, "Emotions and Psychological Survival," 339.
149. For instance, in August and September, 1943, the 8th Guards Army held twenty-one cinema sessions, four concerts, and eighteen lectures for the local population, TsDAGO, f. 57, op. 4, d. 97, l. 1. Similarly, the Seventeenth NKVD Regiment organized fifteen film sessions and held forty-two conversations with civilians, RGVA, f .32900, op. 1, d. 412, l. 24.
150. RGVA, f. 32900, op. 1, d. 402, l. 82.
151. Military commissions were ad hoc bodies established by Red Army to investigate enemy war crimes against the civilian population and Soviet prisoners of war. For the discussion about military commissions, see introduction in F. F. Sverdlov, ed., *Dokumenty obviniaiut. Kholokost: svidetel'stva Krasnoi Armii* (Moscow: Rossiiskaia biblioteka Kholokosta, 1996) and Mordechai Altshuler, "The Holocaust in the Soviet Mass Media," *Yad Vashem Studies* 39:2 (2011): 153–156.
152. Tsentr i fond kholokost, Lichnyi fond V. N. Tosglina ed.xp. No. 1a, l. 23.
153. Il'ia Al'tman, Leonid Terushkin, Irina Brodskaia, eds., *Sokhrani moi pis'ma. Sbornik pisem evreev perioda velikoi otechestvennoi voiny* Vypusk 2 (Moscow: Tsentr i Fond 'Kholokost'. Izdate'stvo MIK, 2010), 121.
154. Abdulin, *Red Road*, 121–122.
155. Ibid., 109.
156. Reese, *Why*, 149.
157. Serhy Yekelchyk, "The Civic Duty to Hate: Stalinist Citizenship as Political Practice and Civic Emotion Kiev, 1943–53," *Kritika: Explorations in Russian and Eurasian History* 7.3 (2006): 531.
158. RGASPI, f. 17, op. 125, d. 104, l. 182.
159. IAN RAN, f. 2, op. 31, d. 31, l. 44.
160. RGVA, f. 32900, op. 1, d. 414, l. 41.
161. Ibid., l. 69.
162. Ibid., l. 69.

163. Jeffrey Burds, "Sexual Violence in Europe in World War II, 1939–1945," *Politics & Society* 37 (March 2009): 50.
164. Beevor, *The Fall*, 169.
165. Reese, *Why*, 218.
166. I. Stalin, *O Velikoi Otechestvennoi voine Sovetskogo Soiuza* (Moscow: Voennoe izdatel'stvo ministerstva vooruzhennykh sil Soiuza SSR, 1948), 30.
167. Berkhoff, *Motherland in Danger*, 271.
168. Brandon Schechter, *The Stuff of Soldiers: A History of the Red Army in World War II Through Material Objects* (Ithaca: Cornell University Press, 2019), 81.
169. For the famine in Soviet interior, see Berkhoff, *Motherland in*, 97. For Leningrad, see Alexis Peri, *The War Within: Diaries from the Siege of Leningrad* (Cambridge: Harvard University Press, 2017), 4.
170. For hunger in the Red Army, see Schechter, *The Stuff*, 87. For prioritization of feeding the Red Army, see Wendy Z. Goldman, "Introduction: The Politics of Food and War," in Wendy Z. Goldman and Donald Filtzer, eds., *Hunger and War: Food Provisioning in the Soviet Union during World War II* (Bloomington & Indianapolis: Indiana University Press, 2015), 12.
171. For improvements in the diet of Soviet troops, see Schechter, *The Stuff*, 89–90. For cannibalism, see Berkhoff, *Motherland*, 97.
172. Donald Filterz, "Starvation Mortality in Soviet Home-Front Industrial Regions during World War II," in Goldman and Filtzer, eds., *Hunger and War*, 266.
173. Mikhin, *Guns*, 8–9.
174. Schechter, *The Stuff*, 83.
175. Slutskii, *Zapiski*, 40.
176. RGVA, f. 32900, op. 1, d. 341, l. 23.
177. TsAMO, f. 1512 (233sd), op. 1, d. 35, l. 20.
178. Timofejev, *Rusi*, 218.
179. Omer Bartov, *The Eastern Front 1941–1945: German Troops and the Barbarisation of Warfare* (Oxford: Oxford University Press, 1985), 144.

2 2nd and 3rd Ukrainian Fronts' Operations and Rampage in Europe

1. BA, Lichnyi Dnevnik 26.8.1944–41.5.1945. El'kinson Pavel Abramovich, 3.
2. Catherine Merridale, *Ivan's War: Life and Death in the Red Army* (New York: Picador, 2006), xxxii.
3. Igor Casu, "Stalinist Terror in Soviet Moldavia, 1940–1953," in Kevin McDermott and Matthew Stibbe, eds., *Stalinist Terror in Eastern Europe: Elite Purges and Mass Repression* (Manchester: Manchester University Press, 2010), 41.
4. Ibid., 43.
5. Mark Axorthy, *Third Axis, Fourth Ally: Romanian Armed Forces in the European War, 1941–1945* (London: Arms and Armour, 1995), 28.
6. Holly Case, *Between States: The Transylvanian Question and the European Idea during WWII* (Stanford: Stanford University Press, 2009), 95.

7. Grant T. Harward, *Romania's Holy War: Soldiers, Motivation, and the Holocaust* (Ithaca: Cornell University Press, 2021), 1.
8. Vladimir Solonari, *Purifying the Nation: Population Exchange and Ethnic Cleansing in Nazi-Allied Romania* (Baltimore: The Johns Hopkins University Press, 2010), 2.
9. Radu Ioanid, *The Holocaust in Romania: The Destruction of Jews and Gypsies under the Antonescu Regime, 1940–1944* (Chicago: Ivan R. Dee, 2000), xii.
10. Solonari, *Purifying the Nation*, 150.
11. Ibid., 150.
12. Olga Kucherenko, "Reluctant Traitors: The Politics of Survival in Romanian-occupied Odessa," *European Review of History* 15.2 (2008): 145.
13. Ibid., 145.
14. Alexander Dallin, *Odessa, 1941–1944: A Case Study of Soviet Territory under Foreign Rule* (Iasi-Oxford-Portland: Center for Romanian Studies, 1998), 164.
15. Dennis Deletant, "Ghetto Experience in Golta, Transnistria, 1942–1944," *Holocaust and Genocide Studies* 18.1 (2004): 19.
16. Grant Harward, "Peasant Armies at Odds: Romanian-Soviet Interaction during the Second World War," *The Journal of Slavic Military Studies* 24.2 (2011): 287.
17. Alexander Werth, *Russia at War: 1941–1945* (London: Barrie and Rockliff, 1964), 816.
18. Diana Dumitru, *The State, Antisemitism, and Collaboration in the Holocaust: The Borderlands of Romania and the Soviet Union* (New York: Cambridge University Press, 2016), 178.
19. TsA FSB Rossii, document reproduced in S. V. Stepashin et al., eds., *Organy Gosudarstvennoi Bezopasnosti SSSR v Velikoi Otechestvennoi Voine. Sbornik Doumentov. Vpered na Zapad. 1 ianvaria – 30 iunia 1944 goda* tom 5 kniga 1 (Moscow: Obshcestvo izucheniia istorii otechestvennykh spetssluzhb, 2007), 307.
20. RGASPI, f.17, op. 125, d. 241, l. 95.
21. Ibid., l. 90.
22. Ibid.
23. TsDAGO, f. 59, op. 1, d. 1614, l. 184.
24. RGVA, f. 32900, op. 1, d. 314, ll. 54–55.
25. RGVA, f. 32900, op. 1, d. 172, l. 31.
26. Ibid., l. 32.
27. TsDAGO, f. 59, op. 1, d. 1614, l. 181.
28. Richard Harrison, ed., *The Iasi-Kishinev Operation: The Red Army's Summer Offensive into the Balkans (20–20 August 1944): Soviet General Staff*, trans. Richard Harrison (Solihull: Helion & Company, 2017), 162.
29. Richard DiNardo, *Germany and the Axis Powers: From Coalition to Collapse* (Lawrence: University Press of Kansas, 2005), 188.
30. S. S. Biriuzov, et al., *Beogradska Operacija*, 2nd ed. (Moscow-Belgrade: Institute for the Military History of the Ministry of Defense of the USSR and Vojnoistorijski Institut JNA, 1989), 36–37.
31. Krivosheev, ed., *Rossiia i SSSR*, 297.

32. V. A. Zolotarev, et al., eds., *Velikaia Otechestvennaia voina 1941–1945 godov: v dvenadtsati tomakh. Krasnaia Armiia v stranakh tsentral'noi, severnoi Evropy i na balkanakh. Dokumenty i materialy 1944–1945* (Moscow, 2000), 15.
33. Case, *Between States*, 93.
34. The advance units of the 3rd Ukrainian Front reached Bulgaria as early as 8 September, P. A. Zhilin, et al., eds., *Osvoboditel'naia missiia sovetksikh vooruzhennykh sil v Evrope VO vtoroi mirovoi voine. Dokumenty i materialy* (Moscow: Voennoe-izdatel'stvo, 1985), 97.
35. TsAMO, f.413 (57A), op. 10372, d.349, l. 53.
36. On the eve of the Iasso-Kishinev Operation, which led to Soviet entry into the Balkans, the 2nd and 3rd Ukrainian Fronts had 1,314,200 troops, Krivosheev, ed., *Rossiia i SSSR*, 297. However, immediately after the operation, on 29 August, the general staff in Moscow permanently recalled the 52nd and the 5th Shock Armies from the two army groups, thereby diminishing the Red Army's manpower to around 1 million troops.
37. Hlihor and Scurtu, *The Red Army in Romania*, 109.
38. Ibid., 145.
39. RGVA, f. 32900, op. 1, d. 458, l. 34.
40. BA, El'kinson dnevnik, 3.
41. TsAMO, f. 1512 (233sd), op. 1, d. 35, l. 243.
42. RGVA, f. 32900, op. 1, d. 458, l. 42.
43. Hlihor and Scurtu, *The Red Army in Romania*, 116.
44. Ibid., 146–147.
45. Csaba Békés, László Borhi, Peter Ruggenthaler, and Ottmar Trașcă, eds., *Soviet Occupation of Romania, Hungary, and Austria, 1944/45–1948/49* (Budapest: Central European University, 2015), 35.
46. Slutskii, *Zapiski*, 52.
47. Ramona Miron and Horia Dumitrescu, "Abuzurile Armatei Rosii in Vrancea" in Horia Dumitrescu, ed., *Chronica Vrancei* (Pallas: Focșani, 2006) 313–314.
48. Madeline Morris, "Force of Arms: Rape, War, and Military Culture," *Duke Law Journal* 45.4 (1996): 665–666.
49. Hlihor and Scurtu, *The Red Army in Romania*, 146–147.
50. Ibid., 145.
51. For the overall population of Romania, see the 1948 census, Dr. A. Golopentia and Dr. D. C. Georgescu, eds., *Populatia Republicii Populare Romane La 25 Ianuarie 1948* (Buchurest: Institut Central de Statistica, 1948), 37; For the population of Arad county, see Ibid., 41; for Iasi and Alba, see Ibid., 39.
52. For Bucharest, see RGVA, f. 32900, op. 1, d. 183, l. 252. For Craiova, see ACNSAS, fond Documentar, dosar nr. 13953, vol. 2, ff. 132–136, document reproduced in Békés, Borhi, Ruggenthaler, and Trașcă, eds., *Soviet Occupation of Romania, Hungary, and Austria* (Budapest: Central European University Press, 2015), 37–38; for Timisoara, see Hlihor and Scurtu, *The Red Army in Romania*, 146.
53. For instance, see AJ KMJ I – 3-b/577, "Pismo šefa kabineta maršala Jugoslavije Mitra Bakića Načelniu Personalnog odeljenja predsednistva nacionalnog komiteta, l. 1."

54. Reported in no author, "Crimele 'eliberatorilor' sovietici în județul Alba. Jafuri, violuri și asasinate în Alba Iulia și împrejurimi" Radio Alba 24 26 February 2022, accessed 10 Octoboer 2024, https://alba24.ro/crimele-eliberatorilor-sovietici-in-judetul-alba-jafuri-violuri-si-asasinate-in-alba-iulia-si-imprejurimi-638279.html.
55. Candace Kruttschnitt, William D. Kalsbeek, and Carol C. House, eds., *Estimating the Incidence of Rape and Sexual Assault* (Washington, DC: The National Academies Press, 2014), 1.
56. David Allen, "The Reporting and Underreporting of Rape," *Southern Economic Journal* 73.3. (2007): 623.
57. Robert Lilly, *Taken by Force: Rape and American GIs in Europe during World War II* (New York, 2007), 12.
58. Sergiu Verona, *Military Occupation and Diplomacy. Soviet Troops in Romania 1944–1958* (Durham: Duke University Press, 1992), 49.
59. RGVA, f. 32900, op. 1, d. 183, ll. 489–490.
60. Hlihor and Scurtu, *The Red Army in Romania*, 239.
61. Mariana-Narcisa Radu, "The Incrimination of Sexual Intercourse with a Minor," *Valahia University* Law Study 20.2. (2012): 45–46.
62. These are some forms of sexual violence, other than rape, identified by Regina Mühlhäuser in her study of German sexual violence in the Soviet Union, Regina Mühlhäuser, "The Unquestioned Crime," 37–38.
63. Harward, *Romania's Holy War*, 81.
64. DiNardo, *Germany and the Axis*, 93.
65. Ibid., 93.
66. Yannis Sygkelos, *Nationalism from the Left: the Bulgarian Communist Party during the Second World War and the Early Post-War Years* (Boston: Brill, 2011), 37.
67. Jozo Tomasevich, *War and Revolution in Yugoslavia 1941–1945: Occupation and Collaboration* (Stanford: Stanford University Press, 2001), 737.
68. This figure is my estimate. When the Red Army advanced units reached Bulgaria, on 5 September, the 3rd Ukrainian Front numbered 258,000 troops, A. G. Khorkov, *Osvoboditelnaia missia sovetskikh vooruzhennykh sil na Balkanakh* (Moscow: Nauka, 1980), 137. In addition, Moscow deployed the Danube Military Flotilla in Bulgaria which numbered 6,500 troops, Krivosheev, ed., *Rossiia i SSSR*, 300. The Soviets also had the bigger Black Sea Fleet at their disposal. However, I cannot find the number of Black Sea Fleet sailors deployed in Bulgaria. Nonetheless, it is reasonable to presume that it was about 10,000 strong, which would bring the total number of Soviet troops to 275,000.
69. M. V. Zakharov et al., eds., *Osvobozhdenie iugo-vostochnoi i tsentral'noi Evropy voiskami 2-go i 3-go Ukrainskikh frontov 1944–1945 gg.* (Moscow: Nauka, 1970), 234.
70. TsAMO, f. 413 (57A), op. 10372, d. 349, l. 29; Khorkov, *Osvoboditelnaia missia*, 143–144; Zakharov et al., eds., *Osvobozhdenie*, 218; B. D. Presniakov, *Pod zvezdami balkanskimi* (Moscow: Moskovskii rabochii, 1985), 21.
71. Gaj Trifković, "Operacije Crvene Armije u Sjevernoj Jugoslaviji 1944–1945. Iz Sovjetskih dokumenata," *Vojnoistorijski glasnik* 2 (2017): 207.
72. VA, f. NOVJ, k. 214, f. 3, d. 44, l. 1.

73. Biriuzov et al., *Beogradska Operacija*, 118.
74. Gaj Trifković, "'The German Anabasis': The Breakthrough of Army Group E from Eastern Yugoslavia 1944," *Journal of Slavic Military Studies* 30.4 (2017): 602–603.
75. Ibid., 611
76. Ibid., 603.
77. Krivosheev, ed., *Rossiia i SSSR*, 300.
78. Timofejev, *Rusi*, 188.
79. Nikola Popović, *Jugoslovensko-sovejtski odnosi u drugom svetskom ratu* (Belgrade: Institut za savremenu istoriju, 1988), 206. In total, during 1944 and the first five months of 1945, the Soviets provided Yugoslavs with 233,607 rifles, 22,154 handguns, 84,260 machineguns of various calibers, 5,053 anti-tank guns, 6,048 mortars, 170 anti-tank cannons, 1,283 field cannons, 172 tanks, 552 airplanes, and 1,329 radio stations.
80. Timofejev, *Rusi*, 191–192.
81. Gaj Trifković, "'Damned Good Amateurs': Yugoslav Partisans in the Belgrade Operation 1944," *Journal of Slavic Military Studies* 29.2 (2016): 267.
82. V. A. Zolotarev, et al., eds., *Krasnaia Armiia v stranakh Tsentral'noi, Severnoi Evropy i na Balkanakh*, 184.
83. Trifković, "Damned Good Amateurs," 268.
84. Schechter, *The Stuff of Soldiers*, 86–87.
85. RGVA, f. 32900, op. 1, d. 341, l. 53.
86. The 3rd Ukrainian Front leadership issued such orders on 16 October 1943 and 21 April 1944, RGVA, f. 32900, op. 1, d. 341, l. 315, and then again following the tragedy in Burgas, RGVA, f. 32900, op. 1, d. 341, l. 108. Lower levels of command issued similar orders. For 233rd Rifle Division order issued on 24 November 1944, see TsAMO, f.1512 (233sd), op. 1, d. 35, l. 295.
87. For example, in the Serbian city of Subotica, there were at least three attempts to impose ban on the sale of alcohol, the last order threatening repeat offenders with six months of forced labor, IAS, f. 68, k.1521, "8 marta 1945 god. Gradskom Narodno Oslobidlačkom Odboru grada Subotica. Od šefa odeljka narodne milicije, kapetan Stevanović." Meanwhile, the municipal authorities in Zaječar revoked the license from a local tavern owner for repeatedly violating the ban on the sale of alcohol to Yugoslav and Soviet soldiers, IAZ, f. Sreski Narodni Odbor Zaječar godina 1944, k.2, "Sreski narodni odbor u Zaječaru dana 25 novembra 1944 godine doneo je sledeće."
88. Norman Naimark, *Russians in Germany: A History of the Soviet Zone of occupation, 1945–1949* (Cambridge: Harvard University Press, 1995), 113.
89. BA, El'kinson dnevnik, 5.
90. TsAMO RF, f. 1512 (233sd), op. 1, d. 93, l. 258; RGVA, f. 32900, op. 1, d. 340, l. 11.
91. Ibid.
92. RGVA, f. 32900, op. 1, d. 337, l. 45.
93. Ibid., l. 27.
94. VA, f. NOVJ, k. 371, f. 6, d. 26, l. 2.
95. Timofejev, *Rusi*, 219–220.
96. IAS, f. 166, k. 27.2 "Privredni odeljak."

97. RGVA, f. 32900, op. 1, d. 341, l. 108.
98. RGVA, f. 32900, op. 1, d. 414, l. 15.
99. RGVA, f. 32900, op. 1, d. 185, l. 240.
100. RGVA, f. 32900, op. 1, d. 192, l. 178.
101. VA, f. NOVJ, k.191, f. 1, d. 11, l. 9 and Ibid., 66.
102. Vladimir Dedijer, ed., *Josip Broz Tito: Prilozi za Biografiju* (Zagreb: Kultura, 1953), 441–443.
103. AJ KPR I-3-a 2/4 "Dokumenta o odnosima FNRJ-SSSR. Postupci sovjetskih vojnika prema narodu i imovini u FNRJ: prilog br30."
104. Naimark, *The Russians*, 70.
105. Ruth Lawlor, "Contested Crimes: Race, Gender, and Nation in Histories of GI Sexual Violence, World War II," *The Journal of Military History* 84.2. (2020): 548–551; Mühlhäuser, *Sex and the Nazi*, 10–12.
106. Ibid., 133.
107. For Hungary, see Peter Kenez, *Hungary from the Nazis to the Soviets. The Establishment of the Communist Regime in Hungary, 1944–1948* (Cambridge: Cambridge University Press, 2006), 41–42. For Austria, see Jill Lewis, *Workers and Politics in Occupied Austria 1945–1945* (Manchester: Manchester University Press, 2007), 40.
108. Interview with Floarea, published in Laura Spariousu and Svenka Savic, eds., *Životne price žena u Vojvodini: Rumunke 1924–1974* (Novi Sad: Futura publikacije i Ženske studije i istraživanja), 44. Author's interviews with Anonymous (woman), Božidar Stojanović, and Bratislav Filipović.
109. For Romanian women, see BA, El'kinson dnevnik, 3. For Hungarian women, see Andrea Peto, "Memory and the Narrative of Rape in Budapest and Vienna in 1945" in Richard Bessel and Dirk Schumann, eds., *Life after Death: Approaches to a Cultural and Social History of Europe during the 1940s and 1950s* (Cambridge: Cambridge University Press, 2003), 139. For Austrian women, see Lewis, *Workers and Politics*, 69.
110. RGASPI, f.17, op.125, d.247, ll. 72–78, document reproduced in V. A. Zolotarev, et al., eds., *Krasnaia Armiia v stranakh Tsentral'noi, Severnoi Evropy i na Balkanakh*, 114.
111. VA, f. NOVJ, k. 1919, f. 31, d. 6, l. 13. I am thankful to Nevenko Vlaisavljević for sharing this document with me.
112. Ibid., 13.
113. Anna Phillips, *Power and Influence after the Cold War: Germany in East-Central Europe* (Lanham: Rowman & Littlefield, 2000), 89.
114. For 1941, see Deborah S. Cornelius, *Hungary in World War II: Caught in the Cauldron* (New York: Fordham University Press, 2011), 377. For 1942 and the Hungarian army's destruction see, Peter Szabo, "Hungarian Soldiers in WWII," in Laszlo Veszpremy and Bela Kiraly, eds., *A Millennium of Hungarian Military History* (Boulder: Social Science Monographs, 2002), 445–446.
115. Krisztián Ungváry, "Hungarian Occupation Forces in the Ukraine 1941–1942: The Historiographical Context," *The Journal of Slavic Military Studies* 20.1 (2007): 84.
116. Ibid.
117. Randolph Braham with Scott Miller, "Preface" in *The Nazis' Last Victims: The Holocaust in Hungary*, eds., Randolph Braham with Scott Miller

(Detroit: Wayne State University Press in association with the USHMM, 1998), 18.
118. Richard Germann, "Austrian Soldiers and Generals in World War II," in Gunter Bischof, Frits Plasser, and Barbara Stelzl-Marx, eds., *New Perspective on Austrians and World War II: Contemporary Austrian Studies* Vol. 17 (New Brunswick: Transaction Publishers, 2009), 29.
119. Thomas R. Grischany, "Mental Aspects of Austrian Wehrmacht Service," in *New Perspective on Austrians*, 46.
120. Kenez, *Hungary from the Nazis to the Soviets*, 38.
121. John Lukacs, "Foreword" in *The Siege*, xviii.
122. Nevenkin, *Take Budapest*, 40.
123. Lewis, *Workers and Politics*, 45.
124. Nevenkin, *Take Budapest*, 12–15.
125. Glantz, *When Titans Clashed*, 221.
126. Nevenkin, *Take Budapest*, 57.
127. Ibid., 55.
128. Liedtke Gregory Liedtke, "Furor Teutonicus: German Offensives and Counter-Attacks on the Eastern Front, August 1943 to March 1945," *The Journal of Slavic Military Studies* 21.3. (2008): 583.
129. I. A. Pliev, *V boiakh za osvobozhdenie Rumynii, Vengrii, Chekhoslovakii* (Ordzhonikidze: Ir, 1971), 24.
130. Aleksandr Georgievich Mikhailik, "Istoriia boevykh deistvii Krasnoi armii na territorii Vengrii (sentiabr' 1944 – aprel' 1945 gg)," (PhD diss., Voronezh State Pedagogical University, 2016), 73.
131. David M. Glantz, "Stalin's Strategic Intentions, 1941–1945: Soviet Military Operations as Indicators of Stalin's Postwar Territorial Ambitions," *Journal of Slavic Military Studies* 27.4 (2014): 676–720.
132. Mikhailik, "Istoriia Boevye deistviia," 116.
133. Ungvary, *The Siege*, xvi.
134. Nevenkin, *Take Budapest*, 29.
135. V. A. Zolotarev, et al., eds., *Krasnaia Armiia v stranakh tsentral'noi, severnoi evropy i na balkanakh*, 290.
136. Richard W. Harrison, ed., *The Budapest Operation 1945: An Operational-Strategic Study Soviet General Staff*, trans. Richard W. Harrison (Solihull: Helion & Company, 2017), 69.
137. Ungvary, *The Siege*, 378.
138. Norbert Számvéber, *The Sword Behind The Shield: A Combat History of the German Efforts to Relieve Budapest 1945 – Operation 'Konrad' I, III, III* (West Midlands: Helion & Company, 2015), 424.
139. Glantz, *Colossus Reborn*, 253.
140. Ibid., 253–254.
141. Zolotarev, et al., eds., *Velikaia Otechestvennaia. Krasnaia Armiia v stranakh tsentral'noi, severnoi evropy i na balkanakh*, 602.
142. Krivosheev, ed., *Rossiia i SSSR*, 449.
143. Ibid., 302.
144. Ungvary, *The Siege*, 375.
145. For the Axis losses, see Nikolai Shefov, *Bitvy Rossii* (Moscow: AST, 2006), 158. For Soviet losses, see Krivosheev, ed., *Rossiia i SSSR*, 316.

146. Ibid., 449.
147. Ungvary, *The Siege*, 331–338.
148. TsAMO, f. 1512 (233sd), op. 1, d. 35, l. 348.
149. RGVA, f. 32900, op. 1, d. 341, l. 130.
150. Merridale, *Ivan's War*, 385.
151. Harward, *Romania's Holy War*, 261.
152. Andrea Peto, "Atvonulo hadsereg, maradando trauma. Az 1945-os budapesti nemi eroszak esetek emlekezete," *Tdrtenelmi Szemle* 41 (1999), 86, cited in Martvin Mevius, *Agents of Moscow: The Hungarian Communist Party and the Origins of Socialist Patriotism 1941–1953* (Oxford: Oxford University Press 2005), 62.
153. Ungvary, *The Siege*, 354.
154. Fruzsina Skrabski, *Silenced Shame*, directed by Fruzsina Skrabski (Budapest, 2013), film.
155. BA, El'kinson dnevnik, 11, and diary excerpts from Abram Shaulovich Shavelev, reproduced in Al'tman, Terushkin, and Brodskaia, eds., *Sokhrani moi pis'ma. Vypusk 2* (Moscow: Tsentr i FGond 'Kholokost'. Izdate'stvo MIK, 2010), 266.
156. Ibid.
157. Slutskii, *Zapiski*, 129–130.
158. Ibid., 127.
159. Alaine Polcz, *One Woman in the War Hungary 1944–1945*, translation and introduction by Albert Tezla (Budapest: Central European Press, 2002); Orme, *Comes the Comrade* and Alexandra Orme, *By the Waters of the Danube* (New York: Duell, Sloan, and Pearce, 1951); Diary of Roza Bodo, which is extensively cited in Gergely Kunt, "Wartime Sexual Economy as Seen through a Hungarian Woman's World War II Diary," *Feminist Studies* 43.1 (2017): 108–133; Skrabski's documentary also features interviews with numerous rape victims, Skrabski, *Silenced Shame*, film.
160. Jeno Farkass, *The Last Winter A Diary of the Siege and Occupation of Budapest, 1944–1945* trans. Maria Farkas Szokolai and Charles Farkas (unpublished manuscript, 29 January 2020), 34–35 and 43.
161. Ibid., 126.
162. Ibid., 131.
163. Ibid., 140–141.
164. Ibid., 142–143.
165. Gunter Bischof, *Austria in the First Cold War, 1945–55* (New York: St. Martin's Press, 1999), 33.
166. Stelzl-Marx, *Stalins Soldaten in Österreich*, 466.
167. Bischof, *Austria in the First Cold War*, 33.
168. Maria Mesner, "Gender and Abortion after the Second World War: the Austrian Case in a Comparative Perspective," in Eleonore Breuning, Jill Lewis, and Gareth Pritchard, eds., *Power and the People: A Social History of Central European Politics, 1945–1956* (Manchester: Manchester University Press, 2005), 254; Lewis, *Workers and Politics*, 70.
169. Mesner, "Gender and Abortion," 254.
170. Ibid.
171. Stelzl-Marx, *Stalins Soldaten*, 466.

172. Edele, *Stalin's Defectors*, 36.
173. Ibid., 37.
174. Document 75, document reproduced in Alexander Hill, ed., *The Great Patriotic War of the Soviet Union, 1941–45: A Documentary Reader* (New York: Routledge, 2009), 103.
175. Charles Glass, *The Deserters: A Hidden History of World War II* (New York: The Penguin Press, 2013), xi.
176. Steven Welch, "Commemorating 'Heroes of a Special Kind': Deserter Monuments in Germany," *Journal of Contemporary History* 47.2 (April 2012): 372.
177. RGVA, f. 32900, op. 1, d. 183, l. 175.
178. RGVA, f. 32900, op. 1, d. 230, l. 43.
179. Interview with Ujj Miklosne in *Silenced Shame* film at 00.51; Hlihor and Scurtu, *The Red Army in Romania*, 145; IAS, f. 83, k. 23, "Mesnim narodnim odborima Pov. Br 145/45 dana 20.IX.1945."
180. RGVA, f. 32905, op. 1, d. 128, ll. 210.
181. TsAMO, f. 413 (57A), op. 10372, d. 349, l. 53.
182. Gabriel Temkin, *My Just War: The Memoir of a Jewish Red Army Soldier in World War II* (Novato: Presidio, 1998), 189–190.
183. RGVA, f. 32900, op. 1, d. 218, l. 43.
184. RGVA, f. 32900, op. 1, d. 183, l. 118; RGVA, f. 32900, op. 1, d. 183, l. 132.
185. RGVA, f. 32900, op. 1, d. 220, l. 207.
186. RGVA, f. 32900, op. 1, d. 183, l. 131.
187. Ibid., 210.
188. VA, f. NOVJ, k. 214, f. 5, d. 21, ll. 1–2.
189. RGVA, f. 3290, op. 1, d. 220, l. 104.
190. RGVA, f. 32905, op. 1, d. 128, ll. 44–45.
191. Ibid.
192. Attacked authorities – RGVA, f. 32905, op. 1, d. 143, l. 80; RGVA, f. 32905, op. 1, d. 143, l. 22. Forged documents – RGVA, f. 32905, op. 1, d. 143, l. 80; RGVA, f. 32905, op. 1, d. 130, l. 205.
193. RGVA, f. 32900, op. 1, d. 220, l. 22.
194. Ibid., l. 103.
195. Ibid., l. 104.
196. Ibid., l. 42–56.
197. RGVA, f. 32900, op. 1, d. 363, ll. 6–7.
198. Ibid., l. 82.
199. For Yugoslavia, see Zolotarev, et al., eds., *Krasnaia Armiia v stranakh tsentral'noi, severnoi evropy i na balkanakh*, 184. For Romania, see Ibid., 15. For Hungary, see Ibid., 291. For Austria, see Ibid., 602.

3 The Kremlin's Policies

1. RGVA, f. 32900, op. 1, d. 172, l. 104.
2. RGASPI, f. 644, op. 2, d. 309, ll. 189–192, document reproduced in Tatiana Volokitina et al., eds, *Sovetskii Faktor v Vostochnoi Evrope 1944–1953. Tom 1 1944–1948. Dokumenty* (Moscow: ROSSPEN, 1999), 55–56.

3. Hill, *The Red Army*, 271.
4. RGASPI, f. 644, op. 2, d. 309, ll. 189–192, document reproduced in Volokitina et al., eds, *Sovetskii Faktor*, 55–56.
5. RGVA, f. 32900, op. 1, d. 172, ll. 104–106.
6. Ibid., ll. 108–109.
7. RGVA, f. 32900, op. 1, d. 172, l. 106.
8. Ibid.
9. Ibid.
10. Ibid.
11. Hlihor and Scurtu, *The Red Army in Romania*, 113.
12. Ibid., 118.
13. Ibid., 119.
14. Ibid., 117.
15. Ibid., 121–122.
16. Arh M.A.p.N., fond 1367, dosar 109, ff.189–190, document reproduced in Hlihor and Scurtu, *The Red Army in Romania*, 202–203.
17. TsAMO, f. 48a, op. 3410, d.14, l. 220, document reproduced in Zolotarev et al., eds., *General'nyi shtab*, 430.
18. Perry Biddiscombe, "Prodding the Russian Bear: Pro-German Resistance in Romania, 1944–5," *European History Quarterly* 23.2 (1993): 230.
19. Dinu Giurescu, *Romania in the Second World War 1939–1945* (Boulder: East European Monographs, 2000), 385.
20. Arh M.Ap.N, fond 1367, dosar 199, ff.310–312, document reproduced in Hlihor and Scurtu, *The Red Army in Romania*, 209–210.
21. Dinu Giurescu, *Romania's Communist Takeover: The Radescu Government* (Boulder: East European Monographs, 1994), 23; 76.
22. For extreme cuts, see Berry Burton, *Romanian Diaries 1944–1947* (Iasi-Portland: Center for Romanian Studies, 2000), 34. Soviets deployed two full NKVD Divisions, GARF, f. 9401, op. 2, d. 92, l. 112, document reproduced in Volokitina et al., eds, *Sovetskii Faktor tom 1, 130–131*. In addition, the Red Army had five regular divisions in Romania in March 1945, Giurescu, *Romania in the Second World War*, 393.
23. Hlihor and Scurtu, *The Red Army in Romania*, 147–148.
24. Arh M.Ap. N., fond 1367, dosar 199, ff. 506–507, document reproduced in Hlihor and Scurtu, *The Red Army in Romania*, 207.
25. RGASPI, f. 644, op. 2, d. 309, ll. 189–192, document reproduced in Volokitina et al., eds, *Sovetskii Faktor v Vostochnoi Evrope tom 1*, 130–131.
26. B. V. Senilov, *Voennyie dengi vtoroi mirovoi voiny* (Moscow: Finansy i Statistika, 1991), 76.
27. TsAMO RF, f. 240, op. 9512, d. 3, l. 6, document reproduced in V. A. Zolotarev, et al., eds., *Krasnaia Armiia v stranakh Tsentral'noi, Severnoi Evropy i na Balkanakh*, 54.
28. R. J. Crampton, *Bulgaria* (Oxford: Oxford University Press, 2007), 309–310.
29. Vesselin Dimitrov, *Stalin's Cold War: Soviet Foreign Policy, Democracy and Communism in Bulgaria, 1941–1948* (New York: Palgrave Macmillan, 2008), 70.
30. G. Nikova, "Bolgariia mezhdu Germaniei i Sovetskim Soiuzom (sotsial'nyi i ekonomicheskii rakurs)," in *Chelovek na Balkanakh*, ed., G. G. Litavrin et al., 284.

31. "The Armistice Agreement with Bulgaria; October 28, 1944," The Yale Law School: The Avalon Project: Documents in Law, History and Diplomacy, accessed 10 May 2014, http://avalon.law.yale.edu/wwii/bulgaria.asp#protocol.
32. Zakharov, *Osvobozhdenie*, 242. In total, the Soviets supplied Bulgarians with 344 airplanes, 65 tanks, 410 field guns, 155 antiaircraft weapons, 370 mortars, 18,800 rifles, 10,616 machine guns, 12,700 submachineguns, 420 heavy machineguns, 280 anti-tank weapons, 369 radio stations, 2,572 telephones, and 370 automobiles.
33. David Stone, "The 1945 Ethridge Mission to Bulgaria and Romania and the Origins of the Cold War in the Balkans," *Diplomacy & Statecraft* 17.1 (1996): 103.
34. VA, f. NOVJ, k. 57, f. 6, d. 17, l. 1.
35. Đilas, *Conversations*, 63–64.
36. Popović, *Jugoslovensko-sovejtski odnosi*, 158.
37. Ibid., 206.
38. Volokitina et al., eds, *Sovetskii Faktor*, 118–133.
39. Ivo Banac, ed., *The Diary of Georgi Dimitrov 1933–1949* (New Haven: Yale University Press, 2003), 353.
40. Alexander Prusin, *Serbia under the Swastika: A World War II Occupation* (Urbana: University of Illinois Press, 2017), 157–158.
41. Author's Interview with Radmila Petković.
42. Ibid.
43. Berkhoff, *Harvest*, Chapter 6.
44. Martvin Mevius, *Agents of Moscow: The Hungarian Communist Party and the Origins of Socialist Patriotism 1941–1953* (Oxford: Oxford University Press, 2005), 52.
45. Nevenkin, *Take Budapest*, 29.
46. Ibid.
47. TsAMO RF, f. 243, op. 2914, d. 215, ll. 44–47, document reproduced in V. A. Zolotarev, et al., eds., *Krasnaia Armiia v stranakh Tsentral'noi, Severnoi Evropy i na Balkanakh*, 309.
48. Rodion Malinovskii, *Budapesht, Vena, Praga* (Moscow: Nauka, 1985), 82.
49. TsAMO RF, f. 4, op. 11, d. 78, ll. 422–424, document reproduced in V. A. Zolatarev, *Prikazy Narodnogo Komissara Oborony*, 333. The regiment was converted back to regular army within three months, "Gaeta 'Pravdy'. Kakimi byli shtrafbaty," Kommunisticheskaia Partiia Rossisskoi Federatsii, accessed 21 October 2014, http://kprf.ru/history/soviet/123513.html.
50. TsAMO RF, f. 148a, op. 3763, d. 213, l. 46–48, document reproduced in V. A. Zolotarev et al., eds. *Stavka VGK*, 207.
51. V. A. Zolotarev, et al., eds., *Krasnaia Armiia v stranakh Tsentral'noi, Severnoi Evropy i na Balkanakh*, 291.
52. Mevius, *Agents of Moscow*, 48.
53. Kenez, *Hungary from the Nazis to the Soviets*, 63.
54. Ibid.
55. Kenez, *Hungary from the Nazis to the Soviets*, 73–74.
56. RGVA, f. 32905, op. 1, d. 130, l. 173.
57. Ibid., 176–177.

58. Ungvary, *The Siege of Budapest*, 340–341.
59. TsAMO RF, f. 243, op. 2914, d. 215, ll. 44–47, document reproduced in V. A. Zolotarev, et al., eds., *Krasnaia Armiia v stranakh Tsentral'noi, Severnoi Evropy i na Balkanakh*, 309.
60. RGVA, f. 32905, op. 1, d. 130, l. 39. The document states "only with the sanction of the special directorate." However, the special directorate was the code word for the directorates for the utilization of internal resources, RGVA, f. 32900, op. 1, d. 172, ll. 108–109.
61. Schechter, *The Stuff of*, 219.
62. RGVA, f. 32900, op. 1, d. 341, 130.
63. RGVA, f. 32900, op. 1, d. 367, l. 31.
64. "Interview with Petr Rudiagin," *Ia pomniu*, accessed 28 November 2024, https://iremember.ru/memoirs/pekhotintsi/rudyagin-petr-timofeevich/.
65. RGVA, f. 32900, op. 1, d. 452, l. 5.
66. Ibid.; Slutskii, *Zapiski*, 42.
67. RGVA, f. 32900, op. 1, d. 367, l. 31.
68. RGVA, f. 32900, op. 1, d. 452, l. 85; Temkin, *My Just War*, 200.
69. Temkin, *My Just War*, 200.
70. RGVA, f. 32900, op. 1, d. 452, l. 85.
71. BA, Dnevnik El'kinson, 22; Temkin, *My Just War*, 200; "Interview with Aleksandr Sedoi," *Ia pomniu*, accessed 28 November 2024, https://iremember.ru/memoirs/artilleristi/sedoy-aleksandr-stepanovich; "Interview with Grigorii Russkikh;" "Interview with Piotr Riudagin," *Ia pomniu*; "Interview with Mikhail Tsurkan," *Ia pomniu*; "Interview with Aleksandr Solov'ev," *Ia pomniu*.
72. RGVA, f. 32900, op. 1, d. 363, l. 95.
73. D. I. Vorontsov, eds., *Vengerskie voennoplennye v SSSR. Dokumenty 1941–1953 godov* (Moscow: Rosspen, 2005), 6–7.
74. RGVA, f. 32900, op. 1, d. 220, l. 94.
75. Pavel Polian, *Against Their Will: The History and Geography of Forced Migrations in the USSR* (Budapest: Central European University, 2004), 266.
76. Agnes Huszar Vardy, "Forgotten Victims of World War II: Hungarian Women in Soviet Forced Labour Camps," in Steven Vardy, Agnes Vardy and Tooley Hunt eds., *Ethnic Cleansing in Twentieth Century Europe* (New York: Columbia University Press, 2003), 508.
77. RGVA, f. 1p, op. 01e, d. 37, ll. 5–6, document reproduced in D. I. Vorontsov, et al., eds., *Vengerskie voennoplennye*, 285–286.
78. Kenez, *Hungary from the Nazis to the Soviets*, 36.
79. Mevius, *Agents of Moscow*, 61.
80. Kenez, *Hungary from the Nazis to the Soviets*, 78.
81. Ibid., 77–78.
82. Kamen Nevenkin, *Fortress Budapest: The Siege of the Hungarian Capital, 1944–45* (Keszthely: PeKo Publishing Kft., 2020), 29–30.
83. Kenez, *Hungary from the Nazis to the Soviets*, 71.
84. Ibid., 37.
85. Charles Farkas, *Vanished by the Danube: Peace, War, Revolution, and Flight to the West*, introduction by Margaret McMullan (Albany: State University of New York Press, 2013), 264; Ungvary, *The Siege*, 349.

86. Jill Lewis, "Dancing on a Tight Rope: The Beginning of the Marshall Plan," in Bischof, Gunther, Anton Pelinka, and Dieter Stiefel, eds., *The Marshall Plan in Austria: Contemporary Austrian Studies*, Volume 8 (New Brunswick: Transaction Publishers, 2001), 140.
87. Robert Knight, "The Carinthian Slovenes" in Eleonore Breuning, Jill Lewis and Gareth Pritchard, eds., *Power and the People: A Social History of Central European Politics, 1945–56* (Manchester: Manchester University Press, 2005), 118.
88. Bischof, *Austria in the First Cold War*, 41.
89. Harold Knoll and Barbara Stelzl-Marx, "Stalin's Judiciary in Austria: Arrests and Convictions during the Occupation" in Karner Stefan and Barbara Stelzl-Marx, eds., *The Red Army in Austria: The Soviet Occupation, 1945–1955*, trans. by Alex J. Kay (Lanham: Lexington Books, 2020), 182–183.
90. Bischof, *Austria in the First Cold War*, 41.
91. Walter M. Iber, "Occupation and Exploitation: Soviet Economic Policy toward Austria from 1945 to 1955/63" in Karner Stefan and Barbara Stelzl-Marx, eds., *The Red Army in Austria: The Soviet Occupation, 1945–1955*, trans. by Alex J. Kay (Lanham: Lexington Books, 2020), 129.
92. Bischof, *Austria in the First Cold War*, 41.
93. For Hungary, see Kenez, *Hungary from the Nazis to the Soviets*, 33. For Austria, see Klaus Eisterer, "Austria under Allied Occupation" in Rolf Steininger, Günter Bischof, and Michael Gehler, eds., *Austria in the Twentieth Century* (New Brunswick, NJ: Transaction Publishers, 2002), 201.
94. Iber, "Occupation and Exploitation," 127.
95. Stelzl-Marx, *Stalins Soldaten in Österreich*, 274.
96. Lewis, *Workers and Politics*, 67.
97. Lewis, "Dancing on a Tight Rope," 141.
98. Ibid., 142.
99. Lewis, *Workers and Politics*, 74.
100. Ibid., 66.
101. Bischoff, *Austria in the First Cold War*, 38.

4 Propaganda

1. K. V. Krainiukov, S. E. Zakharov and G. E. Shabaev, *Partiino-politicheskaiarabota v sovetskikhvooruzhennykhsilakh v godyvelikoiotecehst-vennoivoiny 1941–1945. Kratkiiistoricheskiiobzor* (Moscow: OrdenaTrudo vogoKrasnogoZnameniVoennoeizdatel'stvoministerstvaOborony SSSR Moskva, 1968), 8.
2. G. V. Sredin, *Ideologicheskaiarabota KPSS v deistvuiushceiarmii 1941–1945gg* (Moscow: Voennoeizdatel'stvo, 1985), 14.
3. K. V. Krainiukov, S. E. Zakharov and G. E. Shabaev, *Partiino-politicheskaiarabota*, 8.
4. Anoshin, *Na Pravyiboi*, 2.
5. Berkhoff, *Motherland*, 3–4.
6. Burds, "Sexual Violence in Europe," 47.
7. Berkhoff, *Motherland*, 194.
8. Ibid., 141.

9. I. G. Ehrenburg, *Voina. 1941–1945* (Moscow: KRPA Olimp, 2004), accessed 28 January, 2024, http://militera.lib.ru/prose/russian/erenburg_ig3/177.html.
10. Ibid.
11. TsDAGO, f. 56, op. 1, d. 1194, ll. 1–3.
12. TsDAGO, f. 57, op. 4, d. 96, l. 9.
13. TsAMO RF, f. 32, op. 795436, d. 11, ll. 36–39, document reproduced in V. A. Zolotarev et al., eds., *RusskiiArkhiv: VelikaiaOtechestvennaia. GlavnyePoliticheskieOrganyVooruzhennykh Sil SSSR v VelikoiOtechestvennoivoine 1941–1945gg. DokumentyiMaterialy 1941–1945gg.* 17.6 (1–2) (Moscow: Terra, 1996), 293.
14. TsAMORF, f. 32, op. 795436, d. 11, ll. 36–39, document reproduced in V. A. Zolotarevetal., eds., *GlavnyePoliticheskieOrgany*, 295.
15. TsDAGO, f. 62, op. 2, d. 910, l. 49.
16. "Interview with Mikhail Ivanov," *Ia pomniu.*
17. RGVA, f. 32900, op. 1, d. 412, l. 155.
18. TsDAGO, f. 62, op. 2, d. 910, l 57.
19. TsAMO, f. 3430 (4 gvmk), op. 1, d. 141, l. 27.
20. Ibid., l. 28.
21. TsDAGO, f. 62, op. 2, d. 910, l. 61; RGVA, f. 32900, op. 1, d. 402, l. 240.
22. Aleksandr Krivitskii, *Russkiiofitser za rubezhom* (Moscow: Voenizdat, 1946), 4. That these articles were first published in Ibid., 5.
23. P. G. Kuznetsov, *Dniboevye* (Moscow: Voenizdat, 1959), 311.
24. TsAMO, f. 3430 (4 gvmk), op. 1, d. 141, ll. 29–30.
25. P. G. Kuznetsov, *Marshal Tolbukhin* (Moscow: Voennoeizdatel'stvominster stvaoborony SSSR, 1966), 176–177.
26. RGVA, f. 32900, op. 1, d. 458, ll. 48–49.
27. Anoshin, *Na Pravyiboi*, 91.
28. RGVA, f. 32900, op. 1, d. 458, l. 11.
29. Anoshin, *Na pravyiboi*, 90.
30. K. V. Krainiukov, S. E. Zakharov and G. E. Shabaev, *Partiino-politicheskaiarabota*, 393.
31. Anoshin, *Na pravyiboi*, 93–94.
32. Ibid., 86.
33. TsAMO, f. 1512, op. 1, d. 91, l. 193.
34. Ibid.
35. TsAMO, f. 1512, op. 1, d. 93, l. 207.
36. TsAMO, f. 96 (68sk), op. 1, d. 242, l. 196.
37. VA, f.NOVJ, k. 96, f. 5, d.1, l. 6, originally from TsAMO, f. 243, o. 250987, d.16, no page number.
38. TsAMO, f. 243, op. 2914, d. 73, ll. 102–205, document reproduced in V. A. Zolotarev, et al., eds., *KrasnaiaArmiia v stranakhTsentral'noi, SevernoiEvropyinaBalkanakh*, 223–224.
39. TsAMO, f. 234, op. 2969, d. 28, ll. 43–44, document reproduced in I. V. Bukharin i S. Stoianovich, eds., *OtnosheniiaRossii (SSSR) s Iugoslaviei 1941–1945gg. Dokumentyimaterialy* (Moscow: Terra kniyhniziklub, 1998), 322–324.

40. TsAMO, f. 1512 (233sd), op. 1, d. 34, l. 150.
41. Anita Kondoyanidi, "The Liberating Experience: War Correspondents, Red Army Soldiers, and the Nazi Extermination Camps," *The Russian Review* 69.3 (2010): 438–462.
42. S. S. Biriuzov et al., eds., *BeogradskaOperacija*, 124.
43. Ibid.
44. TsAMO, f. 1512 (233sd), op. 1, d. 93, ll. 197–198.
45. Nikolai Zav'ialov, *Pod zvezdami balkanskimi* (Kyiv: Izdatel'stvopoliticheskoi literaturyUkrainy, 1987), 83.
46. Temkin, *My Just*,194; RGVA, f. 32900, op. 1, d. 413, l. 217.
47. TsAMO, f. 1512 (233sd), op. 1, d. 35, l. 303; TsAMO, f. 1512 (233sd), op. 1, d. 93, l. 256.
48. RGVA, f. 32900, op. 1, d. 442, l. 81.
49. RGVA, f. 32900, op. 1, d. 188, l. 183.
50. Ibid.
51. Ibid.
52. Anoshin, *Na Pravyiboi*, 168.
53. For instance, see USHMM, 22.016, box 3, folder 23, "Statement of 1 April 1944 on examination of body of Soviet soldier found near Moshonsentpeter, Hungary who had evidently been tortured," originally from TsAMO, f. 240, op. 2772, d. 82, l. 29; Ibid., "Statement of 13 March 1945 on examination of body of evidently tortured Soviet officer who was wounded during battle near the village of Godrusha [not further identified]," originally from TsAMO, f.240, op.2772, d.82, l. 22.
54. Anoshin, *Na Pravyiboi*, 168.
55. TsAMO, f. 243, op. 265386, d. 5, ll. 46–50, document reproduced in V. A. Zolotarev, et al., eds., *KrasnaiaArmiia v stranakhTsentral'noi, SevernoiEvropyinaBalkanakh*, 365–367.
56. Ibid., 367.
57. From TsAMO RF (no citation), document reproduced in Nevenkin, *Take Budapest*, 247.
58. A. A. Gromyko et al., eds., *SSSR-Avstriia: dokumentyimaterialy* (Moscow: Politizdat, 1980), 16–17.
59. Ibid., 618.
60. Lewis, *Workers and Politics*, 40–41.
61. TsAMO, f. 32, op. 11306, d. 240, ll. 461–463, document reproduced in V. A. Zolotarev, et al., eds., *Krasnaia Armiia v stranakh Tsentral'noi, Severnoi Evropy i na Balkanakh*, 627.
62. Anoshin, *Na Pravyiboi*, 228–229.
63. RGVA, f. 32900, op. 1, d. 441, l. 62.
64. Ibid., 63.
65. Kuznetsov, *Marshal Tolbukhin*, 176.

5 Disciplinary Policies

1. Glantz, *Colossus Reborn*, 369 and 374.
2. Timoshenko, *Distsiplinarnyi Ustav*, 5.

3. Ibid., 5.
4. Ibid., 6–32.
5. Oleg Budnitskii, "In Parantheses: Extrajudicial Executions during the Great Patriotic War" *Cahiers du Monde Russe* 63.1. (2022): 231, 238.
6. Beevor, *The Fall of Berlin*, 32
7. Ungváry, *The Siege*, 363.
8. Viacheslav Zviagintsev, *Voina na vesakh femidy. Voina 1941–1945gg v materialakh sledstvenno-sudebnykh del* Tom 1 (Moscow: Terra-knizhnyiklub, 2006), 390.
9. Alex Statiev, "Penal Units in the Red Army," *Europe-Asia Studies* 62.5 (2010): 727.
10. Ministerstvo oborony Rossii, *Ukazy Prezdiuma Verkhovnogo Soveta SSSR o voennom polozheniii obutverzhdenii Polozheniia o voennykh Tribunalovot 22 iunia 1941 goda*, accessed 22 December 2021, www.archive.mil.ru/archival_service/central/resources/collection/gallery.htm?id=10967%40cmsPhotoGallery.
11. N. A. Petukhov, *Istoriia voennykh sudov Rossii* (Moscow: Norma, 2003), 327.
12. Marc Jansen and Nikita Petrov, "Mass Terror and the Court: The Military Collegium of the USSR," *Europe-Asia Studies* 58. 4 (2006): 589.
13. Zviagintsev, *Voina*, 25.
14. Ibid., 29.
15. Glantz, *Colossus Reborn*, 384.
16. Vadim J. Birstein, *SMERSH. Stalin's Secret Weapon: Soviet Military Counterintelligence in WWII* (London: Biteback, 2011), 26.
17. Ibid., 1.
18. N. V. Grekov "Deiatel'nost' Kontrrazvedki, SMERSH, po Presecheniiu Izmeny i Dezertirstva v voiskakh vo vremia Velikoi Otechestvennoi Voiny 1941–1945 gg," *Voenno-Istoricheskii Zhurnal* 2 (2006): 42.
19. For Soviet civilians, see A. I. Romanov, *Nights Are Longest There: A Memoir of the Soviet Security Services* (Boston-Toronto: Little, Brown and Company, 1972), 92; Soviet prisoners of war, Ibid., 124; for screeing Soviet officers who worked in occupation apparatus, see Ibid., 163.
20. TsAMO, f. 1512 (233sd), op. 1, d. 93, l. 264; Romanov, *Nights Are Longest There*, 207.
21. N.a., "Voiska NKVD po okhrane tyla deistvuiushchei Krasnoi Armii," *Istorii aotechestvennykh spetssluzhbi pravokhranitel'nykh organov*, accessed 18 August 2023, www.shieldandsword.mozohin.ru/VD3462/troops/vot.htm.
22. RGVA, f. 32905, op. 1, d. 198, l. 300. Although I have not found exact figures for the NKVD Army of the 3rd Ukrainian Front, it had six regiments at this time, which would mean that it had a similar number of soldiers as the NKVD Army of the 2nd Ukrainian Front, RGVA, f. 32900, op. 1, d. 484, l. 54. For June 1945, see Nikita Petrov, "The Internal Troops of the NKVD in the System of Soviets Organs of Rerpression in Austria, 1945–1946," in Gunter Bischof, Frits Plasser and Barbara Stelzl-Marx, eds., *New Perspectives on Austrians and World War II, Contemporary Austrian Studies* Volume 17 (New Brunswick: Transaction Publishers, 2009), 252.
23. RGVA, f. 32900, op. 1, d.172, l. 21.
24. Ibid., l. 104.

25. RGVA, f. 32900, o.1, d. 341, ll. 54–56.
26. Ibid., l. 59. The Commissariat of Defense Order was referenced in Tolbukhin's order from 29 May 1944 below. The order, however, was not published in Zolatarev, *PrikazyNarodnogoKomissaraOborony SSSR 1943–1945gg.*
27. RGVA, f. 32900, op. 1, d. 341, l. 58.
28. Ibid., l. 58–59.
29. For instance, see NKO order "O beschinstvakh, vooruzhennykhgrabezhakh, krazhakh u grazhdanskogonaseleniiaiubiistvakh, tvorimykhotdel'nymivo ennosluzhashcimi v prifrontovoipoloseimeropriatiiakhprotivnikh," which states that the Commissariat of Defense has been receiving reports from the NKVD and Soviet organizations about the criminal conduct by some service personnel, TsAMO RF, f. 4, op. 11, d. 77, ll. 482–484, document reproduced in Zolatarev, *Russkii Arkhiv: Velikaia Otechestvennaia. Prikazy Narodnogo Komissara Oborony*, 290–292.
30. TsAMO, f. 1512 (233sd), op. 1, d. 35, l. 235.
31. Ibid., l. 235.
32. Ibid., 44.
33. Ibid., l. 248.
34. "Interview with Mikhail Ivanov," *Ia pomniu.* Less plausibly, Ivanov claimed that he was not aware of any violation of this order in his regiment until the end of the war.
35. Ibid.
36. "Interview with Nikolai Povov," *Ia pomniu.* 28 November 2024, www .iremember.ru/memoirs/tankisti/popov-nikolay-vasilevich/.
37. TsAMO, f. 48a, op. 3410, d. 14, l. 422, document reproduced in Zolotarev et al., eds., *General'nyi shtab*, 472.
38. Ibid.
39. RGASPI, f. 17, op. 125, d. 247, ll. 72–78, document reproduced in *Krasnaia Armiia v stranakh Tsentral'noi, Severnoi Evropy i na Balkanakh*, 111.
40. I. S. Anoshin, *Na Pravyiboi* (Moscow: Voennoeizdatel'stvo, 1988), 83.
41. RGASPI, f. 395, op. 74, d. 99, ll. 1–7, document reproduced in Zolotarev, et al., eds., *Krasnaia Armiia v stranakh Tsentral'noi, Severnoi Evropy i na Balkanakh*, 116.
42. RGVA, f. 32900, op. 1, d. 185, l. 239.
43. RGVA, f. 32900, op. 1, d. 337, l. 47.
44. Banac, ed., *The Diary of Georgi Dimitrov*, 330–343.
45. For Yugoslav-Bulgarian relations see Ibid., 337 and 343, for the armistice see Ibid., 339 and 341.
46. For the meeting with Biriuzov see Ibid, 341. For the meeting with Anoshin, see Anoshin, *Na pravyiboi*, 84.
47. Timofejev, *Rusi*, 183.
48. VA, f. NOVJ, k. 181, f. 3, d. 6, l. 2.
49. VA, f. NOVJ, k. 27, f. 12, d. 1, l. 2; VA, f. NOVJ, k. 182, f. 1, d. 9, l. 1; VA, f. NOVJ, k. 191, f. 1, d. 11, l. 11.
50. VA, f. NOVJ, k. 191, f. 1, d. 11, l. 11.
51. For October 17 see, Ibid., l. 66. For 26 October, see Ibid., 140. For October 29, see Ibid., 14.

52. Ibid., 9 and Ibid, 66.
53. Đilas, *Conversations with Stalin*, 88.
54. Slutskii, *Zapiski*, 94.
55. Ibid., 94.
56. AJ, f. 836 – KMJ I – 3-b/571, document reproduced in Bukharin and Stoianovich, *Otnosheniia*, 361–362.
57. AJ, KMJ I – 3-b/57, document reproduced in Bukharin and Stoianovich, eds., *Otnoshenia*, 363–364.
58. VA, f. NOVJ, k. 181, f. 3, d. 41.
59. VA, f. NOVJ, k. 26, f. 8, d. 9, 8.
60. VA, f. NOVJ, k. 191, f. 1, d. 11, 13–14.
61. Đilas, *Conversations*, 89.
62. VA, f. NOVJ, k. 26, f. 8, d. 8, l. 2.
63. VA, f. NOVJ, k. 26, f. 8, d. 9, l. 8.
64. AJ, f. 836 – KMJ I – 3-b/101, l. 3.
65. VA, f. NOVJ, k. 181, f. 3, d. 41, l. 1.
66. TsAMO, f. 48a, op. 3410, d. 14, ll. 507, document reproduced in V. A. Zolotarev, et al., eds., *Krasnaia Armiia v stranakh Tsentral'noi, Severnoi Evropy i na Balkanakh*, 483–484.
67. TsAMO, f. 48a, op. 3410, d. 14, ll. 507, document reproduced in Zolotarev et al., eds., *General'nyishtab*, 484.
68. RGVA, f. 32900, op. 1, d. 186, l. 153.
69. Ibid., l. 162.
70. Ibid.
71. Ibid.
72. TsAMO, f. 1512, op. 1, d. 35, l. 285.
73. Ibid.
74. Ungváry, *The Siege*, 344. His source for this claim was a cold-war era book, Siegfried Kogelfranz, *Das Erbe von Jalta* (Paris: n.p., 1985), 96.
75. For common, see Ibid., 332. For humanely, see Ibid., 338.
76. For Malinovskii and Konev see Naimark, *Russians in Germany*, 71. His source was Jan Stransky, *East Wind Over Prague* (New York: Random House, 1950), 38. For Tolbukhin see Naimark, *Russians in Germany*, 70. His source was Jörg K. Hoensch, *Sowjetische Osteuropa-Politik: 1945–1975* (Kronberg/Ts.: Athenäum-Verlag, 1977), 39 n. 7.
77. Kenez, *Hungary from the Nazis to the Soviets*, 40.
78. Lewis, *Workers and Politics*, 40.
79. Mevius, *Agents of Moscow*, 65.
80. Ibid., 61.
81. For instance, in May 1944, Malinovskii was transferred from the position of the commander of the 3rd to 2nd Ukrainian Front, while Tolbukhin was transferred from the 4th to 3rd Ukrainian Front, A. A. Pechenkin, "Komanduiushciefrontami 1944 goda," *Voenno-istoricheskii zhurnal* 10 (2005): 10. Armies moved between fronts more frequently, for instance, the Forty-Sixth Army was transferred at least four times between 2nd and 3rd Ukrainian Fronts from the spring of 1944 until the end of the war, n.a., "46-ia Armiia," *Boevye deistviia Krasnoi armii v VOV*, accessed 31 August 2014, www.bdsa.ru/index.php?option=com_content&task=view&id=2817.

82. Major-General Kuznetsov, the commander of the NKVD Army of the 2nd Ukrainian Front who was also in charge of command posts in the country, received reports every ten days about the activities of command posts in Hungary and northern Transylvania. The last remaining Axis troops capitulated in Budapest on 13 February 1945, which would mean that according to Ungváry, the Red Army troops had a license to do as they pleased from 13 to 15 February, Anoshin, *Na Pravyiboi*, 189. However, the Budapest command post detained 519 Soviet soldiers from 12 February to 22 February, RGVA, f. 32905, op. 1, d. 143, l. 32. Unfortunately, I did not find the day to day reports about the activity of Budapest command post, thus it cannot be established with absolute certainty that no arrests were made between 13 and 15 February. Yet, in the ten-day period from 22 February to 3 March, the patrols of the Budapest command post detained only 86 soldiers, RGVA, f. 32905, op. 1, d. 143, l. 60. Obviously, if soldiers were allowed a free reign of looting and raping from 13 to 15 February, then the patrols should have detained fewer soldiers from 12–22 February than from 23 February to 3 March. In fact, the very opposite was the case.
83. From TsAMO RF (no citation), document reproduced in Nevenkin, *Take Budapest*, 246.
84. Ibid., 247.
85. Ibid.
86. Ungváry, *The Siege*, 338. Ungváry made this claim based on Soviet documents which the Germans captured.
87. RGVA, f. 32900, op. 1, d. 174, l. 14.
88. RGVA, f. 32900, op. 1, d. 363, l. 23.
89. Diary excerpts from Shavelev, Al'tman, Terushkin, and Brodskaia, eds. *Sokhranimoipis'ma. Vypusk 2*, 266; Temkin, *My Just War*, 201; "Interview with Mikhail Tsurkan," *Ia pomniu*; "Interview with Aleksandr Solov'ev," *Ia pomniu.*
90. Ungváry, *The Siege*, 338.
91. See for instance, TsAMO, f. 1512 (233sd), op. 1, d. 35, l. 348.
92. RGVA, f. 32905, op. 1, d. 98, l. 29.
93. Ibid., l. 23.
94. Svenka Savic ed., "Elza" in *Women's Identities in Vojvodina: 1920–1930* (Novi Sad: Futura Publikacije, 2006), 91.
95. For crossing the frontier see TsAMO, f. 1512 (233sd), op. 1, d. 34, l. 163. For trenches see RGVA, f. 32900, op. 1, d. 183, l. 130.
96. Vardy, "Forgotten Victims of World War II," 510.
97. Randolph L. Braham, *The Politics of Genocide: The Holocaust in Hungary* (New York: Columbia University Press, 1981), 51–52.
98. RGVA, f. 1p, op. 01e, d. 37, ll. 5–6, document reproduced in D. I Vorontsov, et al., eds., *Vengerskie voennoplennye*, 285–286.
99. RGVA, f. 1p, op. 01e, d. 27, ll. 162, document reproduced in D. I Vorontsov et al eds., Ibid., 283.
100. V. A. Zolotarev, et al., eds., *KrasnaiaArmiia v stranakhTsentral'noi, SevernoiEvropyinaBalkanakh*, 601.
101. TsAMO, f. 3, op. 11556, d. 18, ll. 85–86, document reproduced in V. A. Zolotarev, et al., eds., *Krasnaia Armiia v stranakh Tsentral'noi, Severnoi Evropy i na Balkanakh*, 610.
102. Gromyko et al., eds., *SSSR-Avstriia*, 16.

103. Ibid., 17.
104. RGVA, f. 32900, op. 1, d. 441, l. 62.
105. RGVA, f. 32900, op.1, d. 188, l. 8.
106. RGVA, f. 32905, op. 1, d. 130, l. 118.
107. Ibid., l. 118.
108. RGVA, f. 32900, op. 1, d. 458, l. 43.
109. RGVA, f. 32900, op. 1, d. 172, l. 201.
110. Temkin, *My Just War*, 201.
111. RGVA, f. 32900, op. 1, d. 172, l. 31.
112. Ibid., l. 32.
113. TsDAGO, f. 59, op. 1, d. 1614, l. 181.
114. VA, f. NOVJ, k. 214, f. 5, d. 21, ll. 1–2.
115. VA, f. NOVJ, k. VA, k. 214, f. 6, d. 19, l. 1.
116. RGVA, f. 32900, op. 1, d. 192, l. 146.
117. Hlihor and Scurtu, *The Red Army in Romania*, 153.
118. The nominal chairman of the Allied Control Commission was Marshal Malinovskii, but his primary concern was commanding the 2nd Ukrainian Front and not governing Romania.
119. Lev Kopelev, *To Be Preserved Forever*, translated and edited by Anthony Austin (Philadelphia and New York: J. B. Lippincott Company, 1977).
120. Slutskii, *Zapiski*, 130.
121. RGVA, f. 32900, op. 1, d. 458, l. 47.
122. Ibid.
123. Istorijski Arhiv Negotin (IAN), Narodno Oslobidalački odbor Štubik, br.2-1944, "Komanda mesta Jabukovac N.O.V.J. 8 oktobra 1944 g."
124. VA, f. NOVJ, k. 191, f. 1, d. 11, l. 66.
125. Bulgarian mothers – Istorijski Arhiv Subotica(IAS), f. 186, k. 64. A Subotica resident received a month-long prison sentence for insulting the honour of an allied army. He was overheard to say, "I'll fuck mothers of Bulgarian soldiers." He was angry that they had urinated and defecated in his basement. Russian mothers – VA, f. NOVJ, k. 225, f. 1, d. 41, l. 1. KNOJ arrested a man who said that Russians were poorly dressed, and cursed their Russian communist mothers.
126. AJ KMJ I – 3-b/577, "Pismo šefa kabineta maršala Jugoslavije Mitra Bakića Načelniku Personalnog odeljenja predsedništva nacionalnog komiteta, l. 1."
127. RGVA, f. 32900, o.1, d. 341, ll. 54–56.
128. RGVA, f. 32900, op.1, d. 220, l. 220.
129. TsAMO, f. 1512 (233sd), op. 1, d. 93, ll. 190–191.
130. Ibid., l. 192.
131. General-Colonel M. G. Vozhakin ed., *Velikaia otechestvennaia komkory: Voennyi biograficheskii slovar' v 2-ukh tomakh* Volume 1 (Moscow-Zhukovskii: Kuchkovo Pole, 2006), 439–440.
132. TsAMO, f. 1512 (233sd), op.1, d.93, l. 196.
133. Ibid.
134. Ibid.
135. Ibid.
136. Ibid.
137. TsAMO, f. 1512 (233sd), op. 1, d. 91, l. 295.
138. TsAMO, f. 1512 (233sd), op.1, d. 34, l. 147.

139. Vozhakin ed., *Velikaia otechestvennaia komkory*, 440.
140. RGVA, f. 32900, op. 1, d. 220, l. 171.
141. For Serov as Beria's deputy during the war see Glantz, *Colossus Reborn*, 379; For the flight to Craiova see GARF, f. 9401, op. 2, d. 66, l. 354, document reproduced in T. V. Volokitina, et al., eds, *Iz istorii sovetsko rumynskikh otnoshenii: tri vizita A. Ia. Vyshinskogo v Bukharest 1944–1946. Dokumenty rossiiskikh arkhivov* (Moscow: Rosspen, 1998), 31.
142. For 2,000 NKVD troops see GARF, f. 9401, op. 2, d. 66, l. 354, document reproduced in T. V. Volokitina, et al. eds. *Izistoriisovetsko-rumynskikhotnoshenii*, 31–32. Soviets had arrested fifty-five anti-Soviet individuals, among them high ranking Romanian civil servants and officers, they confiscated ninety guns, eight hundred radio sets and twelve cars, GARF, f. 9401, op. 2, d. 70, ll. 63–65 document reproduced in T. V. Volokitina, et al., eds., *Iz istorii sovetsko rumynskikh otnoshenii*, 35.
143. GARF, f.9401, op. 2, d. 66, ll. 365–367, document reproduced in T. V. Volokitina, et al., eds. *Iz istorii sovetsko rumynskikh otnoshenii*, 34.
144. Zviagintsev, *Voina*, 455.
145. RGVA, f. 32900, op. 1, d. 412, l. 161.
146. RGVA, f. 32900, op. 1, d. 413, l. 184.
147. Mordvinkin's party characteristic, written in early 1945, stated that he did not have any reprimands and that he was a skilled and a brave soldier, for which he received several government awards. However, the report criticized Mordvinkin for irregularly participating in the Party work, claiming that he did not always conscientiously carry out his assignments and that he fraternized with his subordinates too much, RGVA, f. 32900, op. 1, d. 457, l. 47. Subsequently, on 8 May 1945 Mordvinkin committed suicide. The head of his regiment cited the following reasons for suicide: unbalanced character, instability, and negligent attitude towards operational documents. The latter indicates that there was another incident in which Mordvinkin lost or otherwise mishandled secret documents, a serious violation. Thus, it seems that Mordvinkin's suicide had nothing to do with events in Craiova, RGVA, f.32900, op.1, d. 451, l. 67.
148. RGVA, f. 32900, op. 1, d. 205, l. 73.
149. James Harris, "Was Stalin a Weak Dictator?" *The Journal of Modern History* 75.2 (2003): 376.
150. Polcz, *One Woman in the War Hungary*, 104.
151. Ibid., 105.
152. Farkass, *The Last Winter*,136.
153. VA, f. NOVJ, k. 371, f. 6, d. 26, l. 1.
154. Ibid., 2.
155. Author's interview with BratislavFilipović. The following day, Filipović's father was invited to an interview, presumably by the military prosecutor or SMERSH. He told them that the officer fired the gun accidently. When the guilty officer returned from his interrogation, he started kissing Filipović's father for framing the incident as an accident.
156. RGVA, f. 32900, op. 1, d. 458, l. 34.
157. VA, f. NOVJ, k. 223, f. 13, d. 1, l. 4.
158. RGVA, f. 32900, oo.1, d. 172, l. 248. The document did not specify how the culprit was punished.

159. RGVA, f. 32900, op. 1, d. 192, l. 116. The document did not specify how the culprit was punished.
160. RGVA, f. 32900, op. 1, d. 172, l. 246. The document did not specify how the culprit was punished.
161. RGVA, f. 32900, op. 1, d. 183, l. 220.
162. RGVA, f. 32900, op. 1, d. 412, l. 148.
163. Ibid., 168
164. RGVA, f. 32900, op. 1, d. 337, l. 47.
165. TsAMO, f. 1512 (233sd), op. 1, d. 93, l. 211.
166. Timofejev, *Rusi*, 221.
167. Zviagintsev, *Voina*, 736.
168. Ibid., 736.
169. Petukhov, *Istoriia voennykh sudov*, 337.
170. Zviagintsev, *Voina*, 736.
171. Petukhov, *Istoriia voennykh sudov*, 338.
172. Zviagintsev, *Voina*, 16–17.
173. Lynne Viola, *Stalinist Perpetrators on Trial: Scenes from the Great Terror in Soviet Ukraine* (Oxford: Oxford University Press, 2017), 167.
174. Jan Gross, Neighbors: *The Destruction of the Jewish Community in Jedwabne, Poland* (Princeton: Princeton University Press, 2001); Tanja Penter, "Local Collaborators on Trial: Soviet War Crimes Trials under Stalin (1943–1953)," *Cahiers du Monde russe* 49, no. 4 (2008): 341–364; Alexander Prusin, "'Fascist Criminals to the Gallows!': *The Holocaust and Soviet War Crimes Trials, December 1945–February 1946*," Holocaust and Genocide Studies 17, no. 1 (2003): 1–30; and Oleksandr Melnyk, "Stalinist Justice as a Site of Memory: Anti-Jewish Violence in Kyiv's Podil District in September 1941 through the Prism of Soviet Investigative Documents," *Jahr bücher für Geschichte Osteuropas* 61, no. 2 (2013): 223–48.
175. Oleg Rzheshevskii, "Berlinskaia Operatsiia 1945g.: Diskussia Prodolzhaetsia," *Mir Istorii* 4 (2002), accessed 9 August 2016, www.archive.is/RoR3l.
176. Ibid.
177. Romanov, *Nights are Longest There*, 98–99;Temkin, *My Just War* 201; Mikhin, *Guns*, 2; Alexander V. Pyl'cyn, *Penalty Strike: The Memoirs of a Red Army Penaal Company Commander, 1943–1945*, ed. by Artem Drabkin and trans by Bair Irincheev (Mechanicsburg: Stackpole Books, 2009), 23. "Interview with Nikolai Nadtochii," *Ia pomniu*; "Interview with Aleksandr Solov'ev," *Ia pomniu*; "Interview with Mikhail Tsurkan," *Iapomniu*; "Interview with Mikhail Ivanov."
178. "Interview with Nikolai Nadtochii," *Ia pomniu.*
179. Pyl'cyn, *Penalty Strike*, 23.
180. RGVA, f. 32900, op. 1, d. 337, l. 47.
181. TsAMO, f. 1512 (233sd), op. 1, d. 34, l. 150.
182. RGVA, f. 32900, op. 1, d. 337, l. 47.
183. Hlihor and Scurtu, *The Red Army in Romania*, 116.
184. Romanov, *Nights Are Longest There*, 98–99
185. RGVA, f. 32905, op. 1, d. 248, l. 35; "Interview with Nikolai Nadtochii," *Ia pomniu.*

186. RGVA, f. 32900, op. 1, d. 363, l. 4.
187. RGVA, f. 32900, op.1, d. 341, l. 54.
188. RGVA, f. 32900, op. 1, d. 341, 83.
189. RGVA, f. 32900, op. 1, d. 220, l. 101.
190. RGVA, f. 32900, op. 1, d. 183, l. 220.
191. Ibid.
192. For attempted rape see RGVA, f. 32905, op. 1, d. 241, l. 155. For insubordination see RGVA, f. 32905, op. 1, d. 241, l. 155. For desertion see RGVA, f. 32900, op. 1, d. 452, l. 29.
193. RGVA, f. 32905, op. 1, d. 250, l. 9.
194. Statiev, "Penal Units," 738–739.
195. RGVA, f. 32905, op. 1, d. 250, l. 11.
196. RGVA, f. 32900, op. 1, d. 455, l. 20.
197. RGVA, f. 32900, op. 1, d. 340, l. 19.
198. Ibid., l. 39.
199. RGVA, f. 32900, op. 1, d. 402, l. 325.
200. Ibid., l. 329.
201. RGVA, f. 32900, op. 1, d. 402, l. 330.
202. RGVA, f. 32900, op. 1, d. 412, l. 177.
203. RGVA, f. 32900, op. 1, d. 402, l. 327.
204. Ibid., 325–326.
205. Ibid., l. 326.
206. RGVA, f. 32900, op. 1, d. 402, l. 323–324.
207. For 1944, see RGVA, f. 32900, op. 1, d. 441, l. 123. For first two months of 1945 see RGVA, f. 32900, op. 1, d. 441, l. 132.
208. RGVA, f. 32900, op. 1, d. 441, l. 123.
209. Ibid., l. 127.
210. Ibid., l. 128.
211. RGVA, f. 32905, op. 1, d. 130, l. 41–42.
212. For the dismissed officers see RGVA, f. 32905, op. 1, d. 130, l. 42. For how they were instructed in moral conduct, see RGVA, f. 32905, op. 1, d. 130, l. 24.
213. RGVA, f. 32905, op. 1, d. 128, l. 7; RGVA, f. 32905, op. 1, d. 248, l. 11–12; RGVA, f. 32905, op. 1, d. 130, l. 167–177.
214. RGVA, f. 32905, op. 1, d. 130, l. 169.
215. Ibid.
216. Ibid.
217. Ibid.
218. RGVA, f. 32905, op. 1, d. 250, l. 90.
219. RGVA, f. 32900, op. 1, d. 441, l. 1.

6 Soviet Soldiers' Views of the Countries of the Balkans and Central Europe

1. The vast majority of the available literature focuses mostly on the Soviet soldiers' attitudes and conduct in Germany, such as parts of several chapters in Beevor, *Berlin*; chapter 9 in Merridale's *Ivan's War*; part 8 in

Werth's *Russia at War*; chapter 2 in Naimark, *The Russians in Germany*; chapter 8 "*The Alien World: The Red Army Goes Abroad*" in Schechter, *The Stuff of Soldiers*; and chapter 4 in Nicole Eaton, *German Blood, Slavic Soil: How Nazi Königsberg Became Soviet Kaliningrad* (Ithaca: Cornell University Press, 2023). Many of these authors mention other countries, but the overwhelming focus is on the Red Army in Germany.

2. Hajkova, *The Last Ghetto*, 81–82.
3. Weiner, *Making Sense of War*, 8.
4. Slutskii, *Zapiski*, 46.
5. "Polish," *Washington Post*, 21 December 1981, accessed 21 March 2021, www.washingtonpost.com/archive/politics/1981/12/22/polish/5d7aca6b-c573-42bb-a4b5-99559e062345/?fbclid=IwAR1akHhnc-RyUXiltqEaDRmeoVCjQeUOZtKSxgsAvLOmwtvzxa6Gy5OlfAM; she wrote her book based on wartime notes, see Orme, *Comes the Comrade*, 103.
6. Maren Roger, "The Sexual Policies and Sexual Realities of the German Occupiers in Poland in the Second World War," *Contemporary European History* 23.1 (2014): 5.
7. Stephen Kercher, "Remembering Alice de Barcza – one of the most interesting women to teach at UW Oshkosh" *UW Oshkosh Today*, 10 March 2021, accessed 21 March 2021, https://uwosh.edu/today/95239/remembering-alice-de-barcza-one-of-the-most-interesting-women-to-teach-at-uw-oshkosh/.
8. Orme, *Comes the Comrade*, 59–60.
9. Kercher, "Remembering Alice de Barcza."
10. Orme, *Comes the Comrade*, 57.
11. That the Red Army was peasant mostly, see Hill, *The Red Army*, 51. For standard of life, see Kristy Ironside, *A Full-Value Ruble: The Promise of Prosperity in the Postwar Soviet Union* (Cambridge: Harvard University Press, 2021), 3–5.
12. Ronit Fischer, "Transnistria: The Holocaust in Romania," in *The Routledge History of the Holocaust*, ed., Jonathan C. Friedman (New York: Routledge, 2011), 279.
13. Harward, *Romania's Holy War*, 2.
14. John R. Lampe and Marvin R. Jackson, *Balkan Economic History, 1550–1950: From Imperial Borderlands to Developing Nations* (Bloomington: Indiana University Press, 1982), 7.
15. Vladimri Solonari, *A Satellite Empire: Romanian Rule in Southwestern Ukraine, 1941–1944* (Ithaca: Cornell University Press, 2019), 16, 97–98, and 125.
16. Diana Dumitru, *The State, Antisemitism, and Collaboration in the Holocaust: The Borderlands of Romania and the Soviet Union* (Cambridge: Cambridge University Press, 2016), 177.
17. Solonari, *A Satellite Empire*, 31.
18. "Interview with Mikhail Ivanov," *Ia pomniu*; Alexander Dallin, *Odessa, 1941–1944: A Case Study of Soviet Territory under Foreign Rule* (Iasi-Oxford-Portland: Center for Romanian Studies, 1998), 92; several Soviet sources from Stalingrad maintain that the Romanians who surrendered to the Red Army reminded them of Gypsies, Mansur Abdulin, *Red Road from Stalingrad: Recollections of a Soviet Infantryman* (Mechanicsburg: Stackpole Books, 2004), 16; LubaVinogradova and AntonyBeevor, eds., *A Writer at War: Vasily Grossman with the Red Army, 1941–1945* (London: Harvill Press, 2005), 194.

19. Solonari, *Purifying the Nation*, 266–267.
20. Viorel Achim, *The Roma in Romanian History* (Budapest: Central European University Press, 1998), 179
21. Evgenii Moniushko, *From Leningrad to Hungary: Notes of a Red Army Soldier, 1941–1946* (New York: Frank Cass, 2005), 247.
22. In Russian, the saying is: *vezde khorosho, gde nas net*, Gabriel Temkin, *My Just War: The Memoir of a Jewish Red Army Soldier in World War II* (Novato: Presidio, 1998), 175.
23. Anton Romenskii, *Glazami i serdtsem soldata. Rasskazyvaiut frontoviki 1941–1945* (Moscow: Voennoe izdatel'stvo ministerstva oborony SSSR, 1979), 120.
24. Slutskii, *Zapiski*, 47.
25. BA, El'kinson dnevnik, 7.
26. Petr Mikhin, *Guns against the Reich: Memoirs of a Soviet Artillery Officer on the Eastern Front* (Mechanicsburg, Stackpole Books, 2011), 143.
27. "Interview with Aleksandr Toptygin," *Ia pomniu*, accessed 28 November 2024, https://iremember.ru/memoirs/svyazisti/toptigin-aleksandr-nikolaevich/.
28. RGVA, f. 32900, op. 1, d. 458, l. 42.
29. Đilas, *Conversations*, 140.
30. Mariana Stanciu and Adina Mihailescu, "Poverty in Romania during 1918–1945," *Journal of Community Positive Practices* 18.2 (2018): 26.
31. Ibid., 29; Lampe and Jackson, *Balkan Economic History*, 534–535.
32. Sarah Cameron, *The Hungry Steppe: Famine, Violence, and the Making of Soviet Kazakhstan* (Ithaca: Cornell University Press, 2018), 4
33. Schechter, *The Stuff*, 83; Hill, *The Red Army*, 359.
34. TsAMO RF, f. 67, op. 12022, d. 978, l. 18–20, document reproduced in V. A. Zolotarev, et al., eds., *Russkii Arkhiv: Velikaia Otechestvennaia. Tyl Krasnoi Armii v Velikoi Otechestvnnoi voine 1941–1945gg. Dokumenty i materialy 1944–1945* T. 25.14 (Moscow: Terra, 1998), 625.
35. N. N. Constantinescu, *Romania's Economic History from the Beginnings to World War II* (Bucharest: Editura Academiei Romane, 1994), 253.
36. "Interview with Mstislav Ivanov," *Ia pomniu*, accessed 28 November 2024, https://iremember.ru/memoirs/razvedchiki/ivanov-mstislav-borisovich/.
37. "Interview with Mikhail Tsurkan," *Ia pomniu.*
38. "Interview with Nina Glotova," *Ia pomniu*, accessed 20 December 2023, https://iremember.ru/memoirs/mediki/glotova-nina-ivanovna/.
39. "Interview with Aleksandr Solov'ev," *Ia pomniu.*
40. "Interview with Nikolai Nadtochii," *Ia pomniu.*
41. Ibid.
42. BA, El'kinson dnevnik, 3.
43. Ibid., 8.
44. Harward, *Romania's Holy War*, 169.
45. Grant Harward, "Peasant Armies at Odds: Romanian-Soviet Interaction during the Second World War," *The Journal of Slavic Military Studies* 24.2 (2011): 282; Werth, *Russia*, 209.
46. DiNardo, *Germany and the Axis Powers*, 183.
47. Temkin, *My Just War*, 172.
48. Ibid., 174. This was a play on words that make sense only in the Russian language. The River Prut marked the Romanian–Soviet border, and River

Siret (referred to as Serut by Temkin) is further south in Romania. But na-serut also means to shit oneself. Thus, the song had two meanings: "When Russian come to Prut, Romanians go to (River) Siret" and "When Russians come to Prut, Romanians shit themselves."

49. "Interview with Iosif Lempert," *Ia pomniu,* 28 November 2024, https://iremember.ru/memoirs/drugie-voyska/lempert-iosif-mikhaylovich/.
50. "Interview with Mstislav Ivanov," *Ia pomniu.*
51. "Interview with Aleksei Ustimenko," *Ia pomniu,* accessed 13 August 2016, http://iremember.ru/memoirs/minometchiki/ustimenko-aleksey-petrovich/.
52. Ibid., 216. This assertion confirms the finding by historian Karen Petrone that the Soviet propaganda dehumanized and feminized enemy, at least when it came to Romanians, Karen Petrone, "Masculinity and Heroism in Imperial and Soviet Military-Patriotic Cultures" in B. E. Clements, R. Friedman, & D. Healy, eds., *Russian Masculinities in History and Culture* (New York: Palgrave, 2001), 189.
53. "Interview with Sergei Otroshcenko," *Ia pomniu.*
54. TsAMO RF, f. 395, op. 9134, d. 12, ll. 2–6, document reproduced in V. A. Zolotarev, et al., eds., *Krasnaia Armiia v stranakh tsentral'noi, severnoi evropy i na balkanakh.* 70.
55. Ibid., 72.
56. RGVA, f. 32905, op. 1, d. 98, l. 21.
57. Mark Axworthy, *Third Axis Fourth Ally: Romanian Armed Forces in the European War, 1941–1945* (London: Arms and Armour), 213.
58. "Interview with Vil' Sarychev," *Ia pomniu,* accessed 28 November 2024, https://iremember.ru/memoirs/minometchiki/sarichev-vil-georgievich/.
59. "Interview with Nikolai Nadtochii," *Ia pomniu.*
60. Isaak Rabinovich Moiseevich, "Pis'ma I. Rabinovicha zhene," 14 September 1944, letter reproduced in Il'ia Al'tman, Leonid Terutkin, Elena Testova, et al., eds., So*khrani Moi Pis'ma: Sbornik Pisem Evreev Perioda Velikoi Otechestvennoi Voiny* Vypusk 3 (Moscow: Tsentr i Fond Kholokost, 2013), 122.
61. Slutskii, *Zapiski,* 58.
62. Ibid., 57.
63. BA, El'kinson dnevnik, 3.
64. Slutskii, *Zapiski,* 54.
65. Lazar' Brontman, *Voennyi dnevnik korrespondenta "Pravdy": vstrechi, sobytiia, sud'by, 1942–1945* (Moscow: Tsentrpoligraf, 2007), 351.
66. Ibid., 352–353.
67. The 3rd Ukrainian Front recruited 110,000 soldiers in Odesa and Nikolaev regions, TsDAGO, f. 57, op. 4, d. 314, l. 95. The 2nd Ukrainian Front was reinforced with 330,000 soldiers from the previously occupied territories in Ukraine in the first four months of 1944. Similarly, this data does not specify the number of soldiers from Transnistria as opposed to the Reichskomissariat Ukraine, which was under German control. Yet, there can be no doubt that a sizable portion of these soldiers hailed from parts of the country administered by Bucharest. Vladislav Grinevich, "Voennye mobilizatsii v Ukraine v 1943–1944 godakh."
68. For venality, see Solonari, *A Satellite Empire,* 89; for exploitation, see Ibid., 34. For genocidal, see Dumitru, *The State,* 180–182.

69. "Interview with Mikhail Tsurkan," *Ia pomniu.*
70. "Interview with Aleksandr Solov'ev," *Ia pomniu.*
71. Ibid.
72. BA, Mirain L'vovna Kogan, Interview Odesa 6 February 2009, letters, 4.
73. The 2nd Ukrainian Front reported that it recruited 99,896 people from among the spetskontigent, TsA FSB Rossii, document reproduced in S. V. Stepashin, et al., eds., *Organy Gosudarstvennoi Bezopasnosti* T. 5 K. 2, 502. Additional 6,262 *spetscontigent* were sent to special NKVD camps, presumably for further filtration, 457 joined NKVD-NKGB and 154 were arrested. I did not find comprehensive situation information for the 3rd Ukrainian Front, but the situation seems to have been similar, Matvei Zakharov, *Osvobozhdenie Iugo-vostochnoi i Tsentralnoi Evropy* (Moscow: Nauka, 1970), 215–216.
74. Slutskii, *Zapiski,* 55. That he wrote most of his book in the summer of 1945, see Ibid., 357.
75. Ibid., 55.
76. Milovan Đilas, *Revolucionarni rat* (Belgrade: Književne novine, 1990), 52.
77. Rachel Applebaum, *Empire of Friends: Soviet Power and Socialist Internationalism in Cold War Czechoslovakia* (Ithaca: Cornell University Press, 2019), 4–6.
78. BA, El'kinson dnevnik, 3; Khorkov, *Osvoboditelnaia missia,* 143–144; Zakharov, *Osvobozhdenie,* 218; Presniakov, *Pod zvezdami balkanskimi,* 21; TsAMO, f. 413 (57A), op. 10372, d. 349, l. 29.
79. Slutskii, *Zapiski,* 61.
80. For the 57th Army, see TsAMO, f. 413 (57A), op. 10372, d. 392, ll. 6–7; for the 37th Army, see Zhilin, et al., eds., *Osvoboditel'naia missiia,* 106.
81. BA, El'kinson dnevnik,7.
82. For Belgrade, see VA, f. NOVJ, k. 96, f. 1, d. 17, l. 18. For Subotica, see, IAS, f. 176, k. 10, "Rad i referat antifašističkog fronta žena u Subotici, 1." For Knjaževac, see V. A. Zolotarev, et al., eds., *Krasnaia Armiia v stranakh Tsentral'noi, Severnoi Evropy i na Balkanakh,* 245. For Topola, see V. F. Tolbuko and N. A. Baryshev, *Ot Vidina do Belgrada: istoriko-memuarnyi ocherk o boevykh deistviiakh sovetskikh tankistov v belgradskoi operatsii* (Moscow: Nauka, 1968), 39; for *Zaječar,* see S. S. Biriuzov, et al., eds., *Beogradska Operacija,* 219; for Novi Sad, see Timofejev, *Rusi,* 193; for Požarevac, see Nikolai Zav'ialov, *Pod zvezdami balkanskimi,* 111; for Negotin, see Zhilin, et al., eds., *Osvoboditel'naia missiia,* 335–336; for Vratarnica, see TsAMO, f. 413, op. 10381, d. 16, l. 183, document reproduced in V. A. Zolotarev, et al., eds., *Krasnaia Armiia v stranakh Tsentral'noi, Severnoi Evropy i na Balkanakh,* 225.
83. Đorđe Lobačev, *Kad se Volga ulivala u Savu. Moj zivotni roman* (Belgrade: prosveta, 1997), 124.
84. RGASPI, f. 17, op. 125, d. 247, ll. 72–78, document reproduced in V. A. Zolotarev, et al., eds., *Krasnaia Armiia v stranakh Tsentral'noi, Severnoi Evropy i na Balkanakh,* 111.
85. BA, El'kinson dnevnik, 5.
86. Ibid., 9.
87. "Interview with Mikhail Ivanov," *Ia pomniu.*
88. Author's interview with Nadežda Đurišić.

89. Z. E. Sutrina, "My v Bolgarii (iz voennogo dnevnika)," diary reproduced in *73-ia gvardeiskaia. Sbornik vospominanii, dokumentov i materialov o boevom puti 73-oi gvardeiskoi strelkovoi Stalingradsko-Dunaiskoi Krasnoznamennoi divizii*, ed., A. K. Morozov, et al. (Alma-Ata: Kazahstan, 1986), 187.
90. Author's interview with Bratislav Filipović.
91. Author's interview with Živojin Ilić.
92. Author's interviews with Grgo Bačlija and with Milica Novaković.
93. Author's interview with Divna Protić.
94. TsAMO, f. 32, op. 11309, d. 230, ll. 169–176, document reproduced in V. A. Zolotarev, et al., eds., *Krasnaia Armiia v stranakh Tsentral'noi, Severnoi Evropy i na Balkanakh*, 122.
95. TsAMO, f. 1512, op. 1, d. 93, l. 192.
96. IAS, f. 86, k. 64, "Okrivljeni Voratović Danilo."
97. RGVA, f. 32900, op. 1, d. 192, l. 143.
98. N. I. Iashcenko, "Druzhba, rozhdennaia v boiakh," recollections reproduced in A. K. Morozov, et al., eds, *73-ia gvardeiskaia*, 193.
99. Tolbuko and Baryshev, *Ot Vidina do Belgrada*, 203–204.
100. TsAMO, f. 32, op. 11309, d. 230, ll. 169–176, document reproduced in V. A. Zolotarev, et al., eds., *Krasnaia Armiia v stranakh Tsentral'noi, Severnoi Evropy i na Balkanakh*, 122.
101. "Sećanje crvenoarmejke na oslobađanje Beograda," accessed on 18 September 2013, www.vesti-online.com/Vesti/Srbija/311930/Secanje-crvenoarmejke-na-oslobadanje-Beograda.
102. TsAMO, f. 1512, op. 1, d. 93, l. 200.
103. Mikhin, *Guns*, 143.
104. VA, f. NOVJ, k. 28, f. 1, d. 1, l. 6.
105. Author's interview with Božidar Stojanović.
106. Author's interview with Mihajlo Đurišić.
107. Belgrade citadel, see TsAMO RF (no citation provided), document reproduced in Bukharin and S. Stoianovich, eds., *Otnosheniia Rossii (SSSR) s Iugoslaviei*, 352; for forcing of Sava, see VA, f. NOVJ, k. 28, f. 1, d. 1, l. 7. For Avala, see TsAMO, f. 413, op. 10372, d. 349, l. 410.
108. VA, f. NOVJ, k. 96, f. 1, d. 18, l. 33.
109. Tolbuko and Baryshev, *Ot Vidina do Belgrada*, 226.
110. VA, f. NOVJ, k. 222, f. 1k, d. 20, ll. 1–2.
111. RGVA, f. 32900, op. 1, d. 186, l. 162.
112. IAS, f. 82, k. 95, "Spisi narodne milicije. Telefonski izvesštaj primljen dana 4. juna 1945 god."
113. VA, f. NOVJ, k. 222, f. 1k, d. 50, l. 2.
114. RGVA, f. 32900, op. 1, d. 188, l. 166.
115. Author's interview with Dušan Novaković.
116. Goran Davidović and Miloš Timotijević, "Dan posle: uništavanje JVuO i uspostavljanje vlasti komunista u čačanskom kraju 1944–1945," *Istorija 20. Veka* 22.2 (2004): 27.
117. TsAMO, f. 413 (57A), op. 10372, d. 514, l. 122.
118. Slutskii, *Zapiski*, 91.
119. Ibid., 91.

120. Timofejev, *Rusi*, 195.
121. RGASPI, f. 17, op. 125, d. 247, ll. 72–78, document reproduced in Zolotarev, et al., eds., *Krasnaia Armiia v stranakh Tsentral'noi, Severnoi Evropy i na Balkanakh*, 111. For Vrčin, see TsAMO, f. 1512, op. 1, d. 91, l. 201.
122. For Bulgaria, see, RGVA, f. 32900, op. 1, d. 192, l. 53; for Yugoslavia, see TsAMO, f. 1512 (233sd), op. 1, d. 93, 212.
123. "Interview with Vil' Sarychev," *Ia pomniu.*
124. Zav'ialov, *Pod zvezdami balkanskimi*, 52; BA, El'kinson *Dnevnik*, 5; Presniakov, *Pod zvezdami balkanskimi*, 21; Romenskii, ed., *Glazami i serdtsem soldata*, 118; Vylitok, *Pod zvezdami balkanskimi* (Kishinev: Karta Moldoveiaske, 1984), 28. Yes, Soviet veterans loved referring to the southern Balkan sky and stars in their memoirs.
125. "Interview with Nikolai Nadtochii," *Ia pomniu.*
126. "Interview with Aleksandr Sedoi," *Ia pomniu.*
127. Ibid.
128. BA, El'kinson *Dnevnik*, 4.
129. Ibid., 5.
130. Ibid.
131. "Excerpts from book Andronov, *Mudrost' Pobedy* (Tomsk: Sibirskii proekt, 2006)," *Ia pomniu*, accessed 18 September 2013, http://iremember.ru/svyazisti/mishurov-fedor-mikhaylovich.html.
132. Mikhin, *Guns*, 148.
133. TsGA KAZSSR, f. 1660, op. 1, d. 196, ll. 19–20, document reproduced in K. Morozov, et al., eds., *73-ia gvardeiskaia*, 228.
134. BA, El'kinson dnevnik, 9.
135. Ibid., 10.
136. Zav'ialov, *Pod zvezdami Balkanskimi*, 127–128.
137. S. S. Biriuzov, *Surovye gody* (Moscow: Nauka, 1966), 481.
138. Đilas, *Revolucionarni rat*, 369.
139. Mikhin, *Guns*, 146–147.
140. BA, El'kinson dnevnik, 9.
141. Mikhin, *Guns*, 144. Mikhin attributed these thoughts to one of his comrades, but they clearly reflected his own views.
142. BA, El'kinson dnevnik, 9.
143. N. M. Skomorokhov, *Boem zhivet istrebitel'* (Moscow: Voenizdat, 1975), 201.
144. AJ, KPRII-3-e-2/16, 3, "Informacije o mestima u kojima su trajno sahranjeni paliborci Crvene armije u II svetskom ratu i odavanju počasti palim borcima, VIII 1962."
145. AJ, KPR I-3-a SSSR 2/3, Ad-3, "Gledanje Staljina na našu Armiju i naše kadrove."
146. Slutskii, *Zapiski*, 95.
147. Mikhin, *Guns*, 174.
148. Ibid., 155.
149. VA, f. NOVJ, k.371, f. 6, d. 26, l. 4.
150. VA, f. NOVJ, f. 1919, k. 31, d. 6, l. 13.
151. RGVA, f. 32900, op. 1, d. 412, l. 176.

152. Temkin, *My Just War*, 196–198; Slutskii, *Zapiski*, 109; Lobačev, *Kad se Volga ulivala u Savu*, 162.
153. Letter from Ivan Kuz'mich Parhsikov, document reproduced in Aleksandr Shindel, ed., *Po obe storony fronta: pis'ma sovetskikh i nemets͡kikh soldat, 1941–1945 gg.* (Moscow: Sol′, 1995), 105; BA, El'kinson dnevnik,11.
154. BA, El'kinson dnevnik, 10.
155. Temkin, *My Just War*, 194.
156. Ibid., 194.
157. Kenez. *Hungary from the Nazis to the Soviets*, 38.
158. Temkin, *My Just War*, 196; "Interview with Iurii Favorov," *Ia pomniu*; Interview with Igor' Tupitsyn in *Silenced Shame* at 06.45.
159. Letter from Vladimir Mikhialovich Arkhipov, reproduced in Shindel, ed., *Po obe storony fronta*, 105; letter from Frida Abramovna, reproduced in Al'tman, Terushkin, and Brodskaia, eds., *Sokhrani moi pis'ma. Vypusk 2*, 274; Diary of Khanon Eselevich Kapul, reproduced in Al'tman, Terushkin, and Testova, eds., *Sokhrani moi pis'ma. Vypusk 3*, 185; Mikhin, *Guns*, 184–186; "Interview with Nikolai Aleksandrov," *Ia pomniu*; "Interview with Semen Danich, *Ia pomniu*, accessed 28 November 2024, https://iremember.ru/memoirs/saperi/danich-semen-antonovich/.
160. "Interview with Grigorii Rabinovich," *Ia pomniu*; "Interview with Mikhail Tsurkan," *Ia pomniu.*
161. Nevenkin, *Take Budapest*. 12–15.
162. Krivosheev, ed., *Rossiia i SSSR*, 449.
163. "Interview with Efim Romanov, *Ia pomniu*, accessed 20 December 2020, https://iremember.ru/memoirs/mediki/romanov-efim-mikhaylovich/.
164. For bad people, see "Interview with Pavel Lebedev," *Ia pomniu*, accessed 28 November 2024, https://iremember.ru/memoirs/voditeli/lebedev-pavel-fedorovich/. For hateful, see "Interview with Mikhail Ivanov," *Ia pomniu.* For more perfidious than Germans, see "Interview with Aleksandr Solovev," *Ia pomniu.*
165. BA, El'kinson dnevnik, 10.
166. Ibid., 11.
167. Ibid.
168. Ibid.
169. Ibid., 12.
170. Ibid.
171. Ibid., 11–15.
172. Ibid., 15.
173. Lynne Viola translated the term *baba* as a "hag," "fishwife," and "a woman driver" in the context of rural Russian resistance to collectivization campaign in the 1920s and 1930s, Lynne Viola, "Bab'i bunty and Peasant Protest during Collectivization," *The Russian Review* 45.1 (1986): 23.
174. Alaine Polcz, *One Woman in the War Hungary*, 10.
175. Ibid., 77.
176. Ibid., 96.
177. Ibid., 150.
178. Anonymous, *A Woman in Berlin: Eight Weeks in the Conquered City: A Diary*, trans. by Philip Boehm (New York: Picador/Henry Holt, 2005). I

want to thank Kathryn Barbier for making this point at the Second World War Research Group, North America, where I presented a version of this chapter in March 2021.

179. Atina Grossmann, *Jews, Germans, and Allies: Close Encounters in Occupied Germany* (Princeton: Princeton University Press, 2007), 70.
180. "Interview with Efim Romanov," *Ia pomniu.*
181. "Interview with Aleksandra Aleksandrova (Petrova)," *Ia pomniu*, accessed 21 December 2023, https://iremember.ru/memoirs/mediki/aleksandrova-petrova-aleksandra-mikhaylovna/.
182. Ibid.
183. "Interview with Aleksei Shavrin," *Ia pomniu*, accessed 28 November 2024, https://iremember.ru/memoirs/artilleristi/shavrin-aleksey-fedorovich/.
184. "Interview with Anna Skorobogatova," *Ia pomniu*, accessed 21 December 2023, https://iremember.ru/memoirs/svyazisti/skorobogatova-anna-makarovna/.
185. Diary excerpts from Abram Saulovich Shavelev, reproduced in Al'tman, Terushkin, and Brodskaia, eds., *Sokhrani moi pis'ma. Vypusk 2* (Moscow: Tsentr i FGond 'Kholokost.' Izdate'stvo MIK, 2010), 262–263.
186. "Interview with Sergei Otroshcenkov," *Ia pomniu.*
187. "Interview with Mikhail Ivanov," *Ia pomniu.*
188. "Interview with Boris Tsalik," *Ia pomniu*, accessed 19 December 2020, https://iremember.ru/memoirs/svyazisti/tsalik-boris-moiseevich/.
189. "Interview with Vladimir Bezchastnyi," *Ia pomniu*, accessed 19 December 2020, https://iremember.ru/memoirs/desantniki/bezchastnyy-vladimir-fedorovich/.
190. Moniushko, *From Leningrad to Hungary*, 206–207; Slutskii, *Zapiski*, 112.
191. "Interview with Mariia Rist (Fedorko)," *Ia pomniu.*
192. For calorie intake in Vienna, see Lewis, "Dancing on a Tight Rope," 142.
193. Temkin, *My Just War*, 199.
194. RGVA, f. 32880, op. 2, d. 163, l. 25.
195. Letter from Arkhipov, reproduced in Shindel, ed., *Po obe storony fronta*, 109.
196. Ibid., 109.
197. Slutskii, *Zapiski*, 126.
198. Beevor, *Berlin*, 33.
199. Gromyko, et al., eds., *SSSR-Avstriia*, 16–17.
200. Slutskii, *Zapiski*, 26.
201. Ibid., 126.
202. Ibid.
203. Ibid., 128–130.
204. Letter from Aleksandr Levin, reproduced in Il'ia Altman and Leonid Terushkin, eds. *Sokhrani moi pis'ma. Sbornik pisem i dnevnikov evreev perioda velikoi otechestvennoi voiny* (Moscow: Tsentr i Fond 'Khookost' i izdatel'stvo MIK, 2007), 270. It is not clear whether Levin was in Czechoslovakia or Austria when he used this term; thus, he could have been referring to either Sudeten Germans or Austrians. Either way, there are no indications that he differentiated between the two.
205. BA, Dnevnik El'kinson, 21.
206. "Interview with Sergei Otroshcenkov," *Ia pomniu.*

207. "Interview with Mikhail Ivanov," *Ia pomniu.*
208. BA, Dnevnik El'kinson, 21.
209. Filip Slaveski. *The Soviet Occupation of Germany. Hunger, Mass Violence, and the Struggle for Peace, 1945–1947* (Cambridge: Cambridge University Press, 2013), 11.
210. The Kremlin ordered on 11 May both 2nd and 3rd Ukrainian Front to create camps for a hundred thousand people each. These camps were for several categories of people: Soviets who fought on the side of the Axis and whom the British and the Americans were about to expatriate to the Red Army, as well as liberated prisoners of war and slave laborers, TsAMO, f. 148a, op. 3763, d. 212, ll. 16–19, document reproduced in V. A. Zolotarev, et al., eds., *Stavka VGK*, 236–237.
211. RGVA, f. 32900, op. 1, d. 441, l. 234.

7 Sexual Violence

1. Cited in Oleg Budnitskii, "Muzhchini i zhenshcini v Kransoi armii (1941–1945)," *Cashiers du Monde russe* 52.2 (2011): 405.
2. Mühlhäuser, *Sex and the Nazi Soldier*, 5.
3. Erica L. Fraser, *Military Masculinity and Postwar Recovery in the Soviet Union* (Toronto: University of Toronto Press, 2019), 12.
4. Steven George Jug, "All Stalin's Men? Soldierly Masculinities in the Soviet War Effort, 1938–1945," (PhD diss., University of Illinois at Urbana-Champaign, 2014), 76–77.
5. Ibid., 18.
6. Berkhoff, *Motherland in Danger*, 97. For Leningrad, see Peri, *The War Within*, 4.
7. Filterz, "Starvation Mortality in Soviet Home-Front," 266.
8. Rebecca Manley, *To the Tashkent Station: Evacuation and Survival in the Soviet Union at War* (Ithaca, New York: Cornell University Press, 2009), 1.
9. Pavel Polian, *Ne po svoei vole…istoriia i geografiia prinuditel'nykh migratsii v SSSR* (Moscow: O. G. I. Memorial, 2001), 142.
10. Martin Kragh, "Stalinist Labour Coercion during World War II: An Economic Approach," *Europe-Asia Studies* 63.7 (2011): 1253–1254.
11. Iosif Zalmanovich Kalmanovich, "Otomshcu v sto krat za moego otsa i rodnykh" 15 July 1944, letter reproduced in Al'tman, Terutkin, and Testova eds., So*khrani Moi* Pis'ma. *Vypusk*, 194.
12. Letter from Ivan Kuz'mich Parhsikov, document reproduced in Shindel, ed., *Po obe storony fronta*, 105.
13. I want to thank Janine Holc for suggesting this angle of interpretation of Parshikov's letter.
14. Matt E. Lenoe, "Emotions and Psychological Survival in the Red Army, 1941–42" *Kritika: Explorations in Russian and Eurasian History* 22.1. (Spring 2021): 319.
15. Semen Peisakhovich Mostov, "Ostanovilis' v g. Vanze, prigorode Berlina" 12 November 1944, diary reproduced in Il'ia Al'tman, Leonid Terutkin, Elena Testova, et al., eds., So*khrani Moi Pis'ma* Vypusk 3, 194.

16. Eaton, *German Blood, Slavic Soil*, 119.
17. Louise McReynolds, "Dateline Stalingrad: Newspaper Correspondents at the Front," in *Culture and Entertainment in Wartime Russia*, ed., Richard Stites (Bloomington and Indianapolis: Indiana University Press, 1995), 36.
18. Konstantin Simonov, "Ubei ego (Esli dorog tebe tvoi dom)," accessed 11 January 2023, www.culture.ru/poems/32889/ubei-ego-esli-dorog-tebe-tvoi-dom.
19. Konstantin Simonov, "Zhdi menia i ia vernus…," accessed 11 January 2023, www.culture.ru/poems/32975/zhdi-menya-i-ya-vernus.
20. Robert A. Rothstein, "Homeland, Home Town, and Battlefield: The Popular Song," in *Culture and Entertainment in Wartime Russia*, ed., Richard Stites (Bloomington and Indianapolis: Indiana University Press, 1995), 84.
21. Konstantin Simonov, "Otkrytoe pis'mo Zhenshcine iz g. Vichuga," accessed 11 January 2023, https://simonov.co.uk/openletterru.
22. S. L. Strashnov, "K. Simonov – Lirik v Kontaktakh s Massovoi Auditoriei Voennykh Let," *Vestnik VGU. Seriia: Filologiia. Zhurnalisika* 4 (2018): 85.
23. Merridale's *Ivan's War*, 315–316.
24. Regarding the penis size, Alevtina wrote, "He is taller than you and all of his other bodily parts are greater," Vladimir Bogomolov, "*Zhizn moia ili ty prisnilas'mne…*" (Moscow: Knizhnyi Klub, 2012), 222–224.
25. Ibid., 224.
26. Markwick and Cardona, *Soviet Women*, 8.
27. Hill, *The Red Army*, 325.
28. Anna Krylova, *Soviet Women in Combat: A History of Violence on the Eastern Front* (Cambridge: Cambridge University Press, 2010), 13.
29. Hill, *The Red Army*, 325.
30. Markwick and Cardona, *Soviet Women*, 1.
31. Svetlana Alexievich, *The Unwomanly Face of War: An Oral History of Women in World War II* (New York: Random House, 2017), 212.
32. Ibid., 323.
33. "Interview with Lidiia Gluschenko," *Ia pomniu*, accessed 16 January 2023, https://iremember.ru/memoirs/voditeli/gluschenko-lidiya-mikhaylovna/.
34. "Interview with Mariia Bondarenko (Kataeva)," *Ia pomniu*, accessed 16 January 2023, https://iremember.ru/memoirs/snayperi/kataeva-bondarenko-mariya-dmitrievna/.
35. "Interview with Nina Demesheva (Skvortsova)," *Ia pomniu*, accessed 16 January 2023, https://iremember.ru/memoirs/mediki/demesheva-skvortsova-nina-petrovna/.
36. "Tat'iana Pugacheva (Chertova)," *Ia pomniu*, accessed 16 January https://iremember.ru/memoirs/svyazisti/pugacheva-chertova-tatyana-aleksandrovna/.
37. "Interview with Mariia Bondarenko (Kataeva)," *Ia pomniu.*
38. Kerstin Bischl, "Telling Stories. Gender Relationships and Masculinity in the Red Army 1941–1945," in *Women and Men at War – A Gender Perspective on World War II and Its Aftermath in Central and Eastern Europe*, eds., Maren Röger and Ruth Leiserowitz (Osnabrück: Fibre, 2012), 119.
39. Steven G. Jug, "Red Army Romance: Preserving Masculine Hegemony in Mixed Gender Combat Units, 1943–1944" *Journal of War & Culture Studies* 5.3. (2013): 330.

40. Aleksandr Pyl'tsyn, *Glavnaia kniga o shtrafbatakh* (Moscow: Eksmo, 2009), 154–157.
41. TsAMO, f. 1512 (233sd), op. 1, d. 93, l. 196.
42. Alexievich, *The Unwomanly Face of War*, 235–238. Pregnant servicewomen were demobilized and sent home, which was a way out of war, but was deeply resented by many women as they feared the shame of returning home pregnant as single mothers, Brandon Schechter, "'Girls' and 'Women.'" Love, Sex, Duty and Sexual Harassment in the Ranks of the Red Army 1941–1945, *The Journal of Power Institutions in Post-Soviet Societies* 17 (2016), https://doi.org/10.4000/pipss.4202.
43. The most famous example of a woman agreeing to become a victim of one officer in order to get protection from the rank and file was the German journalist Marta Hiller, Anonymous, *A Woman in Berlin: Eight Weeks in the Conquered City: A Diary*, trans. Philip Boehm (New York: Metropolitan Books/Henry Holt, 2005), 111.
44. Konstantin Somov, *Voina: Uskorennaia zhizn'* (Barnaul: OAO "IPP" "Altai," 2010), 383.
45. BA, *Boris Komsky. Wartime diary, July 1943–January 1945*, 32–32.
46. Ibid., 32.
47. Grigorii Chukhrai, *Moia Voina* (Moscow: Algoritm, 2001), 224.
48. Romanov, *Nights Are Longest There*, 113.
49. Ibid., 113–115.
50. Geoffrey Roberts, *Stalin's General: The Life of Georgy Zhukov* (New York: Random House, 2012), 183.
51. Somov, *Voina*, 386.
52. Ibid., 395.
53. Markwick and Cardona, *Soviet Women on the Frontline*, 79.
54. Merridale, *Ivan's War*, 236.
55. "Interview with Vil' Sarychev," *Ia pomniu.*
56. Budnitskii, "Muzhchini i zhenshcini v Kransoi armii," 411–412.
57. Somov, *Voina*, 383.
58. "Interview with Mstislav Ivanov," *Ia pomniu.*
59. Slutskii, *Zapiski*, 99.
60. Tat'iana Aleksandrovna Repina (Atabek), *K biografii voennogo pokoleniia* (Moscow: Moskovskie uchebniki i Katolitografiia, 2004), 252.
61. Romanov, *Nights Are Longest There*, 78.
62. Diary excerpts from Vladimir Kagarlitskii, reproduced in Al'tman, Terushkin, and Brodskaia, eds., *Sokhrani moi pis'ma. Vypusk 2* (Moscow: Tsentr i FGond "Kholokost." Izdate'stvo MIK, 2010), 43–44.
63. Ibid.
64. Repina (Atabek), *K biografii*, 9–10.
65. Ibid., 90.
66. Ibid.
67. Ibid., 90–107.
68. Repina (Atabek), *K biografii*, 237. For the attacker's identity, see "Ozhidanie schast'ia."
69. Repina (Atabek), *K biografii*, 237.
70. Ibid., 90.

71. "Ozhidanie schast'ia," *Izvestiia*, 21 June 2002, accessed 20 November 2024, https://iz.ru/news/263361.
72. Repina (Atabek), *K biografii*,
73. For instance, see Bruce Myles, *Night Witches: The Untold Story of Soviet Women in Combat* (Edinburgh: Mainstream, 1981).
74. Krylova, *Soviet Women in Combat*, 269.
75. Hill, *The Red Army*, 327–328.
76. Regina Kazyulina, "Women's Antifascist Resistance on German-Occupied Territory through the Lens of Soviet Leaflets, 1941–5," *Journal of Contemporary History* 56. 4: 1145.
77. Daria Rudakova, "Soviet Women Collaborators in Occupied Ukraine 1941–1945" *Australian Journal of Politics and History* 62.4 (2016): 531.
78. Rowe-McCulloch, "Sexual Violence under Occupation," 2.
79. Somov, *Voina*, 452–453.
80. Pavel Luknitskii, *Leningrad deistvuet…frontovoi dnevnik* (Moscow: Sovetksii pisatel, 1971), accessed http://militera.lib.ru/db/luknitsky_pn/03.html.
81. Vanessa Voissin, "The Soviet Punishment of an All-European Crime, 'Horizontal Collboration'" in Gelind Grinchenko, Eleonora Narvselius, eds., *Traitors, Collaborators and Deserters in Contemporary European Politics of Memory* (London: Palgrave Macmillan, 2018), 258–259.
82. RGVA, f. 32900, op. 1, d. 341, l. 58.
83. Ibid., ll. 55–56.
84. Seth Bernstein, *Return to the Motherland Displaced Soviets in WWII and the Cold War* (Ithaca: Cornell University Press, 2023), 112.
85. Wendy Goldman, *Women at the Gates* (Cambridge: Cambridge University Press, 2002), 208.
86. Schechter, *The Stuff of Soldiers*, 216–217.
87. Slutskii, *Zapiski*, 57.
88. BA, El'kinson dnevnik, 3.
89. Ibid., 7.
90. Ibid.
91. Orme, *Comes the Comrade*, 74.
92. Slutskii, *Zapiski*, 78.
93. Author's interview with Vera Protić, the author's grandmother.
94. IAS, f. 83, "Mesnim narodnim odborima Pov. Br 145/45 dana 20.IX.1945."
95. VA, f. NOVJ, k. 371, f. 6, d. 26, l. 1.
96. Ibid., 3.
97. Ibid.
98. A. F. Noskova, "Kem byli v Vostochnoi Evrope soldaty Krasnoi Armii v 1945 godu: svoboditeliami, okkupantami, ili…?" *Vestnik MGIMO Universiteta* 5 (2010): 69.
99. Đilas, *Conversations with Stalin*, 110–111.
100. Ibid.
101. Slutskii, *Zapiski*, 130.
102. For excessive consumption of alcohol, see RGVA, f. 32900, op. 1, d. 341, l. 124. For others, see, RGVA, f. 32900, op. 1, d. 412, l. 26.
103. RGVA, f. 32900, op. 1, d. 441, l. 63.
104. TsDAGO, f. 62, op. 2, d. 910, l. 59.

105. RGVA, f. 32905, op. 1, d. 250, l. 11.
106. For such views in the Japanese military, see Yoshimi Yoshiaki, *Comfort Women: Sexual Slavery in the Japanese Military during World War II* (New York: Columbia University Press, 1995), 66–67; For these attitudes among the German military, see Regina Mühlhäuser "Between 'Racial Awareness' and Fantasies of Potency: Nazi Sexual Politics in the Occupied Territories of the Soviet Union, 1942–1945" in Dagmar Herzog, ed., *Brutality and Desire: War and Sexuality in Europe's Twentieth Century* (Basingstoke: Palgrave Macmillan, 2009), 198.
107. Regina Mühlhäuser, "'You have to Anticipate What Eludes Calculation:' Reconceptualizing Sexual Violence as Weapon and Strategy of War" in Gaby Zipfel, Regina Mühlhäuser, and Kirsten Campell, eds., *In Plain Sight: Sexual Violence in Armed Conflict* (New Delhi: Zubaan Publishers Pvt. Ltd., 2019), 12.
108. Elizabeth Heineman, "Gender, sexuality, and coming to terms with the Nazi past", *Central European History*, 38 (2005): 48.
109. Yoshiaki, *Comfort Women*, 29 and 39.
110. Mary Louise Roberts, *What Soldiers Do: Sex and the American GI in World War II France* (Chicago: The University of Chicago Press, 2013), 160.
111. Ibid., 160.
112. Ibid., Chapter 5; Gebhardt, *Crimes Unspoken*, 87.
113. Lawlor, "Contested Crimes," 554.
114. RGASPI, f. 17, op. 125, d. 241, ll. 90–91; TsDAGO, f. 59, op. 1, d. 1614, l. 184; RGVA, f. 32900, op.1, d. 341, ll. 54–56; RGVA, f. 32900, op. 1, d. 341, l. 76; TsAMO RF, f. 2, op. 795437, d. 12, l. 305, document reproduced in V. A. Zolotarev, et al. eds., *Tyl Krasnoi Armii*, 614; RGVA, f. 32900, op. 1, d. 354, ll. 41–47. It is hard to determine whether the upsurge in venereal diseases was the result of increased instances of rape, prostitution sex, or consensual relations. Most likely, it was the result of all three but especially prostitution sex.
115. "Interview with Nikolai Aleksandrov," *Ia pomniu.*
116. Ibid.
117. Slutksii, *Zapiski*, 47.
118. Ibid.
119. Ibid., 71.
120. Ibid., 177.
121. Ibid., 107.
122. Mikhin, *Guns against the Reich*, 180.
123. "Interview with Nikolai Aleksandrov," *Ia pomniu.*
124. Chukhrai, *Moia Voina*, 258–259.
125. Interview with Palotaine Kali Gabi, in *Silenced Shame* at 35.36.
126. Ibid., at 33.20–37.30.
127. Slutksii, *Zapiski*, 71.
128. Ibid.
129. Ibid., 127.
130. Susan Brownmiller, *Against Our Will. Men, Women and Rape* (Fawcett Books, 1975), 32; Gerda Lerner, *The Creation of Patriarchy* (New York: Oxford University Press, 1986), 80.
131. Naimark, *Russians in Germany*, 114.

132. Yoshiaki, *Comfort Women*, 67.
133. Roberts, What Soldiers Do, 20.
134. Ibid., 115.
135. Doris L. Bergen, "Sexual Violence in the Holocaust: Unique and Typical?" in Dagmar Herzog, ed., *Lessons and Legacies VII* (Evanston: Northwestern University Press, 2007), 180.
136. Svenka Savić, Marija Aleksandrović, Stanka Dimitrov, Jelena Jovanović, eds., *Romani Women: Oral Histories of Romani Women in Vojvodina*, trans. Aleksandra Izgarjan (Novi Sad: Futura Publikacije, 2002), 144.
137. Guy L. Siebold, "The Essence of Military Group Cohesion," *Armed Forces & Society* 33.2 (2007): 287–288.
138. Walter S. Dunn, *Stalin's Keys to Victory: The Rebirth of the Red Army* (Westport: Praeger Security International, 2006), 17.
139. Joshua Goldstein, *War and Gender. How Gender Shapes the War System and Vice Versa* (Cambridge: Cambridge University Press, 2001), 365.
140. Yuki Tanaka, "War, Rape and Patriarchy: The Japanese Experience" in Gaby Zipfel, Regina Mühlhäuser, Kirsten Campell, eds., *In Plain Sight: Sexual Violence in Armed Conflict* (New Delhi: Zubaan Publishers Pvt. Ltd., 2019), 45.
141. Merridale, *Ivan's War*, 267.
142. Mühlhäuser, *Sex and the Nazi Soldier*, 5.
143. Romanov, *Nights Are Longest There*, 156.
144. Ibid., 156.
145. Slutskii, *Zapiski*, 180,
146. Ibid., 178.
147. Sutrina, "My v Bolgarii (iz voennogo dnevnika)," 185.
148. Ibid.
149. Author's interview with Divna Protić.
150. TsAMO, document reproduced in Bukharin and Stoianovich, eds., *Otnosheniia Rossii (SSSR) s Iugoslaviei*, 367.
151. BA, El'kinson dnevnik,10.
152. VA, f. NOVJ, k. 222, f. 1k, d. 4, l. 1.
153. RGVA, f. 32900, op. 1, d. 183, l. 131.
154. TsAMO, f. 1512, op. 1, d. 93, l. 261.
155. RGVA, f. 32900, op. 1, d. 402, l. 245.
156. Ibid.
157. Romanov, *Nights Are Longest There*, 201–202.
158. Ibid., 201.
159. Ibid., 206–207.
160. Slutskii, *Zapiski*, 45.
161. RGVA, f. 32900, op. 1, d. 441, l. 234.
162. RGVA, f. 32900, op. 1, d. 192, l. 81.
163. RGVA, f. 3290, op.1, d. 220, l. 211.
164. Stelzl-Marx, *Stalins Soldaten*, 498.
165. Ibid., 501–502.
166. Ibid., 503.
167. Ibid., 502–504.
168. Ibid., 503.

8 After the War

1. Temkin, *My Just War*, 220.
2. Colonel General Biriuzov, the 3rd Ukrainian Front's Chief of Staff, was the chairmen of the ACC in Bulgaria, Michael Boll, "Reality and Illusion: The Allied Control Commission for Bulgaria as a Cause of the Cold War," *East European Quarterly* 17.4 (1983): 417; in Romania, it was Marshal Malinovskii, the commander of the 2nd Ukrainian Front, Hlihor and Scurtu, *The Red Army in Romania*, 46; in Hungary, it was Marshal Voroshilov, one of Stalin's closest allies from the period of Civil War, Geoffrey Swain and Nigel Swain, *Eastern Europe Since 1945* (New York: Palgrave Macmillan, 2009), 51.
3. Overall, 2,365,474 soldiers from the four Ukrainian fronts survived Vienna and Prague Vienna Strategic Operations, which ended the war, Krivosheev, ed., *Rossiia i SSSR*, 306–308. I say that there were almost 3 million troops in total because these soldiers participated in fighting, but there were hundreds of thousands of soldiers in the rear carrying out occupation duties. Their number can only be guessed.
4. M. Zakharov, "Marshal Sovetskogo Soiuza Rodion Malinovskii" in *Polkovodtsy i voenachal'niki Velikoi Otechestvennoi. Vypusk 1*, ed., A. N. Kiselev (Moscow: Molodaia Gvardiia, 1971), 251.
5. For 586,000 troops, see V. I. Achakso, et al., eds., *Istoriia mirovoi voiny, 1939–1945 v 12 tomakh, Porazhenie militaristskoi Iaponii. Okonchanie vtoroi mirovoi voinyvol. 11* (Moscow: Voenizdat, 1980), 192–193.
6. For age, see Robert Dale, "Re-Adjusting to Life After War: The Demobilization of Red Army Veterans in Leningrad and the Leningrad Region 1944–1950" (PhD Thesis, Queen Mary University of London. 2010), 40. For a slow and loosely organized process, see Sheila Fitzpatrick, "Postwar Soviet Society: The Return to Normalcy, 1945–1953" in Lee Lloyd, ed., *Social Impact of War in World War II: Crucible of the Contemporary World: Commentary and Readings* (London: M. E. Sharpe, 1991), 256.
7. Mark Edele, *Soviet Veterans of the Second World War: A Popular Movement in an Authoritarian Society 1941–1991* (Oxford: Oxford University Press, 2008), 26.
8. RGVA, f. 32900, op. 1, d. 441, l. 234.
9. Verona, *Military Occupation and Diplomacy. Soviet Troops in Romania 1944–1958* (Durham: Duke University Press, 1992), 44. This estimate seems plausible since, according to my research, only the 37th Army stayed in Bulgaria after September 1944 when the rest of the 3rd Ukrainian Front went to Yugoslavia.
10. Swain and Swain, *Eastern Europe*, 4.
11. For the number of troops in Austria, see Eisterer, "Austria under Allied Occupation," 201. Her source for this claim is unclear. For when the Soviet troops left, see Ingrid Bauer and Renate Huber, "Sexual Encounters Across (Former) Enemy Borderlines," in Günter Bischof, Anton Pelinka, and Dagmar Herzog, eds., *Sexuality in Austria* (New Brunswick: Transaction Publishers, 2007), 69.
12. Verona, *Military Occupation and Diplomacy*, 49.
13. Hlihor and Scurtu, *The Red Army in Romania*, 39.

14. Swain and Swain, *Eastern Europe Since 1945*, 4.
15. For the unpopularity of reparations in Austria, see RGASPI, f. 17, op. 128, d. 749, ll. 2–24, document reproduced in Gennadii Bordiugov, et al., eds., *Sovetskaia politika v Avstrii. 1944–1955gg. Sbornik Dokumentov* (Moscow: Seriia 'Airo – pervaia publikatsiia,' 2006), 97. For Vienna specifically, see AVP, f. 07, op. 10, p. 154, d. 13, ll. 2–10, document reproduced in document reproduced in Zolotarev, et al., eds., *Krasnaia Armiia v stranakh Tsentral'noi, Severnoi Evropy i na Balkanakh*, 668. For Gratz, see RGASPI, f. 17, op. 128, d. 35, ll. 45–51, document reproduced in Gennadii Bordiugov, et al., eds., *Sovetskaia politika v Avstrii*, 81. For Hungary, see RGASPI, f. 17, op. 128, d. 783, ll. 35–36, document reproduced in Zolotarev, et al., eds., *Krasnaia Armiia v stranakh Tsentral'noi, Severnoi Evropy i na* Balkanakh, 394.
16. RGASPI, f. 17, op. 128, d. 35, ll. 45–51, document reproduced in Bordiugov, et al., eds., *Sovetskaia politika v Avstrii*, 81.
17. For Transylvania, see RGASPI, f. 17, op. 128, d. 783, ll. 35–36, document reproduced in Zolotarev, et al., eds., *Krasnaia Armiia v stranakh Tsentral'noi, Severnoi Evropy i na Balkanakh*, 394. For Bačka, see USHMM RG 22.008M*3, original from TsAMO RF, f. 240, op. 2772, d. 35, l. 50.
18. Case, *Between States*.
19. For Austria, see AVP, f. 07, op. 10, p. 154, d. 13, ll. 2–10, document reproduced in document reproduced in V. A. Zolotarev, et al., eds., *Krasnaia Armiia v stranakh Tsentral'noi, Severnoi Evropy i na Balkanakh*, 668 and RGASPI, f. 17, op. 128, d. 749, ll. 2–24, document reproduced in Gennadii Bordiugov, et al., eds., *Sovetskaia politika v Avstrii*, 123. For Romania, see RGVA, f. 32900, op. 1, d. 441, l. 212. For Yugoslavia, see RGVA, f. 32900, op. 1, d. 220, l. 210. For Hungary, see Kenez, *Hungary from Nazis to Soviets*, 44–45.
20. RGASPI, f. 17, op. 125, d. 316, ll. 81–82, document reproduced in Gennadii Bordiugov, et al., eds., *Sovetskaia politika v Avstrii*, 106–107.
21. RGVA, f. 32900, op. 1, d. 441, l. 233.
22. lya Ehrenburg and Vasily Grossman, *The Complete Black Book of Russian Jewry*, translated and edited by David Patterson (New Brunswick: Transaction Publishers, 2002), vii.
23. Georgi Aleksandrov, "Tovarishch Ehrenburg uproshcaet," *Pravda* 89, 14 April 1945, 2.
24. RGVA, f. 32900, op. 1, d. 452, l. 113.
25. Gromyko, et al., eds., *SSSR-Avstriia*, 16–17.
26. RGVA, f. 32905, op. 1, d. 91, l. 17.
27. RGVA, f. 32900, op. 1, d. 451, l. 80.
28. RGVA, f. 32900, op. 1, d. 441, 212.
29. RGVA, f. 32900, op. 1, d. 363, l. 136.
30. USHMM RG 040.050 file 9, 1 originally from TsAMO, f. 32, op. 11289, d. 592, l. 365.
31. Slutskii, *Zapiski*, 130.
32. RGVA, f. 32900, op. 1, d. 363, l. 236; RGVA, f. 32900, op. 1, d. 363, l. 64; RGVA, f. 32900, op. 1, d. 363, l. 189; RGVA, f. 32900, op. 1, d. 363, l. 136; RGVA, f. 32900, op. 1, d. 220, ll. 203–204; RGVA, f. 32900, op. 1, d. 363, l. 132; RGVA, f. 32900, op.1, d. 441, ll. 233–237; RGVA, f. 32900, op. 1, d. 363, l. 163.

33. For an order by the NKVD Army, see RGVA, f. 32900, op. 1, d. 357, l. 93. For the order issued by the commander of the 57th Army, see TsAMO, f. 57A, op. 10372, d. 667, l. 67; for the order by Colonel-General Biriuzov, the commander of the 37th Army, see RGVA, f. 32900, op. 1, d. 363, l. 200; RGVA, f. 32900, op. 1, d. 361, l. 65.
34. RGVA, f. 32900, op. 1, d. 363, l. 163.
35. Ibid., l. 189.
36. RGVA, f. 32900, op. 1, d. 367, l. 39.
37. RGVA, f. 32900, op. 1, d. 361, l. 63.
38. Such orders were issued for Vienna on 3 August, Petrov, "The Internal Troops of the NKVD," 267. The order was reiterated on 18 September, RGVA, f. 32900, op. 1, d. 361, l. 63.
39. RGVA, f. 32900, op. 1, d. 363, l. 189.
40. RGVA, f. 32900, op. 1, d. 484, l. 54; Nikita Petrov, "The Internal Troops," 252.
41. RGVA, f. 32900, op. 1, d. 452, l. 170.
42. RGVA, f. 32900, op. 1, d. 441, l. 231.
43. Ibid., l. 233.
44. RGVA, f. 32900, op. 1, d. 363, l. 192.
45. Slaveski, *The Soviet Occupation of Germany*, xi.
46. Naimark, *Russians in Germany*, 79.
47. Matthew Paul Berg, "'Caught between Iwan and the Weihnachtsmann:' Occupation, the Marshall Plan, and Austrian Identity," in Bischof, Gunther, Anton Pelinka, and Dieter Stiefel, eds., *The Marshall Plan in Austria: Contemporary Austrian Studies*, Volume 8 (New Brunswick: Transaction Publishers, 2001), 140.
48. Ibid., 162.
49. Martin Mevius wrote that violence continued well after the war in Hungary, Mevius, *Agents of Moscow*, 64. For Romania, see the note from the Romanian delegation to the ACC dated 25 May 1946, which makes it clear that the Red Army's behavior did not become correct more than a year after the war ended, Arh M.Ap.N., fond 136, dosar 460, ff. 709–711, document reproduced in document reproduced in Hlihor and Scurtu, *The Red Army in Romania*, 238–240.
50. RGASPI, f. 82, op. 2, d. 816, l. 61.
51. Ibid., l. 61.
52. For 2,132 deserters, see RGVA, f. 32905, op. 1, d. 91, l. 290. For 314 deserters, see RGVA, f. 32905, op. 1, d. 91, l. 176.
53. RGVA, f. 32900, op. 1, d. 220, l. 198.
54. RGVA, f. 32900, op. 1, d. 218, l. 67.
55. Moniushko, *From Leningrad to Hungary*, 202 and 212; BA, El'kinson dnevnik, 22.
56. There were 2 million Soviet troops in Romania in May 1945, Hlihor and Scurtu, *The Red Army in Romania*, 123.
57. RGVA, f. 32900, op. 1, d. 441, l. 234–235.
58. RGVA, f. 32900, op. 1, d. 452, l. 185.
59. Edele, *Soviet Veterans*, 27–29.
60. RGVA, f. 32900, op. 1, d. 220, l. 203.
61. BA, El'kinson dnevnik, 21.
62. Moniushko, *From Leningrad to Hungary*, 202.

63. BA, El'kinson dnevnik, 21.
64. Ibid., 22.
65. Slutskii, *Zapiski*, 127.
66. Ibid., 52.
67. Arh M.Ap.N., fond 1367, dosar 460, ff. 44–46, document reproduced in Hlihor and Scurtu, *The Red Army in Romania*, 223–225 and Arh M.Ap.N., fond 136, dosar 460, ff. 709–711, document reproduced in Hlihor and Scurtu, ibid., 238–239.
68. Ibid., 26.
69. For Austria, see RGVA, f. 32900, op. 1, d. 220, l. 195–196; for Romania, see Hlihor and Scurtu, *The Red Army in Romania*, 155; for Yugoslavia, see IAS, f. 86, k. 64 (Okružni sud Subotica), Posl. broj k. 22, 1945–1947.
70. For instance, see Marshal Tolbukhin's order to the 3rd Ukrainian Fronts on 20 May 1945, decreeing the seizure of all weapons from Hungarian civilians, in which he enumerated a series of attacks on Soviet troops, RGVA, f. 32900, op. 1, d. 364, l. 50. Mevius claimed that the enmity of Hungarians to the Soviets sometimes took violent form, and he specified several such incidents, Mevius, *Agents of Moscow*, 64.
71. "Interview with Aleksandr Solov'ev," *Ia pomniu.*
72. Slaveski, *The Soviet Occupation of Germany*, 11.
73. The Kremlin ordered both 2nd and 3rd Ukrainian Front on 11 May to create camps for a hundred thousand people each. These camps were for several categories of people: Soviets who fought on the side of the Axis and whom the British and the Americans were about to expatriate to the Red Army, as well as liberated prisoners of war and slave laborers, TsAMO, f. 148a, op. 3763, d. 212, ll. 16–19, document reproduced in V. A. Zolotarev, et al., eds., *Stavka VGK*, 236–237.
74. RGVA, f. 32900, op. 1, d. 441, l. 234.
75. Letter from Aleksandr Levin, reproduced in Altman and Terushkin, eds., *Sokhrani moi pis'ma*, 270.
76. Bischof, *Austria in the First Cold War*, 37.
77. Edele, *Soviet Veterans*, 31.
78. Moniushko, *From Leningrad*, 219.
79. Edele, *Soviet Veterans*, 33.
80. Beevor, *Berlin*, 407.
81. RGVA, f. 32900, op. 1, d. 363, l. 170.
82. RGVA, f. 32905, op. 1, d. 414, l. 20.
83. Edele, *Soviet Veterans*, 31.
84. Ibid., 33.
85. RGVA, f. 32900, op. 1, d. 363, l. 199.
86. RGVA, f. 32900, op. 1, d. 220, l. 220.

Conclusion

1. Alexander Victor Prusin, *Nationalizing a Borderland: War, Ethnicity, and Anti-Jewish Violence in East Galicia*, 1914–1920 (Tuscaloosa: The University of Alabama Press, 2005), xi.

2. Berkhoff, *Harvest*, 164–187.
3. For Vienna, see Lewis, *Workers and Politics*, 66–67; For Berlin, see Beevor, *The Fall of Berlin*, 392.
4. Noskova, "Kem byli,": 69; Đilas, *Conversations with Stalin*, 110–111.
5. Timofejev, *Rusi*, 221.
6. Rzheshevskii, "Berlinskaia Operatsiia."
7. Merridale, *Ivan's War*, 12–14.
8. Roberts, *What Soldiers Do*, 174; Pannacci, "Sex, Military Brothels," 81; Mühlhäuser, *Sex and the Nazi Soldier*, 129–130.
9. For the threat of forced labor, see Jeffrey Burds, "Sexual Violence in Europe in World War II, 1939–1945," *Politics & Society* 37 (March 2009): 39; for gunpoint, see Gertjejanssen, "Victims," 177; for staving, see Ibid., 208.
10. Mühlhäuser, *Sex and the Nazi Soldier*, 155.
11. Rowe-McCulloch, "Sexual Violence under Occupation,"10 and 14.
12. Ibid., 3.
13. Pannacci, "Sex, Military Brothels," 84–85.
14. Sabine Fruhstuck, "Sexuality and Sexual Violence" in Cambridge History of World War II, Volume 3, *Total War: Economy, Society, and Culture*, eds., Michael Geyer and Adam Tooze (Cambridge: Cambridge University Press, 2015), 431.
15. Roberts, *What Soldiers Do*, 160.
16. Ibid., 172.
17. For Italy, see Francesca Ruvolo, "American Soldiers and Italian Women: The Sexual Economy of Occupied Naples, 1943–1945" (M.A. Thesis: Rutgers University, 2016), 145–146. For France, see Roberts, *What Soldiers Do*, 160.
18. Ibid., 169.
19. Ibid, 160.
20. Isobel Williams, *Allies and Italians under Occupation: Sicily and Southern Italy, 1943–45* (Basingstoke: Palgrave Macmillan, 2013), 201.
21. History of the Judge Advocate General's Office, European Theater, 18 July 1942–1 November 1945. Vol. I. (St. Cloud, France, 1945), 241–242. Thanks to Ruth Lawlor for sharing this document with me.
22. Morris, "Force of Arms," 665–666; Ruth Lawlor, "The Wartime Battlefield of Sex" Modern American History 4.2. (2021): 210.
23. Ibid., 209.
24. Ibid., 210.
25. Ruth Lawlor, "The Stuttgart Incident and the Uses of History" *Diplomatic History* 46.1. (2022): 70.
26. Roberts, *What Soldiers Do*, 162–163.
27. Ibid., 169.
28. Williams, *Allies and Italians*, 196–197.
29. Ibid., 195.
30. Ruth Lawlor and Vojin Majstorovic, "Ideology and Legitimacy: A Comparative Account of Sexual Violence in the U.S. and Red Armies in the Second World War" (unpublished manuscript, 15 June 2025).
31. Mühlhäuser, *Sex and the Nazi Soldier*, 85–86.
32. Ibid., 86–88.

33. David Raub Snyder, *Sex Crimes under the Wehrmacht* (Lincoln: University of Nebraska Press, 2007), 101.
34. Ibid., 136.
35. Ibid., 81, 147.
36. Lawlor and Majstorovic, "Ideology and Legitimacy."
37. Ibid.
38. Zviagintsev, *Voina*, 736.
39. Rzheshevskii, "Berlinskaia Operatsiia."
40. Oleg Khlevniuk, "Stalin and the Generals: Reconstructing Trust during World War II," *Europe-Asia Studies* 74.4 (2002): 527, 531, and 533.
41. Budnitskii, "In Parantheses: Extrajudicial Executions," 229.
42. For instance, see RGVA, f. 32900, o. 1, d. 341, ll. 54–56.
43. For instances of sexual violence in Cherkassy, see Gertjejanssen, "Victims," 262; for Rostov, see Rowe-McCulloch, "Sexual Violence under Occupation," 21–26; For Riga and Berdychev, see Mühlhäuser, *Sex and the Nazi Soldier*, 35–36; for Pskov, see Ibid., 43.
44. Mühlhäuser, *Sex and the Nazi Soldier*, 117–120.
45. Lilly, *Taken by Force*, 11.
46. Olivier Wieviorka, *Normandy the Landings to the Liberation of Paris*, trans. M. B. DeBevoise (Cambridge: Belknap Press of Harvard University Press, 2008), 329.
47. "Historique de la Manche Le SPLAF," *Site sur la Population et les Limites Administratives de la France*, accessed 25 October 2024, http://splaf.free.fr/50his.html.
48. Gebahrdt, *Crimes Unspoken*, 2.
49. Ibid., 18–19.
50. Ibid., 18–19.
51. Estimate made by German filmmaker Helke Sander in her film *Liberators Take Liberties*, cited in Atina Grossmann, "A Question of Silence: The Rape of German Women by Occupation Soldiers," October 72 (1995): 46.
52. Lawlor and Majstorovic, "Ideology and Legitimacy."
53. On 8 May 1945, there were 1,622,000 US Army personnel in Germany, out of a total of 3,077,000 in Europe, Earl F. Ziemke, *The U.S. Army in the occupation of Germany, 1944–1946* (Washington, D.C.: Center of Military History United States Army, 2003), 320. In the second quarter of 1945, the average size of the Red Army in Europe was 6,135,300 Krivosheev, ed., *Rossiia i SSSR*, 261. At different time periods from 1944 to 1945, the forces of the 1st Belarusian Front, 2nd Belarusian Front, 3rd Belarusian Front, and 1st Ukrainian Front were present on the territory of pre-1945 Germany, numbering at least 2,622,700 soldiers, Ibid., 304, 307.

Bibliography

Archives

Archive of Yugoslavia, Belgrade, Serbia (AJ)
Blavatnik Archive, New York City, United States (BA)
Central State Archives of Public Organizations of Ukraine, Kiev, Russia (TsDAGO)
Historical Archive of Negotin, Negotin, Serbia (IAN)
Historical Archive of Subotica, Subotica, Serbia (IAN)
Historical Archive of the Russian Academy of Sciences, Moscow, Russia (IAN RAN)
Historical Archive of Zaječar, Zaječar, Serbia (IAZ)
Russian State Archive of Social and Political History, Moscow, Russia (RGASPI)
The Central Archive of the Ministry of Defense of the Russian Federation, Podol'sk, Russia (TsAMO, RF)
The Military Archive of Serbia, Belgrade, Serbia (VA)
The Russian State Military Archive, Moscow, Russia (RGVA)
The United States Holocaust Memorial Museum, Washington DC, United States (USHMM)
Tsentr i fond kholokost, Moscow, Russia.

Published Archival Documents

Békés, Csaba, Borhi, László, Ruggenthaler, Peter and Trașcă, Ottmar, eds. *Soviet Occupation of Romania, Hungary, and Austria, 1944/45–1948/49*. Budapest: Central European University, 2015.

Bordiugov, Gennadii, et al., eds. *Sovetskaia politika v Avstrii. 1944–1955gg. Sbornik Dokumentov*. Moscow: Seriia 'Airo – pervaia publikatsiia', 2006.

Brontman, Lazar'. *Na linii fronta: Pravda o voine. Voennyi dnevnik korrespondenta 'pravdy'. Vstrechi. Sobytiia. Sud'by 1942–1945*. Moscow: Tsentrpoligraf, 2007.

Bukharin, I. V. and Stoianovich, S., eds. *Otnosheniia Rossii (SSSR) s Iugoslaviei 1941–1945gg. Dokumenty i materialy*. Moscow: Terra kniyhnizi klub, 1998.

Bushaeva, T. S. *Sovetskie liudi v osvoboditel'noi bor'be iugoslavskogo naroda 1941–1945gg. Vospominiia, dokumenty i materialy*. Moscow: Nauka, 1973.

Dedijer, Vladimir, ed. *Josip Broz Tito: Prilozi za Biografiju*. Zagreb: Kultura, 1953.

Erenburg, Il'ia. *Voina. 1941–1945.* Moscow: KRPA Olimp, 2004. Accessed 28 January, 2024, http://militera.lib.ru/prose/russian/erenburg_ig3/177.html.

Ehrenburg, lya and Grossman, Vasily. *The Complete Black Book of Russian Jewry*, translated and edited by David Patterson. New Brunswick: Transaction Publishers, 2002.

Farkas, Charles. *Vanished by the Danube: Peace, War, Revolution, and Flight to the West.* Introduction by Margaret McMullan. Albany: State university of New York Press, 2013.

Golopentia, A. and Georgescu, D. C., eds. *Populatia Republicii Populare Romane La 25 Ianuarie 1948.* Buchurest: Institut Central de Statistica, 1948.

Hill, Alexander, ed. *The Great Patriotic War of the Soviet Union, 1941–1945: A Documentary Reader.* New York: Routledge, 2009.

Kopelev, Lev. *To Be Preserved Forever.* Edited and translated by Anthony Austin. Philadelphia and New York: J. B. Lippincott Company, 1977.

Morozov, A. K., et al., eds. *73-ia gvardeiskaia. Sbornik vospominanii, dokumentov i materialov o boevom puti 73-oi gvardeiskoi strelkovoi Stalingradsko-Dunaiskoi Krasnoznamennoi divizii.* Alma-Ata: Kazahstan, 1986.

Savić, Svenka, ed. *Women's Identities in Vojvodina: 1920–1930.* Novi Sad: Futura Publikacije, 2006.

Savić, Svenka, Aleksandrović, Marija, Dimitrov, Stanka and Jovanović, Jelena, eds., *Romani Women: Oral Histories of Romani Women in Vojvodina.* Translated by Aleksandra Izgarjan. Novi Sad: Futura Publikacije, 2002.

Shindel, Aleksandr. *Po obe storony fronta: pis'ma sovetskikh i nemetskikh soldat, 1941–1945 gg.* Moscow: Sol', 1995.

Spariousu, Laura and Savic, Svenka, eds., *Životne price žena u Vojvodini: Rumunke 1924–1974.* Novi Sad: Futura publikacije i Ženske studije i istraživanja.

Stalin, I. *O Velikoi Otechestvennoi voine Sovetskogo Soiuza.* Moscow: Voennoe izdatel'stvo ministerstva vooruzhennykh sil Soiuza SSR, 1948.

Stepashin, S. V., et al., eds. *Organy Gosudarstvennoi Bezopasnosti SSSR v Velikoi Otechestvennoi Voine. Sbornik Doumentov. Vpered na Zapad. 1 ianvaria – 30 iunia 1944 goda* tom 5 kniga 1. Moscow: Obshcestvo izucheniia istorii otechestvennykh spetssluzhb, 2007.

Stepashin, S. V., et al., eds. *Organy Gosudarstvennoi Bezopasnosti SSSR v Velikoi Otechestvennoi Voine. Sbornik Doumenov. Granitsy SSSR Vosstanovleny 1 iulia – 31 dekabria 1944 goda.* T.5, K.2. Moscow: Obshcestvo izucheniia istorii otechestvennykh spetssluzhb, 2007.

Sverdlov, F. F., ed. *Dokumenty obviniaiut. Kholokost: svidetel'stva Krasnoi Armii.* Moscow: Rossiiskaia biblioteka Kholokosta, 1996.

Timoshenko, Semen. *Distsiplinarnyi Ustav Krasnoi Armii.* Leningrad: Voenizdat, 1941, 3.

Volokitina, T. V., et al., eds. *Iz istorii sovetsko-rumynskikh otnoshenii: tri vizita A. Ia. Vyshinskogo v Bukharest 1944–1946. Dokumenty rossiiskikh arkhivov.* Moscow: Rosspen, 1998.

Volokitina, T. V., et al., eds. *Sovetskii Faktor v Vostochnoi Evrope 1944–1953. T.1 1944–1948. Dokumenty.* Moscow: ROSSPEN, 1999.

Volokitina, T. V., et al., eds. *Vostochnaia Evropa v dokumentakh rossiiskikh arkhivov.1944–1953gg. Tom 1 1944–1948gg.* Moscow-Novosibirsk: Sibirskii khronograf, 1997.

Vorontsov, D. V., ed. *Vengerskie voennoplennye v SSSR. Dokumenty 1941–1953 godov*. Moscow: Rosspen, 2005.

Zabarko, Boris, ed. *Zhivymi ostalis' tol'ko my. Svidetel'stva i dokumenty*. Kiev: Biblioteka instituta iudaiki, 1999.

Zhilin, P. A., et al., eds. *Osvoboditel'naia missiia sovetksikh vooruzhennykh sil v Evrope vo vtoroi mirovoi voine. Dokumenty i materialy*. Moscow: Voennoe-izdatel'stvo, 1985.

Zolotarev, V. A., et al., eds. *Russkii Arkhiv: Velikaia Otechestvennaia. General'nyi shtab v gody Velikoi Otechestvennoi voine 1941–1945gg. Dokumenty i Materialy 1941–1945gg*. T.23.12(4). Moscow: Terra, 2001.

Zolotarev, V. A., et al., eds. *Russkii Arkhiv: Velikaia Otechestvennaia. Glavnye Politicheskie Organy Vooruzhennykh Sil SSSR v Velikoi Otechestvennoi voine 1941–1945gg. Dokumenty i Materialy 1941–1945gg*. T.17-6(1–2). Moscow: Terra, 1996.

Zolotarev, V. A., et al., eds. *Russkii Arkhiv: Velikaia Otechestvennaia. Krasnaia Armiia v stranakh Tsentral'noi, Severnoi Evropy i na Balkanakh. Dokumenty i materialy 1944–1945*. T.14-3(2). Moscow: Terra, 2000.

Zolotarev, V. A., et al., eds. *Russkii Arkhiv: Velikaia Otechestvennaia. Prikazy i Direktivy Narodnogo Komissara VMF v gody velikoi otechestvennoi voiny, 1944–1945*. T.21.10. Moscow: Terra, 1996.

Zolotarev, V. A., et al., eds. *Russkii Arkhiv: Velikaia Otechestvennaia. Prikazy Narodnogo Komissara Oborony SSSR 1943–1945gg*. T.13.2(3). Moscow: Terra, 1997.

Zolotarev, V. A., et al., eds. *Russkii Arkhiv: Velikaia Otechestvennaia. Stavka VGK. Dokumenty i materialy 1944–1945*. T.16.5(4). Moscow: Terra, 1999.

Zolotarev, V. A., et al., eds. *Russkii Arkhiv: Velikaia Otechestvennaia. Tyl Krasnoi Armii v Velikoi Otechestvnnoi voine 1941–1945gg. Dokumenty i materialy 1944–1945*. T. 25 (14). Moscow: Terra, 1998.

Memoirs, Diaries, Letters, Literature

Abdulin, Mansur. *Red Road from Stalingrad: Recollections of a Soviet Infantryman*. Mechanicsburg: Stackpole Books, 2004.

Altman, Il'ia and Terushkin, Leonid, eds. *Sokhrani moi pis'ma. Sbornik pisem I dnevnikov evreev perioda velikoi otechestvennoi voiny*. Moscow: Tsentr i Fond 'Khookost' i izdatel'stvo MIK, 2007.

Altman, Il'ia and Terushkin, Leonid, eds. *Sokhrani moi pis'ma. Sbornik pisem evreev perioda velikoi otechestvennoi voiny* Vypusk 2. Moscow: Tsentr i Fond 'Kholokost'. Izdate'stvo MIK, 2010.

Altman, Il'ia and Terushkin, Leonid, eds. *Sokhrani moi pis'ma. Sbornik pisem evreev perioda velikoi otechestvennoi voiny* Vypusk 3. Moscow: Tsentr i Fond 'Kholokost'. Izdate'stvo MIK, 2013.

Anonymous, *A Woman in Berlin: A Diary*. Edited by Antony Beevor. London: Virago, 2005.

Anoshin, I. S. *Na Pravyi boi*. Moscow: Voennoe izdatel'stvo, 1988.

Banac, Ivo, ed., *The Diary of Georgi Dimitrov 1933–1949*. New Haven: Yale University Press, 2003.

Biriuzov, S. S. *Surovye gody*. Moscow: Nauka, 1966.

Burton, Berry. *Romanian Diaries 1944–1947*. Edited by Cornelia Bodea. Iasi, Oxford, Portland: The Center for Romanian Studies, 2000.

Chukhrai, Grigorii. *Moia Voina*. Moscow: Algoritm, 2001.

Đilas, Milovan. *Conversations with Stalin*. Translated from the Serbo-Croat by Michael B. Petrovich. New York: Harcourt, Brace & World, Inc., 1962.

Đilas, Milovan. *Revolucionarni rat*. Belgrade: Književne novine, 1990.

Farkass, Jeno. "The Last Winter A Diary of the Siege and Occupation of Budapest, 1944–1945." Translated by Maria Farkas Szokolai and Charles Farkas. Unpublished Manuscript, 29 January 2020.

Gurvits, L. A. *Vospominaniia frontovogo radista. Ot KV-radiostantsii – do morskikh krylatykh raket*. St. Petersburg: Ku'tInformPress, 2008.

Lobachev, Djordje. *Kad se volga ulivala u Savu. Moj zivotni roman*. Belgrade: Prosveta, 1997.

Marin, Vasilii. *Ia pomniu, vospominaniia veteranov VOV* [vspominania]. Accessed 27 May 2016, http://iremember.ru/memoirs/pulemetchiki/marin-vasiliy-vladimirovich/.

Mikhin, Petr. *Guns against the Reich. Memoirs of a Soviet Artillery Officer on the Eastern Front*. Mechanicsburg: Stackpole Books, 2011.

Moniushko, Evgenii. *From Leningrad to Hungary. Notes of a Red Army Soldier, 1941–1946*. Translated by Oleg Sheremet. Edited by David M. Glantz. New York: Frank Cass, 2005.

Orme, Alexandra. *Comes the Comrade*. New York: William Morrow & Company, 1950.

Polcz, Alaine. *One Woman in the War Hungary 1944–1945*. Translation and Introduction by Albert Tezla. Budapest: Central European Press, 2002.

Presniakov, B. D. *Pod zvezdami balkanskimi*. Moscow: Moskovskii rabochii, 1985.

Romenskii, Anton, ed. *Glazami i serdtsem soldata. Rasskazyvaiut frontoviki 1941–1945*. Moscow: Voennoe izdatelstvo minsterstva oborony SSSR, 1979.

Simonov, Konstantin. "Otkrytoe pis'mo Zhenshcine iz g. Vichuga." Accessed 11 January 2023, https://simonov.co.uk/openletterru.

Simonov, Konstantin. "Ubei ego (Esli dorog tebe tvoi dom)." Accessed 11 January 2023, www.culture.ru/poems/32889/ubei-ego-esli-dorog-tebe-tvoi-dom.

Simonov, Konstantin. Zhdi menia i ia vernus…." Accessed January 11, 2023, www.culture.ru/poems/32975/zhdi-menya-i-ya-vernus.

Slutskii, Boris. *Zapiski o Voine. Stikhotvoreniia i ballady*. St. Petersburg: Logos, 2000.

Strashnov, S. L. "K. Simonov – Lirik v Kontaktakh s Massovoi Auditoriei Voennykh Let." *Vestnik VGU. Seriia: Filologiia. Zhurnalisika* 4 (2018): 83–85.

Temkin, Gabriel. *My Just War: The Memoir of a Jewish Red Army Soldier in World War II*. Novato: Presidio, 1998.

Zav'ialov, N. I. *Pod zvezdami balkanskimi*. Kiev: Izdatel'stvo politicheskoi literatury Ukrainy, 1987.

Interviews

Ia pomniu, vospominaniia veteranov VOV

Aleksandrov, Nikolai. *Ia pomniu*, 4 April 2011. Accessed 28 November 2024, https://iremember.ru/memoirs/voditeli/aleksandrov-nikolay-filippovich/.

Aleksandrova (Petrova), Aleksandra. Interview by I. Vershinin. *Ia pomniu*, 30 June 2013. Accessed 21 December 2023, https://iremember.ru/memoirs/mediki/aleksandrova-petrova-aleksandra-mikhaylovna/.

Bezchastnyi, Vladimir. Interview by I. Vershinin. *Ia pomniu*, 29 April 2015. Accessed 19 December 2020, https://iremember.ru/memoirs/desantniki/bezchastnyy-vladimir-fedorovich/.

Bondarenko (Kataeva), Mariia. Interview by Iu. Trifonov. *Ia pomniu*, 30 October 2016. Accessed 16 January 2023, https://iremember.ru/memoirs/snayperi/kataeva-bondarenko-mariya-dmitrievna/.

Danich, Semen. Interview by N. Chobanu. *Ia pomniu*, 28 August 2007. Accessed 28 November 2024, https://iremember.ru/memoirs/saperi/danich-semen-antonovich/.

Demesheva (Skvortsova), Nina. Interview by I. Vershinin. *Ia pomniu*, 1 January 2013. Accessed 16 January 2023, https://iremember.ru/memoirs/mediki/demesheva-skvortsova-nina-petrovna/.

Favorov, Iurii. Interview by A. Drabkin and S. Anisimov. *Ia pomniu*, 9 September 2011. Accessed 28 November 2024, http://iremember.ru/minometchiki/favorov-uriy-leonidovich.html.

Glotova, Nina. Interview by A. B. Brovtsin and I. G. Koshchev. *Ia pomniu*, 4 October 2007. Accessed 20 December 2023, https://iremember.ru/memoirs/mediki/glotova-nina-ivanovna/.

Gluschenko, Lidiia. Interview by A. Drabkin. *Ia pomniu*, 25 December 2008. Accessed 16 January 2023, https://iremember.ru/memoirs/voditeli/gluschenko-lidiya-mikhaylovna/.

Ivanov, Mikhail. Interview by N. Chobanu. *Ia pomniu*, 13 May 2012. Accessed 28 November 2024, https://iremember.ru/memoirs/artilleristi/ivanov-mikhail-nikolaevich/.

Ivanov, Mstislav. Interview by A. Drabkin. *Ia pomniu*, 28 January 2010. Accessed 28 November 2024, https://iremember.ru/memoirs/razvedchiki/ivanov-mstislav-borisovich/.

Lebedev, Pavel. Interview by N. Chobanu. *Ia pomniu*, 10 June 2013. Accessed 28 November 2024, https://iremember.ru/memoirs/voditeli/lebedev-pavel-fedorovich/.

Lempert, Iosif. Interview by G. Koifman. *Ia pomniu*, 10 April 2007. Accessed 28 November 2024, https://iremember.ru/memoirs/drugie-voyska/lempert-iosif-mikhaylovich/.

Nadtochii, Nikolai. Interview by N. Chobanu. *Ia pomniu*, 12 April 2012. Accessed 7 February 2023, https://iremember.ru/memoirs/razvedchiki/nadtochiy-nikolay-danilovich/.

Otroshcenkov, Sergei. Interview by N. Domrachev. *Ia pomniu*, 26 December 2012. Accessed 27 May 2016, http://iremember.ru/memoirs/tankisti/otroschenkov-sergey-andreevich/.

Papish, Mark. Interview by G. Koifman. *Ia pomniu*, 13 September 2012. Accessed 27 May 2016, http://iremember.ru/memoirs/pekhotintsi/papish-mark-abramovich/.

Povov, Nikolai. Interview by Iu. Trifonov. *Ia pomniu*, 13 May 2009. Accessed 28 November 2024, https://iremember.ru/memoirs/tankisti/popov-nikolay-vasilevich/.

Pugacheva (Chertova), Tat'iana. Interview by A. Drabkin. *Ia pomniu*, 25 December 2008. Accessed 16 January 2023, https://iremember.ru/memoirs/svyazisti/pugacheva-chertova-tatyana-aleksandrovna/.

Rabinovich, Grigorii. Interview by G. Koifman. *Ia pomniu*, 25 April 2014. Accessed 28 November 2024, http://iremember.ru/pekhotintsi/rabinovich-grigoriy-alekseevich.html.

Rist (Fedorko), Mariia. Interview by I. Vershinin. *Ia pomniu*, 1 October 2014. Accessed 28 November 2024, https://iremember.ru/memoirs/svyazisti/rist-fedorko-mariya-kuzminichna/.

Romanov, Efim. Interview by G. Koifman. *Ia pomniu*, 29 September 2013. Accessed 20 December 2020, https://iremember.ru/memoirs/mediki/romanov-efim-mikhaylovich/.

Rudiagin, Petr. Interview by N. Chobanu. *Ia pomniu*, 17 October 2010. Accessed 28 November 2024, https://iremember.ru/memoirs/pekhotintsi/rudyagin-petr-timofeevich/.

Russkikh, Grigorii. Interview by N. Chobanu. *Ia pomniu*, 17 October 2010. Accessed 28 November 2024, http://iremember.ru/pekhotintsi/russkikh-grigoriy-antonovich.html.

Sarychev, Vil'. Interview by Iu. Trifunov. *Ia pomniu*. Accessed 28 November 2024, https://iremember.ru/memoirs/minometchiki/sarichev-vil-georgievich/.

Shavrin, Aleksei. Interview by Iu. Trifonov. *Ia pomniu*, 29 May 2010. Accessed 28 November 2024, https://iremember.ru/memoirs/artilleristi/shavrin-aleksey-fedorovich/.

Sedoi, Aleksandr. Interview by Iu. Trifonov. *Ia pomniu*, 22 April 2013. Accessed 28 November 2024, https://iremember.ru/memoirs/artilleristi/sedoy-aleksandr-stepanovich.

Siniavskii, Georgii. Interview by G. Pernavskii. *Ia pomniu*, 24 April 2007. Accessed 7 February 2023; https://iremember.ru/memoirs/drugie-voyska/sinyavskiy-georgiy-evtikhievich/.

Skorobogatova, Anna. Interview by A. O. Korytov and K. Chirkin. *Ia pomniu*, 7 December 2010. Accessed 21 December 2023, https://iremember.ru/memoirs/svyazisti/skorobogatova-anna-makarovna/.

Solov'ev, Aleksandr. Interview by N. Chobanu. *Ia pomniu*, 3 February 2009. Accessed 27 May 2016, http://iremember.ru/memoirs/razvedchiki/solovev-aleksandr-ivanovich/.

Toptygin, Aleksandr. Interview by A. Chuprov and S. Oleinik. *Ia pomniu*, 26 February 2013. Accessed 28 November 2024, https://iremember.ru/memoirs/svyazisti/toptigin-aleksandr-nikolaevich/.

Tsalik, Boris. Interview by A. Ivashin. *Ia pomniu*, 27 March 2014. Accessed 19 December 2020, https://iremember.ru/memoirs/svyazisti/tsalik-boris-moiseevich/.

Tsurkan, Mikhail. Interview by N. Chobanu. *Ia pomniu*, 28 September 2008. Accessed 28 November 2024, http://iremember.ru/saperi/tsurkan-mikhail-antonovich.html.

Ustimenko, Aleksei. Interview by S. Smoliakov. *Ia pomniu*, 7 October 2016. Accessed 13 August 2016, http://iremember.ru/memoirs/minometchiki/ustimenko-aleksey-petrovich/.

Zubko, Nikolai. Interview by Iu. Trifonov. *Ia pomniu*, 31 July 2012. Accessed 27 May 2016, http://iremember.ru/memoirs/pekhotintsi/zubko-nikolay-yakovlevich/.

Author's Interviews

Bačlija, Grgo. *Interview by Vojin Majstorović*, 16 May 2012.
Đurušić, Mihajlo. *Interview by Vojin Majstorović*, 19 April 2012.
Đurišić, Nadežda. *Interview by Vojin Majstorović*, 19 April 2012.
Filipović, Bratislav. *Interview by Vojin Majstorović*, 13 March 2012.
Ilić, Živojin. *Interview by Vojin Majstorović*, 17 April 2012.
Novaković, Dušan. *Interview by Vojin Majstorović*, 4 April 2012.
Novaković, Milica. *Interview by Vojin Majstorović*, 4 April 2012.
Petković, Radmila. *Interview by Vojin Majstorović*, 27 May 2012.
Protić, Divna. *Interview by Vojin Majstorović*, 31 May 2012.
Protić, Vera. *Interview by Vojin Majstorović*, 13 March and 27 May 2012.
Stojanović, Božidar. *Interview by Vojin Majstorović*, 20 April 2012.

Newspapers/Journals

Aleksandrov, Georgi. "Tovarishch Ehrenburg uproshcaet." *Pravda* 89, 14 April 1945.

Secondary Sources

Achakso, V. I., et al., eds. *Istoriia mirovoi voiny, 1939–1945 v 12 tomakh, Porazhenie militaristskoi Iaponii. Okonchanie vtoroi mirovoi voinyvol. 11*. Moscow: Voenizdat, 1980.

Allen, David. "The Reporting and Underreporting of Rape." *Southern Economic Journal* 73.3. (2007): 623–641.

Al'tman, Il'ia. *Zhertvy nenavisti. Kholokost v SSSR 1941–1945*. Moskva: Kovcheg, 2002.

Alison, Miranda. "Wartime Sexual Violence: Women's Human Rights and Questions of Masculinity." *Review of International Studies* 33 (2007): 75–90.

Applebaum, Rachel. *Empire of Friends: Soviet Power and Socialist Internationalism in Cold War Czechoslovakia*. Ithaca: Cornell University Press, 2019.

Arad, Yitzhak. *The Holocaust in the Soviet Union*. Lincoln: University of Nebraska Press, 2009.

Artem'ev, A. P. *Bratskii boevoi soiuz narodov SSSR v Velikoi Otechestvennoi voine*. Moscow: Mysl, 1975.

Axorthy, Mark. *Third Axis, Fourth Ally: Romanian armed forces in the European war, 1941–1945*. London: Arms and Armour, 1995.

Bartov, Omer. *The Eastern Front 1941–1945: German Troops and the Barbarisation of Warfare*. Oxford: Oxford University Press, 1985.

Bauer, Ingrid and Huber, Renate. "Sexual Encounters across (Former) Enemy Borderlines." In *Sexuality in Austria: Contemporary Austrian Studies*. Volume 15. Edited by Gunter Bischof, Anton Pelinka and Dagmar Herzog. New Brunswick: Transaction Publishers, 2007.

Bellamy, Chris. *Absolute War: Soviet Russia in the Second World War: A Modern History*. London: Macmillan, 2007.

Beevor, Anthony. *Ardennes 1944: The Battle of the Bulge*. New York: Penguin, 2016.

Beevor, Anthony. *The Fall of Berlin 1945*. New York: Viking, 2002.
Beevor, Anthony and Vinogradova, Luba, eds. *A Writer at War: Vasily Grossman with the Red Army, 1941–1945*. New York: Pantheon Books, 2005.
Berg, Matthew Paul. "'Caught Between Iwan and the Weihnachtsmann:' Occupation, the Marshall Plan, and Austrian Identity." In *The Marshall Plan in Austria: Contemporary Austrian Studies*. Volume 8. Edited by Gunther Bischof, Anton Pelinka and Dieter Stiefel. New Brunswick: Transaction Publishers, 2001.
Bergen, Doris. "Sexual Violence in the Holocaust: Unique and Typical?" in *Lessons and Legacies VII*. Edited by Dagmar Herzog. Evanston: Northwestern University Press, 2007.
Bergen, Doris. *War & Genocide: A Concise History of the Holocaust*, 3rd ed. Lanham: Rowman & Littlefield, 2016.
Berkhoff, Karel. *Harvest of Despair: Life and Death in Ukraine under Nazi Rule*. Cambridge: Belknap Press of Harvard University Press, 2004.
Berkhoff, Karel. *Motherland in Danger: Soviet Propaganda during World War II*. Cambridge: Harvard University Press, 2012.
Berkhoff, Karel and Bernstein, Seth. "Remembering War, Remaining Soviet: Digital Commemoration of World War II in Putin's Russia." *Memory Studies*, forthcoming fall 2016.
Berkhoff, Karel. *Return to the Motherland Displaced Soviets in WWII and the Cold War*. Ithaca: Cornell University Press, 2023.
Biddiscombe, Perry. "Prodding the Russian Bear: Pro-German Resistance in Romania, 1944–1945." *European History Quarterly* 23.2 (1993): 193–232.
Bischl, Kerstin. "Telling Stories. Gender Relationships and Masculinity in the Red Army 1941–1945." In *Women and Men at War – A Gender Perspective on World War II and its Aftermath in Central and Eastern Europe*. Edited by Maren Röger and Ruth Leiserowitz. Osnabrück: Fibre, 2012.
Bischof, Gunter. *Austria in the First Cold War, 1945–1955*. New York: St. Martin's Press, 1999.
Biriuzov, S. S., et al. *Beogradska Operacija*, 2nd ed. Moscow-Belgrade: Institute for the Military History of the Ministry of Defense of the USSR and Vojnoistorijski Institut JNA, 1989.
Birstein, Vadim J. *SMERSH. Stalin's Secret Weapon: Soviet Military Counterintelligence in WWII*. London: Biteback, 2011.
Boll, Michael. "Reality and Illusion: The Allied Control Commission for Bulgaria as a Cause of the Cold War." *East European Quarterly* 17.4 (1983): 417–436.
Bogomolov, Vladimir. *'Zhizn moia ili ty prisnilas'mne…'* Moscow: Knizhnyi Klub, 2012.
Boshyk, Yury, ed. *Ukraine during World War II: History and its Aftermath: A Symposium*. Edmonton: Canadian Institute of Ukrainian Studies, 1986.
Braham, Randolph. "Preface." In *The Nazis' Last Victims: The Holocaust in Hungary*. Edited by Randolph Braham with Scott Miller. Detroit: Wayne State University Press in association with the USHMM, 1998.
Brandenberger, David. *National Bolshevism: Stalinist Mass Culture and the Formation of Modern Russian National Identity, 1931–1956*. Cambridge, Massachusetts: Harvard University Press, 2002.
Browning, Christopher. *Ordinary Men: Reserve Police Battalion 101 and the Final Solution in Poland*. New York: HarperCollins, 1992.

Brownmiller, Susan. *Against Our Will. Men, Women and Rape*. New York: Fawcett Books, 1975.

Budnitskii, Oleg. "In Parantheses: Extrajudicial Executions during the Great Patriotic War." *Cahiers du Monde Russe* 63.1 (2022): 223–239.

Budnitskii, Oleg. "Muzhchini i zhenshcini v Kransoi armii (1941–1945)." *Cashiers du Monde russe* 52.2 (2011): 405–422.

Budnitskii, Oleg and Rupp, Susan, "The Intelligentsia Meets the Enemy: Educated Soviet Officers in Defeated Germany, 1945." *Kritika* 10.3 (2009): 629–682.

Burds, Jeffrey. "Sexual Violence in Europe in World War II, 1939–1945." *Politics & Society* 37 (2009): 35–73.

Cameron, Sarah. *The Hungry Steppe: Famine, Violence, and the Making of Soviet Kazakhstan* Ithaca: Cornell University Press, 2018.

Carmack, Roberto J. *Kazakhstan in World War II: Mobilization and Ethnicity in the Soviet Empire*. Lawrence: University Press of Kansas, 2019.

Case, Holly. *Between States: The Transylvanian Question and the European Idea during WWII* Stanford: Stanford University Press, 2009.

Casu, Igor. "Stalinist Terror in Soviet Moldavia, 1940–1953." In *Stalinist Terror in Eastern Europe: Elite Purges and Mass Repression*. Edited by Kevin McDermott and Matthew Stibbe. Manchester: Manchester University Press, 2010.

Chambers, John, ed., *The Oxford Companion to American Military History*. Oxford University Press, 1999.

Constantinescu, N. N. *Romania's Economic History from the Beginnings to World War II* Bucharest: Editura Academiei Romane, 1994.

Cornelius, Deborah. *Hungary in World War II: Caught in the Cauldron*. New York: Fordham University Press, 2011.

Crampton, R. J. *Bulgaria*. Oxford: Oxford University Press, 2007.

Dale, Robert. "Re-Adjusting to Life after War: The Demobilization of Red Army Veterans in Leningrad and The Leningrad Region 1944–1950." PhD Thesis, Queen Mary, University of London, 2010.

Dallin, Alexander. *German Rule in Russia, 1941–1945*. London: MacMillan, 1957.

David-Fox, Michael. *Revolution of the Mind: Higher Learning among the Bolsheviks, 1918–1929*. Ithaca: Cornell University Press and Studies of the Harriman Institute, 1997.

David-Fox, Michael. *Showcasing the Great Experiment: Cultural Diplomacy and Western Visitors to the Soviet Union, 1921–1941*. New York: Oxford University Press, 2012.

Davidović, Goran and Timotijević, Miloš. "Dan posle: uništavanje JVuO i uspostavljanje vlasti komunista u čačanskom kraju 1944–1945." *Istorija 20. Veka* 22.2 (2004): 23–45.

Dean, Martin. *Collaboration in the Holocaust: Crimes of the Local Police in Belorussia and Ukraine, 1941–1944*. New York: St. Martin's Press, 2000.

Dear, I. C. "France." In *The Oxford Companion to World War II*. Oxford: Oxford University, 2001.

Deletant, Dennis. "Ghetto Experience in Golta, Transnistria, 1942–1944." *Holocaust and Genocide Studies* 18.1 (2004): 1–26.

Dimitrov, Vesselin. *Stalin's Cold War: Soviet Foreign Policy, Democracy and Communism in Bulgaria, 1941–1948*. New York: Palgrave Macmillan, 2008.

DiNardo, Richard. *Germany and the Axis Powers: From Coalition to Collapse*. Lawrence: University Press of Kansas, 2005.

Dumitru, Diana. *The State, Antisemitism, and Collaboration in the Holocaust: The Borderlands of Romania and the Soviet Union*. New York: Cambridge University Press, 2016.

Dunn, Walter S. *Stalin's Keys to Victory: The Rebirth of the Red Army*. Westport: Praeger Security International, 2006.

Eaton, Nicole. *German Blood, Slavic Soil: How Nazi Königsberg became Soviet Kaliningrad* Ithaca: Cornell University Press, 2023.

Edele, Mark. *Soviet Veterans of the Second World War: A Popular Movement in an Authoritarian Society 1941–1991*. Oxford: Oxford University Press, 2008.

Edele, Mark. *Stalin's Defectors: How Red Army Soldiers became Hitler's Collaborators*. Oxford: Oxford University Press, 2017.

Edele, Mark. "Take (No) Prisoners! The Red Army and German POWs, 1941–1943." *The Journal of Modern History* 88.2 (June 2016): 342–379.

Edele, Mark. "'What Are We Fighting for?' Loyalty in the Soviet War Effort, 1941–1945." *International Labor and Working-Class History* 84 (2013): 248–268.

Edele, Mark and Geyer, Michael. "States of Exception: The Nazi-Soviet War as a System of Violence, 1939–1945." In *Beyond Totalitarianism: Stalinism and Nazism Compared*. Edited by Sheila Fitzpatrick and Michael Geyer. Cambridge: Cambridge University Press, 2009.

Eisen, George and Stark, Tamás. "The 1941 Galician Deportation and the Kamenets-Podolsk Massacre: A Prologue to the Hungarian Holocaust." *Holocaust and Genocide Studies* 27.2 (2013): 207–241.

Eisterer, Klaus. "Austria under Allied Occupation." In *Austria in the Twentieth Century*. Edited by Rolf Steininger, Günter Bischof and Michael Gehler. New Brunswick: Transaction Publishers, 2002.

Filterz, Donald "Starvation Mortality in Soviet Home-Front Industrial Regions during World War II." In *Hunger and War: Food Provisioning in the Soviet Union during World War II*. Edited by Wendy Z. Goldman and Donald Filtzer. Bloomington & Indianapolis: Indiana University Press, 2015.

Fischer, Ronit. "Transnistria: The Holocaust in Romania." In *The Routledge History of the Holocaust*. Edited by Jonathan C. Friedman. New York: Routledge, 2011.

Fitzpatrick, Sheila. "Postwar Soviet Society: The Return to Normalcy, 1945–1953." In *Social Impact of War in World War II: Crucible of the Contemporary World: Commentary and Readings*. Edited by Lloyd Lee. London: M. E. Sharpe, 1991.

Fraser, Erica L. *Military Masculinity and Postwar Recovery in the Soviet Union*. Toronto: University of Toronto Press, 2019.

The French military casualties were 210,000, I. C. Dear, ed., "France" in The Oxford Companion to World War II (Oxford: Oxford University Press, 2001), accessed 27 May 2016, www.oxfordreference.com.myaccess.library.utoronto.ca/view/10.1093/acref/9780198604464.001.0001/acref-9780198604464-e-637?rskey=dnviOy&result=643.

Fruhstuck, Sabine. "Sexuality and Sexual Violence." In *Cambridge History of World War II Volume 3 Total War: Economy, Society, and Culture*. Edited by Michael Geyer and Adam Tooze. Cambridge: Cambridge University Press, 2015.

Gebhardt, Miriam. *Crimes Unspoken. The Rape of German Women at the End of the Second World War*. Translated Nick Somers. Malden: Polity Press, 2017.

Germann, Richard. "Austrian Soldiers and Generals in World War II." In *New Perspective on Austrians and World War II: Contemporary Austrian Studies*. Edited by Gunter Bischof, Frits Plasser and Barbara Stelzl-Marx. 17. New Brunswick: Transaction Publishers, 2009.

Gertjejanssen, Wendy. "Victims, Heroes, Survivors: Sexual Violence on the Eastern Front during World War II." PhD Disseration, University of Minnesota, 2004.

Giurescu, Dinu. *Romania's Communist Takeover: The Radescu Government*. Boulder: East European Monographs, 1994.

Goldstein, Joshua. *War and Gender. How Gender Shapes the War System and Vice Versa*. Cambridge: Cambridge University Press, 2001.

Grischany, Thomas R. "Mental Aspects of Austrian Wehrmacht Service." In *New Perspective on Austrians and World War II: Contemporary Austrian Studies*. Edited by Gunter Bischof, Frits Plasser and Barbara Stelzl-Marx. 17. New Brunswick: Transaction Publishers, 2009.

Grischany, Thomas R. *Romania in the Second World War 1939–1945*. Boulder: East European Monographs, 2000.

Glantz, David. *Colossus Reborn: The Red Army at War, 1941–1943*. Lawrence: University Press of Kansas, 2005.

Glantz, David. *Red Storm over the Balkans*. Kansas: University Press of Kansas, 2007.

Glantz, David. *When Titans Clashed: How the Red Army Stopped Hitler*. Lawrence: University Press of Kansas, 1995.

Glantz, David. "Stalin's Strategic Intentions, 1941–1945: Soviet Military Operations as Indicators of Stalin's Postwar Territorial Ambitions." *Journal of Slavic Military Studies* 27.4 (2014): 676–720.

Glass, Charles. *The Deserters: A Hidden History of World War II*. New York: The Penguin Press, 2013.

Goedde, Petra. *GIs and Germans: Culture, Gender and Foreign Relations, 1945–1949*. New Haven: Yale University Press, 2003.

Goldman, Wendy. "Introduction: The Politics of Food and War." In *Hunger and War: Food Provisioning in the Soviet Union during World War II*. Edited by Wendy Z. Goldman and Donald Filtzer. Bloomington & Indianapolis: Indiana University Press, 2015.

Goldman, Wendy. *Women at the Gates*. Cambridge: Cambridge University Press, 2002.

Grekov, N. V. "Deiatel'nost' Kontrrazvedki, SMERSH, po Presecheniiu Izmeny i Dezertirstva v voiskakh vo vremia Velikoi Otechestvennoi Voiny 1941–1945 gg." *Voenno-Istoricheskii Zhurnal* 2 (2006): 42–48.

Grinevich, Vladislav. "Z istorii formuvannia ukrains'kogo radians'koi patriotizmu u roki radians'ko-nimets'koi viinii 1941–1945 rr." *Problemi istorii Ukraini: fakti, suzhdennia, poshuki* 13 (2005): 419–433.

Grinevich, Vladislav. "Voennye mobilizatsii v Ukraine v 1943–1944 godakh. 'Vy dolzhny smyt' svoei krov'iu vinu pered Rodinoi i ee velikim vozhdem tovarishcem Stalinym,'" *Zerkalo nedeli Ukraina*, 2 September 2005, accessed 23 March 2014, http://gazeta.zn.ua/SOCIETY/voennye_mobilizatsii_v_ukraine_v_19431944_godah_vy_dolzhny_smyt_svoey_krovyu_vinu_pered_rodinoy_i_ee.html.

Gromyko, A. A., et al., eds. *SSSR-Avstriia: dokumenty i materialy*. Moscow: Politizdat, 1980.

Gross, Jan. *Neighbors: The Destruction of the Jewish Community in Jedwabne, Poland*. Princeton: Princeton University Press, 2001.

Grossman, Atina. "The 'Big Rape': Sex and Sexual Violence, War, and Occupation in Post-World War II Memory and Imagination." In *Sexual Violence in Conflict Zones: From the Ancient World to the Era of Human Rights*. Edited by Elizabeth Heineman.137–151. Philadelphia: University of Pennsylvania Press, 2011.

Grossman, Atina. "A Question of Silence: The Rape of German Women by Occupation Soldiers." *October* 72 (1995): 42–63.

Hajkova, Anna. *The Last Ghetto: An Everyday History of Theresienstadt*. Oxford: Oxford University Press, 2020.

Harris, James. "Was Stalin a Weak Dictator?" *The Journal of Modern History* 75.2 (2003): 375–386.

Harrison, Richard, ed. *The Budapest Operation 1945: An Operational-Strategic Study Soviet General Staff*. Translated by Richard W. Harrison. Solihull: Helion & Company, 2017.

Harrison, Richard, ed. *The Iasi-Kishinev Operation: The Red Army's Summer Offensive into the Balkans (20–20 August 1944): Soviet General Staff*. Translated Richard Harrison. Solihull: Helion & Company, 2017.

Harward, Grant T. *Romania's Holy War: Soldiers, Motivation, and the Holocaust*. Ithaca: Cornell University Press, 2021.

Harward, Grant T. "Peasant Armies at Odds: Romanian-Soviet Interaction during the Second World War." *The Journal of Slavic Military Studies* 24.2 (2001): 274–298.

Heineman, Elizabeth D. "Introduction: The History of Sexual Violence in Conflict Zones." In *Sexual Violence in Conflict Zones: From the Ancient World to the Era of Human Rights*. Edited by Elizabeth D. Heineman. Philadelphia: University of Pennsylvania Press, 2011.

Heineman, Elizabeth D. "Gender, Sexuality, and Coming to Terms with the Nazi Past." *Central European History* 38.1 (2005): 41–74.

Hellbeck, Jochen. *Stalingrad: The City that Defeated the Third Reich*. Translated by Christopher Tauchen and Dominic Bonfiglio. New York: Public Affairs, 2015.

Herzog, Dogmar. "Introduction: War and Sexuality in Europe's Twentieth Century." In *Brutality and Desire: War and Sexuality in Europe's Twentieth Century*. Edited by Dogmar Herzog. 1–15. London: Palgrave Macmillan, 2009.

Hill, Alexander. *The Red Army and the Second World War*. Cambridge: Cambridge University Press, 2017.

Hlihor, Constantin and Scurtu, Ion. *The Red Army in Romania*. Iasi, Oxford, Portland: The Center for Romanian Studies, 2000.

Iber, Walter M. "Occupation and Exploitation: Soviet Economic Policy toward Austria from 1945 to 1955/63." In *The Red Army in Austria: The Soviet Occupation, 1945–1955*. Edited by Karner Stefan and Barbara Stelzl-Marx. Translated by Alex J. Kay. Lanham: Lexington Books, 2020.

Ioanid, Radu. *The Holocaust in Romania: The Destruction of Jews and Gypsies under the Antonescu Regime, 1940–1944*. Chicago: Ivan R. Dee, 2000.

Ironside, Kristy. *A Full-Value Ruble: The Promise of Prosperity in the Postwar Soviet Union*. Cambridge: Harvard University Press, 2021.

Jansen, Marc and Petrov, Nikita. "Mass Terror and the Court: The Military Collegium of the USSR." *Europe-Asia Studies* 58.4 (2006): 589–602.

Johnson, Daniel. "Red Army troops raped even Russian women as they freed them from camps." *The Telegraph* 24 January 2002, accessed 9 August 2016, www.telegraph.co.uk/news/worldnews/europe/russia/1382565/Red-Army-troops-raped-even-Russian-women-as-they-freed-them-from-camps.html.

Johnson, Daniel. "Russian angry at war rape claims." *The Telegraph* 25 February 2002, accessed 9 August 2016, www.telegraph.co.uk/news/worldnews/europe/russia/1382682/Russians-angry-at-war-rape-claims.html.

Johnston, Timothy. *Being Soviet: Identity, Rumour, and Everyday Life under Stalin, 1939–1953*. Oxford: Oxford University Press, 2011.

Jug, Steven. "All Stalin's Men? Soldierly Masculinities in the Soviet War Effort, 1938–1945." PhD Dissertation, University of Illinois at Urbana-Champaign, 2014.

Jug, Steven. "Red Army Romance: Preserving Masculine Hegemony in Mixed Gender Combat Units, 1943–1944." *Journal of War & Culture Studies* 5.3 (2013): 321–334.

Kay, Alex. "'The Purpose of the Russian Campaign is the Decimation of the Slavic Population by Thirty Million,' the Radicalization of German Food Policy in Early 1941." In *Nazi Policy on the Eastern Front eds., 1941: Total War, Genocide, and Radicalization*. Edited by Alex J Kay, Jeff Rutherford and David Stahel. Rochester: University of Rochester Press, 2012.

Kazyulina, Regina. "Women's Antifascist Resistance on German-Occupied Territory through the Lens of Soviet Leaflets, 1941–1945." *Journal of Contemporary History* 56.4 (2021): 1126–1146.

Kenez, Peter. *Hungary from the Nazis to the Soviets. The Establishment of the Communist Regime in Hungary, 1944–1948*. Cambridge: Cambridge University Press, 2006.

Kercher, Stephen. "Remembering Alice de Barcza – one of the most interesting women to teach at UW Oshkosh." UW Oshkosh Today, 10 March 2021. Accessed 21 March 2021, https://uwosh.edu/today/95239/remembering-alice-de-barcza-one-of-the-most-interesting-women-to-teach-at-uw-oshkosh/.

Khlevniuk, Oleg. "Stalin and the Generals: Reconstructing Trust during World War II." *Europe-Asia Studies* 74.4 (2002): 523–544.

Kirsanov, N. A. and Drobiazko, S. I. "Velikaia Otechestvennaia voina 1941–1945 gg: natsional'nye i dobrovol'cheskie formirovaniia po raznye storony fronta." *Otechestvennaia Istoriia* 6 (2001): 60–75. Accessed 27 May 2016, http://militera.lib.ru/research/1/art/card41557.html.

Knight, Robert. "The Carinthian Slovenes." In *Power and the People: A Social History of Central European Politics, 1945–1956*. Edited by Eleonore Breuning, Jill Lewis and Gareth Pritchard. Manchester: Manchester University Press, 2005.

Knoll, Harold and Stelzl-Marx, Barbara. "Stalin's Judiciary in Austria: Arrests and Convictions during the Occupation." In *The Red Army in Austria: The Soviet Occupation, 1945–1955*. Edited by Karner Stefan and Barbara Stelzl-Marx. Translated by Alex J. Kay. Lanham: Lexington Books, 2020.

Kondayanidi, Anita. "The Liberating Experience: War Correspondents, Red Army Soldiers, and the Nazi Extermination Camps." *Russian Review* 69.3 (2010): 438–462.

Krainiukov, K. V. *Partiino-politicheskaia rabota v sovetskikh vooruzhennykh silakh v gody velikoi otechestvennoĭ voiny 1941–1945: kratkii istoricheskii obzor*. Moscow: Voenizdat, 1968.

Kragh, Martin. "Stalinist Labour Coercion during World War II: An Economic Approach." *Europe-Asia Studies* 63.7 (2011): 1253–1273.

Krivitskii, Aleksandr. *Russkii ofitser za rubezhom*. Moscow: Voenizdat, 1946.

Krivosheev, Georgiĭ, ed. *Rossiia i SSSR v voĭnakh XX veka. Poteri vooruzhennykh sil. Statisticheskoe issledovanie*. Moskva: Olma Press, 2001.

Krivozhin, Gennadii, Nosov, Aleksei and Romanov, Dmitrii. *Zolotye Zvezdy Poles'ia. Ocherki o Geroiakh Sovetskogo Soiuza*. Kiev: Izdatel'stvo Politicheskoi literatury Ukrainy, 1978.

Krylova, Anna. *Soviet Women in Combat: A History of Violence on the Eastern Front*. Cambridge: Cambridge University Press, 2010.

Kruttschnitt, Candace, Kalsbeek, William D and House, Carol C., eds., *Estimating the Incidence of Rape and Sexual Assault*. Washington DC: The National Academies Press, 2014.

Kucherenko, Olga. "Reluctant Traitors: The Politics of Survival in Romanian-occupied Odessa." *European Review of History* 15.2 (2008): 143–155.

Kunt, Gergely. "Wartime Sexual Economy as Seen through a Hungarian Woman's World War II Diary." *Feminist Studies* 43.1 (2017): 108–133.

Kuznetsov, P. G. *Dni boevye*. Moscow: Voenizdat, 1959.

Kuznetsov, P. G. *Marshal Tolbukhin*. Moscow: Voennoe izdatel'stvo minsterstva oborony SSSR, 1966.

Lawlor, Ruth. "Contested Crimes: Race, Gender, and Nation in Histories of GI Sexual Violence, World War II." *The Journal of Military History* 84.2 (2020): 541–569.

Lawlor, Ruth. "The Stuttgart Incident and the Uses of History." *Diplomatic History* 46.1 (2022): 70–96.

Lawlor, Ruth. "The Wartime Battlefield of Sex." *Modern American History* 4.2 (2021): 209–212.

Lawlor, Ruth and Majstorović, Vojin. "Ideology and Legitimacy: A Comparative Account of Sexual Violence in the U.S. and Red Armies in the Second World War." Unpublished manuscript, 15 June 2025.

Liedtke, Liedtke Gregory. "Furor Teutonicus: German Offensives and Counter-Attacks on the Eastern Front, August 1943 to March 1945." *The Journal of Slavic Military Studies* 21.3 (2008): 563–587.

Lilly, Robert. *Taken by Force: Rape and American GIs in Europe during World War II*. New York: Palgrave Macmillan, 2007.

Lenoe, Matt E. "Emotions and Psychological Survival in the Red Army, 1941–1942." *Kritika: Explorations in Russian and Eurasian History* 22.1 (Spring 2021): 313–344.

Lewis, Jill. *Workers and Politics in Occupied Austria 1945–1945*. Manchester: Manchester University Press, 2007.

Loew, Keith. *Savage Continent: Europe in the Aftermath of World War II*. New York: St. Martin's Press, 2012.

Lopukhovsky, Lev and Kavalerchik, Boris. *The Price of Victory: The Red Army's Casualties in the Great Patriotic War*. Translated by Harold Orenstein. Barnsley: Pen and Sword Military, 2017.

Lower, Wendy. *Nazi Empire Building and the Holocaust in Ukraine*. Chapel Hill: University of North Carolina Press, 2005.

Luknitskii, Pavel. *Leningrad deistvuet...frontovoi dnevnik*. Moscow: Sovetksii pisatel', 1971. Accessed 10 January 2023, http://militera.lib.ru/db/luknitsky_pn/03.html.

Majstorovic, Vojin. "The Red Army in Yugoslavia, 1944–1945." *Slavic Review* 75.2 (2016): 396–421.

Manley, Rebecca. *To the Tashkent Station: Evacuation and Survival in the Soviet Union at War*. Ithaca: Cornell University Press, 2009.

Mark, James. "Remembering Rape: Divided Social Memory and the Red Army in Hungary 1944–1945." *Past & Present* 188 (2005): 133–161.

Markwick, Roger and Cardona, Euridice. *Soviet Women on the Frontline in the Second World War*. New York: Palgrave Macmillan, 2012.

Marples, David, Baidaus, Eduard and Melentyeva, Mariya. "Causes of the 1932 Famine in Soviet Ukraine: Debates at the Third All-Ukrainian Party." *Canadian Slavonic Papers* 56.3 (2014): 291–312.

Matsulenko, V. A. "Combat Activities by the Forces of the Third Ukrainian Front's 37th Army in the Iasi-Kishinev Operation (August 1944)" (Candidate Dissertation [Soviet equivalent of doctoral dissertation], Frunze Military Academy, 1951)." Reproduced in *The Iasi-Kishinev Operation: The Red Army's Summer Offensive into the Balkans (20–20 August 1944): Soviet General Staff*. Edited by Richard Harrison. Translated by Richard Harrison. Solihull: Helion & Company, 2017.

McReynolds, Louise. "Dateline Stalingrad: Newspaper Correspondents at the Front." In *Culture and Entertainment in Wartime Russia*. Edited by Richard Stites. Bloomington and Indianapolis: Indiana University Press, 1995.

Melnyk, Oleksandr. "Political Identity under Invasion: Kherson Oblast in Summer 1941." *Journal of Ukrainian Studies* 30.1 (2005): 47–73.

Melnyk, Oleksandr. "Stalinist Justice as a Site of Memory: Anti-Jewish Violence in Kyiv's Podil District in September 1941 through the Prism of Soviet Investigative Documents." *Jahrbücher für Geschichte Osteuropas* 61.2 (2013): 223–248.

Melnyk, Oleksandr. *World War II as an Identity Project: Historicism, Legitimacy Contests, and the (Re-) Construction of Political Communities in Ukraine, 1939–1946*. New York: Columbia University Press, 2023.

Merridale, Catherine. "Culture, Ideology and Combat in the Red Army 1939–1945." *Journal of Contemporary History* 41 (April 2006): 203–209.

Merridale, Catherine. *Ivan's War: Life and Death in the Red Army*. New York: Picador, Henry Holt and Company, 2006.

Merridale, Catherine. "Masculinity at War: Did Gender Matter in the Soviet army?" *Journal of War & Culture Studies* 5.3 (2013): 307–320.

Mesner, Maria. "Gender and Abortion after the Second World War: the Austrian Case in a Comparative Perspective." In *Power and the People: A Social History of Central European Politics, 1945–1956*. Edited by Eleonore Breuning, Jill Lewis and Gareth Pritchard. Manchester: Manchester University Press, 2005.

Mevius, Martvin. *Agents of Moscow: The Hungarian Communist Party and the Origins of Socialist Patriotism 1941–1953*. Oxford: Oxford University Press, 2005.

Mikhailik, Aleksandr Georgievich. "Istoriia boevykh deistvii Krasnoi armii na territorii Vengrii (sentiabr' 1944 – aprel' 1945 gg)." PhD Dissertation, Voronezh State Pedagogical University, 2016.

Milesku, Spetarul, et al., eds. *Istoriia Respubliki Moldova. S drevneishikh vremen do nashikh dnei*. Kishinev: Elan-Poligraf, 2002.

Miron, Ramona and Dumitrescu, Horia. "Abuzurile Armatei Rosii in Vrancea." In *Chronica Vrancei*. Edited by Horia Dumitrescu. Pallas: Focșani, 2006.

Moeller, Robert G. *War Stories: The Search for a Usable Past in the Federal Republic of Germany*. Berkeley: University of California Press, 2001.

Morris, Madeline. "Force of Arms: Rape, War, and Military Culture." *Duke Law Journal* 45.4 (1996): 651–781.

Mukhin, Iuri. *Po povetske i po prizyvu. Nekadrovye Soldaty Velikoi Otechestvennoi Voine*. Moscow: Iuaza/Eksmo, 2005.

Mühlhäuser, Regina. "Between 'Racial Awareness' and Fantasies of Potency: Nazi Sexual Politics in the Occupied Territories of the Soviet Union, 1942–1945." In *Brutality and Desire: War and Sexuality in Europe's Twentieth Century*. Edited by Dagmar Herzog. Basingstoke: Palgrave Macmillan, 2009.

Mühlhäuser, Regina. *Sex and the Nazi Soldier: Violent, Commercial and Consensual Encounters during the War in the Soviet Union, 1941–45*. Translated by Jessica Spengler. Edinburgh: Edinburgh University Press, 2021.

Mühlhäuser, Regina. "'You have to Anticipate What Eludes Calculation:' Reconceptualizing Sexual Violence as Weapon and Strategy of War." In *Plain Sight: Sexual Violence in Armed Conflict*." Edited by Gaby Zipfel, Regina Mühlhäuser and Kirsten Campell. New Delhi: Zubaan Pubishers Pvt. Ltd., 2019.

Myles, Bruce. *Night Witches: The Untold Story of Soviet Women in Combat*. Edinburgh: Mainstream, 1981.

Myles, Bruce. "The Unquestioned Crime: Sexual Violence by German Soldiers during the War of Annihilation in the Soviet Union, 1941–1945." In *Rape in Wartime*. Edited by Raphaëlle Branche and Fabrice Virgili. New York: Palgrave Macmillan, 2012.

Naimark, Norman. *The Russians in Germany: A History of the Soviet Zone of Occupation, 1945–49*. Cambridge: Harvard University Press, 1995.

Nevenkin, Karmen. *Take Budapest: The Struggle for Hungary Autumn 1944*. Stroud: The History Press, 2012.

Noskova, A. F. "Kem byli v Vostochnoi Evrope soldaty Krasnoi Armii v 1945 godu: svoboditeliami, okkupantami, ili…?" *Vestnik MGIMO Universiteta* 5 (2010): 65–72.

Overy, Richard. *Russia's War*. New York: Penguin Books, 1998.

Pannacci, Raffaello. "Sex, Military Brothels and Gender Violence during the Italian Campaign in the USSR, 1941–3." *Journal of Contemporary History* 55.1 (2020): 75–96.

Penter, Tanja. "Local Collaborators on Trial: Soviet War Crimes Trials under Stalin (1943–1953)." *Cahiers du Monde russe* 49.4 (2008): 341–364.

Peri, Alexis. *The War Within: Diaries from the Siege of Leningrad*. Cambridge: Harvard University Press, 2017.

Petrone, Karen. "Masculinity and Heroism in Imperial and Soviet Military-Patriotic Cultures." In *Russian Masculinities in History and Culture*. Edited by B. E. Clements, R. Friedman and D. Healy. New York: Palgrave, 2001.

Petrov, Nikita. "The Internal Troops of the NKVD in the System of Soviets Organs of Repression in Austria, 1945–1946." In *New Perspective on Austrians and World War II, Contemporary Austrian Studies*. Volume 17. Edited by Gunter Bischof, Frits Plasser and Barbara Stelzl-Marx. New Brunswick: Transaction Publishers, 2009.

Petrov, Nikita. *Kto rukovodil organami gosbezopasnosti, 1941–1954: Spravochnik*. Moscow: Zven'ia, 2010.

Petukhov, N. A. *Istoriia voennykh sudov Rossii*. Moscow: Norma, 2003.

Phillips, Anna. *Power and Influence after the Cold War: Germany in East-Central Europe*. Lanham: Rowman & Littlefield, 2000.

Pliev, I. A. *V boiakh za osvobozhdenie Rumynii, Vengrii, Chekhoslovakii*. Ordzhonikidze: Ir, 1971.

Polian, Pavel. *Against Their Will: the History and Geography of Forced Migrations in the USSR*. Budapest: Central European University, 2004.

Popov, I. G. *Batal'ony idut na zapad*. Moscow: Izdatel'stvo Moskovskogo universiteta, 1985.

Popović, Nikola. *Jugoslovensko-sovejtski odnosi u drugom svetskom ratu*. Belgrade: Institut za savremenu istoriju, 1988.

Portugal'skii, R. M., Domank, A. S. and Kovalenko, A. P. *Marshal S. K. Timoshenko*. Moscow: Izdatel'stvo MOF 'Pobeda-1945 god', 1994.

Prusin, Alexander. "'Fascist Criminals to the Gallows!': The Holocaust and Soviet War Crimes Trials, December 1945–February 1946." *Holocaust and Genocide Studies* 17.1 (2003): 1–30.

Prusin, Alexander. *Nationalizing the Borderland: War, Ethnicity, and Anti-Jewish Violence in East Galicia, 1914–1920*. Tuscaloosa: University of Alabama Press, 2005.

Prusin, Alexander. *Serbia under the Swastika: A World War II Occupation*. Urbana: University of Illinois Press, 2017.

Pyl'cyn, Alexander V. *Penalty Strike: The Memoirs of a Red Army Penaal Company Commander, 1943–1945*. Edited by Artem Drabkin. Translated by Bair Irincheev. Mechanicsburg: Stackpole Books, 2009.

Radu, Mariana-Narcisa. "The Incrimination of Sexual Intercourse with a Minor." *Law Study* 20.2 (2012): 44–53.

Reese, Roger. *The Soviet Military Experience: A History of the Soviet Army, 1917–1991*. New York: Routledge, 2001.

Reese, Roger. *Why Stalin's Soldiers Fought: The Red Army's Military Effectiveness in World War II*. Kansas: University of Kansas Press, 2011.

Roberts, Geoffrey. *Stalin's General: The Life of Georgy Zhukov*. New York: Random House, 2012.

Roberts, Mary Louise. *What Soldiers Do: Sex and the American GI in World War II France*. Chicago: The University of Chicago Press, 2013.

Roger, Maren. "The Sexual Policies and Sexual Realities of the German Occupiers in Poland in the Second World War." *Contemporary European History* 23.1 (2014): 1–21.

Romanov, A. I. *Nights Are Longest There: A Memoir of the Soviet Security Services*. Boston-Toronto: Little, Brown and Company, 1972.

Rossino, Alexander. *Hitler Strikes Poland: Blitzkrieg, Ideology and Atrocity*. Lawrence: University Press of Kansas, 2003.

Rothstein, Robert A. "Homeland, Home Town, and Battlefield: The Popular Song." In *Culture and Entertainment in Wartime Russia*. Edited by Richard Stites. Bloomington and Indianapolis: Indiana University Press, 1995.

Rudakova, Daria. "Soviet Women Collaborators in Occupied Ukraine 1941–1945." *Australian Journal of Politics and History* 62.4 (2016): 529–545.

Rutherford, Jeff. *Combat and Genocide on the Eastern Front: The German Infantry's War, 1941–1944*. Cambridge: Cambridge University Press, 2014.

Ruvolo, Francesca. "American Soldiers and Italian Women: The Sexual Economy of Occupied Naples, 1943–1945." M.A. Thesis: Rutgers University, 2016.

Rzheshevskii, Oleg. "Berlinskaia Operatsiia 1945g.: Diskussia Prodolzhaetsia." *Mir Istorii* 4 (2002). Accessed 9 August 2016, http://archive.is/RoR3l.

Schechter, Brandon. *The Stuff of Soldiers: A History of the Red Army in World War II through Material Objects*. Ithaca: Cornell University Press, 2019.

Shefov, Nikolai. *Bitvy Rossii*. Moscow: AST, 2006.

Shternshis, Anna. *Soviet Jews, Soviet and Kosher: Jewish Popular Culture in the Soviet Union, 1923–1939*. Bloomington: Indiana University Press, 2006.

Shternshis, Anna. "Between Life and Death: Why Some Soviet Jews Decided to Leave and Others to Stay in 1941." *Kritika* 15.3 (2014): 477–504.

Siebold, Guy L. "The Essence of Military Group Cohesion." *Armed Forces & Society* 33.2 (2007): 286–295.

Slaveski, Filip. *The Soviet Occupation of Germany: Hunger, Mass Violence and the Struggle for Peace, 1945–1947*. Cambridge: Cambridge University Press, 2013.

Snyder, David Raub. *Sex Crimes under the Wehrmacht*. Lincoln: University of Nebraska Press, 2007.

Sokolov, Boris. *Marshal Malinovskii: Hero of the Soviet Union: Architect of the Modern Soviet Army*. Translated by Richward W. Harrison. Solihull: Helion & Company, 2017.

Solonari, Vladimir. *A Satellite Empire: Romanian Rule in Southwestern Ukraine, 1941–1944*. Ithaca: Cornell University Press, 2019.

Solonari, Vladimir. *Purifying the Nation: Population Exchange and Ethnic Cleansing in Nazi-Allied Romania*. Washington DC: Johns Hopkins University Press, 2010.

Stanciu, Mariana and Mihailescu, Adina. "Poverty in Romania during 1918–1945." *Journal of Community Positive Practices* 18.2 (2018): 13–31.

Statiev, Alex. "Penal Units in the Red Army." *Europe-Asia Studies* 62.5 (2010): 721–747.

Stelzl-Marx, Barbara. *Stalins Soldaten in Österreich: Die Innensicht der sowjetischen Besatzung 1945–1955*. Vienna: Böhlau Verlag Wien, 2012.

Stone, David. "The 1945 Ethridge Mission to Bulgaria and Romania and the Origins of the Cold War in the Balkans." *Diplomacy & Statecraft* 17.1 (1996): 93–112.

Streit, Christian. "Soviet Prisoners of War in the Hands of the Wehrmacht." In *War of Extermination: The German Military in World War II, 1941–1944*. Edited by Hannes Heer and Klaus Naumann. New York: Berghahn Books, 2000.

Swain, Geoffrey and Swain, Nigel. *Eastern Europe since 1945*. New York: Palgrave Macmillan, 2009.

Sygkelos, Yannis. *Nationalism from the Left: The Bulgarian Communist Party during the Second World War and the early Post-War Years*. Boston: Brill, 2011.

Számvéber, Norbert. *The Sword behind the Shield: A Combat History of the German Efforts to Relieve Budapest 1945 – Operation 'Konrad' I, III, III*. West Midlands: Helion & Company, 2015.

Tanaka, Yuki. "War, Rape and Patriarchy: The Japanese Experience." In *Plain Sight: Sexual Violence in Armed Conflict*. Edited by Gaby Zipfel, Regina Mühlhäuser and Kirsten Campell. New Delhi: Zubaan Pubishers Pvt. Ltd., 2019.

Timofejev, Aleksej. *Rusi i drugi svetski rat u Jugoslaviji: Uticaj SSSR-a i ruskih emigranata na događaje u Jugoslaviji 1941–1945*. Belgrade: Institut za noviju istoriju Srbije, 2011.

Tolbuko, V. F. and Baryshev, N. A. *Ot Vidina do Belgrada: istoriko-memuarnyi ocherk o boevykh deistviiakh sovetskikh tankistov v belgradskoi operatsii*. Moscow: Nauka, 1968.

Tomasevich, Jozo. *War and Revolution in Yugoslavia 1941–1945: Occupation and Collaboration*. Stanford: Stanford University Press, 2001.

Trifković, Gaj. "'Damned Good Amateurs': Yugoslav Partisans in the Belgrade Operation 1944." *Journal of Slavic Military Studies* 29.2 (2016): 253–278.

Trifković, Gaj. "Operacije Crvene Armije u Sjevernoj Jugoslaviji 1944–1945. Iz Sovjetskih dokumenata." *Vojnoistorijski glasnik* 2 (2017): 205–233.

Trifković, Gaj. "'The German Anabasis': The Breakthrough of Army Group E from Eastern Yugoslavia 1944." *Journal of Slavic Military Studies* 30.4 (2017): 602–629.

Uldricks, Teddy. "War, Politics and Memory: Russian Historians Reevaluate the Origins of World War II." *History & Memory* 21.2 (2009): 60–82.

Ungváry, Krisztián. "Hungarian Occupation Forces in the Ukraine 1941–1942: The Historiographical Context." *The Journal of Slavic Military Studies* 20.1 (2007): 81–120.

Ungváry, Krisztián. *The Siege of Budapest: 100 days in World War II*. Translated by Ladislaus Lob. New Haven: Yale University Press, 2005.

Valeva, E. L. "Bolgariia v nachale vtoroi mirovoi voiny: drama strany i tsaria Borisa III." In *Chelovek na Balkanakh v epokhu krizisov i etnopoliticheskikh stolknovenii XX V*. Edited by G. G. Litavrin, et al., St. Petersburg: Aleteiia, 2002.

Vardy, Agnes Huszar. "Forgotten Victims of World War II: Hungarian Women in Soviet Forced Labour Camps." In *Ethnic Cleansing in Twentieth Century Europe*. Edited by Steven Vardy, Agnes Vardy and Tooley Hunt. New York: Columbia University Press, 2003.

Verona, Sergiu. *Military Occupation and Diplomacy. Soviet Troops in Romania 1944–1958*. Durham: Duke University Press, 1992.

Viola, Lynne. "Bab'i bunty and Peasant Protest during Collectivization." *The Russian Review* 45.1 (1986): 23–42.

Viola, Lynne. *Stalinist Perpetrators on Trial: Scenes from the Great Terror in Soviet Ukraine*. Oxford: Oxford University Press, 2017.

Voissin, Vanessa. "The Soviet Punishment of an All-European Crime, 'Horizontal Collboration.'" In *Traitors, Collaborators and Deserters in Contemporary European Politics of Memory*. Edited by Gelind Grinchenko and Eleonora Narvselius. London: Palgrave Macmillan, 2018.

Vozhakin, M. G., et al., eds. *Velikaia Otechestvennaia. Komandarmy. Voenni biograficheskii slovar'*. Moscow: Kuchkovo Pole, 2005.

Weiner, Amir. *Making Sense of War: The Second World War and the Fate of the Bolshevik Revolution*. Princeton: Princeton University Press, 2001.

Welch, Steven. "Commemorating 'Heroes of a Special Kind': Deserter Monuments in Germany." *Journal of Contemporary History* 47.2 (2012): 37–401.

Werth, Alexander. *Russia at War 1941–1945*. London: Barrie and Rockliff, 1964.

Wieviorka, Olivier. *Normandy the Landings to the Liberation of Paris*. Translated by M. B. DeBevoise. Cambridge: Belknap Press of Harvard University Press, 2008.

Williams, Isobel. *Allies and Italians under Occupation: Sicily and Southern Italy, 1943–45*. Basingstoke: Palgrave Macmillan, 2013.

Wood, Elizabeth. "Performing Memory: Vladimir Putin and the Celebration of World War II in Russia." *The Soviet and Post-Soviet Review* 38 (2011): 172–200.

Wood, Elisabeth Jean. "Sexual Violence during War: Toward an Understanding of Variation." In *Order, Conflict, and Violence*. Edited by Ian Shapiro, Stathis Kalyvas and Tarek Masaud. Cambridge: Cambridge University Press, 2008.

Wood, Elisabeth Jean. "Variation in Sexual Violence during War." *Politics & Society* 34.3 (September 2006): 307–341.

Yekelchyk, Sergy. "The Civic Duty to Hate: Stalinist Citizenship as Political Practice and Civic Emotion Kiev, 1943–53." *Kritika: Explorations in Russian and Eurasian History* 7.3 (2006): 529–556.

Yekelchyk, Sergy. *Stalin's Empire of Memory: Russian-Ukrainian Relations in the Soviet Historical Imagination*. Toronto: University of Toronto Press, 2004.

Zakharov, M. V. "Marshal Sovetskogo Soiuza Rodion Malinovskii." In *Polkovodtsy i voenachal'niki Velikoi Otechestvennoi. Vypusk 1*. Edited by P. M. Andriianov. Moscow: Molodaia gvardiia, 1971.

Zakharov, M. V. *Osvobozhdenie iugo-vostochnoi i tsentral'noi Evropy voiskami 2-go i 3-go Ukrainskikh frontov 1944–1945 gg*. Moscow: Nauka, 1970.

Zakić, Mirna. "The Price of Belonging to the Volk: Volksdeutsche, Land Redistribution and Aryanization in the Serbian Banat, 1941–1944." *Journal of Contemporary History* 49.2 (2014): 320–340.

Zhilin, V. A. *Tankisty-geroi 1943–1945 gg*. Moscow: Iauza i Eksmo, 2008.

Ziemke, Earl F. *The U.S. Army in the Occupation of Germany, 1944–1946*. Washington DC: Center of Military History United States Army, 2003.

Zviagintsev, Viacheslav. *Voina na vesakh femidy. Voina 1941–1945gg v materialakh sledstvenno-sudebnykh del* Tom 1. Moscow: Terra-knizhnyi klub, 2006.

Films

Fruzsina Skrabski, *Silenced Shame*. Directed by Fruzsina Skrabski, Budapest, 2013.

Digital Resources

"Aleksei Sergeevich Zheltov." *Pamiat' Naroda*. Accessed 23 May 2020, https://pamyat-naroda.ru.

"Auschwitz Holocaust memorial ceremonies begin without Putin, Obama," RT. Accessed 27 May 2016, www.rt.com/news/226543-poland-auschwitz-commemoration-putin/.

"Crimele 'eliberatorilor' sovietici în județul Alba. Jafuri, violuri și asasinate în Alba Iulia și împrejurimi." Radio Alba 24 26 February 2022. Accessed 10 October 2024, https://alba24.ro/crimele-eliberatorilor-sovietici-in-judetul-alba-jafuri-violuri-si-asasinate-in-alba-iulia-si-imprejurimi-638279.html.

"Historique de la Manche Le SPLAF." Site sur la Population et les Limites Administratives de la France. Accessed 25 October 2024, http://splaf.free.fr/50his.html.

History of the Judge Advocate General's Office, European Theater, July 18, 1942–November 1, 1945. Volume I. St. Cloud: France, 1945.

"Kuz'ma Nikolaevich Derevianko." *Pamiat' Naroda*. Accessed 23 May 2020, https://pamyat-naroda.ru/commander/340/.

Ministerstvo oborony Rossii, https://archive.mil.ru/archival_service/central/resources/collection/. Accessed 22 December 2021.

"Polish." Washington Post. 21 December 1981. Accessed 21 March 2021, www.washingtonpost.com/archive/politics/1981/12/22/polish/5d7aca6b-c573-42bb-a4b5-99559e062345/?fbclid=IwAR1akHhnc-RyUXiltqEaDRmeoVCjQeUOZtKSxgsAvLOmwtvzxa6Gy5OlfAM.

"Putin podpisal zakon o nakazanii za reabilitatsiiu natsizma." *Novaya Gazeta* 5 May 2014. Accessed 9 August 2016, www.novayagazeta.ru/news/1681716.html.

"Ulične borbe u Beogradu, 15–20. oktobra 1944. Povodom 68 godina od oslobođenja grada." *Istorija u pokretu*. Accessed 10 May 2014, www.fpi.rs/blog/ulicne-borbe-u-beogradu-15-20-oktobra-1944-povodom-68-godina-od-oslobodenja-grada/gradjani-i-vojnici-i-oficiri-crvene-armije-knez-mihajlova/.

"Voiska NKVD po okhrane tyla deistvuiushchei Krasnoi Armii." *Istoriia otechestvennykh spetssluzhb i pravokhranitel'nykh organov*. Accessed 18 August 2023, https://shieldandsword.mozohin.ru/VD3462/troops/vot.htm.

"Welcoming the Liberation: Soviet Army during WW II." *English Russia*. Accessed 10 May 2014, http://englishrussia.com/2012/01/28/welcoming-the-liberation-soviet-army-during-wwii/.

Index

Printed in the United Kingdom by TJ Clays Ltd.